D1744735

Debt Management for Development

Fürs Ch. and to our dear friend Hans (1910–2006), whom we both remember

Debt Management for Development

Protection of the Poor and the Millennium Development Goals

Kunibert Raffer

Department of Economics, University of Vienna, Austria

Edward Elgar

Cheltenham, UK • Northampton, MA, USA

© Kunibert Raffer 2010

All rights reserved. No part of this publication may be reproduced, stored in a retrieval system or transmitted in any form or by any means, electronic, mechanical or photocopying, recording, or otherwise without the prior permission of the publisher.

Published by
Edward Elgar Publishing Limited
The Lypiatts
15 Lansdown Road
Cheltenham
Glos GL50 2JA
UK

Edward Elgar Publishing, Inc.
William Pratt House
9 Dewey Court
Northampton
Massachusetts 01060
USA

A catalogue record for this book
is available from the British Library

Library of Congress Control Number: 2009940752

Mixed Sources
Product group from well-managed
forests and other controlled sources
www.fsc.org Cert no. SA-COC-1565
© 1996 Forest Stewardship Council
FSC

ISBN 978 1 84980 108 9 (cased)

Printed and bound by MPG Books Group, UK

Contents

Preface

Unsustainable debts have been an important development barrier and a heavy burden for most Southern countries (SCs), restricting their policy space and causing avoidable misery to the poorest. Over decades creditors have dictated 'solutions' unhampered by the Rule of Law or basic legal principles and without solving the problem. Interestingly Southern sovereign debtors were once treated fairly decently: before the Bretton Woods Institutions and the Paris Club, a creditor cartel took over as 'debt managers'. The present financial crisis caused by neoliberal greed and 'liar loans' (in the USA, not the South) is likely to impact very negatively on Southern debtor nations.

Adequate protection of debtors in distress, their human dignity and human rights, part and parcel of any civilized legal system, were totally denied to the South over decades. The 'lemon squeezer' model of debt management put debt service over human needs, causing part of the misery the MDGs are now to reduce. Changes for the better have occurred recently. Anti-poverty measures have become part and parcel of creditor dominated 'solutions'. After being forced by creditors to introduce school fees or cost recovery schemes in the basic health sector in order to be capable of repaying a few dollars more, SCs are meanwhile encouraged by the same creditors to reduce or abolish these charges. Official creditors continue to deny the fundamental right to neutral and disinterested judges to SC debtors and the globe's poorest, the cornerstone of the Rule of Law and a matter of course for anyone else. Legal standards at the time of debt slavery or even in very ancient Rome were perceptibly higher than those that official creditors uphold vis-à-vis SCs nowadays. Public creditors have been eager to benefit from debtors' duress, creating a new form of dependency, which one may call neo-Listian.

This book shows how debt management should be reformed to prevent debts from crowding out development and human needs, to facilitate reaching the Millennium Development Goals (MDGs). An analysis of the history of sovereign Southern debts shows the differences in SC debtor treatment before 1945 and describes debt accumulation after World War II as a Ponzi scheme that eventually crashed. Proposals on how to solve the never-ending debt story are discussed, especially Rule of Law-based sovereign insolvency. It is shown that fundamental legal principles are still not observed when it comes to SCs. The MDGs are interpreted as a generally agreed and accepted minimum standard of debtor protection that must be reached. In line with official declarations by public creditors, financing the MDGs must therefore enjoy priority. The important role of non-governmental organizations (NGOs) and civil society in bringing about reforms for the better, largely against recalcitrant official creditors, is described. Basic concepts such as sustainability, macroeconomic forecasts, ownership and preferred creditor status are analysed in view of their relevance to the MDGs. Finally the question of how best to finance these Goals is tackled. A caveat regarding the reliability of official data produced by creditors, used by virtually everyone, be they academics or political decision makers, is presented in the Annex.

I particularly wish to thank Ann Pettifor and Jürgen Kaiser for their most valuable help regarding Chapter 10, which I could not have written the way it is without their advice, help and comments. I am indebted to Jomo K.S. and Sara Burke for their inputs.

This book is the final outcome of a course on sovereign debt and the MDGs that I have taught at the University of Vienna and at the UN Institute of Training and Research (UNITAR). I thank my students for their questions and remarks.

Abbreviations

AFRODAD	African Network on Debt and Development
BWIs	Bretton Woods Institutions
CAC	collective action clause
CDS	credit default swap
CIRRs	commercial interest reference rates
CONAIE	Confederación de Nacionalidades Indigenas del Ecuador
CPIA	Country Policy and Institutional Assessment
DAC	Development Assistance Committee
DSF	Debt Sustainability Framework
DSR	debt service ratio
E(E)C	European (Economic) Community/-ies
(E)SAF	(Enhanced) Structural Adjustment Facility
EU	European Union
FTAP	fair transparent arbitration process (Raffer proposal)
GATT	General Agreement on Tariffs and Trade
GDP	gross domestic product
GMR	*Global Monitoring Report*
GNP	gross national product
GPG	global public good
GSP	gross social product
HDR	*Human Development Report*
HIPC	highly indebted poor country
IBRD	International Bank for Reconstruction and Development (the Bank)
IDA	International Development Association
IDB	Inter-American Development Bank
IEO	Independent Evaluation Office (IMF)
IFI	international financial institution
IFF	international finance facility
IMF	International Monetary Fund (the Fund)
ISR	interest service ratio
LLDC	least developed country
MDB	multilateral development bank
MDG	millennium development goal
MDRI	Multilateral Debt Relief Initiative

NAFTA	North American Free Trade Agreement
NFIDCs	net food-importing developing countries
NGO	non-governmental organization
NIEO	New International Economic Order
NPV	net present value
ODA	Official Development Assistance
OECD	Organisation for Economic Co-operation and Development
OED	Operations Evaluation Department (IBRD)
OPEC	Organization of Petroleum Exporting Countries
OTC	over the counter (trade)
PRGF	Poverty Reduction and Growth Facility
PRSP	Poverty Reduction Strategy Paper
PSI	policy support instrument
RTA	Retroactive Terms Adjustment
SA(L)	structural adjustment (loan)
SAPRI(N)	Structural Adjustment Participatory Review Initiative (Network)
SC	Southern country
(SD)DRF	(Sovereign Debt) Dispute Resolution Forum
SDR	special drawing right
SDRM	Sovereign Debt Restructuring Mechanism
SILIC	severely indebted low income country
SIV	structured investment vehicle
SLF	Short-term Liquidity Facility
SPV	special purpose vehicle
TRIPS	Trade Related Intellectual Property Rights
UN	United Nations
UNCITRAL	United Nations Commission on International Trade Law
UNCTAD	United Nations Conference on Trade and Development
UNDP	United Nations Development Programme
UNICEF	United Nations International Children's Emergency Fund
WTO	World Trade Organization
WTO	World Tourist Organization

1. Brief history of debt management until 1989

SOVEREIGN DEBTS BEFORE 1945

Initially, sovereign debts of Southern countries (SCs) were largely a phenomenon of Latin America and those few countries, such as the Ottoman Empire, that were not colonies. Like at present, bonds were the preferred instrument. Financing their wars of independence with British loans, most Latin American nations came into existence with huge debts. Debt servicing problems soon surfaced. In 1846 creditors even financed an unsuccessful Spanish invasion, hoping that Spain would repay those loans that had helped its colonies gain independence.

Characterized by high effective interest rates and frequent defaults Southern debt was roughly comparable to modern junk bonds. Only fractions of face values were actually disbursed, the rest going into front-end fees and prepaid interest. Typically, around one third of an English loan would actually reach Latin America during 1822–26. In 1825 Greece received 13.75 per cent of a loan's face value, carrying a front-end discount of 43.5 per cent. Such terms make one suppose that full repayment was not expected anyway.

Creditors tolerated massive buy-backs by debtor countries. Many countries could buy back up to half of their distressed bonds at secondary market prices. Bolivia in 1886 or Ecuador in 1898 stand out as especially successful cases. Chile even had special entries in her budget that provided funds to effect buy-backs (Acosta, 2001, p. 25).

The USA – then a developing country – has an interesting history of non-payment. Quasi sovereign with regard to debts pursuant to the 11th Amendment, US states have an impressive record of defaulting, which is even reflected in Dickens's *A Christmas Carol*. One night Scrooge suffers a nightmare: his solid British assets might have turned into a 'mere United States' security'. Mississippi seems to have coined the term repudiation when it simply refused to honour its debts. It was not the only case though. Some of the states defaulting during the 1840s paid – though not always all money due – when the situation improved, some never paid anything. The US railway system was largely financed by Europeans. Railway companies that enjoyed government support routinely went bankrupt, leaving foreign creditors with worthless papers and the USA with the infrastructure. There once was a specific insolvency procedure for railways. Specific legal norms for such companies still exist today. Established in 1868, the British Council of Foreign Bondholders has tried to get compensation for damages suffered because of unilateral breach of contract. In the 1940s nine US states suspended interest payments on loans they had received to build railways and canals, when the price of their main export good, cotton, left them short of resources.

It might be of interest to note that the 11th Amendment and court decisions based on it do not preclude the federal government or other US states from filing suits. Foreigners, though, are explicitly barred from suing US states. Foreign bondholders circumventing it by suing at state courts, such as in Arkansas and Mississippi, did win their cases. The states, however, simply refused to obey their own courts and pay.

Military interventions occurred every now and then. The 'Roosevelt Corollary' of 1904 demanded a right of the USA to intervene in Latin American countries that were unstable or not honouring their debts. Such 'chronic wrongdoing', Theodore Roosevelt declared, would 'ultimately require intervention by some civilized nation' – the USA. Apparently Roosevelt did not think of sovereign US states. Mostly, though, economic mechanisms prevailed before 1945. Risk was allowed to play its role. Even debtor protection and debtor rights were generally accepted. After some negotiations and feet-dragging, claims were in most cases reduced by agreement. Generally sovereign debtors including SCs were treated much more generously before the Bretton Woods Institutions (BWIs) became debt managers. One reason seems to be the dispersion of creditors (bondholders).

Especially during the 19th century international tribunals held that states were not bound by contracts made by someone without proper authority, so-called ultra vires contracts. When Venezuela's President Páez had his consul improperly enter into contracts that fell within the legislature's authority, claims under these contracts were rejected. In 1922 Costa Rica refused to honour a contract between the former dictator Federico Tinoco and a British oil company, a concession granted by him and approved by the Chamber of Deputies. The constitution would have required approval by both chambers. The new government repudiated the contract on the grounds that those who had entered it had acted ultra vires. It also challenged odious debts entered into between Tinoco and the Royal Bank of Canada, passing a law to renounce them. Arbitration was invoked by Great Britain. Chief Justice Taft, of the US Supreme Court, was the sole arbitrator. While holding that Tinoco's government was a legitimate de facto government, capable of binding the state to international obligations, he held that the Royal Bank of Canada 'knew' that the funds in question were to be used for the personal expenses of the retiring ruler and his brother. Thus the bank could not expect repayment by Costa Rica (Adams, 1991, pp. 167ff.). If the Royal Bank of Canada had been able to prove that its funds had been used for legitimate government use, its claim would have been upheld. Comparing this decision with present debt management, one cannot help noting differences.

The concept of 'odious debts' was introduced by the USA around 1900. During the peace negotiations after Cuba's war against her colonial ruler, won with strong US support, the Spanish argued that the USA, which now held Cuban sovereignty, should assume Cuba's debt. The USA argued that these debts were not only incurred by Spain without Cuban consent, but indeed against the very interest and will of Cubans in order to finance repression: such odious debts must not be repaid.

When the Soviet Union repudiated tsarist debts A.N. Sack wrote his seminal work. After Costa Rica odiousness fell into oblivion. It was taken up again by the USA after overthrowing Saddam Hussein. Obviously by coincidence, Cuba and Iraq were characterized by strong political US interests and very low, if any, US claims. The enthusiastic reception of this proposal by non-governmental organizations (NGOs) apparently made the US government reconsider its argument with regard to Iraq (see Chapter 3).

The management of the Egyptian debt crisis of 1876 is an economic success story contrasting vividly with present BWI policies. How this debt accumulated is not of interest here, nor its role in Anglo-Egyptian relations, only the technicalities of the solution. The representatives of private bondholders decided to use Egyptian insolvency law as the yardstick to solve the crisis. The administrator appointed to protect creditor interest, Evelyn Baring, did not apply the 'lemon squeezer' approach of the BWIs. He lowered, for example, taxes and postal fees, financed expenditures in public health and education, and encouraged improvements in irrigation. Wages and pensions were paid out in full. After a surprisingly short time his concept was economically successful for creditors and the debtor alike. A hard nosed nineteenth-century capitalist managed this crisis much better and more quickly than international public sector institutions at present.

After Mexico's default of 1914 the US Ambassador proposed following Egypt's example, but did not prevail against creditors. The USA invaded Mexico and occupied Veracruz, although the Hague Convention of 1907 had outlawed the use of force in the case of sovereign debts. After years of debt management – the country was practically run by creditors at times – debt service was finally geared to Mexico's capacity to pay. Eventually creditors received less than 10 per cent of face values. The Egyptian solution would most probably have delivered a better result more quickly and cheaply for everyone involved.

The final outcome of Latin America's debt crisis in the 1930s may be called de facto insolvency. After negotiations Brazil's debts were reduced by over 75 per cent in 1943. 'Debt default eased' Chile's 'payments constraints' (Maddison, 1985, p. 28). Colombian local governments pioneered debt default, central authorities followed. Some big European debtors were themselves delinquent regarding their debts after World War I. The USA has still not received full repayment from many European countries for loans during this war. The British and French governments defaulted in the 1930s, considering the needs of their peoples more important than legal obligations to creditors. The essence of this argument is familiar to bankruptcy specialists.

One lesson from history is that, one way or another, economic facts finally assert themselves. Debt reductions are unavoidable. It is particularly interesting that sovereign debtors were treated better than at present – occasional military interventions, such as the bombing of Venezuela's harbours in 1903 or the Roosevelt Corollary, not withstanding.

TWO DE FACTO INSOLVENCIES AFTER 1945

Two spectacular cases of de facto composition occurred after 1945: Germany's London Accord and Indonesia's reduction in 1969. Both roughly halved the present values of debts.

Comparing Germany's debt indicators when it got relief with those considered 'generous' under HIPC II shows a technically inexplicable difference. Germany's debt service ratio (DSR) before reduction was below 4 per cent, the ratio debt stock/exports below 100 per cent. Unlike 150 per cent under HIPC II, 85 per cent in 1952 was considered unsustainable for Germany. No doubt Germany's reparations after World War I, which the country had to pay against Keynes's advice, were one important reason why Germany's debt burden (negligible compared with SCs at present) was considered unbearable and stifling Germany's economy. But if so, why is an even larger burden sustainable for poorer countries? Germany's debt indicators (measured as percentages of export earnings) improved steeply after 1949.

Scheduled DSR fell from 3.06 (1953) to 1.84 (1956), only once exceeding 2 per cent slightly after 1956 (2.07 in 1958) when amortization started after five years grace. Creditors accepted a German trade surplus, agreeing that debt service cannot generally exceed this surplus. Germany was only expected to pay if it had such surpluses. Germany's economy boomed so dynamically that the country outdid its schedule, using contractual possibilities of early repayment. Still, it always paid less than 5 per cent of export earnings, never more than 60 per cent of its trade surplus. Therefore the German Jubilee campaign (Erlaßjahr 2000) demanded an upper debt service limit of 5 per cent for SCs in the 1990s. Germany was not forced to adopt 'structural adjustment' programmes, but could pursue the very opposite, successful economic policies characterized by the term 'social market economy' (*Soziale Marktwirtschaft*), which triggered the German 'economic miracle'. Independent arbitration was stipulated for any disagreements. Neither the International Monetary Fund (IMF) nor the International Bank for Reconstruction and Development (IBRD) estimated Germany's capacity to pay, but a German national, Hermann J. Abs, was asked to tell creditors how much they should cancel. Among the creditors forgiving Germany's debts were SCs: Ceylon (now Sri Lanka), Pakistan and Iran. The Republic of South Africa was a creditor. So were Yugoslavia, Greece and Spain, considered 'developing countries' in those days and on the Organisation for Economic Co-operation and Development's (OECD) list of aid recipients when it was formed, remaining there over many years.

Abs was also the mastermind behind Indonesia's debt reduction around 1970, which resembled Germany's. Both creditors and the debtor accepted him in this role. He did not formally have an arbitrator's decision power, but it was clear that both parties were willing to implement his advice. While Indonesia held mostly public debts, the composition also covered private claims. Abs insisted on strictly equal treatment of all (including private) creditors as 'indispensable for any settlement of debts'. Since Indonesia had substantial debts to communist governments, this demand was also politically important. It is of interest to note that Germany, as a creditor, strongly opposed Indonesia's debt reduction on the high moral grounds that debts have to be repaid. When 'the' debt crisis broke in 1982 Germany had not yet paid everything it owed – in accordance with the London Accord.

As creditors did not want to establish Indonesia as a precedent Abs had to find special reasons why this was a singular case, inapplicable to other debtors. These 'special characteristics' were:

- All old debts were contracted by the previous government.
- Indonesia's debts consisted predominantly of credits with little or no economic usefulness; practically the whole debt service had to be financed by the central budget.
- High inflation could only be brought under control by energetic policy and exceptionally generous help from without.
- The country was unable to repay its debts in the future.

Indonesia's creditors, especially the Paris Club, obviously recognized these as valid reasons for debt reduction. Logic suggests applying this solution to any similar case – without creating legal precedents if necessary. When Ghana demanded 'Indonesian type' relief a little later creditors were reluctant to grant comparable terms, explaining this by the desire to avoid precedents. Eventually Ghana was granted very 'generous' terms that have remained undisclosed until this day.

SOUTHERN DEBT PROBLEMS EMERGING IN THE 1960S

The Pearson report (Pearson et al., 1969, pp. 153ff.), prepared at the request of the IBRD's president, identified structural origins of the debt problem. Apparently inequalities in the global economy, putting SCs at a disadvantage exist, such as the structural resource gaps to which the Prebisch-Singer thesis (secularly falling terms of trade of raw materials) had drawn attention. The report warned of 'many serious difficulties' that could result from 'very large scale lending', emphasizing: 'The accumulation of excessive debts is usually the combined result of errors of borrower governments and their foreign creditors. Failures on the part of the debtors will be obvious. The responsibility of foreign creditors is rarely mentioned' (ibid., p. 156). This sounds as modern as the report's finding that debt management had emphasized spending cuts and credit restrictions while neglecting the need to sustain sound development outlays. Had it been written nowadays, the millennium development goals (MDGs) would in all likelihood have featured here as well.

The Pearson report considered the debt problem already so urgent that it suggested the application of a unique feature of the $3.75 billion US-UK loan in 1945 (at 2 per cent interest), the so-called Bisque clause, to provide 'a timely policy alternative to moratoria or debt rescheduling when a country is in temporary balance of payments difficulty' (ibid., p. 159). This clause allowed the debtor (the UK) to waive or cancel interest payments unilaterally contingent on certain conditions. It was agreed to change it in 1957: the UK was then entitled to postpone up to seven instalments of principal and interest. Four of these seven deferrals had been used when the Pearson report was written. Deferred payments were to be paid after 2001, carrying an interest of 2 per cent. The report called for debt reduction, proposing that SCs should be allowed to waive or cancel interest payments unilaterally contingent on their economic situation.

To contain debt problems the report also demanded softer terms of

Official Development Assistance (ODA), considering the average terms (1968: 3.3 per cent, 24.8 years) as problematic. Specifically emphasizing that the terms had worsened (1964: 3.1 per cent, 28.4 years on average) the Commission recommended interest rates of 2 per cent (like the British loan) or less and maturities of 25 to 40 years in order to defuse the building up debt debacle.

The OECD reacted. Several annual reports on aid (so-called 'Chairman's Reports') discussed the debt problem. The proposal of softening ODA terms was flatly rejected. ODA terms hardened. The *Review 1970* on development cooperation (OECD, 1970, p. 153) found that debt difficulties for a number of 'developing countries' had worsened. The *Review 1972* (p. 77) warned that 'rolling over debt requires increasingly large *gross* amounts of resources transferred', which may create problems of overborrowing in the hope of 'payments from a larger future income stream' (p. 74), pointing out that such hopes had resulted in debt problems.

In 2000 the OECD's annual report *Development Co-operation 1999* (OECD, 2000, p. 43) on ODA started a 30-year retrospective on aid, recalling some of the findings of the 'pathbreaking' Pearson report as 'still relevant today'. However, the report's recommendations regarding overindebtedness were not mentioned, even though highly topical at the time.

This early debt problem resulted from official lending constituting 75 per cent of total sovereign debts in 1968. Debts were perfectly in line with development theory that had identified two gaps as impediments to development: the 'savings gap' (insufficient savings to finance investments) and the 'foreign exchange gap' (insufficient resources to import needed capital goods). Thus capital from the capital abundant North had to flow to capital scarce SCs where theory assumed it to earn higher returns. The 'growth-cum-debt' concept or the model of the 'debt cycle' express the perception of an SC's theoretical trajectory. After first increasing, net borrowing eventually declines and turns negative. Finally the now no longer 'underdeveloped country' becomes a net capital exporter. Apparently this approach does not work as smoothly as assumed. The first wave of lending by official creditors after 1945 produced a huge debt problem.

THE EUROMARKET: COVERING UP THE WIDELY KNOWN DEBT CRISIS

The Pearson report was published at the very time when another wave of lending was about to start: the Euromarket took off. In spite of the report's warnings Southern debts exploded during the 1970s. A Ponzi scheme took off, covering existing problems with new inflows – precisely in the way that the OECD had warned against. Nevertheless OECD countries favoured this evolution, later incorrectly calling it the 'recycling of petro-dollars'. This second wave rested on a nearly universal convergence of interests of borrowers, lenders and OECD governments.

Several factors fuelled this borrowing and lending spree:

- Pressure caused by the heavy existing debt burden that could be eased by new credits from a new class of creditors.
- Negative real interest rates and relatively high commodity prices encouraged SCs to borrow.
- Spreads fell dramatically. Differences between North and South, supposedly reflecting differences in risk, were perceptibly reduced.

Commercial loans offered an opportunity to diversify sources of finance, to improve the position of SCs vis-à-vis official, especially multilateral, lenders by reducing creditor power to impose conditions. Declining ODA, the practice of tying aid, the frequent use of ODA for political purposes or to gain economic advantages must have made commercial loans attractive. Apart from very few exceptions confirming the rule, commercial banks have not tried to dictate their clients' policies.

During the second half of the 1970s SC shares in publicized eurocredits were always well above 50 per cent of the total, peaking at roughly 63 per cent. This growth of SC debts occurred at a time of slack demand in the North, high liquidity of commercial banks, strong inflation in the OECD countries and negative real interest rates. Commercial bank loans, however, were strongly concentrated on richer SCs.

If doubtful loans had not been urged upon SCs, excess supply would have driven interest rates down towards an equilibrium allowing investments that were unprofitable under actual interest rates. The assumption that sovereign debtors can at most become illiquid, but not insolvent, and the knowledge that their claims would be protected against the market by Northern governments, on which commercial banks disobeying the most elementary rules of banking operated during the 1970s, led to massive misallocations of resources.

The handling of small crises in the 1970s, such as Zaire or Indonesia, convinced commercial banks that sovereign lending was riskless. Indonesia illustrates this very clearly. Shortly after Indonesia's generous debt reduction, the Indonesian national oil company Pertamina had amassed uncontrollable debts. According to a report by the US Senate Committee on Foreign Relations (1977) no one, including commercial banks themselves, seemed to know how much precisely. A one-year stand-by agreement was concluded with the IMF, putting a ceiling on Indonesia's external borrowing and a specific sub-ceiling on Pertamina's. Foreign banks rushed in to go on lending, using technical tricks (such as rolling over short-term loans) to escape those ceilings. Warnings and 'direct representation' (ibid., p. 22) by the US embassy went unheeded. Convinced that they would be bailed out, banks went on lending. When the crisis broke the US government immediately helped. The committee concluded that 'the Indonesian situation' could be repeated any time and Senator Sarbanes expressed his fears that the Senate would soon be forced to vote for payments to debtor governments to bail out US banks. The committee concluded: 'Conceptually, the independence of private bank lending activities overseas would be fine if the banks were actually made to bear the ultimate risk.' Intervention of creditor governments 'calls into question the justification – the high degree of risk involved . . . for the high rate of interest banks charge to developing countries. Thus it is the creditor governments, not the banks, which are really bearing the risk.'

Economically, bank behaviour was perfectly rational – a clear case of moral hazard, produced by OECD governments. Banks apparently charged what they could get and lent as much as they could, being very annoyed when Colombia, a prudent borrower, refused to borrow money that she did not need. Nevertheless Colombia did not get new loans any easier than other Latin American countries after 1982.

WARNING SIGNS DURING THE 1970S

Warning voices were raised throughout the 1970s. G. Abbott saw the roots of the debt crisis in sub-Saharan Africa in the 1960s, when foreign debts began to accumulate faster than economies or foreign exchange earnings were growing. Defining insolvency rather than illiquidity as the problem, he proposed (like the Pearson report) debt cancellation ten years before the official start of the debt crisis.

Accepting the need for debt alleviation the major creditors adopted the so-called Retroactive Terms Adjustment (RTA) in 1978 to provide debt relief and improve the net flow of bilateral official aid to low-income countries. These debts were mostly caused by official flows, including aid, clearly documenting the co-responsibility of official creditors deciding and monitoring where and how resources are spent. The long-winded, clumsy name documents the creditors' desire to avoid the words debt relief or debt reduction, not to mention insolvency. This steadfast refusal to recognize realities officially has remained the most important hindrance to proper debt management and to a viable solution of the crisis to the present day.

Creditor governments are still unwilling to accept insolvency procedures to solve Southern debt problems.

The Latin American *dependencia* school warned of debt problems. In 1968 M.S. Wionczek thought a debt crisis comparable to the 1930s possible. Participants at a conference in Mexico City in 1977 (its papers were published by *World Development*, **7** (2) in 1979) discussed solutions to the debt problem. G.K. Helleiner demanded rules for debt relief, including the reduction of present values of repayments. The IBRD's C.S. Hardy warned of debt problems, classifying refinancing as 'not really a credible alternative'. The coordinator of the conference, M.S. Wionczek, explained the post-1977 wave of optimism in the face of a deteriorating situation 'in terms of institutional interests and social psychology rather than economic and financial analysis'.

The BWIs started structural adjustment lending well before 1982. After 1973 the IMF had already started in Africa. Officially the Bank started programme lending in 1980, but it had exerted its influence in connection with projects before. The Bank always used its leverage to support the IMF and its policy against resistance by SCs.

During the early phase, when the Fund was apparently glad to find clients, conditionality was considered lenient in relation to the required adjustment effort. At that time adjustment programmes were usually planned for one year, which fitted in best with administrative time horizons. In 1979 conditionality became stricter. Eighty eight arrangements were approved by the IMF between January 1979 and December 1981, to support adjustment policies, particularly measures to reach a sustainable balance of payments position. All countries asking for rescheduling in 1981 had adopted an 'adjustment programme' with the Fund when negotiating with their creditors. In spite of RTA, the Pearson report and other explicit warnings, the fact that new loans were mostly used to service old ones on time well before August 1982, or their own experience with macroeconomic interventions and adjustment programmes, the BWIs strongly encouraged SCs to borrow.

Without ignoring the co-responsibility of SC governments that borrowed eagerly, it must be recalled that Third World leaders warned repeatedly of the dangers inherent in debt accumulation and proposed relief measures, for instance, at UNCTAD IV and V, or during the negotiations of the Conference on International Economic Cooperation in Paris. When demanding a New International Economic Order (NIEO) during the early 1970s, the South demanded debt relief and a new framework to resolve debt issues, focusing on reforms of debtor-creditor relations, such as an appropriate role of debtors in rescheduling or an international commission on debts.

CAN THE CAUSES OF THE 1982 CRISIS SIMPLY BE REDUCED TO OPEC'S PRICE INCREASES?

It is important to recall that debts took off at the end of the 1960s, when international liquidity increased due to an oversupply of US dollars, possibly connected with financing the Vietnam war. As the debt crisis following Euromarket borrowing is routinely and uniquely ascribed to the Organization of Petroleum Exporting Countries' (OPEC) price increases, some facts must be mentioned. The OECD's *Review 1983* on development cooperation stated on p. 57:

> At the beginning of the 1970s . . . a major jump in private bank lending occurred . . . . It is evident from the tables that it was in this period, essentially before the first oil shock, that the decisive increase in the role of bank lending occurred, both in absolute terms and proportionally . . . . In the wake of the first oil shock, capital market financing of developing countries fell away in 1974 . . . the period 1975–1978 can be regarded in retrospect as almost a repetition of the early 1970s . . . [but] the rise in bank lending was not as dramatic as in 1971–1973.

This does not support the present routine of blaming OPEC, that is, Southern exporters, for the debt crisis in 1982. The General Agreement on Tariffs and Trade's (GATT) annual publication *International Trade 1979/80* found: 'The overall trade deficit of the non-oil developing countries grew steadily from $15 billion in 1973 to $40 billion in 1975. The largest part of this increase resulted from an increased deficit in manufactures, essentially in trade with industrial countries; the rise of the deficit in fuels, while substantial, was relatively less important' (GATT, 1980, pp. 8f.; for details and quotes, see Raffer and Singer, 2001, pp. 133ff.). The impact of interest rates at the end of the 1980s is shown by the findings of the IMF's Padma Gotur. Of the total increase of current account deficits of non-oil SCs ($66 billion for 1978–81), $18 billion was caused by oil trade, $24 billion by net interest payments and $21 billion were traced to terms of trade changes. In spite of the 'second oil crisis' the impact of interest rates was 1.33 times the impact of oil.

Data published by the Bank of England show that oil surpluses were a visible chunk of liquidity but by no means the only source fuelling the Euromarket. Rough estimates of the balance of payments effects of the oil price hike of 1973–74 by Raffer show that increased costs of oil imports of the group of least developed countries were roughly compensated by generous transfers from OPEC countries until the beginning of the 1980s, when their ODA measured as GNP percentages was on average a multiple of the OECD's. Naturally these transfers did not follow the pattern of price impacts. The Arab Republic of Yemen experienced huge net inflows, while Tanzania, for example, was severely hit by uncompensated price increases. OPEC members financed the IMF's oil facility established in 1974. Ranking amongst the largest beneficiaries, Britain and Italy were ironically among the first countries benefitting from this facility aimed at helping SCs. The blanket blame laid at OPEC's door by OECD countries is definitely at odds with the facts.

Balance of payments surpluses of some OPEC countries, classified as 'capital surplus oil exporters' by the IBRD, increased international liquidity further after 1973–74. Undeniably one important factor influencing the Euromarket, its quantitative impact, has often been exaggerated. Some OPEC members were themselves big borrowers. Indonesia, for instance, borrowed roughly as much in the Euromarket in 1979 as all other low-income countries. The net amount of OPEC money available for the Euromarket was thus much less than the trade surpluses of oil exporters.

THE OPEN CRISIS OF THE EARLY 1980S

When the Federal Reserve adopted a restrictive monetary policy to fight inflation at the end of the 1970s and US budget deficits increased under the Reagan administration to finance military expenditures, interest rates increased swiftly and dramatically. Previously negative real interest rates turned into historically high positive levels. LIBOR went above 16 per cent and real interest rates, still around −7 per cent in 1980, peaked at around 22 per cent in 1982 according to the IBRD. Large shares of debts at variable interest rates quickly transmitted this increase to borrowers, pushing up debt service considerably.

At about the same time raw material prices started to fall dramatically, and terms of trade with them. Between 1980 and 1982 the latter reached historic lows, comparable only to the 1930s. Increased Northern protectionism was one reason for falling export receipts according to the IBRD. Debtors suddenly faced a situation where interest rates (the cost of borrowing) skyrocketed while their income plunged. Until August 1982 the unsustainable situation was covered by new loans made to allow debtors to service their debts. After the Mexican crash syndicated bank lending fell sharply. Between 1982 and 1984 the stock of syndicated loans outstanding was reduced by nearly 25 per cent. With the exception of East Asia 'spontaneous' lending ceased. 'Concerted' or 'involuntary' lending occurred in conjunction with debt restructuring. No bank was willing to increase its share in total exposure. Concerted action assured that the burden of additional exposure would be shared by all.

Some facts corroborate the impression that commercial banks must have been convinced that no real risk to the banking system existed. First, spreads increased drastically after the Mexican crash in 1982. Commercial banks were reluctant to agree to multi-year rescheduling until 1984, which does not allow them to charge front-end fees every year. Pressure had to be used to make commercial banks participate in the Mexican rescue package of 1982. If they had thought that Mexico could trigger a major banking crisis they would have been eager to avoid it. However, reliance on bail-outs by the official sector would explain such behaviour. Profits from early rescheduling were enormous. It was believed in 1983 that some US lawmakers might try to require banks to refund excessive fees already collected from Latin American sovereign obligors. If banks had actually feared losing money due to a collapse of their debtors they would not have charged these high fees, worsening their debtors' position further.

Even the amount of debts of big debtors was first unknown and remained so for some time. Verifying past due interest claimed by creditors loan by loan, Costa Rica managed to save almost 10 per cent of the interest in arrears. Unfortunately such checks were not routinely made.

The BWIs, particularly the IMF, did not arrive on the scene after August 1982 to solve a problem created by others, but they had been part of the process leading to it. Their type of adjustment did not prevent the debt crisis. The first unsuccessful adjustment programmes existed before 1982. The IMF might counter by pointing out that it did not have sufficient leverage then to force countries into necessary reforms. Then one would have to ask why programmes were financed if and when the IMF was aware that necessary reforms were not undertaken and the money could thus not be put to good use. The argument of lack of leverage would be at odds with the claim that debtors themselves 'own' programmes only 'supported' by the BWIs. The claim of country 'ownership' is more often heard recently. But both official sources and publications by leading BWI staff show that countries do not 'own' programmes. Depending on occasions and audiences the BWIs have either claimed only to support a country's own programme or to make a country adopt 'sensible' policies, a clear logical inconsistency.

Structural adjustment measures privileged repayment over debtor protection, as shall be discussed in detail later. Austerity measures cut down social expenditure causing misery and economic decline in debtor economies. Based on empirical evidence, the famous UNICEF study *Adjustment with a Human Face* (Cornia et al., 1987) demanded a thorough rethinking of adjustment policies. Its demands were immediately qualified as a *cri du cœur* rather than a serious guideline for economic policy. During this period financing the MDGs – had they already been declared – would clearly have been subordinated to higher payments in favour of creditors.

The BWIs completely failed to realize in time how serious the situation was. It took them an embarrassingly long time to acknowledge the nature and the dimension of the debt problem, as a host of evidence from their own publications proves. As late as 1982 a paper in their official quarterly allayed fears that private banks might not cover SC deficits. These widespread concerns of 'two years ago' had become unfounded 'nowadays', although it could not be excluded that some groups of non-oil exporting SCs might not be able to borrow all the funds they might need in the future. This echoed the findings of an IMF working group on international capital markets published in *Finance and Development* in March 1981 in an unsigned article and as an Occasional Paper. The BWIs thought for some time that there was no crisis, stating that the money market functioned well, seeing no signs of liquidity bottlenecks, nor of restrictions regarding the capital base of private banks limiting lending to SCs, which was supposed to continue on a large scale. The Task Force on Non-concessional Flows established by the BWIs in 1979 presented its findings in May 1982. Pointing out that the conclusions had been presented before the crisis and there was presently even less reason for optimism, a paper in *Finance & Development* insisted that they did still hold (cf. Raffer and Singer, 2001, pp. 164ff.). But relatively soon the BWIs skilfully used this crisis to increase their importance dramatically. After the demise of the Bretton Woods system economic reason would have suggested dissolving its supporting mechanism, the IMF too. The debt crisis provided a unique chance to find a new justification for its existence as a debt manager.

CHILE'S DEBACLE: A CONVENIENTLY FORGOTTEN CASE

Mexcio's debt crisis in 1982 was not the only crisis of neoliberal policies at that time. Liberalizing and opening Chile's economy produced a financial crash. The military dictatorship provided an ideal precondition to implement neoliberal ideas. Price controls were eliminated, public expenditure was reduced, state enterprises privatized and the economy opened up. As the market knows best, banking supervision was cut down – as happened in the USA recently. Moral backing came from the BWIs. The IMF's Director of the Western Hemisphere, E. Walter Robichek, had assured Latin Americans that exchange and other risks would presumably be taken into account as private firms can be expected to be careful. Private borrowers (as opposed to governments) were very unlikely to overborrow, even with official guarantees (Diaz-Alejandro, 1985, p. 9). Briefly, private, voluntary transactions were the private sector's own business and presumably Pareto optimal. This view is sometimes called the Robichek doctrine. The bulk of booming credit expansion went into speculation, the trade deficit in 1982 was 70 per cent of export revenues. After bailing out the Banco Osorno authorities realized that practically no inspection or supervision of bank portfolios existed. Reserve requirements had been steadily reduced, and 'apparently little effort was spent on investigating the banking credentials of new entrants' when banks were privatized (ibid.) The 'Chilean miracle' of 1981 turned into a catastrophe in 1982, GDP fell by more than 14 per cent. The government was forced to socialize private losses, another parallel to the present US crisis.

THE ILLIQUIDITY 'THEORY' – DELAYING AT ANY COSTS

When the existence of a crisis had finally been recognized, debt management after 1982 was based on the so-called illiquidity theory, the assumption that there was no fundamental crisis, only a temporary inability to pay. William R. Cline, the US Treasury Secretary James Baker, as well as the BWIs firmly defended this thesis. Based on optimistic assumptions regarding debtors' export volumes and prices, or relatively high growth in OECD countries, Cline (1985) claimed just before the 1985 IMF/IBRD meeting that by the late 1980s debt-export ratios would be back to levels previously associated with creditworthiness. Optimistically he concluded: 'The emerging evidence in 1983–84 has tended to confirm the analysis that the debt problem is one of illiquidity and subject to improvement as international recovery takes place' (ibid., p.187).

During this meeting in Seoul James Baker expressly called on international financial institutions (IFIs) to support comprehensive macroeconomic and structural policies in SCs, demanding a continued central role of the IMF together with multilateral development banks and more intensive IMF and IBRD collaboration. As countries would grow out of debts, Baker insisted that not a single cent of debts should be forgiven. Financial help was proposed in the form of additional net lending of $29 billion over three years for some countries. Commercial banks were supposed to lend $20 billion, IFIs $9 billion. To put this amount into perspective: Mexico alone paid $9.4 billion in interest in 1985, her total debt service was $14.5 billion, Brazil's 10.3 billion.

Supported by all creditors Baker firmly rejected any general solution, insisting on solving SC problems case by case. Eventually a group of debtors was singled out, called highly indebted countries (HICs) but sometimes dubbed 'Baker countries', on which debt initiatives were to focus. Membership in this group clearly reflected US economic and political interests. It was unclear how many countries were eligible. For some time two lists existed. To overcome the debt problem during the perceived period until recovery, 'involuntary lending' by commercial banks was seen as the solution, which appeared a good policy on the assumption that debtors would grow out of the problem. Officially favoured was the so-called menu approach: as on a menu banks were supposed to choose their options. Small banks with relatively little money in SCs could chose a way out: exit bonds allowing them not to participate in further concerted lending. Larger banks might sell their claims on the secondary market to reshuffle their portfolios.

The most popular instrument 'on the menu' was debt equity swaps. They allowed investors to buy from banks at secondary market discounts and to finance direct investments worth the face value of acquired claims. Unlike in the past, debtor countries themselves were officially barred from the secondary market. Somewhat later a fee was charged by SC authorities, which could eventually become quite substantial. However, with austerity programmes restricting domestic demand and Northern protectionism restricting export possibilities, debt equity swaps have usually not exceeded relatively modest levels. Exceptions were most notably Mexico and Chile. Chile's military junta introduced a special programme for nationals. One may assume the junta and its supporters to have benefitted more from this preferential treatment than the opposition. If effected on a larger scale (political resentment against selling out to foreigners apart) they only postpone balance of payments problems. Once the repatriation of profits starts foreign exchange pressures make themselves felt again. The effect is thus the same as a grace period. Further problems were mentioned in the literature: inflationary effects and subsidizing investments that would take place anyway. It is interesting to note that Mexico, which introduced debt equity swaps in 1986 on a significant scale, suspended its scheme for exactly these reasons in November 1987. Irrespective of one's opinion on direct investment in general these swaps were not a viable tool to solve a debt crisis, as the relation of debt stocks and available swap opportunities documented.

Crises were frequently reported at quarters' ends during the 1980s due to US quarterly accounting, triggered by awkward and economically debatable regulatory constraints, such as the 90 days clause, the impossibility of capitalizing interest arrears, or unpredictable and allegedly discriminatory decisions of regulators. On one occasion the hands of the clock were reportedly held back to book payments 'in time'. In contrast, legal rules governing loan loss provisioning on the European continent proved to be stabilizing.

The IBRD's (1988, p.xxix) *World Debt Tables* complained that concerted lending by banks since 1982 had just been sufficient to refinance around a quarter of interest payments by HICs (also called 'Baker Countries'), making the IBRD 'the principal net lender to HICs'. Jeffrey Sachs called the substantial bail out of private banks by multilaterals an 'implicit taxpayers' subsidy'. In a major process of risk shifting, risk was reallocated to public multilaterals, increasing their share of debts substantially. The third wave of debts – multilateral flows – hardened conditions for debtors since multilaterals, in marked contrast to private banks, refused to reschedule or reduce their claims. A financial merry-go-round started to keep up the pretence that multilaterals do not reschedule. Funds from, say, the IBRD were used to repay the IMF, allowing it in turn to lend again to the debtor, so that the IBRD loan could be serviced 'in time'. Not infrequently, OECD governments participated as intermediary financiers. The whole bill had to be picked up by debtors.

Apart from shifting risk to official IFIs, this also shifted risk from the USA to other countries. US banks were much more heavily exposed in HICs than others, accounting for a higher percentage of total bank debts than the US share in IFIs. Seen as a country the USA could thus reduce its risks, being bailed out by other countries. The idea that other countries should use their money directly to allow the USA to reduce their exposure was advocated for some time. In particular, the idea was propagated that balance of payments surplus countries, such as Japan or Germany, should use their surpluses to become larger creditors. The USA accused Japan of not properly sharing the burden of necessary international expenditures, which were mainly military expenditures, although Japan's low military outlays were due to the restrictions imposed by the USA itself after World War II. Japan's Capital Recycling Programme of 1986 is one result of this pressure.

In May 1987 US money centre banks finally acknowledged that some money was irretrievably lost. In a spectacular move Citicorp set aside $3 billion in additional reserves to cover loan losses. Without doing so Citicorp would have expected profits of $2 billion. This move and favourable reaction of the stock exchange set the stage for other banks to follow. The argument that default by Latin America (it was routinely assumed that the whole region would behave like one country) would wipe out the primary capital of major banks and lead to a crash of the banking community was no longer valid. The fact that US banks, unlike banks on the European continent, had not used their high incomes from SC loans to build up reserves for quite some time is not what one would expect if higher spreads had actually been charged because of higher (perceived) risk. Backed by their new strength, US banks started to favour tougher bargaining.

EVENTUALLY RECOGNIZING THE NEED FOR DEBT REDUCTION

Already Baker recognized de facto that debt reduction was necessary. The US Treasury actively backed a deal between Mexico and her creditors in 1987–88, involving a reduction of the principal owed. The idea was to use US Treasury zero coupon bonds as collateral for securitized Mexican debt amounting to $20 billion. The outcome was very modest, though, falling far short of the quantitative target; interest rate increases eroded the result already during the same year.

The 'Venice Terms' of the Paris Club still insisted on full repayment in 1987 but stretched maturities for poor debtors. Opposition against initiatives to reduce the debt burden of poor countries was eventually overcome at the Toronto summit in 1988. The UK proposal, called 'Toronto Terms', involved debt reduction of some official debts owed by poor (so-called 'IDA-only') SCs to members of the Paris Club (Northern governments). Official creditors were to cancel either one third of the stock of eligible debts or grant an equivalent reduction of the rate of interest. On US insistence a third option was agreed on, which was considered equal: stretched maturities and grace periods of 14 years.

At the 1988 IMF/World Bank conference in Berlin, the new US Treasury Secretary, N. Brady, referred to the necessity of debt reduction. The 'Brady Plan', presented on 10 March 1989 after violent riots in Venezuela, called explicitly for debt reduction, although only commercial banks were supposed to lose money.

1988 was the year when creditors gave up the pretension that everything would eventually be repaid. The 'illiquidity theory' was finally dead – after causing considerable damage to debtor economies.

2. Brief history of debt management after 1989

After the need for debt reduction had finally been officially recognized – much too late, and after considerable damage had been inflicted on debtors by creditors delaying this decision – reality still remains to be faced fully. One important weak point of the 'Brady Plan' was that only one group of creditors, commercial banks, had to face losses. Official creditors remained exempt. In spite of the routinely used name, this proposal originated in a debtor country. It was first made by the Brazilian Finance Minister, Bresser Pereira, and immediately turned down by the US Treasury. Later Japan's Finance Minister, Miyazawa Kiichi, supported it before it became the 'Brady Plan'. 'Brady reductions' were implemented under BWI guidance, a new task for the BWIs which made them discard the illiquidity theory immediately.

Understandably, banks were not keen to follow Brady's proposal. Treasury Under-Secretary Mulford warned commercial banks that they might face 'a legislated or mandated solution to the problem that may be very much more unpleasant' if they refused to reduce parts of their loans 'voluntarily'. The first tangible product of the Brady initiative, the Mexican agreement, was reached under prolonged pressure by the US government. With some prodding commercial banks exchanged old syndicated debt for new bonds (securitization) at a discount of 35 per cent. Three options existed: capital stock reduction, equivalent reduction in interest rates ('par bonds') and new money (chosen by 13 per cent). It remains difficult to see how new money can be equivalent to debt reductions – either via cuts of stock or flows – unless one assumes that (most of) the new money would be lost anyway. As official money poured in to 'finance debt relief', Mexico's total debts changed little. The effect was negligible.

Other countries, such as Argentina, Costa Rica, Brazil, Venezuela, the Philippines or Ecuador, benefitted from Brady schemes – called debt and debt service reduction schemes after Brady's term at the US Treasury. The results were not encouraging. The early 'Brady countries' still could not service their debts as due afterwards, not even in the Philippines which had a second helping. When Ecuador, encouraged by the IMF, officially defaulted on her 'Brady bonds' in 1999 the illusion that Brady deals had worked was finally dead. Although private creditors had granted 45 per cent reduction, Ecuador's debt time series only show a small blip downwards. If all creditors had reduced by only 30 per cent, Ecuador would in all probability have been economically afloat again.

Like Baker before, Brady strengthened IFI 'supervision' of debtors further. Given the fact that IFI control had not been able to improve the economic situation of Southern debtors over more than a decade, and considering the amount of well-founded critique of BWI debt management this was a debatable strategy. The BWIs embraced the 'Brady Plan' as fully as the 'Baker Plan', although it was the exact opposite of their own opinion upheld so far, possibly so because they gained increased importance. Their austerity policies called 'structural adjustment' went on, increasing poverty and steering economies away from goals later to become part of the MDGs. After defending the illiquidity theory for some years the BWIs seemed to have forgotten their own arguments and analyses, as well as that the policies advised to (or forced on) debtor countries by them were based on this error.

A portion of policy-based loans should be set aside to support transactions involving significant debt reduction. This part of the proposal contains two bail-outs. First, private banks are bailed out by public institutions. Second, as the US share in both IFIs was smaller than the share of US banks in the debts of Brady beneficiaries, it also involves a bail out of the USA at the expense of other countries. Similar ideas of international burden sharing in favour of the USA had been voiced on Capitol Hill before. The Bill H.R. 1453 introduced in the House of Representatives on 5 March 1987, for example, demanded a deconcentration of SC debts 'now unnecessarily concentrated in United States commercial bank holdings'. It went unmentioned that this concentration resulted from free, profit maximizing decisions by US money centre banks. To stretch the financial limits of IFIs, Brady called upon other governments to provide bilateral financial support: countries with current account surpluses – in particular Japan, Germany and Taiwan – were asked to bail out the Americans.

Although it involved losses, the bail-out was the carrot. The stick was a change in IFI disbursement practices. Disbursement by the BWIs would no longer depend on prior completion of full commercial bank financing packages, thus weakening the position of commercial banks. The IMF's executive board stated that a loan package to a heavily indebted country could be approved before the completion of a debt reduction agreement with its commercial creditors provided the Fund felt such prompt support to be essential, and negotiations were already started with commercial banks with an agreement expected within a reasonable time. The Fund also softened its position on arrears to commercial banks, recognizing that a debtor's financing situation might not allow them to be avoided. The policy of non-toleration of arrears to IFIs remained unchanged.

While of limited financial importance, the Brady initiative definitely opened the door for debt reduction. In 1989 IDA introduced a Debt Reduction Facility. In 1990 President Bush declared debt reduction an option under the 'Enterprise for the Americas' initiative.

In early 1991 Senate Resolution No. 84 praised the people and the government of Poland for their efforts in trying to transform their economy, noting specifically: 'there is precedent for the reduction of debt of a nation under special circumstances, including the London accord after World War II, in which the allies forgave the new German Government the debt incurred by the Nazi Government, as well as the recent forgiveness by the United States Government of the military debt of the Egyptian Government'. The resolution urged private and public creditors to reduce Polish debt 'by at least 50 percent', arguing that 'the success of the people and the Government of Poland in the rebuilding of their economy is dependent on the Government of Poland receiving a reduction in their foreign debt burden'. As the USA had virtually no claims, this request addressed other countries. It also noted that Western aid had not been 'sufficient to the magnitude of the problems confronting the people and the Government of Poland', and that 'the burden of foreign debt has made the process of economic transformation more difficult'.

After Toronto bilateral creditors also started to grant larger and larger relief. Nevertheless, the myopia of official creditors is shown by the example of the Paris Club's debt relief terms. In 1991 the UK Chancellor of the Exchequer, John Major, urged that Paris Club debts should be reduced by two thirds. These 'Trinidad Terms' were considered so radical that OECD governments refused to apply them. A compromise of 50 per cent reduction was agreed on, the 'Intermediate Trinidad Terms' or 'Enhanced Toronto Terms'. The 'Naples Terms' adopted three years later by the G7 were still less generous than the UK Trinidad proposal: 50 per cent to 67 per cent debt reduction. Eventually the discussion on the multilateral debt overhang brought about reductions surpassing the original British proposal. Meanwhile 100 per cent has been reached, which proves that granting necessary relief in time would have avoided many economic and social problems.

The Paris Club's high percentages of debt reduction are misleading though. As a matter of principle only so-called pre-cut-off debts are eligible for debt relief, such as the 'Naples Terms'. The cut-off date is when the debtor asked the Paris Club the first time for debt relief, which can be quite early. As time goes by, post-cut-off debts are logically likely to grow, as they have in fact done. Uganda's cut-off date, for instance, is in 1981. If the cut-off date is early enough 100 per cent 'debt forgiveness' may mean a reduction of total debts by less than 1 per cent. Mathematically, debt relief converges to 100 per cent while actually cancelled debts converge to zero. EURODAD, an NGO campaigning for debt relief, quoted IBRD calculations for 20 countries, according to which 80 per cent Paris Club debt relief would mean a mere 17 per cent actual reduction for all debts. Announcing its 'Evian Approach' for non-highly indebted poor countries on 29 October 2003 the Paris Club eventually declared that the 'adjustment of the "cut-off date" will also be actively considered.'

THE EUPHORIA OF THE EARLY 1990S

After the 'lost decade' of the 1980s, the 1990s began with officially heralded hope and recovery, at least for debtors with 'prudent' economic policies, meaning those implementing BWI advice. This optimism was based on huge capital inflows, especially to Latin America, and conventional debt indicators, such as the debt service ratio, at pre-1982 levels. As the Annex on data shows in detail, correct interpretation of IFI data did not at all justify any optimism: 'improvements' simply resulted from 'forgetting' huge arrears. Directly put, if creditors had been prepared to accept much lower, let alone similar arrears in 1982, be it in percentages of long-term debts or in current dollars, there would have been no debt crisis. Apparently no one recalled the enthusiasm about private flows to the South during the 1970s, when OECD governments, the IMF, the IBRD and private banks were all equally enthusiastic about increasing private lending.

Once again the 'market worked' according to official sources. Until the Mexican crash Latin America was used by IFIs as the practical vindication of their 'adjustment' policies based on the so-called Washington Consensus emphasizing globalization and deregulation (Raffer, 1996). This time the IBRD took greater care to place occasional, cautious caveats about volatility and sustainability – possibly a fine example of learning by doing. After some 15 years of IMF 'structural adjustment' measures, sub-Saharan Africa (SSA) had experienced the first wave of official optimism in 1989, characterized by the famous statement of a high ranking IBRD official: 'Recovery has begun' (IBRD and UNDP, 1989, p. iii). This statement had to be withdrawn quickly because of massive criticism even from within the United Nations (UN) family, most notably the Economic Commission for Africa. Quite rightly so, as the present state of SSA debtors proves. The Inter-American Development Bank's report *Economic and Social Progress in Latin America* of 1992 started with the ominous formulation 'The Recovery Begins', strongly recalling the words heralding SSA's alleged economic recovery, which was so obviously at odds with SSA's state. In Latin America, however, euphoria was allowed to last longer. The Mexican crash of 1994–95 put an end to this enthusiasm entirely based on high capital inflows, without regard to balance of payments data, GDP/head figures at the level of 1977 or the drastic fall in standards of living.

In spite of all euphoria, commercial banks did not resume lending, as one might have expected if debtors had actually recovered. A new group of creditors was ushered in: bondholders, who had been the main lenders to Southern sovereigns before 1940 – the fourth and last Ponzi wave. Euphoric statements by multilateral institutions and the OECD, as well as regulatory changes opened the door. Such changes, and a trend toward explicitly rating borrowing SCs, at least partially triggered by them, allowed institutional investors to place money there. Bringing in the public at large (including pension funds) allowed 'old' creditors (including IFIs) to receive more repayments than otherwise possible. Debts kept growing but their structure changed perceptibly. Commercial banks could reduce their exposure. IFIs could receive debt service without problems for a while. Whereas bondholders were practically non-existent in 1982, they are now an important class of creditors in quite a few countries. In Argentina, for example, the share of bonds in public and publicly guaranteed long-term debt rose from 8.2 per cent to 74.23 per cent and the share of commercial banks declined from 59.6 per cent to 8.3 per cent during 1980–99. The securitization of claims by 'Brady deals' set the course for this last Ponzi wave. Paving the way for bonds, regulators in OECD countries relaxed guidelines for bond issues and lowered minimum credit ratings. These regulatory changes, the IMF's insistence on liberalizing capital accounts – in plain violation of its own Articles of Agreement – and official euphoria made the crises of the 1990s possible. Finally, as Brady bonds already 'incorporated' a haircut, it was understood that they would not have to suffer additional losses in the future. It was even stipulated contractually that a further restructuring of 'Bradies' would not be sought. This might have supported the belief that bonds – new debt after the crash – would generally enjoy priority. Including bonds in her restructuring agreement of 2000, Pakistan finally shattered this perception of preference.

An important external factor contributed. As capital flooded back to different emerging markets at more or less the same rate irrespective of the pace of domestic reform, Eichengreen and Mody (1998, p. 39) identified declining interest rates in the major money centres as an important trigger: 'U.S. interest rates fell by 50 per cent between 1989 and 1991. By 1992 short-term rates in the United States were at their lowest level since the early 1960s.' One should expect such flows to react in a highly unstable way vis-à-vis changes in interest rate differentials. This danger was clearly seen by Eichengreen and Mody before the 'Tequila Crisis' erupted at the end of 1994, warnings were even published in IFI publications. The rise in Northern interest rates occurred in 1994 as predicted. It 'was associated with a curtailment of capital flows and the sharp shock to confidence now known as the Tequila crisis' (ibid.). Official optimism about renewed market access and claims that the debt crisis had been overcome – often backed by Mexico's example – were crashed by the new Mexican crisis and the rescue package required to defuse it. As usual, the BWIs had not foreseen the crash of their model debtor, a country which had implemented BWI 'recommendations' faithfully, as the BWIs had proclaimed, readily claiming credit for what they had announced to be their success. Debt management, however, had simply shifted some risk on to the public at large, such as mutual funds and pension funds. The crisis broke in the very debtor always enjoying privileged treatment, showing excellent traditional debt indicators, but a rapidly and steeply increasing deficit of the current account balance (179 per cent per annum for Mexico; however less than the 230 per cent for Latin America according to official BWI data; Raffer, 1996, p. 36), which hardly suggested sustainability.

Mexico was left to pick up the bill, the costs of a \$50 billion rescue package. Her *tesobonos* happened to be rated BBB, beyond the reach of 'small guy investors' and pension funds before the regulatory changes mentioned above, without which the Tequila crisis could not have occurred as it did. Investors were once again bailed out – saving 'small guy investors' figured prominently in the political debate within the USA. Roughly five years later the IBRD drew attention to striking similarities between Mexico's crisis and Chile's debacle of the early 1980s described in Chapter 1.

Recalling the Mexican fiasco of 1994–95 and the problems of sustainability and stability of large global financial market intermediated resource flows, the OECD (1996, p. 57) quickly identified systemic risks requiring 'the provision of a much larger officially provided safety net'. Economically this amounts to an invitation to speculate, an offer gladly accepted, as the Asian crash showed or the crises in Brazil and Russia immediately following. Less diplomatic and elegant language might simply speak of the prospect of officially subsidized speculation. Catastrophic private failures were interpreted as the manifest need for even more taxpayer's money, incidentally at the same time, when the OECD was concerned about abolishing 'state-led' development. As financial assistance by OECD countries and IFIs is not free of charge, SCs would also have to face steep costs of fighting the crises their 'helpers' triggered, having to pick up the bill of bail-outs plus interest on the money lent to finance them.

THE HIPC INITIATIVES

Many SCs, particularly the poorest, remained burdened with high shares of multilateral debts they had to service with priority. Other creditors had to wait as IFIs received the lion's share of debt service payments actually made. At the end of 1993 IFIs received more than half the payments made by poor SCs. Sixty two per cent of all multilateral debts were owed to the BWIs. According to the IBRD's *World Debt Tables* (1996, p. 170): 'Seventy percent of outstanding debt [in SSA] at the end of 1995 was owed to official creditors – 90 percent if Nigeria and South Africa are excluded.' The share of the IBRD group, the IMF, the African Development Bank and its Fund was 30 per cent of long-term debt outstanding. Despite high net transfers HIPCs often had to reschedule since 1980. The IBRD's *Global Development Finance* (1997, p. 42) admitted the effects of delaying relief: 'The surge in borrowing, coupled with increasing reliance on rescheduling and refinancing, increased the nominal stock of debts of HIPCs from $55 billion in 1980 to $183 billion in 1990 . . . by the end of 1995 it had reached $215 billion.'

The slowdown from an annual growth rate of 12.77 per cent to 3.28 per cent in the 1990s was achieved by a shift towards more grants, higher concessionality and 'forgiving' ODA debts. This clearly shows that wrong debt management by creditors unwilling to accept economic facts and powerful enough to keep debtors from making reality felt has exacerbated the problem. Trying to avoid smaller write-offs to go easy on their budgets official creditors allowed debts to grow further, thus forcing themselves eventually to accept much bigger write-offs. One can protect the illusion that bankrupt borrowers will eventually repay by going on lending or by capitalizing interest arrears on paper for quite a while. On paper one increases one's claims, although this does not make the money actually repaid. Such new claims are not recouperable, 'phantom debts' without any economic base, just making the 'costs' of debt relief look higher on paper.

Until September 1995 the BWIs officially denied that multilateral debts were a problem. If they had actually financed viable projects and programmes, these debts would have been self-liquidating, thus really no problem. Unfortunately, multilateral claims were not earning their own debt service. A pervasive preoccupation with new lending, identified for the IBRD through internal documents is certainly one reason. A discussion document leaked from the IBRD acknowledged for the first time that something had to be done since multilateral debt was a heavy burden on many poor countries. Breaking the taboo of the multilateral debt overhang, which is of particular relevance to the poorest countries, is a great merit of IBRD president, James Wolfensohn, proposing and backing a Multilateral Debt Facility against strong internal opposition. The IMF opposed Wolfensohn's idea at least with equal fervour, a fact not fully reflected by the present official assertion that HIPC is a 'joint' BWI initiative.

In early 1996 the BWIs assessed the outlook for debt sustainability in 38 heavily indebted IDA only countries, projecting the likely availability of external finance and estimating the effects of 'Naples Terms' debt relief from the Paris Club and similar treatment from other bilateral and commercial creditors. Former BWI success stories, such as Ghana and the Côte d'Ivoire, were among the countries assessed. The debt burden was classified as sustainable if the net present value (NPV) of debt to exports was expected to fall below 200 per cent, and the debt service ratio below 20 per cent within five years. Eight countries were found to have unsustainable debts defined as ratios above 250 per cent and 25 per cent after ten years. Twelve countries falling between these categories were classified as 'possibly stressed'. Liberia, Nigeria and Somalia were finally not assessed, the remaining 18 considered 'sustainable'.

After the G7 had agreed on up to 80 per cent debt relief by the Paris Club – thus finally going further than Britain's Trinidad proposal – the highly indebted poor countries (HIPC) Initiative was adopted by the Bank's Development Committee and the Fund's Interim Committee in the autumn of 1996. Its declared aim was to bring debts of eligible countries to sustainable levels, to enable a country 'to meet its current and future external debt-service obligations in full without recourse to debt relief, rescheduling of debts, or the accumulation of arrears, and without unduly compromising growth' (Boote and Thugge, 1997, p. 10). This objective of reaching overall debt sustainability, allowing countries to exit from continuous reschedulings was also confirmed by the 1997 issue of the IBRD's *Global Development Finance* (p. 44). HIPC was meant to provide a durable exit strategy from debt problems. The need to reduce multilateral debts was officially recognized. HIPC relief was initially limited to a two-year period to avoid it becoming a permanent facility, but an extension was possible. The 1998 review proposed a two-year extension. After several extensions HIPC was to 'close' by the end of 2006 (which would have excluded some countries from HIPC) when the G8 summit 2005 introduced the Multilateral Debt Relief Initiative (MDRI; see Chapter 4). In June 2006 'options to deal with the expiration of the sunset clause' were examined.

Wolfensohn's proposed fund became the HIPC Trust Fund established by the IBRD, allocating $500 million as its initial contribution. IDA, the IBRD's 'soft window', was assigned the task of administering it on the basis of decisions made by donors and multilateral creditors. Contributions can be earmarked for a particular debtor or a particular IFI. The HIPC Trust

Fund may pre-pay debts, cover debt service when it falls due, or purchase and subsequently cancel debts. The IBRD was also prepared to provide enhanced support in the form of IDA grants during the interim period. Getting bilateral contributions to the HIPC Trust Fund was faced with the difficulty that countries willing to contribute hesitated to make large payments as long as some major creditors did not pay up as well.

Initially the IMF refused to contribute cash, wanting its 'contribution' to be financed by bilateral donors, a proposal attacked as unacceptable by many NGOs. Then it proposed to contribute by replacing Enhanced Structural Adjustment Facility (ESAF) loans (5.5 years grace, 10 years maturity) with softer ESAF loans (10 years grace, 20 years maturity) or a permanent ESAF. The IMF wanted to expand its monitoring and control-ling of cash strapped debtors in the future. Eventually it agreed to establish a Trust Fund for HIPC's concessional part, hoping other creditors would contribute and agreed to grants. These are to be used to repay the IMF itself to pretend that the IMF is not reducing debts. The proposal to sell some of the IMF's gold to finance its contribution to the HIPC Initiative was particularly strongly supported by NGOs. Historically some IMF gold had been sold in the 1970s, after the decision to demonetize gold. The IMF Trust Fund was established with those proceeds in 1976. But in the case of debt relief, sales were declared impossible by hardliners among offi-cial creditors. Resistance by major shareholders but also smaller members, such as Austria, prevented it at first. When opposition was overcome, several countries, most notably Britain, decided to sell large portions of their gold reserves at precisely the same time. Finally, it was agreed to 'sell' gold in 'off-market' operations, which basically meant revaluing gold with a low book value.

In contrast, when the IMF lost so many customers that it had become unable to cover its own operating costs, gold sales to finance the Fund ('new and sustainable income and expenditure framework') were quickly agreed. Apparently, the IMF's owners are prepared to sell gold for any purpose provided that this does not help the globe's poorest.

To qualify for HIPC I countries had to have a good track record with the BWIs. It was composed of two stages. During stage one countries must carry out economic and social reforms under BWI programmes, after which eligibility for HIPC debt relief is assessed. This was called the decision point. Economic analysis would suggest that appropriate debt reduction follows suit once an overhang has been assessed. All the more so as a track record of faithful implementation of 'structural adjustment' is demanded as a precondition, which means that creditors must be satisfied with the debtor's economic policy. But reduction is not granted on assessment. A three-year period follows before the so-called completion point is reached, which means before debt reduction actually takes place. Of course during this period 'good behaviour' (which equals obeying official creditors) is necessary. These three years have apparently no other function but to preserve intervention possibilities into domestic affairs, particularly so as the record of 'adjustment' successes is quite underwhelming. During stage 1 relief was granted, but the BWIs continued to lend, increasing debts and making more relief necessary at completion point. Why countries already classified as 'unsustainable' had to wait six more years for reductions remains a mystery. If the preliminary analysis by the BWIs is correct there is no economic justification for delaying relief further, most evidently so for countries in the 'unsustainable' category. Delay only means allowing debts to grow further, as the history of debt management in general as well as of HIPCs proves.

The relevant analysis was to be done by Bank, Fund and the HIPC according to the same criteria – 200–250 per cent debt exports (in present value terms) and 20–25 per cent debt service ratios. Specific vulnerability indicators, such as export concentration and variability, were to be taken into account. Fiscal indicators, such as debt (NPV) to fiscal revenue, were added due to French pressure in favour of the Côte d'Ivoire. Officially this modification was introduced to take the specificities of 'highly open economies' into account.

The HIPC Initiative relied heavily on non-IFI creditors. Paris Club members would commit up to 80 per cent reduction of eligible debt in present value terms. Other non-multilateral creditors were expected to provide relief on 'at least comparable terms' (Boote and Thugge, 1997, p. 14), even though they had had no say in determining reductions. Only if this should prove insufficient at completion point IFIs would reduce their claims in a way preserving their wrongly claimed 'preferred creditor status'. This allows IFIs to reduce their own claims less than other creditors having to bail out IFIs.

In April 1997 Uganda became the first country to benefit from the initiative. Bolivia, Burkina Faso (initially categorized as 'sustainable'), Guyana, Ethiopia, Côte d'Ivoire – a country with an unusually large share of private debts still dating back to the time when it was widely presented as a 'success' – and Mozambique followed.

HIPC II

HIPC I fell short of official expectations. At Cologne the G7 decided to change HIPC substantially. The debt-export ratio was lowered to 150 per cent, still substantially higher than the burden once considered acceptable to Germany. Officially HIPC II is called 'Enhanced HIPC Initiative'. This

'Cologne Initiative' was granted under strong NGO pressure, supported by more than 17 million signatures collected worldwide, after the G7 allegedly had wanted to close down HIPC I.

An official anti-poverty focus was established, eventually introducing at least the idea of debtor protection, not necessarily always fully honoured by practice. Although HIPC I had already paid some lip service to anti-poverty measures, this was an important innovation. ESAF was renamed Poverty Reduction and Growth Facility (PRGF) to emphasize the new, official anti-poverty focus. Whether this was more than just a change of name is an interesting question. Even years later the Fund's home page informed: 'The Poverty Reduction and Growth Facility (PRGF), formerly known as the Enhanced Structural Adjustment Facility (ESAF) provides loans . . . .' (IMF, 2003a).

Arguably, HIPC II was even more disappointing than HIPC I. NGOs immediately challenged its viability. Already in 2000 the NGO community spoke of the 'betrayal of Cologne: twelve months of failure' (Raffer and Singer, 2001, p. 190). It soon proved that reductions were too small. The Zedillo report written at the request of the UN Secretary General concluded in 2001 that HIPC II had 'in most cases' (Zedillo et al., 2001, p. 21) not gone far enough to reach sustainable debt levels, suggesting a 're-enhanced' HIPC III (ibid., p. 54).

'Topping up' had to be invented, in the words of the G7 at their Kananaskis summit in 2002 with 'additional assistance (or topping up) at the Completion Point'. In plain English this means that the embarrassment of inviability at 'completion point' was to be tackled by additional relief above what estimations under HIPC II had produced as 'necessary' reductions. It may well be called HIPC III. The MDRI could be counted as HIPC IV. This new acronym helpfully avoids the possibility that HIPC counting might eventually surpass the number of French kings named Louis (of whom there were only 18).

Like HIPC I, HIPC II and 'debt management' by creditors in general have suffered from two fundamental shortcomings:

- 'Overoptimistic' projections (discussed in detail in Chapter 12), 'proving' that objectively too small reductions would suffice and 'justifying' highly insufficient payment cuts (HIPCs), thus prolonging the problem.
- Pure arbitrariness of creditors in deciding which countries would receive HIPC treatment.

Nigeria, a severely indebted low income country (SILIC), was classified a HIPC initially, but removed from the list in 1998 as no longer meeting the criteria. She had a debts/export ratio of 250.14 and a debt service ratio (DSR) of 11.22 in 1998. However, the low DSR, helpfully below the HIPC limit due to arrears, results exclusively from the fact that Nigeria – unable to pay as due – had accumulated huge arrears. Since 1993 debt service was a fraction of interest arrears on long-term debt. Arrears of principal were always much higher than these interest arrears during that period. Simply by adding interest arrears Nigeria's DSR would have been slightly above 35 per cent in 1997. Adding all principal arrears shown by the IBRD's *Global Development Finance* for 1997 (calculating as though all contractual obligations had been honoured as stipulated) would produce a DSR of 90.93 per cent. The lack of 'IDA-only' status, a criterion wholly dependent on arbitrary creditor decisions 'excluded' Nigeria. Before getting substantial Paris Club debt relief in 2005, Nigeria had suddenly been moved again to official IDA-only status.

Indonesia, once presented as a miracle by the BWIs eagerly taking credit for another success, became a SILIC as a result of BWI advice that produced the Asian crisis. She was denied HIPC status, although simple divisions of total debts in present value terms and debt service by export revenues showed a debt/exports ratio of 251.75 and a DSR of 33 in 1998. Economically and judged by HIPC-relevant debt indicators Indonesia was a HIPC. But as in Nigeria's case, the amount of debt was substantial ($150.8 billion). Seeing HIPC reductions as costly creditors denied HIPC treatment on economically unconvincing, bureaucratic grounds (Raffer and Singer, 2001, pp. 191–92).

THE ASIAN CRISIS 1997

Soon after the 'Tequila crisis' the old cycle of euphoria and doom repeated itself, producing the Asian crisis, with 'striking similarities' to the Mexican crash (Ortiz Martinez, 1998). East Asian countries were hailed as model economies right into the crash. More recently Argentina was still praised for its economic policies while already crashing. Asians were said to be successful because they had embraced globalization and orthodox economic teachings so fully – model pupils like Mexico before 1994–95 or pre-crash Chile.

It must not be forgotten that the risk weight given by the Basle Committee to short-run flows encouraged those risky short-term flows that brought about the Asian crash. The Basle system accorded a low risk weight of 20 per cent to claims vis-à-vis private banks in non-OECD countries with maturities up to and a weight of 100 per cent if maturities exceeded one year. At a hearing at the German *Bundestag* on 14 March

2001 Andrew Crockett, the head of the Bank for International Settlement, explained this problematic decision as 'a micro-macro problem'. For any individual loan a shorter maturity means *ceteris paribus* less risk than a longer one. He admitted, however, that there is a problem if 'all loans to Thailand are with three-months maturity': their effect becomes highly destabilizing – a correct observation. As rules and norms are made for all lenders rather than for the single, odd out loan, this macro effect should have been foreseen. Not doing so, Basle I became one major cause of the Asian crash.

Much later the IBRD (1999, p. 2) acknowledged having known 'the relevant institutional lessons' years before. A report by its Operations Evaluation Department on Chile's structural adjustment loans 'highlighted the lack of prudential supervision of financial institutions in increasing the economy's vulnerability to the point of collapse' (ibid.). The 'key lesson' that 'prudential rules and surveillance are necessary safeguards . . . rather than unnecessary restrictions' (ibid.) did not keep the BWIs from encouraging undue liberalization, the very policies leading to Chile's crash, in Mexico and in Asia. The problem had been recognized years before. The unfolding of the Asian crisis could be watched like a movie whose script is known. Argentina's crisis in 1995 goes unmentioned, although it was of a similar variety.

One has indeed to ask: 'Why did not policymakers and international financial institutions give these weaknesses appropriate weight?' (ibid.). Why did neither IBRD nor IMF (both not normally known for their restraint in giving advice) warn Asian countries to proceed more slowly with cautious sequencing as they do, meanwhile pointing at already available evidence, instead of supporting too quick liberalization and applauding inflows of volatile capital? IBRD (1999, p. 2) fails to produce a credible answer, stating instead that 'decisionmakers overlooked the failure of the Asian countries to comply with the basic tenets of the much abused Washington consensus'. Summarizing that Mexico fulfilled most of the consensus conditions, but East Asia did not, the IBRD presents 'The conclusion: Washington consensus policies were neither the cause of high growth, nor the cause of the crisis' (ibid.). This begs the question why debtors have been forced to adopt them, and why Bank and Fund had propagated them so forcefully. One also wonders about the rapid U-turn in the evaluation of a region whose success as an 'Asian miracle' orthodoxy and the BWIs had claimed to result from the policies they advise (cf. Raffer and Singer, 2001, pp. 53, 138ff.).

If Asian countries had not liberalized their economies so strongly, the crisis could not have happened. Money that cannot enter a country can hardly leave it. Sticking to the old, successful Asian model would have prevented the crisis, as it prevented the debt crisis of the 1980s – or control-led debt problems as Korea did in the early 1980s. High debt/equity ratios (for instance, 5:1 for Daewoo) which posed no problem under government protection in the Asian system make an enterprise extremely vulnerable in a Western type financial system, even without the additional risk of volatile short-term inflows. These ratios alone were enough reason not to liberalize so speedily, exposing actors to an environment for which they were extremely ill-equipped.

As in the case of Mexico the bail-out of international investors followed immediately. Although debts had been incurred by private companies the governments of the borrowing countries were taken to task – as in Chile some 15 years ago, someone had to finance the bail-out. As private busi-ness can go bankrupt, governments had to guarantee that speculators got paid. Stiglitz (2000b, p. 2) puts it in a nutshell. While 'reckless lending by international banks and other financial institutions combined with reckless borrowing' and 'fickle investor expectations' led to the crash, the 'costs – in terms of soaring unemployment and plummeting wages – were borne by workers. Workers were asked to listen to sermons about "bearing pain" just short after hearing, from the same preachers, sermons about how globalization and opening up capital markets would bring them unprecedented growth.' The present US crisis could not be described more aptly. Wages suffer definitely more than bonus payments in the sector causing the crisis.

Although the budgetary situation was excellent by international stand-ards, the IMF insisted on its usual austerity measures. During 1990–94 average budget deficits of Korea, Malyasia and the Philippines were 0.4, 0.7 and 1.4 per cent of GDP, respectively, which compared favourably with the deficits of most European countries. Indonesia and Thailand had surpluses. During 1995–96 all five countries had budget surpluses. Nevertheless, and although the problem was private debts, the IMF imme-diately called for budget restraint. The room for manoeuvring that the governments had could thus not be used to soften the crisis by increasing public expenditure. Naturally, as private debts had to be socialized, public money was needed for bail-outs rather than for cushioning the impact of the crash on the populations. Foreign exchange borrowed from the IMF was used to allow speculators to leave the countries with smaller losses than they would have had to suffer without cover. The Asian crisis of 1997 moved well over $100 billion in bail-out funds. IFIs once again came unconditionally down on the side of creditors. Living standards deterio-rated drastically. Nevertheless the issue of the right of workers to partici-pate in the decisions which did affect their lives so thoroughly was never raised, as Stiglitz notes. Naturally, no foreign creditor would ever enjoy such 'implicit government guarantees' in any OECD country. Money lost with Enron is certainly not refunded by the US Treasury.

Due to its size the Asian crisis of 1997 was the first real challenge to the virtually unchallenged rule of neoliberalism. Grave errors and misjudgement in crisis management (Raffer and Singer, 2001, pp. 150ff.) damaged the credibility of the BWIs. Strong critique was heard from more conservative quarters as well. The crises in Russia and Brazil that followed quickly, and possibly the crash of the LTCM hedge fund, certainly intensified doubts. Although critically important for global economic policy, the Asian crash was nothing generically special. Liberalization and deregulation had triggered a host of crises before. Inflation adjusted losses due to the US Savings & Loans debacle, which cost US taxpayers hundreds of billions of dollars, were 'several times larger than the losses experienced in the Great Depression' as J. Stiglitz pointed out. Yet in relation to GDP it is dwarfed by crises in SCs and formerly communist countries: 'This debacle would not make the list of the top 25 international banking crises since the early 1980s', Stiglitz noted at the UN University in 1998. This means that there was more than one such major crisis per year on average, effects of the Washington Consensus that had simply been repressed by official thinking for nearly two decades. Crises were not confined to the financial sector, as the deregulation of British beef production shows, where the public had to pick up the bill of neoliberal policies when BSE erupted. All this indicates the strength of interests behind the Washington Consensus.

The Asian crisis did trigger hard feelings. As distinguished an economist as Jagdish Bhagwati spoke of a 'Wall-Street-Treasury complex' dictating the agenda, drawing a parallel to the Savings & Loans crisis in the USA. Attempts to establish an Asian Monetary Fund, disliked by the IMF and the US Treasury, were seen as the explanation of why the BWIs had not warned their Asian members. Conspiracy theories emerged, also fuelled by cheap sales of Asian assets to Euro-American foreigners. The fact that the IMF even identified foreign buyers for Korean banks certainly did not counteract such perceptions. Expanding Bhagwati's expression to 'Wall Street-Treasury-IMF complex' Robert Wade asked why the IMF insisted on further capital account opening in countries 'awash with domestic savings', and why it did 'so little to organize debt *rescheduling* negotiations'. Since 1990 Wade had repeatedly warned of precisely such a crisis, of 'speculative inflows', '[U]ncontrolled outflows' and vulnerability to an 'investment collapse'.

In 1999 Michael Dobbs and Paul Blustein (1999) reported in the *Washington Post* that the 'wide spread belief that the West would bail out Russia encouraged foreign investors to pour billions' into risky investments 'setting the stage for a catastrophic reversal'. The authors quote an IMF official working on Russia who received a 'deluge of phone calls from investment bankers and portfolio managers lobbying for a new IMF bailout'. After earning returns 'upwards of 50 percent' they 'wanted the fund to use taxpayer-backed resources' to ensure that they would not face losses. One person called 'three, four times a day'.

An interesting change should not go unnoticed. In the early days of 'structural adjustment' the BWIs routinely insisted on devaluations by debtor countries as a necessary element to solve crises. Some years later the IMF especially came to favour currency boards and fixed pegs. During the new crises brought about by capital account liberalization in the 1990s, such as in Asia or Brazil, the BWIs insisted on defending fixed exchange rates. This change occurred in line with changed capital flows. In the 1980s debts were in foreign currencies. Devaluing the debtor's currency increased the debt burden in domestic currency, without impairing debt stocks in dollars or yens. The short-term placements of the 1990s were often in the debtor's currency. Speculators would have had to take losses if the old recipe had still been applied. Keeping the peg fixed allows them to leave the country without or with reduced losses. Financing this outflow with money borrowed from IFIs, debtor countries socialize speculators' losses.

One cannot exclude that high real interest rates may attract highly speculative, extremely short-term capital hoping for a quick buck made within a (few) day(s) before leaving again, particularly so if speculators expect to be protected by official bail-outs socializing losses. But such inflows are a far cry from capital needed to finance development, and likely to aggravate rather than to defuse crises. On the other hand, high real interest rates that might go beyond 40 per cent are no doubt erratic disruptions as bankruptcies of domestic corporations and entrepreneurs prove.

Malaysia, the one country that introduced capital controls against neoliberal warnings and pressures, did not fare that badly, as IMF documents meanwhile admit (cf. Raffer and Singer, 2001, pp. 156f.). The reduction of interest rates that accompanied controls helped contain increases in non-performing loans. According to Standard & Poor's these would have risen to above 30 per cent of total loans, if interest rates had not been cut sharply. Legally Malaysia simply used her membership right: any IMF member may exercise capital controls in a manner which will not restrict payments for current transactions, defined as 'not for the purpose of transferring capital' by the Fund's Articles of Agreement, although even restricting such flows is legal. Article VI(1)(a) goes further, stating that a 'member may not use the Fund's general resources to meet a large and sustained outflow of capital except as provided in Section 2 of this Article [referring exclusively to reserve tranche purchases] and the Fund may request a member to exercise controls to prevent such use of the general resources of the Fund'. The mechanisms to control speculation established under Bretton Woods and legally still in place, have been eroded and virtually abolished in practice. Asian countries had not only the right to control capital outflows – as the IMF had to admit when Malaysia exercised it (ibid., p.157) – but in forcing members to finance large and sustained outflows by speculators the IMF openly violated its own constitution, protecting speculators from those countries that control the Fund by their votes.

Corrective measures affecting the balance of payments should be done 'without resorting to measures destructive of national or international prosperity' (Article I(v)). This would have been easily possible in Asia if speculators had not been bailed out. Article IV(1)(ii) requests the IMF to foster stability and a monetary system that does not produce 'erratic disruptions'. The policy of high real interest rates forced on clients did the opposite.

The history of the Asian crisis displays the typical pattern of any neoliberal crisis, including the present US crisis. Euphoric eulogies on the efficiency and benevolence of shedding national boundaries and regulatory constraints right until the crash. Once the crisis breaks, attitudes towards public intervention change totally: socializing private losses created by deregulated markets is welcome and demanded. The huge US bail-outs in and after 2008 are another example, differing only in sheer dimension. But so does this crisis. Southern governments had to socialize private debts repeatedly. Taxpayers, especially vulnerable and politically powerless groups, are left to bear the brunt. In contrast to domestic markets, mechanisms protecting the poor do not exist. Globalization has not replicated the structures of domestic civilized legal and political systems – considered useless at best to creditors and speculators. For a sovereign debt overhang no crisis resolution procedure with proper debtor protection exists yet.

Both BWIs gained dramatically in importance. Acting as judges, jury, expert and bailiff in their own cause, public creditors forced debtors to accumulate further unpayable debts and to 'open' their economies much more than creditor governments themselves would accept. Debt management driven liberalization reduced tariff revenues on which especially poorer countries depend critically, thus often aggravating debt problems. It weakened the position of debtor countries in the World Trade Organization (WTO) because liberalization measures already taken under 'structural adjustment' can no longer be used as a bargaining chip in multilateral negotiations.

The fact that the tigers did demonstrably not follow the Washington

Consensus (Rodrik, 1996; Raffer and Singer, 2001, p. 53) was downplayed at best, but mostly disregarded. The IBRD's conclusion on the irrelevance of the Washington Consensus strongly corroborates Rodrik's view that bringing about changes in economic policy was the real reason. Rodrik (1996, p. 17) interprets the debt crisis as an opportunity seized by ortho- dox economists for a 'wholesale reform of prevailing policies' offering the chance 'to wipe the slate clean and mount a frontal attack on the entire range of policies in use'. A crisis brought about by overspending and over- lending in globalized credit markets and the sudden change of Northern economic policy sending interest rates skyrocketting was simply declared to stem from too little globalization: import substitution and 'inward looking' policies. Distinctions between bad and proper import substitu- tion were not made, even though the Asian tigers had used these discred- ited policies to good effect before they started neoliberal globalization. The crash of the globalized credit market provided leverage for further globalization in the South.

THE END OF THE PONZI SCHEME

Two decades after 1982 BWI debt management reached the end of the flagpole. After shifting lending from bilateral creditors to commercial banks to public IFIs after August 1982 and then on to bondholders, no further shift is possible. After the wave of privatization enforced by debt management there is little left to sell or swap. The game of debt-musical chairs is over, reality has to be faced. Debt reduction to sustainable levels can no longer be avoided.

One cannot exclude that IFIs themselves might still be prepared to finance one further shift towards more multilateral lending if they get enough resources and remain protected from losses. During the Asian crisis the IMF's First Deputy Managing Director argued – using Thailand's crisis of 1997 and Mexico's of 1994–95 as supporting evidence – that the prospect of larger crises caused by capital account liberalization would call for more resources for the IMF to cope with the very crises the Fund's liberalization drive would create in the future (Fischer, 1997). From the narrow point of view of institutional self-interest (which one, of course, hopes to be irrelevant) such crises are better than using the membership right to capital controls guaranteed by the IMF's Articles of Agreement, which would not require increased IMF resources nor generate addi- tional IMF income. Even though the huge bail-out of creditors in Brazil in August 2002 may be interpreted as a different signal, solvent member countries are unlikely to go on financing increasingly larger bail-outs.

Unfortunately the G20 London decision in 2009 changed this for the worse, shifting the balance again in favour of IFIs. Those whose policies have contributed to the crisis are asked to fight it. Dracula is in charge of guarding the blood bank.

3. In quest of solutions: sovereign insolvency proposals, collective action clauses and recent country cases

In November 2001 the IMF performed a sudden and unexpected U-turn. After nearly two decades of fiercest opposition, it suddenly advocated the very idea of sovereign insolvency that it had opposed bitterly just the day before. The new First Deputy Managing Director, Anne Krueger (2001a), joined those proposing to copy domestic insolvency laws to solve sovereign debt problems. Although the titles of Krueger's first papers speak of a 'new approach' and she did initially not quote any of the many authors advocating this approach much earlier, the idea of sovereign insolvency is not new at all. Meanwhile Rogoff and Zettelmeyer (2002b) compiled a comprehensive survey on earlier publications.

Arguably before Krueger, Adam Smith advocated sovereign insolvency in 1776 – the only author given academic credit by her. In 1981 an international lawyer, C.G. Oechsli, published the proposal to use corporate insolvency (Chapter 11, Title 11 of the US Code) as the analogy to renegotiate the debts of SCs. Soon after 1982 a British banker, David Suratgar, came up with this idea (cf. Raffer, 2001b; Rogoff and Zettelmeyer, 2002b). Krueger's first speech followed several statements in favour of sovereign insolvency by the Secretary of the US Treasury, Paul O'Neill, the British Chancellor of the Exchequer, Gordon Brown, and the Canadian Finance Minister, Paul Martin. Even the IMF's former Managing Director, Michel Camdessus, had once suggested 'some sort of Super Chapter 11 for countries' (*Financial Times*, 17 September 1998). Two employees of the Bank of England and the Bank of Canada, Andy Haldane and Mark Kruger, proposed a standstill in 2001, arguing that sovereign debtors need the safe harbour which bankruptcy law provides in a corporate context. Last and by no means least, in 2000 the Secretary General of the UN, Kofi Annan (2000, p. 38), had called for a 'debt arbitration process to balance the interests of creditors and sovereign debtors and introduce greater discipline into their relations' in his Millennium Report. Unfortunately he took back his courageous demand relatively soon – possibly so under strong pressure, certainly after advice.

While sovereign insolvency is hardly a new idea, Anne Krueger is to be commended for having broken the taboo of pronouncing the word insolvency. This brought about a long needed change in the IMF's own attitude. She provided street cred, in particular in 19th and H Streets. Once she had presented the idea, many opponents of sovereign insolvency, especially IMF staff, lost any recollection of their own grave reservations. Like being touched by Harry Potter's wand, 'arguments' used to assert that the principles of insolvency could not be applied to sovereign debtors disappeared. The IMF's special variant, called Sovereign Debt Restructuring Mechanism (SDRM), differs perceptibly from earlier proposals though. It is totally shaped by the IMF's institutional self-interest, aimed at protecting the IMF rather than at solving the problem. Understandably, strong reservations were heard from creditors, including the US Treasury (Taylor, 2002), academics and NGOs.

By proposing its SDRM for relatively richer countries the IMF itself admitted that its own and the IBRD's debt management could not solve the problem. With the Ponzi scheme definitely over and the sharing of unavoidable losses looming over all creditors, the IMF tried to secure itself privileges early on, immunizing itself legally against losses.

CREDITOR-CAUSED DELAYS AND DAMAGES

Krueger rightly pointed out that delays cause costs and that avoiding such damages is one reason for sovereign insolvency procedures. One has to concur fully with Krueger (2001a, p. 8):

> For debtor countries, the new approach would clearly reduce the costs of restructuring and would encourage countries to go down that road earlier than they do now. This is not a bad thing. At the moment too many countries with insurmountable debt problems wait too long, imposing unnecessary costs on themselves, and on the international community that has to help pick up the pieces.

As someone having advocated sovereign insolvency since 1986, repeatedly drawing attention to this kind of damage, I might recall that countries were not allowed by creditors to choose that road. The IMF especially had opposed it fiercely.

One should recall that the IBRD (1992a, pp. 10ff.) had acknowledged insolvency as the root of the problem during the euphoria of the early 1990s, when the end of the debt crisis was proclaimed and it could be argued that insolvency relief was no longer necessary. In spite of its own embarrassing record the IBRD lectured on prudent borrowing. Its *World Debt Tables 1992–93* explained that 'the principal policy lesson of the debt crisis is that domestic resources and policy, not external finance per se are the key to economic development'. After drawing attention to vulner-abilities, adverse external shocks and changes in interest rates, the IBRD declared as early as in 1992:

> *In a solvency crisis, early recognition of solvency as the root cause and the need for a final settlement are important for minimizing the damage.* . . . protracted rene-gotiations and uncertainty damaged economic activity in debtor countries for several years . . .. It took too long to recognize that liquidity was the visible tip of the problem, but not its root. (IBRD, 1992a, p. 10ff., emphasis in original)

In *Finance & Development* of September 1992, two IBRD economists, M. Ahmed and Larry Summers quantified the costs of delaying recogni-tion of the 'now' generally acknowledged solvency crisis as 'one decade' lost in development. The Bank failed to mention that this delay had been caused by defenders of the illiquidity theory, notably the BWIs. In spite of the IBRD's insight about damaging delays, the HIPC Initiative delayed solutions again for six years; insolvency remained shunned by the Bank. After timid attempts to propose Indonesia as a model during the 1980s, the IBRD later tried to create the impression that Indonesia had not received debt reduction. According to the IBRD and Krueger this delay damaged poor debtor economies further. Neither Bank, Fund, nor other official creditors see their delaying tactics as a reason for compensating at least part of the damage they caused.

All historical cases of sovereign debt overhang prove that debts must eventually be reduced by substantial amounts. The IMF's *World Economic Outlook* of September (2003b, p. 140) presented research results for the period 1970–2002 that 'suggest that while large debt reductions have often occurred in conjunction with debt defaults there are cases where they have been brought about by a combination of strong economic growth and fiscal consolidation'.

Nineteen out of 26 cases 'were associated with a debt default'. Obviously reductions were insufficient. The IMF suggests that a 'sustainable public debt level for a typical emerging economy may only be about 25 percent of GDP' (ibid., p. 142), much less than present debt burdens of problem cases. This passage recalls well-known facts from insolvency procedures: while some debtors believed to be insolvent can overcome their problem, most cannot.

Logically debts have grown further by capitalized arrears, adding further unpayable debts on top of those obligations an insolvent debtor is already unable to honour. If a debtor has to pay n per cent interest, but is only able to pay m per cent (m $<$ n) the stock of debts grows by $(n - m)$ per cent every year. With n and m assumed constant (5 and 2.5, respectively) debts would, for example, increase by 28 per cent over a decade. The example could be complicated, for example, by introducing repayments of principal, variable interest rates or inflation, but the basic mechanism remains unchanged. If the debtor is insolvent rather than illiquid, debts start accumulating on paper, further beyond an insolvent debtor's economic capacity to repay. Debts that can never be repaid because of increasing gaps between economic capacity and payments contractually due – I called them 'phantom debts' – must increase eventually. As anyone familiar with basic mathematics can verify, creditors unwilling to grant sufficient relief when necessary increase irrecouperable debts. Total debts are pushed to ever more unrealistic heights, making reductions to economically sustainable levels appear costlier and costlier on paper as the share of phantom debts increases. Existing only on paper they nevertheless compromise the debtor's economic future. They also allow creditors to exert pressure. 'Forgiving' them may mean losing political power but certainly not money. One cannot lose money already lost. Deleting phantom debts simply means to stop playing the 'Emperor's New Clothes', acknowledging the naked economic truth.

While debt management has not provided a solution, it has affected North-South relations fundamentally. It provided political leverage to the North, allowing creditors to change the policies of debtors. The economic sense behind 'solutions' such as the debt service option, under which Cologne Terms with 90 per cent NPV reduction on eligible debts are achieved 'through concessional interest rates and a repayment period of 125 years, including 65 years of grace', as calculated by the IBRD's *Global Development Finance 2000* (2000b, vol.1, p.171), remains unclear at best. Similarly the 'bullet option' with an interest rate of 0.0001 per cent (the IBRD did not dare write over how many years) would be ridiculed in the case of all other debtor-creditor relations. Politically, though, such solutions provide long-term leverage over poor countries.

In the end creditors as a group must accept larger losses, but not all creditors are necessarily worse off. The structure of creditors has changed dramatically, as described in Chapter 2. Bondholders again account for the bulk of claims in quite a few cases. Noteworthy distributional effects exist, exacerbated by the fact that IFIs were able to secure a privileged status of de facto preferred creditors. Therefore others have to lose more. One of the main goals of the SDRM was to secure legally preferred creditor status for IFIs.

THE SDRM – ANOTHER FORM OF SIMPLY DISASTROUS RESCHEDULING MANAGEMENT?

The main difference between the SDRM and earlier proposals of sovereign insolvency, which understandably raised highly justified concerns, is the role of the Fund. If implemented Krueger's proposal would increase the IMF's role and importance dramatically. After the loss in reputation caused by the Asian crisis and the Meltzer report this might not be unwelcome. The IMF would not only become the undisputed overlord of sovereign insolvency, but its present de facto treatment as a preferred creditor would be legally enshrined by treaty.

Naturally Krueger does not present the SDRM this way. A lot of lip service is paid to the alleged influence of private creditors. In her first speech Krueger (2001a, p. 7) admits that adjudicating disputes among creditors, verifying claims (as I proposed in 1990, see Chapter 5) and confirming the integrity of voting 'are not things the Fund could do well'. It is alleged that a 'supermajority' of creditors should have the right to take important decisions. This is the majority of all creditors demanded to reduce their claims, able to bind dissenting creditor minorities. The outcome of the process would 'remain where it should be – in the hands of the debtor and creditors' (ibid., p. 5).

In spite of such statements, Krueger's model assures that the IMF would absolutely dominate and determine the outcome. In reaction to critique, especially by Wall Street, IMF staff churned out many different versions after November 2001. Space prohibits discussing all details raised and revised. However the important elements remained unchanged. The IMF's crushing dominance would be assured by several features:

1. The IMF Alone Decides

The IMF's Executive Board alone determines sustainability and decides on the adequacy of the debtor's economic policy. These decisions cannot be challenged. By determining sustainability the IMF would automatically determine the amount of debt reduction. The most important – and in all likelihood most contentious – decision would be taken by the Fund, a creditor both in its own right and controlled by a majority of official creditors. Neither other creditors nor the debtor would have any say, including on which policies the debtor is to adopt. In contrast to the insolvency procedure of public debtors in the USA, where overindebted municipalities have the right to present a plan, the IMF, not the debtor, would submit the plan. The IMF later suggested that the debtor may choose which part of debts to include into an SDRM, a choice which would be 'influenced' by the Fund, whose conditionality would 'enhance' the 'incentives to assure equitable treatment' of creditors. The IMF even considered enshrining the board's authority to define a debtor's behaviour as a breach of its obligations under the Articles of Agreement and to determine sanctions against this member country.

Krueger (ibid., p. 5) suggested that the Fund give 'implicit support to a temporary standstill'. This would 'allow a country to come to the Fund and request' a stay, enabling the debtor to 'negotiate a rescheduling or restructuring with its creditors, given the Fund's consent to that line of attack' [sic]. Krueger suggested that the Fund be given the right to endorse the stay triggered by the debtor's demand for insolvency relief. Practically this means no SDRM – no 'attack' on creditors – without the IMF's permission.

Put in a nutshell: 'Like an IMF-supported adjustment program, the standstill could be endorsed for limited periods and renewed following reviews of the country's economic policies and its relations with creditors' (ibid., p. 7). She suggests a 'maximum period beyond which the stay could not be maintained without the approval of a required majority of creditors'. As Krueger's wording allows more than one renewal creditors might have to wait before they get a chance to vote. During this period the Fund alone would decide.

The passage on relations with creditors raises the question of why the Fund would have to evaluate it. Are creditors themselves not able to judge whether their relations with a debtor are good? What if their view differs from the IMF's? What happens if – for the sake of argument – all creditors accept a stay, but the IMF does not agree? Would the Fund endorse the stay all the same?

Massive Wall Street opposition against stays and standstills produced changes. In an attempt to please the private sector the IMF eventually proposed in 2002 that activation would not automatically trigger any suspension of creditor rights (for details and the quotes of various IMF documents, see Raffer, 2006 as well as Chapter 5). There would be no generalized stay on enforcement and no suspension of contractual provisions, including on interest accrual. Assuaging a concern expressed by many Wall Street investors, any creditor would formally retain the right to litigation. But the so-called 'hotchpot' rule and the possibility of enjoining specific enforcement actions would render this right useless. The 'hotchpot' rule means that any amount recovered due to litigation would be deducted from the sum this creditor would finally be entitled to receive. If successful litigants had to pay their legal fees they would be worse off than by not litigating. Litigation becomes pointless. So this was not really a fundamental change.

2.   Protecting the IMF's Own Claims

The present de facto status of IFIs is to change into a *de jure* preference. Official declarations and assertions have perfectly obfuscated this fact: legally and even according to their own statutes IFIs have no preferred creditor status. This technical concept does not formally apply to the IBRD, nor to regional multilateral banks or the IMF. Suffice it here to point out that the IMF knows that it enjoys no legal or contractual preferred creditor status, as can be read on its very own home page (Boughton, 2001, pp. 820ff.; for details see Chapter 13). Preferential treatment of IFIs makes the ongoing discussion about bailing in the private sector – or private sector involvement – particularly obfuscating. Under various Brady schemes private creditors accepted losses, for example, 35 per cent in the case of Mexico. Reductions were quite generous but did not solve the problem as new official money immediately increased debts again. Although private creditors granted 45 per cent reduction, Ecuador's first Brady deal only shows as a small blip downwards in the country's debt time series. This obviously does not result from private sector stinginess but from the fact that private creditors alone granted reductions. Finally in 1999 Ecuador was unable to honour her Brady bonds, the first undeniable failure of this initiative. If all creditors had reduced by only 30 per cent commercial banks would have saved 15 percentage points and Ecuador would in all probability have been economically afloat again – a prime example of the necessity of equal treatment repeatedly demanded by the private sector.

Regarding its own major shareholders, the members of the Paris Club, the IMF remained undecided. The Fund suggested both that they could participate as a separate class of creditors or that these bilateral official creditors might not participate at all. Apparently the choice of whether to remain exempt from the SDRM was left to the IMF's major shareholders. Should they decide to opt out, the private sector alone would have to accept reductions of their claims. The following passage (IMF, 2002a, p. 21) definitely deserves quoting. It allows an evaluation of the Fund's repeated assertions of wanting to empower private creditors in a very clear light. Paris Club members: 'would presumably continue their current policy of requiring that the debtor seek comparable treatment from private creditors when private claims on the sovereign are judged to be material, and would also continue to assess whether the agreement of private creditors meet this requirement'.

As projections and advice by the BWIs usually form the basis for decisions by the Paris Club, contradictions between the sustainability assessed within the SDRM and Paris Club decisions might not be considered too likely. The Paris Club would in this case continue to determine reductions to be granted by private creditors. These would be expected to implement its decisions.

3. Making the IMF's Statutes the Basis of the SDRM

The whole mechanism, down to details, is to be enshrined into the IMF's statutes. Krueger uses the problem of so-called 'vulture funds' to claim that the IMF is necessary to implement sovereign insolvency, arguing that laws barring 'vultures' from interfering with the mechanism 'must have the force of law universally' (Krueger, 2001a, p. 7). Otherwise creditors would deliberately seek out jurisdictions where they can enforce claims against creditor majorities. As 'Getting every country to amend its domestic bankruptcy law – let alone to enforce it in a uniform way – would be a heroic undertaking', Krueger (2001b, p. 3) recommends an amendment of the IMF's statutes. This 'statutory approach' would oblige all member states to change their domestic laws in a way that opposition of creditor minorities can be overruled. 'Supermajorities' would then be able to bind dissenting creditors. As both changing the Fund's statutes and the process of ratification would take time, her proposal would have 'no implications for our current negotiations with member countries – Argentina and Turkey, for example' (ibid., p. 2). This 'statutory approach' would firmly and officially install the IMF as the overlord of sovereign debt relief. Private creditors and debtors would have to pick up the bill. The results are likely to match those of HIPC I, HIPC II, 'structural adjustment', Paris Club Terms and the 'Brady deals', all characterized by a leading role of the IMF. One may, in fact, call the SDRM 'Brady II', another Brady Plan incorporating appropriate modifications made necessary by the new debt structure with many bondholders.

The argument is altogether flawed. Not all countries and territories are IMF members. The Cayman Islands, for example, are not a member but enjoy enough autonomy to offer itself as a place for creditors shopping for jurisdictions where unanimity is required and any single hold-out creditor can try to get more than accepted by all other creditors. It should be recalled that these three minuscule islands have routinely been used against the Tobin tax opposed by the IMF, arguing that it could not be introduced because universal acceptance could not be assured. 'Tobin tax paradises' such as the Cayman Islands would preclude implementation. The same concern would logically hold with regard to Krueger's 'shopping for jurisdictions'. Conveniently, though, this point was not discussed.

Krueger (2002b, p. 4) assures that this amendment would be used 'only as a tool to empower creditors and debtor, not as a way to extend the

IMF's legal authority'. This is difficult to believe, considering that there is an easy way to assure that 'vultures' cannot disturb negotiations between creditors and the debtor. Krueger (2001a, p.4) herself points out that it is not absolutely clear whether Elliott's strategy would 'survive legal challenge in future cases'. Legally there are several suggestions on how to preclude vulture funds from operating, but there is – as Raffer (2002c) showed – a water tight way of doing so.

Krueger's assertions that decisions should be left in the hands of creditors and that adjudicating disputes, verifying claims and confirming the integrity of voting are not things the Fund could do well sounded too good to be true. It soon turned out not to be true. Krueger changed her mind, demanding the role of the arbiter for the IMF. A Dispute Resolution Forum (DRF), later called Sovereign Debt Dispute Resolution Forum (SDDRF) was proposed. This new IMF organ without authority to challenge decisions made by the Executive Board but 'independent' from the Executive Board and the Board of Governors was to be established by an amendment of the IMF's Articles of Agreement. The selection criteria for its members or even classification rules for the many creditor classes the IMF imagines would all become enshrined into the Fund's statute. Its decisions resolving disputes between the debtor and its creditors or among creditors could not be challenged (an appeals panel was suggested at one time). Itself subject to the IMF Board's decision, the SDDRF would hold substantial powers over private creditors and the debtor. It could recognize or void any claim in full or in part. It could practically wipe out claims, which is the ultimate authority over creditors. In 2002 Krueger proposed a complicated, clumsy and unnecessary five-stage process again dominated by the IMF. Variants and changes were proposed and discussed at length.

Krueger's 'statutory approach' would assure that the IMF can continue to take the important decisions as it has done so far. Krueger (2002b, p.4) puts it in a nutshell: 'The Fund would only influence the process as it does now, through its normal lending decisions.' Considering that the first adjustment measures were implemented in sub-Saharan Africa some 30 years ago and the Fund's success there and in other debtor countries, this is hardly encouraging. The whole SDRM procedure, down to absolutely minor details, was to become part of the Fund's Articles of Agreement, which would have further empowered the Fund. It was also considered that either the (SD)DRF or a separate private institution might administer a sovereign claims registry. This useful detail soon disappeared from the discussion.

The rejection of the SDRM during the 2003 spring meeting by the US and emerging markets precluded the introduction of an unfair, self-serving, inefficient system. The discussion will definitely erupt again with the next big crisis, especially so if and when the sums needed for further bail-outs are large. Economic logic suggests that the IMF will advocate its SDRM once again – the advantages it would confer to the Fund are simply too great to assume anything else.

Discriminated private creditors have voiced strong and understandable reservations against a leading role of the IMF in determining debt reductions. It seems easy to guess what private creditors think about phrases such as involving or bailing in the private sector, considering that the private sector has repeatedly granted, sometimes substantial, debt reductions, while the IMF has been protected and would be bailed out totally by the SDRM.

COLLECTIVE ACTION CLAUSES

John Taylor (2002), Under-Secretary for International Affairs of the US Treasury, opposed an increase in the IMF's importance, proposing a package of new collective action clauses (CACs) instead. US corporate bond issuers had used majority action as a means to 'replicate the attractive feature of a formal bankruptcy (the ability to force changes on a dissident minority), without actually putting a company into Chapter 11' (Buchheit and Gulati, 2000, p. 68). Unlike English law that allows changing any terms by appropriate creditor majority, US law has precluded any change in amounts of and dates for payments without the consent of each affected bondholder since the 1930s. Non-payment terms, however, can by changed, often by simple majority. Debtors can combine the offer to tender existing bonds in exchange for new instruments reflecting the new financial terms of the restructuring with changing non-payment terms of the old bonds, so that creditors unwilling to participate in the exchange will soon hold bonds of sharply reduced or virtually no value. Creditors consenting to the exchange and the amendments 'exit' their old bonds, holding only new bonds after 'exit'. Terms that can be changed include, for example, the waiver of immunity, submission to jurisdiction, financial covenants such as negative pledge restrictions or the issuer's obligation to keep bonds listed on a stock exchange (ibid., pp. 81–82). Apart from incentives that may be offered by debtors, any creditor accepting the offer has every economic reason to want other bondholders to accept as well. As hold-outs are a threat to consenting creditors too, these are interested in exit amendments precluding hold-out action as much as possible.

Although not widely used then, exit amendments were occasionally part of 'Brady deals' (for example, Brazil in 1992). Ecuador was the first debtor to use them for Brady bonds when she defaulted on Brady and eurobond debts in 1999, less than five years after Brady bonds had been issued. As in the case of corporations, incentives to consent had to be offered. Ecuador offered principal reinstatement (automatic issuance of additional bonds if another payment default should occur within the next ten years and continue uncured during one year; bonds to be newly issued would decline over this period) and slow reduction of debts before maturity. Interestingly this can also be done by cash buy-backs at prevailing market discounts. After 1982 direct buy-backs by debtors had been strongly opposed. Cross-default and negative pledge clauses were removed, old bonds were delisted. Ecuador was allowed to reacquire some of her Brady bonds, which made acceleration by remaining bondholders after exchange impossible. Obviously Ecuador's promise of 1995 that she would never default on her Brady bonds was removed. Roughly 97 per cent accepted the offer.

As any rumour that the debtor may finally give in to demands by hold-outs would obviously reduce or destroy chances for successful exit offers, debtors do whatever they can to clarify that they would never settle any amounts due under old bonds on terms more favourable than those of the exchange offer (for example, Pakistan in 1999, Ukraine in 2000, see Buchheit and Gulati, 2000, p. 64).

CACs were not anything new. Under English law contracts containing CACs are fairly common, as well as the appointment of trustees. As the British government has traditionally supported the City's interest, the request for CACs obviously reflected experiences with sovereign debt problems in the past. Because of the shift of jurisdictions from London to New York and possibly the belief that the costs of trustees could be economized, their use had declined. Thus bondholders were left without mechanisms of organizing themselves. Reintroducing CACs into sovereign bonds floated in New York was thus a homecoming. The private sector, for example, the International Primary Market Association, sees trustees meanwhile as an effective way of coordinating creditors. No bondholder can take unilateral action without involving the trustee, who has to carry out litigation and would assure pro rata sharing among bondholders of any recoveries.

Although CACs have been a customary feature in international lending before they largely fell out of use, it was claimed for some time that inserting CACs would increase the costs of borrowing for SCs. Eichengreen and Mody (2000) found that CACs reduce the cost of borrowing for more creditworthy issuers, but less creditworthy issuers pay higher spreads. It appears that for the latter advantages of orderly restructuring are offset by the moral hazard and default risk associated with the presence of renegotiation-friendly loan provisions.

CACs prove that negotiated debt reduction is possible because creditor majorities within the private sector are prepared to recognize economic facts and to help shield their new claims against hold-outs. What they also prove (see Ecuador's Brady reduction) is that (substantial) relief might not be sufficient if only private creditors grant it. The SDRM would have perpetuated this shortcoming, adding the additional shortcoming compared with CACs that debt reductions would not be negotiated between the parties, but imposed by the IMF.

CACs in future loan contracts could bar disruptive litigation from the start and include any of the useful CACs proposed so far or agree on arbitration instead of waivers of immunity, as already stipulated by some contracts between sovereigns and private creditors. One could agree on a traditional waiver of immunity combined with the stipulation that no creditor is allowed to sue during insolvency proceedings. Trustees could be stipulated as well. Any of these options puts vultures out of business, solving the problem that the IMF, in pursuit of its institutional self-interest, presented as so threatening and urgent.

Taylor's proposal was an alternative to the SDRM, but it does not preclude appropriate mechanisms of sovereign insolvency. Helping creditors to organize, to be able to act more quickly and efficiently, CACs are a helpful component of any insolvency rather than a contradiction to it. The proper functioning of fair insolvency procedures depends on the full ability of parties to defend their legal and economic interests. Creditors must be able to act efficiently – whatever helps them to do so is welcome.

Although the SDRM and CACs were not the only proposals on the table, only CACs were readily used. A voluntary Code of Good Conduct for debt renegotiation first proposed by the Banque de France was also promoted. My proposal of internationalizing the basic features of US municipal insolvency, so-called Chapter 9 (of Title 11 US Code, Bankruptcy) has been widely supported by NGOs. It is presented in detail in Chapter 5. The Code of Good Conduct demands fair representation of creditors, an expeditious and cooperative process, fair burden sharing, preserving the debtor's financial situation, reaching debt sustainability as soon as possible and also arbitration – briefly, many elements of Chapter 9 insolvency.

Whenever CACs or the code should be able to prevent formal insolvency procedures this would be great. The very existence of an insolvency mechanism would be helpful in making these options more efficient. Sovereign insolvency is a solution of last resort, a thorny choice, not least to the debtor. However the two models of sovereign insolvency, the IMF's SDRM and my Chapter 9 based debt arbitration contradict each other, as shown in Chapter 5.

Obviously Taylor is not against arbitral awards as such, but against centralizing the process with the IMF. He does not object to arbitration as a means to handle inconsistencies between different types of issues or jurisdictions. One may conclude that he is against one specific model, not necessarily against any form of insolvency.

The G10 recommended CACs. Canada and the UK incorporated clauses regarding creditor actions into their debt contracts as a useful and commendable way of breaking the ice. Eventually the Institute of International Finance supported CACs. In March 2003 Mexico was the first SC debtor issuing bonds with CACs under New York law. With 75 per cent the majority action level was lower than some investors might have liked, but the market dissipated any fears. Since 2003 the number of emerging market issuers using CACs has continued to grow. Eichengreen and Mody have been proven right: fears about increased borrowing costs were unfounded. Logically there is no reason why costs should increase. Signing a fire insurance does not normally increase the likelihood of fire, unless the signing party already holds a lit match next to the insured object.

Uruguay

In March 2003 Uruguay sought a reprofiling of her debt obligations, a move attracting a great deal of attention because it was also seen as an attempt by the critics of the SDRM to show that the private sector could deliver solutions without the SDRM. A high-ranking Uruguayan official formulated: 'from Uruguay's view point' the SDRM 'was divorced with the principles applied in a voluntary debt exchange strategy' (Steneri, 2003, p. 8). Therefore the IMF opposed Uruguay's move. It had supported Ecuador's exit consent, which signalled the need for debt reduction even for Brady bonds, thus supporting the call for an SDRM.

A relatively small debtor, Uruguay merely sought an extension of maturities. Most amortization initially due during 2003–10 was shifted beyond 2010. The Samurai bond already included CACs. These were applied, the first time a sovereign did so in Japan. Unsurprisingly, the exercise was successfully completed within less than two months, resulting in the reprofiling of over 90 per cent of Uruguay's $5.2 billion of outstanding foreign currency bonds. All new external bonds were issued under a trust indenture and included an aggregation clause: if 85 per cent of all affected series agreed to an amendment of the payment terms, then the vote required for the amendment at the level of each individual bond was reduced from 75 per cent to two thirds. Uruguay's maturity extension was implemented at original interest rates, that is, at pre-crisis rates when Uruguay had enjoyed investment grade status. Comparing this with an imputed 'crisis market rate' one may calculate an implicit, small 'haircut'.

Steneri feels that Uruguay's exit amendments 'in some sense were more aggressive than Ecuador's'. They eliminated the ability of hold-outs to attach payments made on new bonds, deleted cross-default and cross-acceleration provisions and removed listing requirements on the old bonds. In October 2003 Uruguay was again able to place a new bond issue.

THE ONGOING SEARCH FOR SOLUTIONS

While helpful, CACs cannot always solve situations of debt distress. In the absence of viable general solutions, different strategies of debt reduction have emerged, all of them based on highly specific circumstances rather than on any general model or rule, let alone the Rule of Law. A wave of retiring Brady bonds occurred recently, bringing their outstanding (dollar-denominated) volume down to less than $50 billion in 2006. Mexico rebought all 'Bradies' as early as 2002, giving important savings in debt service as the reason.

Introducing the MDRI for some poor SCs in 2005, official creditors progressed towards deeper debt relief. In 2005 the present Norwegian government went further, explicitly expressing the intention to support arbitration on illegitimate debts and to 'adopt an even more offensive position in the international work to reduce the debt burden of poor countries. The UN must establish criteria for what can be characterized as illegitimate debt and such debt must be cancelled.' (Norwegian Government, 2005) The government firmly opposes undue conditionality regarding privatization. Finally Norway 'will support the work to set up an international debt settlement court that will hear matters concerning illegitimate debt' (Norwegian Government, 2005).

Three recent cases stand out because of very distinct specificities marking further evolution in the absence of one general framework of rules: Iraq, Argentina and Nigeria. Their experiences underline the need for a proper mechanism.

Iraq

This case is highly instructive for two reasons: the USA revived their odious debt doctrine and Iraq showed how quickly one hotly debated problem of the SDRM, used by the IMF to allege the necessity of amending its statues, can be solved if this is wanted.

On 22 May 2003 UN Security Council Resolution 1483 immunized all of Iraq's oil and gas wealth from legal process until the end of 2007, also directing all UN members to transfer any Iraqi assets in their jurisdictions to the immune Development Fund for Iraq. On the same day Presidential Executive Order no. 13303 gave this resolution force of law within the USA, though without any time limit. In 2004 it was expanded to cover the assets of the central bank. The US President vested seized assets in the US Treasury (GAO, 2005, p. 10) to be passed on to be used in Iraq. In 2004 the UK and the USA drafted a provision containing a global stay in all members' jurisdictions. It did not make it into the final text because it was excessive and 'redundant since the practical utility of litigation was already near zero after Resolution 1483' (Gelpern, 2005, p. 396). Gelpern immediately connects to the sovereign insolvency debate, pointing out that 'With nary a peep from the markets' Iraq's prime assets were put outside creditors' reach, 'the most controversial early aspiration of the IMF's Sovereign Debt Restructuring Mechanism (SDRM), shelved just weeks before' was implemented. Its most hotly debated element, a stay on lawsuits, was simply implemented at the stroke of a pen, without discussion or resistance. One may ask whether the fact that the US private sector had hardly any claims was helpful. James Baker, who had once categorically opposed any debt reduction was sent to creditor governments to advocate debt write-offs. Interestingly the amount of debts was not clear for some time, as regional creditors were not sure whether billions of dollars were loans and grants.

Once the USA realized what it had done by reviving its own odious debt doctrine, the administration started to back-pedal vigorously. The damage of giving credibility to the doctrine was done though. It could only be limited.

The word (odious) is shunned. The Paris Club decision does not use it. It can, by the way, not be found on the Paris Club's home page. Officially Iraq's debts were not reduced because of odiousness. A CRS report for Congress (Weiss, 2005) does not mention odiousness as the reason for US efforts to achieve debt relief for Iraq. It introduces odious debts in the following way:

> Proponents of a doctrine of 'odious' debt assert that some of Iraq's debts could potentially be classified as non-legitimate under international law since they were undertaken during the Hussein regime and that international law should be able to expunge these debts. The concept of 'odious' debt does not appear to be well established in international law. (Weiss, 2005, p. 6)

It is conspicuous that the pertaining footnotes (omitted here) quote demands to apply 'Iraqi Terms' to other debtors, for example, S. Raghavan

'African Advocates to U.S.: Reduce Our Debt Like Iraq's', in *The Miami Herald* of 20 February 2004. The US government's forceful advocating of odiousness goes completely and conspicuously unmentioned as though it had never occurred. Instead the source informs: 'Moreover, the U.S. government has made clear its intention to restructure its Iraqi debt through the Paris Club process, and parallel negotiations with non-Paris Club countries in the Middle East and Asia, and Iraq's private creditors.'

As the Paris Club only accounted for a third of all debts (the USA roughly for 3.3 per cent), this means that the Paris Club also set the course for the bulk of debt owed to other creditors.

On 21 November 2004 Paris Club members agreed on a debt relief programme for Iraq providing a total reduction of 80 per cent in three phases (30-30-20). As usual, the debtor has to assure comparability: 'The Republic of Iraq has committed to seek comparable treatment from its other external creditors.' Weiss (2005, p. 4) remarks: 'Under traditional Paris Club guidelines, Iraq's petroleum and gas reserves would render it ineligible for debt relief.' Critics wonder whether such exceptional relief was really needed, to what extent it really benefitted the people and whether much better economic and social results could have been achieved if all expenditures had been scrupulously accounted for. An official document of the US House of Representatives (2005, p. 20) concluded:

> After the invasion of Iraq, the U.S.-run Coalition Provisional Authority took control of more than $22.4 billion in Iraqi resources and spent or disbursed $19.6 billion. While these Iraqi assets were under U.S. control, unprecedented sums were withdrawn in cash from the Federal Reserve and shipped to Iraq, where they were spent or disbursed by the CPA with virtually no financial controls. Partial audits of these expenditures have disclosed evidence of substantial waste, fraud, and abuse.
>
> Because of the lack of oversight and accounting, the extent of wasteful and corrupt spending during the period of U.S. control is not known.

Argentina

Only three months after the final futile IMF attempt to rescue Argentina in September 2001, followed by the government's desperate move to restructure its domestic debts, Argentina had to declare default. It should be recalled that one reason for the dimension of the crisis was the peso-dollar parity, introduced by Argentina in line with the IMF's fad at that time, currency boards and fixed pegs. The Ministry of Finance's attempts to put together a programme covering financial needs for 2001–02, while country spreads were about to reach 1000 basis points, was supported by nearly $20 billion of multilateral credits, $13.7 billion from the IMF alone. When refinancing becomes that prohibitively expensive, delaying a solution makes things worse. So it was in Argentina, even though short-lived optimism brought down the spread to 700 points. A final attempt to stave off default, the 'Mega Swap', failed to avert the crisis. In 2001 the IMF granted further money. In its report on Argentina the IMF's Independent Evaluation Office (IEO) concluded: 'The September 2001 augmentation suffered from a number of weaknesses in program design, which were evident at the time. If the debt were indeed unsustainable, as by then well recognized by IMF staff, the program offered no solution to that problem' (IMF, 2004, pp. 54–55). According to this view the IMF aggravated the problem.

In 2003 a first offer was made to creditors in Dubai: writing off 75 per cent of nominal values. This was five percentage points below the secondary market. As no past due interest would be recognized, economic losses were higher. It was flatly rejected, although 'some observers argued that the Argentine government's position was not unreasonable' Helleiner (2005, p. 955). The New York third district court refused to grant attachments, arguing that this would disrupt negotiations with other creditors. The US government presented an amicus curiae brief supporting Argentina's request for a stay to all enforcement. One might add that years of privatization had left no assets to attach anyway. However the critical role of the US administration was once again highlighted. Unlike during the SDRM discussion, there was no problem connected with keeping creditors from enforcing their rights. In 2004 Argentina modified her initial offer (Buenos Aires proposal) somewhat. Payments were linked to growth. Conditions would vary with the degree of acceptance (more or less than 70 per cent).

On 3 May 2005 the government announced that the acceptance had reached 76.15 per cent of the debt in default. The haircut was roughly 70 per cent (ibid., p. 959). Taking the amounts exchanged into account (without hold-outs) sceptics calculate an overall reduction of roughly 14.2 per cent, predicting that this haircut – once again suffered by only one class of creditors – will in the end be insufficient. A value of $62.3 billion of old bonds was exchanged for about $35.3 billion dollars of new instruments plus the corresponding GDP growth-linked coupons. A substantial percentage of bondholders did not accept, organizing themselves into bondholders' associations, without recovering, however, anything so far. The neoliberal privatization drive now protects Argentina. There is practically nothing left to attach.

Meeting President Bush in 2004, Argentina's President Kirchner compared Enron paying its investors only '14 cents on the dollar' (ibid.) with Argentina. While Argentina caused an angry outcry, Enron did not but was considered a matter of course. What annoyed creditors was Argentina's strategy of setting the terms in a take it or leave it way. After the exit consent even some market participants felt that the cuts were reasonable. Creditors themselves had proposed a write-off of 40 per cent – 45 per cent in NPV terms. In its desperate situation Argentina had no other chance but to get relief. As no formal framework existed, it chose this strategy. This precedent, in turn, may well encourage other sovereigns to become bolder, to return to pre-BWIs debtor-creditor relations.

It is finally important to note that Argentina openly opposed the IMF, even threatening not to pay the Fund as due. On several occasions Argentina prevailed against the IMF. Seeing President Kirchner, President Bush reportedly 'joked to a group of other foreign leaders: "here comes the conqueror of the IMF"' (ibid., p.955). While this seems exaggerated, Argentina certainly stood its ground against the IMF in an unprecedented way. Helleiner argues that political support by the USA allowed Argentina to act as it did. Meanwhile Argentina and Brazil have also spearheaded a new drive by SC debtors: early repayments to the IMF, which already started to create problems with the Fund. The neoliberal US crisis, starting from its subprime mortgages, has again turned the tables, again saving the IMF as the debt crisis did after the demise of Bretton Woods.

Nigeria

In October 2005 Nigeria received (in the words of the Paris Club) an 'exceptional treatment', a 67 per cent debt reduction in two phases, which amounted to $18 billion (including moratorium interest) or about 60 per cent of total Paris Club debts. Nigeria had chosen not to have a programme with the IMF, following her own economic reforms called National Economic Empowerment and Development Strategy (NEEDS) instead. Compared with the qualm over HIPC, this was serious: it once again challenged the IMF's rule over debtors. This led to the invention of a totally new IMF instrument, called the policy support instrument (PSI), which allows Nigeria ample policy space. Considering that even Iraq had to sign an IMF programme, this is path-breaking.

High oil prices allowed Nigeria to pay arrears to the Paris Club and to announce a market buy-back of the debt stock remaining after the Paris Club write-off. While this means a large outflow immediately, savings would soon be substantial. Kersley et al. (2005) quote British negotiators, saying that 'a combination of write-off, the payment of arrears, and a market buy-back would mean that "100 per cent of Nigeria's debt would be eliminated" by the end of 2005'. However multilateral debts of some $2.8 billion would remain. Substantial debt service savings due to the agreement with the Paris Club can translate into substantial increases of social spending, a central focus of NEEDS.

This unprecedented deal followed a resolution by Nigeria's House of Representatives calling on the President to repudiate Nigeria's debt on the grounds that Nigeria's external debts are odious and illegitimate. Legislators also sent a team to Europe to canvass debt cancellation in the continent's leading financial centres. The mover of the resolution to repudiate debt was present in Paris when Nigeria negotiated. The decision by creditors may well have had the intention to quell any public discussion initiated by a debtor nation and backed by parliament, even though the Nigerian Senate later voted in favour of honouring debt servicing for that year.

US DEBTS – A REASON TO RECONSIDER DEBT MANAGEMENT?

Strongly increasing debts of the USA triggered an IMF reaction unheard of so far. To fight this debt's driving engine, the current account deficit (IMF code: 'global imbalances'), the IMF exhorts SCs, such as oil exporters with balance of payments surpluses, to import more from the USA. The prudent use of large current account surpluses by Arab countries after 2000, first lauded as an improvement over the 1970s, came again under attack.

The IMF's *World Economic Outlook* (September 2005, pp. 113–14) demands a '5 percent of GDP permanently higher investment rate' of oil producers and East Asian economies to reduce the US current account deficit visibly, since the recent increase in oil prices added to 'global imbalances'. The *Regional Economic Outlook* of the IMF's Middle East and Central Asia Department published in the same month points out that 'these countries may need to increase spending on imported goods'. Petrodollar recycling is demanded again: countries with low absorption capacity should recycle their petrodollars through capital outflows to the rest of the world; in other words, OPEC is now requested to do another 'recycling of petrodollars', the very policy which continues to be used to blame OPEC for the 1982 debt crisis. Speaking again of an 'oil shock', an IMF employee demanded higher government spending by oil exporters to increase imports, the very policy that landed OPEC countries in trouble after 1973. The fact that oil exporters import relatively little from the USA, having turned into large buyers of goods from Asia is of particular concern to this author, even though that could simply be a clear sign of Asia's revealed comparative advantage and consumer preferences – in other words, an indication that the global market functions well.

Such demands on surplus countries differ markedly from the usual

IMF strategy to adjust balance of payments deficits. One may wonder whether this is the first sign of a fundamental reorientation of the Fund's 'adjustment' policies, whether we should expect the IMF soon to request higher imports of Argentine beef or African cotton by OECD countries in order to correct imbalances, just in the way that Keynes had wanted it. With regard to its Northern members, the IMF has meanwhile turned Keynesian: deficit spending to fight the crisis is lauded, even demanded. The enormous sums of money spent by the USA now are a commendable way of fighting the US-caused crisis. Europe is sometimes even criticized for spending too little. In stark contrast to its policies in the North, the IMF keeps demanding SCs to implement more or less the same austerity policies that proved unable to solve the debt crisis. Quite openly, the IMF has adopted a double standard. There is one law for the rich and another law for the poor.

4. Gleneagles, the Multilateral Debt Relief Initiative and the US crisis

After more than three decades of 'debt management' (the IMF implemented its first 'adjustment measures' after 1973), first insufficient debt reductions for poor countries shortly later (disguised under the name retroactive terms adjustment), and then after two HIPCs plus one topping up, the G8 finally admitted that debt reductions so far had been insufficient. Thus the MDRI might well be called HIPC IV if one counted properly. Unfortunately, it might once again not provide the exit from debt problems. A EURODAD report (Hurley, 2007, p. 18) had already expressed concerns about how 'to avoid an "MDRI II" ten years down the line'. The effects of the present US crisis are likely to render another initiative (HIPC V) necessary.

Countries 'eligible' for MDRI support are 'HIPC countries that have reached completion point' as the IBRD (2007, p. 2) pocket brochure formulates. As with HIPC, 40 countries qualify. On the publication's cover the MDRI's goal is defined as: 'To provide additional support to HIPCs to reach the MDGs.' Permanent exit or external viability are not mentioned. They seem no longer intended. The serious debt problem already recognized by the Pearson Commission in the 1960s drags on. The solutions offered still lag behind this commission's generous proposals made nearly 40 years before the MDRI was launched in 2006.

Logically the additional support, which is now the goal of the MDRI, is only necessary because the initially announced goal of HIPC was not met: enabling SCs 'to meet its current and future external debt-service obligations in full without recourse to debt relief, rescheduling of debts, or the accumulation of arrears, and without unduly compromising growth' (see Chapter 2). Meanwhile, the cover page of the IBRD (2007) pocket brochure redefines HIPC's goal: 'To ensure deep, broad and fast debt relief and thereby contribute toward growth, poverty reduction, and debt sustainability in the poorest, most heavily indebted countries.' Rewriting history, it is now claimed that HIPC was only planned to 'contribute' toward sustainability, or that the officially declared aim, which was not achieved by a considerable amount, had never been HIPC's officially declared aim.

As in the case of HIPC II (Cologne) and topping up (Kananaskis) the G7/8 again initiated the MDRI at Gleneagles. On all occasions massive NGO pressure was at least one important reason for this decision. Debt servicing problems in spite of HIPC were another.

Further debt reductions and the MDRI framework were announced well before the meeting of the G8 finance ministers. In a press conference on the 2005 spring meeting of the International Monetary and Financial Committee, its chairman, Gordon Brown, also Chancellor of the Exchequer of the host G8 country, informed that '[f]or the relief of poverty' this IMF Committee had 'agreed on the importance of moving further and faster on debt relief, and that there will be more funds needed additional to those that exist at the moment to achieve a lasting exit from debt for the poorest countries'. Honouring deplorable tradition, the British Chancellor once again officially announced a goal that was quickly downgraded from 'lasting exit' to 'additional support' (IBRD, 2007). Referring to the upcoming 'G-7 and G-8 summit at Gleneagles', he told the press: 'We believe we can make substantial progress over the course of the next months in relieving both the debts and the poverty of people in the poorest countries of the world.' This would 'certainly require further debt relief'.

Reading the Chancellor's statements with the benefit of hindsight, the MDRI already emerges. Speaking about how to finance 'the next stage of multilateral debt relief', he expressly mentioned the claims of the BWIs and the African Development Bank. Brown expected that 'at the next meeting of the G-7 Finance Ministers and at Gleneagles there will be announcements about additional sums of money for debt relief for the multilateral debts owed by the poorest countries'.

Obviously debt servicing problems caused by too little relief under HIPC were also one triggering factor. Taking once again the lead in debt matters, Britain had announced that she would service her 'share' of debts owed by the poorest countries to the concessional financing arms of the IBRD and the African Development Bank, bailing out these IFIs. Canada had followed suit, announcing the extension to debts owed to the IMF. Shortly before the press conference the Netherlands had joined, servicing their share of the multilateral debts owed by the poorest countries to the IBRD and the African Development Bank. This need to finance multilateral debt service in spite of the officially declared efficiency of the policies that IFIs force debtors to pursue, as well as the US proposal to cancel debts rather than paying for debt service proved the failure of debt reductions so far and the necessity of further debt reductions. In March 2005 the USA proposed 100 per cent debt relief for HIPCs by cancelling reflows and adjusting gross assistance flows by the amount 'forgiven', so as not to reduce net flows. The US proposal in 2001 to replace IFI loans to the poor with grants on a substantial scale may have been another trigger. All these ideas proved that debt had again become unsustainable.

The three IFIs mentioned by the G8 obviously resulted from arbitrary creditor decisions. Apparently no one had thought of the Inter-American Development Bank (or its soft window). What the Chancellor did mention, though, was that IFIs would not be required to finance debt reductions but that this would be done by 'additional money from the richest countries'. Although all IFIs had established loan loss reserves, and multilateral development banks (MDBs) are required by their statutes to grant debt relief, they would not be required to touch these reserves. IFIs would be bailed out.

In a letter to the IBRD's president dated 23 September 2005 the G8 finance ministers reaffirmed their commitment 'to cover the full cost to offset dollar for dollar the forgone principal and interest repayments' (IDA, 2006a, p. 13) for IDA and the African Development Fund. They pledged to:

> make available immediately additional funds to cover the full cost during the IDA 14 period and these funds will be fully additional to the resources already agreed during the IDA 14 replenishment. For the period after IDA 14, we are committed to cover the full costs for the duration of the cancelled loans and we will make contributions additional to regular replenishments of IDA.

While the public remains sceptical about progress actually achieved by the G8 and other official creditors, one should not deny that – compared with the 1980s – considerable progress has occurred. Although highly critical of the G8, especially of their promise to increase ODA substantially, Oxfam (2007, p. 4) also commended progress during the recent past: 'Debt cancellation continues to deliver progress.' A significant fall in debt and a corresponding switch from debt service towards financing education, health and so on can be seen: 'To date, 24 countries have benefited.' In more concrete terms this may be expressed as additional teachers (Malawi), abolishing education fees or 'Twenty more million children are in [sic] school' (ibid., p. 2).

ELIGIBLE COUNTRIES, CREDITORS AND DEBTS

Although another commendable step towards necessary relief, and although the specific reference to the MDGs clearly shows that the idea of debtor protection has made further progress, the MDRI suffers from serious shortcomings. Sadly its implementation corroborates the perception that creditors are not at all prepared to accept and apply the Rule of Law, to recognize debtor rights, and to end creditor domination and arbitrariness. This is reflected in the choice of countries, creditors to grant relief and debts to be covered as outlined below.

An Arbitrary List of Countries

The G8 finance ministers emphasize their agreement 'to complete the process of debt relief for' HIPCs 'by providing additional development resources' to 'provide significant support for countries' efforts to reach the goals of the Millennium Declaration (MDGs)'. Although some non-HIPCs suffer from relatively heavier debt burdens, official creditors arbitrarily restricted eligibility to HIPCs after completion point. If the decision had been based on objective criteria and debtor rights – as mandated by the Rule of Law – this could not have happened. Once again arbitrariness has overcome legal, logical, economic and humane principles, which would require treating all countries subject to the same debt pressure in the same way.

MDRI eligibility makes HIPC's sunset clause again relevant because only SCs entering HIPC can go on to the MDRI, a fact positively suggesting HIPC IV as the more appropriate name. The boards of IDA and the IMF had extended the sunset clause four times. When extending it to 31 December 2006, it was decided to 'close the Initiative to new entrants by ring fencing its application to those countries meeting the Initiative's income and indebtedness criteria based on end-2004 data' (IMF and IDA, 2006a, pp. 2–3). 'In April 2006, the Boards endorsed and closed the list of countries assessed to have met' (ibid., p. 3) the two criteria (income and indebtedness). A country is considered potentially eligible for debt relief under HIPC if:

1. It is IDA-only and PRGF eligible.
2. Its end-December 2004 debt burden indicators are above the thresholds established under the HIPC Initiative after full application of traditional debt relief mechanisms.

However the document goes on clarifying that the 'closed list' is somehow not really closed: 'Only countries in that list, henceforth referred to as the "identified countries," *and others that are subsequently assessed to have met the relevant criteria using end-2004 data,* could be considered for future HIPC Initiative debt relief' (ibid., emphasis added). Thus 'the list could subsequently be amended to include other countries whose data are verified to have met the income and indebtedness criteria at end-2004' (ibid.,

p. 18). 'Countries satisfying the three eligibility criteria could qualify for debt relief under the HIPC Initiative even after the sunset clause expires' (ibid., p. 9). The BWIs qualify the need for a sunset clause, which they propagated before based on the argument that the window of opportunity of debt relief must be closed to avoid HIPC becoming a permanent institution: 'Since the list of countries that have been assessed to meet the Initiative's income and indebtedness criteria based on end-2004 data is closed, there is less need for a sunset clause' (ibid.). Grandfathered poor countries can always be included if analysis of their 'end-2004 data' identifies them as eligible at some point of time in the future. Considering substantial changes in BWI data over time (see Annex on data) one cannot exclude that happening. Therefore 'even if the sunset clause were to take effect, the HIPC Initiative would still not be closed, as eligible pre-decision point and remaining interim countries face no deadline to reach either the decision or completion point under the HIPC Initiative' (ibid., p. 7). One may speak of a sunset clause without a sunset.

In April 2006 three (Bhutan, Laos, Sri Lanka) of the 14 countries that had been assessed to have met the HIPC criteria based on end-2004 data declared they would not wish to participate. In February 2007 the Kyrgyz Republic announced that she would not join HIPC despite being classified as eligible. However such express, official declarations by debtor countries are considered irrelevant by the BWIs: 'Under the current rules of the Initiative, these countries remain eligible or potentially eligible for the Initiative, with the result that they can change their intent at any point in the future and decide to apply for debt relief if otherwise eligible and qualified to do so at that time' (ibid., p. 9).

The document explains that from an IMF perspective, a country's current indication of its intention not to avail itself of HIPC relief cannot provide the basis for making the country ineligible under the HIPC Initiative. The Fund's Articles of Agreement are used to 'argue' that member countries cannot decide against the wishes of the IMF, a clumsily constructed, ridiculous argument. The document's conclusion does not convincingly follow from the quoted Article V, Section 12(f)(ii): 'balance of payments assistance may be made available on special terms to developing members in difficult circumstance, and for this purpose the Fund shall take into account the level of per capita income'. Apart from the fact that 'may' is not 'must', this formulation certainly does not contain any obligation on the part of the member country. It does not oblige the IMF to act at all ('may'), let alone implement one specific programme, although one may argue that the IMF is encouraged to do something. In contrast, the IMF is much less concerned about its own statutes when they explicitly prohibit financing 'a large and sustained outflow of capital' (Article VI.1.a) as the IMF did during the Asian crisis to bail out speculators, or with regard to any member's statutory right to exercise capital controls necessary to regulate capital flows, unless such controls would restrict current transactions.

Unsurprisingly, the BWIs are prepared to reassess data in order to allow a country to qualify. Afghanistan's debt burden indicators based on verified end-2004 debt are below the HIPC indebtedness thresholds. But this is not necessarily the end. 'Staffs could not reach a conclusion on Afghanistan's classification because a large part of the country's potential external obligations is either unverified or in dispute' (IMF and IDA, 2006b, p. 7). It was thus proposed to reassess Afghanistan's debt indicators once the disputes are resolved. Should Afghanistan's end-2004 debt ratio be found to be above the relevant thresholds, staffs would then propose Afghanistan to be included in the list. IMF and IDA (ibid.) assure that if 'other countries are found in the future to face a similar situation, it is proposed that they receive the same treatment as Afghanistan'. However 'To the best of staffs' knowledge, only Afghanistan has unverified debts and debts under dispute whose resolution could have an impact on the country's classification in terms of potential eligibility under the HIPC Initiative.' Stating that this special treatment would in principle be available to any country in a similar situation helpfully destroys any potential suspicion that Western interest in Afghanistan, as well as its invasion, might have anything to do with this special though objective treatment.

An Arbitrary List of IFIs

The choice of IFIs – the Inter-American Development Bank group was initially not included – also reflects creditor arbitrariness. Hurley (2007, p. 5) points out that only three multilateral creditors of a total of 23 which participate in the HIPC Initiative were addressed. Only one further IFI, the Inter-American Development Bank, joined the MDRI thus far, covering claims vis-à-vis Latin American HIPCs. Hurley singles out 'significant political pressure by some Latin American Governments as well as civil society organizations in Latin America, Europe, the United States and Canada' as the reason.

An Arbitrary List of Debts

The G8 announced a 100 per cent reduction of multilateral claims of three arbitrarily picked IFIs. It soon emerged that 100 per cent cancellation of this reduced sample was too good to be true. By any normal understanding of this announcement, 100 per cent would mean all debts incurred up to the announcement or the formal decision to implement it, at most with the small, bureaucratic adjustment of cutting off at the end of the last full fiscal year. This is by no means the case. Thus 100 per cent is at severe odds with the truth.

Once again, earlier cut-off dates were introduced. IDA's cut-off date is end-2003, a decision that cannot be reconciled at all with the 100 per cent relief claim. Furthermore, 'Undisbursed credit balances as of the cutoff date would not be eligible for cancellation' (IDA, 2005, p.3). IDA also clarifies that debt service payments made by HIPCs between the cut-off date (31 December 2003) 'and the country's debt cancellation start date will not be covered under the MDRI' (ibid., p. 4).

In contrast, the IMF and the African Development Bank chose end-2004 as their cut-off date, as did the Inter-American Development Bank later on. Since the G8 declaration was made in 2005 this seems somehow IDB defensible. Still this too is not strictly speaking 100 per cent off, as announced.

Finally, MDRI debt relief will reduce annual IDA allocations to countries receiving it by the amount of relief in that year. Additional resources provided to IDA by the donors (to pay this country's debt service) are reallocated to all IDA recipients on the basis of the BWIs' 'performance-based allocation mechanism'. IDA flows will increase (including new IDA commitments and forgone reflows) thanks to donor additionality, but new IDA commitments to most eligible HIPC countries would decrease: 'Beyond IDA 14, when forgone credit reflows increase considerably, new IDA assistance commitments may become negligible in a number of countries with high debt service to IDA' (ibid., p. 8).

CONTINUING CONTROL: MAKING DEBT MANAGEMENT PERMANENT

Eligibility criteria for MDRI debt relief reflect HIPC completion point criteria, including a public expenditure management that meets BWI approval. Information gathered in the context of the ongoing 2005 Country Policy and Institutional Assessment (CPIA) forms one base of assessing its standard (ibid., p. 5). Countries are classified according to their policy performance (three categories: strong, medium, poor) using the IBRD's CPIA index. Corresponding to these categories, the framework establishes three indicative thresholds for each debt burden indicator. Thresholds corresponding to strong policy performers are highest. A 'traffic light' mechanism, resting on policy-dependent indicative debt thresholds of the Debt Sustainability Framework (DSF), was introduced to determine the risk of debt distress (red: high risk of debt distress and so on). According to IMF and IBRD (2006, p. 21) the allocation of IDA grants will soon be affected by the MDRI and a 'transition from the current traffic light system, which is essentially a static assessment based on the latest available debt indicators, to a more dynamic assessment based on the joint DSAs'. These 'tend to be somewhat more conservative than the static assessments under the traffic light system' (ibid., p. 20). In short, a whole new system to control SCs' budgets, expenditures and macroeconomic policies is being put in place.

'The CPIA index has been criticized for its partiality of its assessments – relying on the subjective judgments of World Bank staff – and the lack of empirical evidence and rigour of the criteria upon which such evaluations are based' (Tan, 2006, p. 29). Such licence is not new: confronted with embarrassing shares of 'satisfactory' projects found by its own controllers, the IBRD introduced a new methodology in the 1980s, a 'less mechanical and somewhat subjective judgement as to performance', characterized by '*subjectivity of assessments, which increased the weight given to evaluators' perceptions, some of which were difficult to explain fully*' (IBRD, 1989, pp. 15ff., emphasis added). This somewhat subjective method reduced the share of unsatisfactory projects from 28 per cent according to the old method to 12 per cent with unsatisfactory or uncertain performance in 1987. 'Uncertain' was a euphemism, defined as: 'Project achieves few objectives, if any, and has no foreseeable worthwhile results' (ibid., p. 15). In spite of this innovative change the share of satisfactory operations went on declining perceptibly. The Bank changed its method again in 1997. 'Soft' criteria became more important. In contrast to the first reform, this new method increased the share of satisfactory projects sustainably, 'a remarkable improvement', according to the Bank (cf. Raffer, 2005d, pp. 190ff.). Like subjective judgements producing better results, controlling debtors via conditions and so-called prior actions has a long tradition. These mechanisms of domination have been further developed over time.

To evaluate the economic sense of multilateral monitoring, one has to recall that especially in the case of the poorest countries that were not really flooded by private, commercial creditors, the large bulk of debts are claims by official creditors. In contrast to the private sector, these creditors have always keenly monitored the use of their funds. They have used assessments, product cycle models and various forms of checks on the use of the money received. In short, they are as responsible for the fact that these expenditures did not generate appropriate rates of returns as debtors. IFIs especially have financed without applying proper duty of care, as many examples prove, from 'criminal debts' (as in Indonesia) to going on lending to Argentina, increasing the country's debt burden in spite of staff estimates that a debt reduction of between 15 and 40 per cent would be required. Shortcomings published by the Wapenhans report

(IBRD, 1992b), such as that beauty of language was more important than on the ground benefits, could be added. Evidence, including evidence published by IFIs themselves, shows that the multilateral debt debacle is at least as much the fault of lenders as borrowers. It also shows that IFIs are definitely not qualified to go on controlling debtors' borrowing decisions.

After three HIPC helpings and several Paris Club measures since the Toronto Terms, IFI claims have obviously become the dominating type of debts in poor countries: 'For the 18 post-completion point HIPCs participating in the MDRI, about 80 percent of the debt outstanding after HIPC debt relief is owed to multilateral creditors' (IMF and IBRD, 2006, p. 17). This document expects debt relief under the MDRI to reduce recipients' debt ratios significantly: the average NPV debt/exports ratio would fall from 140 per cent after HIPC debt relief to a projected 52 per cent. However the BWIs expect quick increases in debts: 'The reduction in the risk of debt distress as a result of MDRI relief raises the prospect that IDA will switch from grants to loans in MDRI countries, leading to a quick reaccumulation of debt.' Under IDA 14 IDA-only countries classified at high risk of debt distress receive 100 per cent grant financing, countries with a moderate risk 50 per cent, and low risk countries 100 per cent loan financing on IDA terms (ibid., p. 6).

Logically the present multilateral debt problem means that programmes and projects financed under IFI supervision have not generated a sufficient share of self-liquidating investments to avoid the difficult situation these countries are in now. IFI monitoring, quite strict and down to details, is part of the problem, not of the solution.

IFIs see the MDRI as a framework to achieve two objectives: deepening debt relief to HIPCs to help them reach the MDGs, while safeguarding the long-term financial capacity of IDA and the African Development Bank; and encouraging the best use of additional donor resources for development by allocating them to low income countries on the basis of policy performance. This performance is evaluated under CPIA. Demands on debtors are not always consistent. Thus IFIs used to demand the introduction of school fees in the past; now under the MDRI debtor countries have to eliminate these fees again, undoing under IFI pressure what IFIs had forced them to do first. Honduras, for example, pledged to eliminate fees for public schools under the initiative (Hurley, 2007, p. 7). While introducing fees was good policy once – at least in the eyes of stern IFIs – eliminating them is now good policy, which begs the question whether forcing debtor SCs to introduce them was indicated.

The CPIA assigns a value between 1 and 6 to capture perceived performance of economic variables. Applying this framework to the IBRD, *The Economist* (21–27 April 2007, p. 62) pointed out:

Where people are promoted according to personal ties rather than merit, the bank gives a score of only two out of six; where ombudsmen and auditors exist, but lack authority, the bank gives a score of just three. So by its own measure, the bank might not now deserve much support.

The Economist refers to the Wolfowitz affair, where the IBRD president most vocally campaigning against corruption, favouritism and dubious governance practices finally had to resign over his behaviour regarding an unusual wage increase granted to his girlfriend, who was an IBRD employee.

Total control by creditors during the phase of debt reductions is quite unique and can only be found in the case of discriminated SC debtors. All civilized insolvency laws see creditors and debtors as two parties, conferring the power to decide on independent courts. The fact that progress in debt reduction has been so extremely slow and that recognizing the very need for cancelling substantial parts of debts took so long makes this creditor domination even worse. However, again in stark contrast to civilized laws that allow reorganized debtors after a fresh start again to take their own decisions, official creditors plan to go on controlling debtors after debt reduction. This seems to explain why several countries have already refused to participate.

The BWIs want 'to monitor the evolution of a country's debt burden indicators and to guide financing strategies' (IMF and IBRD, 2006, p. 7). The BWIs conclude that the 'key question . . . how fast debt should accumulate' depends theoretically on 'virtually the entire range of micro- and macroeconomic factors governing growth and stability' (ibid., p. 20). Logically that means total control. The argument recalls the statement that good projects cannot prosper in a bad environment, thus the whole range of SCs' policies have to be addressed by IFIs. The very same argument was used to defend the monitoring of whole economies under 'structural adjustment'. Recalling that the IBRD had to admit in 1990 that 'structural adjustment' had not encouraged investments nor enabled debtors to grow out of debt, using this 'justification' for control again is hardly convincing.

'FREE RIDING'

The understanding that IFIs have of the expression 'free riding' is arguably most clearly expressed by a document prepared by the African Development Bank (AfDB, 2006, p. 3) for the Commonwealth HIPC Ministerial Forum:

The term free rider in public economics refers to 'a person who receives the benefits of a good without paying for it'. Free-riding in this brief is therefore

> a shorthand for situations in which non-concessional lenders indirectly obtain financial gain from ADF and IDA's debt forgiveness, grants and concessional financing activities without paying for it. This is undesirable because it means that creditors, rather than the recipient country, are receiving at least part of the benefit of ADF and IDA grants and debt relief, and the development effectiveness of these institutions is thereby reduced. At the same time, countries indebtedness would not decline as intended by the grants and MDRI framework.

This is a remarkably unusual understanding of free riding, distinct from the term's meaning in economic textbooks. No one would dream of thinking that commercial banks lending to a company, an individual or a municipality after these had enjoyed the fresh start provided by insolvency protection would have to 'pay for it', which can only mean compensating former creditors that got a 'haircut', simply because of lending after debtors have again become viable. This argument recalls the IMF's clumsy attempts to convince people that the SDRM would only work if enshrined in its statutes because of 'vulture funds'. The same villains of the piece are used as 'justification' once again.

IDA and IMF (2006, p. 11) explain: '"Free-riding" concerns could arise if creditors increase lending to post-MDRI HIPCs, thereby "free riding" on the fiscal and balance-of-payments space created by debt relief.' The MDRI is seen as increasing the potential for free riding. It is one favourite 'argument' for tight control of poor debtors even after MDRI relief. To the extent that debt reduction would significantly lower debt ratios of eligible countries after implementation, they would again enjoy increased creditworthiness.

The BWIs seem to use the word free riding in several ways:

1. Referring to 'old creditors' that simply refuse to accept the same haircut and/or get court awards for payment (ibid., p. 29). This 'hold-out' problem could be easily solved by a meaningful sovereign insolvency framework. Such a framework would also be fair to those creditors who are expected to grant comparable treatment without having been allowed to participate meaningfully in negotiations. So far, however, official creditors have not tried to stop such behaviour, although it would have been as easy as a stroke of a pen. One may thus assume that this is not really a major concern. Only very recently, just before the G8 at Heiligendamm in 2007, Gordon Brown deplored the 'activities of so-called vulture funds that seek to profit from debts owed by the poorest countries in the world'. In this written ministerial statement on 10 May 2007, available on the Parliament's home page, he declared: 'I am determined to limit the damage done by such funds.' However his proposed measures are ineffective. Thus

'talks with leading commercial creditors on a voluntary code of conduct that will set out the actions that responsible creditors should take to help reduce the risk of litigation, including the requirement to participate in collective action to reduce unsustainable debts' or working 'with our G8 partners to develop a Charter on Responsible Lending that includes a commitment to protect developing countries from vulture fund activity' will never work. While most non-Paris Club creditors have accepted the decisions in which they had not been allowed to participate, 'aggressive creditors' (Brown's wording) have the business purpose of not doing so. They will accept nothing but a legal prohibition to litigate, as would be part and parcel of the Raffer Proposal. Nevertheless, once again Britain has taken the leadership role in addressing another debt problem – a progressive attitude that does deserve to be commended, especially so as a 'growing number of commercial creditors and distressed debt funds are engaging in litigation against HIPCs' (ibid., p. 33). On 22 May 2007 the Paris Club followed. Its press release 'urge[d] . . . all official and commercial creditors and debtor countries to take the necessary steps to implement this initiative'. Paris Club creditors 'are committed to avoid selling their claims on HIPC countries to other creditors who do not intend to provide debt relief under the HIPC initiative, and urge other creditors to follow suit'. As examples, especially Iraq, have shown, stopping hold-outs is easy if important creditor countries want it.

2. Such 'old' non-participating creditors grant new loans after losses by participating creditors have removed the debt overhang. In that case both an insolvency framework and appropriate actions by Paris Club members would also solve this problem.

3. After the fresh start, the debtor is again creditworthy. Uniquely in the case of SCs this may also be characterized as 'free riding on the fiscal and balance-of-payments space created by debt relief' (ibid., p. 11). In plain English, this means that creditors that had not lent before (and had thus no claims) are now accused of not having granted the same reductions as the SC's creditors having claims before debt reduction. In any other case but an SC that would be considered patently absurd. The BWIs have repeatedly expressed strong concern that debt reductions may attract new creditors, as absolutely normal after any successful corporate, private or municipal restructuring. Again one notes that new creditors are considered normal in the case of all other debtors having enjoyed insolvency relief. The existence of a sovereign insolvency framework would again be helpful, as the risk of losing money would work as a disincentive to loose lending.

Both explanations (2) and (3) assume that SCs have insufficient competence to run their own economies, that they need a guardian after meaningful debt relief, to keep them from immediately accumulating unsustainable debts once again. Arguably this need for a protecting guardian is best expressed by this passage: 'A key concern is the risk that some non-concessional creditors may be willing to finance even low-return investments, since lowered debt ratios post-MDRI and the prospect of future IDA grants provides reassurance to creditors that post-MDRI borrowers will be able to service their loans' (IDA, 2006b, p. 2). Logically this means either that SCs would knowingly borrow at a loss just because they are able to 'afford' it or that SC governments are so corrupt that one can normally bribe them into doing so. Some form of economic protectorate is thus needed, and the BWIs are ready to take up this new form of the white person's burden: 'the DSF treatment is likely to require strengthening policies aimed at curbing free riding behavior' (IDA, 2005, p. 8). One has to 'ensure that the DSF remains an effective tool in stemming an excessive buildup of debt in low-income countries while not unnecessarily constraining access to resources for development' (IMF and IBRD, 2006, p. 18).

Mechanisms to address free riding already exist according to IMF and IDA (2006a, p. 6): 'the track record of policy performance necessary to reach the decision point requires countries to abide by stringent limits on non-concessional borrowing'. IDA's board approved a 'two-pronged package' of measures addressing free riding on future borrowing by IDA grant recipients as well as post-MDRI countries.

Non-concessional lending is usually singled out as the free rider concern, although 'Private net debt flows to low-income countries have declined from already low levels since the mid-1980s' (IMF and IBRD, 2006, p. 26). However the document informs: 'Private debt flows are to a large degree related to natural resource-based economies.' If financing commodity production and exports, such credits should be self-liquidating or in any case not routinely cause problems. Especially new creditors eager to establish trade relations, such as China and India, automatically provide export markets too. While sharply falling raw material prices might still create problems, such credits, if properly invested, should normally have rates of return that allow servicing them.

Although focusing on non-concessional lending, the BWIs include any form of new lending. IMF and IBRD (2006, p. 18) ask: 'What is the role of new financing (including of [sic] nonconcessional debt) and how can the "free-rider" problem be addressed?' They regret that IFI surveillance cannot 'require members to provide loan-by-loan data with a view to characterizing creditors as "free riders" on concessional debt or grants' (ibid., p. 27). However 'Loan-by-loan accounting of all new loans contracted or

guaranteed by the public sector on a quarterly basis is part of the reporting obligations of countries to the IMF under a Fund-supported program'
(IDA, 2006b, p. 11). Such programmes are not rare in the poorest SCs.
This document proposes 'that a loan-by-loan approach rather than
an aggregate approach be adopted to identify instances of free riding',
arguing this 'would be consistent with the Fund's minimum concessionality approach, which applies on a loan-by-loan basis'.

According to IDA (2006b, p. 28) 'It is important to acknowledge that
there may be cases where IDA has very little leverage to reduce instances
of free riding, even with strong disincentives.' Resource-rich countries
are singled out as examples. IDA might still deter free riders, though, if
other official creditors introduced 'similar measures', and donors took
'these IDA measures as a signal for their own grant programs'. IMF programmes have been a deterrent for non-concessional borrowing so far.
The document sees a need that, 'as more countries move beyond Fund-
financed programs, the interest of countries in the newly-created Policy
Support Instrument (PSI), which would help maintain non-concessional
borrowing at an appropriate level' (ibid., p. 4) be established. The DSF is
seen as a means to address concerns about unsustainable post-relief borrowing. 'However, the DSF treatment is likely to require strengthening
policies aimed at curbing free riding behavior' (IDA, 2005, p. 8). The DSF
could also 'facilitate creditor coordination' (IMF and IDA, 2006a, p. 7). In
short, one united creditor cum donor cartel could enforce its views.

The concern about overborrowing is particularly interesting if one
recalls that the BWIs expect pre- and post-MDRI debt ratios to converge
in the long run: 'For example, MDRI debt relief reduces the NPV of
debt-to-export ratio on average by about 40 percent over 2006–10, but by
2025 the difference between pre- and post-MDRI debt ratios declines to
just over 10 percentage points' (IMF and IBRD, 2006, p. 17). A sample of
African completion point HIPCs shows a similar long-term convergence.
'In all cases, long-term convergence occurs because of the growing importance with time of accumulated debt from new borrowing' (ibid.; see also
pp. 31ff.). The statements on free riding and on increased borrowing can
only be reconciled in a consistent way if one assumes that new creditors,
not new credits are the problem. New lenders are to be kept out. Finally
poor countries with institutions and policies qualified by the BWIs as
medium or strong are now assumed to be able to manage much higher
debts than under HIPC II, in some cases even HIPC I. This, too, can
hardly be explained by the desire to avoid large new inflows of loans.

Hurley (2007, p. 17) argues that the concern about free riding 'is compounded by a rapidly changing creditor landscape. Countries such as
China, India, Brazil and Venezuela are stepping forward with offers of

rapidly-disbursed and almost condition-free cash to low-income African and Latin American nations, especially those rich in natural resources.'

But more 'traditional' creditors also want to take advantage of some low income countries' new-found creditworthiness: 'On 15 March this year at a roundtable in Washington DC, the U.S. Export Import Bank briefed more than 70 U.S. exporters on the potential for sales to Nigeria now that that country "is experiencing economic stability through improved debt management, privatization, deregulation, banking and trade policy reform, and government and institutional measures to create transparency and fight corruption"' (ibid., p. 17). Judging from IFI documents this latter effort to induce new borrowing or similar efforts by other Northern national export credit agencies are not what the BWIs are concerned about.

THE DAWN OF A 'NEO-LISTIAN' WORLD?

Efforts to gain permanent control over SCs through debt management, even after debt reduction schemes are 'fully' implemented, raises concerns, especially so because this comes on top of other factors limiting the policy pace of SCs, as analysed by Chang (see Chapter 9).

Increasingly the present situation fits List's recommendation of North-South relations. Better known for his opposition to the 'English philosophy' of free trade as harmful to Germany in its early development stages some 150 years ago (but advocating free trade once Germany would be economically as strong as or stronger than the British), List ([1841]1920, p. 211) advocated joint exploitation of the South as 'promising much richer and more certain fruits than the mutual enmity of war and trade regulations'. The title of Chang's (2002) book *Kicking Away the Ladder* quotes List, who recommended this policy vis-à-vis the South, or what he called without much elegance (and failing to be politically perfectly correct) 'barbarian and half-barbarian . . . peoples' (List [1841] 1920, p. 211). This new form of dominance may thus be called neo-Listian (Raffer, 1987, 2000). From a Listian perspective of gaining control – or Rodrik's interpretation of the debt crisis as an opportunity seized to enforce certain policies – IFIs were successful. Their 'debt management' caused substantial social costs to debtor economies, particularly to vulnerable groups, but conquests and taking control can hardly occur without some collateral damage.

From a purely logical point of view, this agenda would plausibly explain why creditor countries – in spite of assuring their strong concern for economic efficiency and accountability – allow IFIs to go on being totally exempt from the most basic rules of law, economics and ethics (see

Chapter 13). This attitude cannot be explained by official declarations of creditor/donor governments.

It makes perfect sense, though, if one assumes that IFIs are supposed to serve as Listian administrators. While they have not brought about sustainable recovery in debtor countries and the economic success of IFI projects is poor according to their own official documents, they have successfully done two things:

1. In particular during the 1980s they have squeezed money out of SCs, at high social and economic costs as the IMF and the IBRD admitted long ago. Compromising future growth and causing misery, they have acted very much in the creditors' interest of recovering as much money as possible.
2. Creditors in their own right as well as institutions controlled by creditor governments, the BWIs have made debtors totally dependent on creditor wishes, subjecting them to a status minds more critical than I might possibly call neo-colonial dependence. Furthermore most donors allow the BWIs to play the role of coordinators and demand their 'seal of approval' before granting debt reductions or new aid. IFI leverage is thus compounded by the collective power of the North.

Critics might point out that no decent and efficient solution has been sought, because present debt management is such a convenient means of ruling debtor economies. In spite of his great popularity with orthodoxy even Adam Smith's advice – given before Krueger's 'new approach' in his *Wealth of Nations* – was not heeded. He stated that with states as with private individuals 'a fair, open, and avowed bankruptcy is always the measure which is both least dishonourable to the debtor, and least hurtful to the creditor'. This solution may be economically, legally and ethically advised, but it fails to confer the same power and control to official creditors as present strategies.

As orthodox scientists are often eager to speak of 'conspiracy' theories to 'disprove' unwelcome reasoning, it must be pointed out that no conspiracy at all is necessary to achieve these results. All that is needed are clear and consistent efforts to increase one's influence, as well as an ability to use emerging opportunities to one's advantage. Good politicians have done just that over centuries. It would not be surprising if this had happened in the case of sovereign debts too. One may well agree that an 'increase in external financing combined with adverse terms of trade shocks and macroeconomic mismanagement, lead to a build up of the debt burden and a deterioration of debt indicators in LICs [low income countries], providing the onset for the debt problems of the 1980s' (IBRD,

2006, p. 11), and extend this conclusion to SCs in general. Especially for middle income countries, one should add the strong and abrupt increase in real interest rates – called 'skyrocketing' by the OECD – triggered by the Federal Reserve's monetary policy and the huge US budget deficits incurred in order to finance armaments. Both policies were doubtlessly determined by internal US concerns with complete disregard for SCs. But they triggered the debt crisis in the South. There is no reason why opportunities such as the debt crisis should not have been immediately seized by IFIs and official creditors. The IMF in particular would have had to be dissolved after the demise of Bretton Woods for which it had been specifically created, because its task had disappeared. Finding a new role as debt manager also allowed it to purport to having a new *raison d'être*. As the dominated have to pay for the 'services' of their administrators, a neo-Listian system is cheap.

SCs have become perceptibly more dependent at present than even during the heydays of the dependency school. The present situation is much more conducive to dependency analysis, but there are no longer any *dependentistas*. The few SCs that could temporarily escape this advanced form of dependence, such as South Korea, did so by following the advice of Raúl Prebisch and dependency thinkers. This successful way to economic development seems now largely closed. While some richer SCs have managed to increase their importance, the poorest countries in the South have lost virtually all their policy space.

In any case, democracy seems to have lost out. Hurley reports that at the annual conference of the Parliamentary Network on the World Bank in March 2007 a Zambian member of Parliament asked the IMF's Managing Director, Rodrigo Rato, whether he would support the development of a *'responsible lending and borrowing framework under the scrutiny of parliamentarians, with the terms of the framework agreed jointly by both debtors and creditors'* (Hurley, 2007, p. 17, emphasis in original). Rato replied that he '"*understood the question to be about debt sustainability*" and the Bank/ Fund debt sustainability framework for low-income countries was an important positive development. But this response ignores the heart of the issue.' Clearly parliamentary scrutiny could not find the managing director's support. It is not advised by IFI documents either.

THE EFFECTS OF THE US CRISIS ON SCS

The large US financial crisis erupting in 2007 resulted from deregulating and liberalizing the financial sector. Although much larger, it is a crisis such as other neoliberal crises in Chile, Mexcio, Asia or the Savings &

Loans crisis in the USA. Those BWI policies forced on or recommended to SCs were carried to their logical extreme, including practices such as 'liar' or 'ninja' (no income, no job or assets) loans that can only be explained by the fact that securitized debt was quickly sold on. Allowing techniques to reduce capital requirements – special vehicles, such as SIVs (structured investment vehicles), SPV (special purpose vehicles), which emerged to keep activities off banks' books and to avoid related capital requirements – increasing the role of private rating agencies to push back official regulators or a booming intransparent over the counter (OTC) market are further characteristics. The basis on which this happened was again the Robichek (now rather Greenspan) doctrine: markets know best and should not be 'overregulated'. The usual result ensued. Credit default swaps (CDSs) emerged as a new form of covering the risk of loan losses, a large market growing dramatically within a short period of time. Economically CDSs are simply default insurances. Selling was easy. But it turned out that protection sellers were not so easily able to pay as stipulated. As no one had bothered to maintain the quality standards of institutions selling CDSs, this is no surprise.

Although SCs did not buy US toxics as eagerly as the Europeans, and the direct link via holding US papers is not a problem at all, SCs are suffering from this US-made crisis (cf. Barry and Peterson, 2009). Exports have dropped because of reduced global demand due to the crisis, remittances as well, though less pronouncedly. Credits get more expensive (to those SCs still getting any). It becomes all the more dubious whether aid promises will be held this time, considering the enormous amount of money mobilized to save the banking system and to stimulate Northern economies. To put this into perspective: as the *Guardian* (17 October 2008) reported, Wall Street banks were to pay bonus payments worth more than $70 billion to staff, or 'Pay and bonus deals equivalent to 10% of US government bail-out package', which had been $700 billion. In comparison, US ODA was $26 billion in 2008 and $21.8 billon in 2007, roughly one third of the bonus payments earmarked for the banking sector that had produced the crisis. Bankers could have financed all US ODA and would still have come out ahead of the game by tens of millions of dollars. Admittedly these bonus payments are less than the total OECD ODA, $119.8 billion in 2008 and $103.5 billion in 2007, though around two thirds of it.

Meanwhile the fault for the US crisis is busily shifted on to the South. This recalls the 1970s, when OPEC was quickly and wrongfully blamed for the debt crisis of 1982. Global imbalances, the mantra goes, are at least the main, if not the real cause. China and OPEC are to blame rather than US regulators, financial institutions or even US overconsumption.

The worst result, though, is that IFIs were granted more power without any reform, and are now allowed to continue as before. They were not even requested to obey their own statutes. 'Reform' is limited to a few basis points of voting being shifted between regions, which is one tangible though economically irrelevant outcome. The IMF, in particular, was saved by the crisis, triggered by those neoliberal policies the IMF recommends. On the brink of bankruptcy by early repayments and a corresponding shrinking of its outstanding claims from the 2002 peak of SDR 70 billion to some SDR 15.5 billion (end-2006) as well as income shortfalls projected to surpass 40 per cent during 2008-10 (Torres, 2007, p. 9), this crisis once again saved the Fund. As in the early 1980s, it was an international debt crisis the IMF helped bring about.

Iceland broke the ice. On 24 October an IMF package totalling $2.1 billion was announced under the Fund's fast-track emergency financing mechanism. A stand-by arrangement for Hungary was approved in November. The neoliberal crisis has revived business of the neoliberal Fund. In March 2009 the IMF 'overhauled' its lending structure, also establishing a Flexible Credit Line (FCL). When the first country, Mexico, availed herself of the FCL, IMF First Deputy Managing Director, John Lipsky, spoke of

> a historic occasion . . . . The IMF Executive Board has approved the first Flexible Credit Line arrangement and, at the same time, the largest financial arrangement in the Fund's history. The approval of this arrangement for Mexico represents the consolidation of a major step in the process of reforming the IMF and making its lending framework more relevant to member countries' needs. (IMF Survey online, 17 April 2009)

This is correct. First, the IMF overcame the existential problem of having no clients. Second, as Mexican authorities stated their intention not to draw on the line, the Fund has opened a new business line, insuring against external crisis, naturally at the political and economic costs of accepting the Fund's ideological demands.

In December 2008 the IBRD created a Financial Crisis Response Fast Track Facility. In January 2009 its president called for a vulnerability fund to be financed by Northern governments devoting 0.7 per cent of their stimulus packages to supporting the poor. Naturally the IBRD could manage the distribution of cash – as Zoellick suggested in the *Financial Times* (25 January 2009) –with the UN and regional development banks. He specified, though, that one 'could use existing mechanisms to deliver the funds fast and flexibly, backed by monitoring and safeguards so the money is well spent'. In plain English this means channelling these funds largely via the IBRD.

Zoellick's idea to finance 'investments' in safety net programmes, such as conditional cash transfers that make it possible for people to keep their children at school, get adequate nutrition and seek health care by this vulnerability fund repeats old perceptions. The wording 'investment' does not suggest grants at all. But poor overindebeted countries cannot afford to finance food by loans. If they could, they would not be poor and overindebted. The vulnerability fund thus threatens to assure that the debt problem will be dragged on further, keeping IFIs in business.

Not all SCs went back to the IMF. In October 2008 Korea and Singapore established temporary reciprocal currency arrangements (swap lines) with the Federal Reserve to assure foreign exchange liquidity. So did Brazil and Mexico. OECD countries such as the UK, Japan or Switzerland as well as the European Central Bank had already concluded such swaps. Incidentally the same press release on 29 October 2008 by the Fed that announced these four swaps also welcomed the IMF's announcement to establish its Short-term Liquidity Facility (SLF). The SLF is officially designed to help member countries facing liquidity problems arising from developments in external capital markets. ASEAN members, China, Japan and South Korea revived the idea of an Asian Monetary Fund. After committing themselves to a \$80 billion crisis fund, an increase to \$120 billion was set to be approved at a regional summit in February 2009. Apparently East Asia has once and for all turned away from the BWIs, as Western European countries or Japan had done long ago.

The foreseeable result of the US crisis is that sub-Saharan African countries will remain under the thumb of unreformed IFIs. Some Latin American countries will again become IFI victims. Continuity of the never-ending story of sovereign Southern debts is assured, although some countries have been able to free themselves from multilateral institutions.

5. The Raffer Proposal: an international Chapter 9 for countries

As pointed out in Chapter 3, emulating corporate insolvency (in the US Chapter 11, Title 11 US Code) was repeatedly advocated early on in the 1980s. The late Alfred Herrhausen, then CEO of the Deutsche Bank, was among the most vocal advocates of negotiated debt reduction, well ahead of many others. It was also advocated by UNCTAD (1986) and several economists, such as myself. In Germany Thomas Kampffmeyer (1987) drew attention to Germany's forgotten de facto insolvency (London Accord) and Indonesia, proposing this solution for SCs. The historical examples of Chapter 1 show that this is economically a perfectly sound idea.

This idea met fierce opposition, not least from the IMF meanwhile advocating corporate insolvency as its 'new approach'. A legalistic, formal killer argument came in handy: Chapter 11 cannot be applied to sovereigns, because corporate insolvency does not address sovereignty, nor governmental powers in general. This argument is right as far as it goes. But there is an easy way out. The USA knows insolvency procedures for debtors with governmental powers, so-called municipalities, granting debtor protection to municipalities and their inhabitants: Chapter 9, Title 11 US Code (USC). Reacting to this legalistic counterargument against Chapter 11, Raffer (1989) proposed internationalizing municipal bankruptcy (so-called Chapter 9) at a conference in Zagreb in 1987, proving that there is no legal argument against insolvency type protection for public debtors, including sovereigns. Designed and used for decades in the USA to solve debt problems of debtors vested with governmental powers, its essential points can be adapted to sovereign borrowers with minor formal changes, granting them the benefits of the only efficient solution, generally accepted with all other debtors. Like all good insolvency laws it combines the need for a general framework with the flexibility necessary to deal fairly with individual debtors. There exists no more technical problem to heed Adam Smith's economically sound advice.

Although I had proposed Chapter 9 initially to defend the emulation of insolvency, I have meanwhile come to see that the specificities of sovereigns need a special form of insolvency dealing with the problem of sovereignty and the specific situation of inhabitants affected by debt management. Rather than seeing Chapter 9 as a means to defend the idea of insolvency, I have come to see it as the only appropriate type of insolvency mechanism. Legal systems with full-fledged public insolvency procedures for public debtors are rare. However, encouraged by a private consulting firm, Hungary introduced insolvency proceedings for municipalities after the demise of communism.

NGOs soon supported my proposal (see Chapter 10), which J.K. Galbraith (2003) named the Raffer Proposal. Mexico's crash of 1994–95 did not only trigger the OECD's call for a larger 'officially provided safety net' for speculators, but also a short-lived revival of insolvency. The Chairman of the Federal Reserve System, Alan Greenspan, suggested thinking about international insolvency as an appropriate mechanism to settle debt problems. The *Financial Times* reported that Treasury Secretary Robert Rubin said he carefully avoided the term 'international bankruptcy court' but that some procedures to work out the debt obligations of debtors were needed. In the *Wall Street Journal* (10 April 1995) Representative Jim Leach of Iowa, the Chairman of the House Banking and Financial Services Committee, recommended international insolvency proceedings: 'What is needed today is a Chapter 11 process for the global financial system, a technique to keep nation-states and their people from the impoverishing implications of insolvency.' Mentioning the little known Chapter 9 proceedings briefly, he specifically pointed out its implicit understanding that local government must continue to function. It was even considered informally to bring the issue to the table of the Halifax G7 summit, but this was not done. New euphoria on capital flows to East Asia soon eclipsed the Mexican shock. The problem faded away from public interest again.

THE ESSENCE OF INSOLVENCY

Since insolvency is a fact of life, any legal system knows insolvency procedures. While early insolvency laws did not take human rights or debtor protection into account, civilized insolvency laws do. Debt prisons are a thing of the past; insolvent debtors can no longer be cut into pieces to be distributed to creditors as under very ancient Roman law. All debtors, except SCs and their inhabitants, enjoy protection. Their human dignity and their human rights are guaranteed by insolvency proceedings. They are not at the mercy (or rather lack thereof) of their creditors. In the USA, for example, one even speaks of 'insolvency protection'. The important point is applying the fundamental principles of insolvency protection to any debtor.

The basic function of any insolvency procedure is the resolution of a conflict between two fundamental legal principles. In a situation of a debt overhang the right of creditors to payments collides with the principle recognized generally (not only in the case of loans) by all civilized legal systems that no one must be forced to fulfil contracts if that leads to inhumane distress, endangers one's life or health or violates human dignity. Although their claims are recognized as legitimate, insolvency exempts resources from being seized by bona fide creditors. Human rights, human dignity and the debtor's 'fresh start' enjoy unconditional priority. Unless they happen to be SCs, debtors cannot be forced to starve themselves or their children to be able to pay. Human rights and human dignity are given unconditional priority over repayment, even though insolvency only deals with claims based on a solid and proper legal foundation. A fortiori this is valid for less well-founded claims. The sanctity of contracts, often rightly referred to, is always overridden by human rights (debtor protection).

Although the sanctity of contracts ('*pacta sunt servanda*') is a fundamental legal, economic and ethical principle, all legal systems recognize circumstances where contractual rights can no longer be enforced, or indeed cease to exist. Human rights might make perfectly legal claims unenforceable, '*pacta sunt servanda*' is overruled. Using the sanctity of contracts to defend present debt management and against applying the same principles to all borrowers is abuse. It is speaking up against equal treatment of all human beings and in favour of discriminating those having the 'wrong' passport.

Insolvency relief is not an act of mercy but of justice and economic reason. This is apparent down to negligible details such as the fact that 'forgive' is not commonly used when insolvency procedures reduce debts. Reduction is a right of insolvent debtors, even if they are not 'deserving, good children', while SCs have to beg for 'forgiveness'.

The other base of insolvency is the most fundamental principle of the Rule of Law: no one must be allowed to be judge in one's own cause. Civilized insolvency laws applicable to all debtors except SCs demand a neutral institution assuring fair settlements. Creditors must not decide on their own claims. Even at the time of debt slavery creditors were not allowed to decide whether to enslave debtors. Only judges could do so. The unrestricted creditor domination, routine in present sovereign debt management, is an open breach of the Rule of Law, a principle presently preached to SCs by creditor governments. It is also inefficient from a purely economical perspective, as the prolonged debt crisis proves.

Present insolvency laws have developed over centuries. While national laws differ in details, the mechanism of insolvency provides the only economically efficient way to solve the problem. Demanding an appropriate insolvency mechanism for SCs simply means that people anywhere on the globe must be treated equally, irrespective of their passports, nationality or colour of their skin.

SPECIFIC FEATURES OF MY PROPOSAL

The specific features of my proposal making it fundamentally different from creditor dominated 'solutions' discussed so far are:

- impartial decision making and respecting the Rule of Law
- debtor protection
- right to be heard (which may be seen as part of debtor protection)
- treating the problem of sovereignty
- fair and equal treatment of all creditors
- improved sustainability
- perceptibly improved stability of the international financial architecture.

Impartial Decision Making and the Rule of Law

With good reason, any decent legal system demands an impartial entity without any self-interest to be vested with the authority to preside legal procedures, to decide if and when necessary, as well as to guarantee certain fundamental rights to any human being. Courts, not creditors nor debtors, are vested with this authority. The very foundation of the Rule of Law demands that one must not be judge in one's own cause. So far, international public creditors have been judge, jury, experts, bailiff, occasionally even the debtor's lawyer all in one, not just violating the Rule of Law but also mocking the very foundation of any legal system. In stark contrast to all civilized legal systems, some international creditors have decided on debt reductions with perfect arbitrariness. This is unfair to debtors and other creditors and economically unsuccessful. Someone with a vested interest is unlikely to decide objectively and thus efficiently. Decades of debt management drive this point home. One important and fundamental principle creditors preach to debtor countries is brushed aside when it comes to dealing with Southern debts.

My international Chapter 9 respects the very foundation of the Rule of Law: impartial decision making. National courts are not the optimal solution. Understandably, creditors fearing political influence on courts insist on stipulating jurisdictions outside debtor countries. However, courts in creditor countries might be problematic too. In 1984 the US Court of Appeals for the Second Circuit granted US insolvency protection to Costa Rica, based in part on the assumption that this was consistent with US policy. The Second Circuit reheard the matter in *Allied Bank International v Banco Credito Agricola de Cartago* (757 F2d 516; 2d Cir 1985) and reversed itself when the executive branch, as amicus curiae, clarified that supporting Costa Rica was not US policy. This reversal occurred in spite of the Court's own legal arguments and what it had called 'principles recognized by all civilized nations' (UNCTAD, 1986, p. 142; cf. also Raffer, 2005c), subordinating legal principles to administrative whim.

It is particularly worrying that administrative wishes in the USA may change court judgements even against the Court's own materially legal arguments. Although it was always explicitly acknowledged that Costa Rica's capital controls were effected 'in response to escalating economic problems', the Court specifically named US 'interest in maintaining New York's status as one of the foremost commercial centers in the world' as one reason for the final judgement. Grave economic problems and legal reasoning were subordinated to this commercial interest, even though it seems unlikely that a different judgement would have done perceptible harm to New York's standing as a financial centre. It is quite rare that interest of a third, technically not involved institution or the wishes of regional governments can shape court verdicts beside or even against legal considerations.

As national courts in debtor or creditor countries might not be totally beyond political influence, I propose international arbitration. Following established international law practice, each side (creditors and the debtor) would nominate one or two persons, who in turn elect one more person to achieve an odd number. While institutionalized, neutral entities are technically feasible, ad hoc panels are preferable. Assuming that new cases will be rare once the present backlog will have been handled, any standing institution would be severely underemployed. Also arbitration panels established by creditors and the debtor for each case might be more acceptable as parties can nominate impartial arbitrators they trust, unlike within the SDRM. In contrast, the IMF would lose importance. Like the SDDRF, these panels could recognize or void individual claims. My proposal confers the same authority on arbitrators as the SDDRF, but not more. My transparent procedure protects bona fide creditors. Ad hoc panels, a traditional mechanism of international law, show that the IMF's statutory approach is not necessary. The procedure need not be enshrined in the Fund's Articles of Agreement.

My arbitration panel could sit anywhere, including the debtor or neighbouring countries, which would make participation by organizations representing the population easier. I have never demanded that it 'be headquartered in a neutral country that is neither an active international lender nor borrower' (Eichengreen, 1999, p. 126). Few, if any, such countries exist. This error probably stems from a misinterpretation of the following passage: 'The reason why no court, whether located in a creditor or debtor country, should chair the procedures is self-evident: its impartiality is not guaranteed' (Raffer, 1990, pp. 304–305). This remark refers to courts of law, not courts of arbitration. Language apart, the illustrating example of *Allied Bank International* does definitely not involve a court of arbitration. It is important to note that nominating arbitrators does not make them representatives of those who nominate them, for example, a Supreme Court judge nominated by the president does not represent the president but the law.

Filing for insolvency protection would trigger a stay. The panel must endorse or reject this stay immediately upon being formed. It must reject the debtor's demand if unfounded, denying this debtor any advantage from starting the procedure. Initially the IMF suggested that it should be given the right to endorse the stay triggered by the debtor's demand for insolvency relief. It later tried to assuage private sector resistance with several variants, including one allowing litigation by dissenting creditors, but preventing any pecuniary advantage by deducting any amount recovered by litigation from the sum such creditors would finally be entitled to receive as a result of insolvency proceedings. Reduced to a *nudum ius*, the right to litigation would become meaningless (Raffer, 2006, p. 250), in fact, a practical joke. Assuming that this creditor would have to pay their legal fees they would be worse off than by not litigating.

Arbitrators would have to mediate between the parties, chair and support negotiations by advice, provide adequate possibilities to be heard for the affected population (see below) and – if necessary – decide.

The panel should verify claims, just as domestic courts routinely do. This proposal (Raffer 1990, p. 309), initially classified as impracticable and utopian by IMF staff, is now part of Krueger's 'new approach'. This gives hope that basic legal principles, such as checking whether those signing loan contracts on behalf of debtors actually have the authority to do so, might eventually be applied when it comes to SCs.

Naturally the debtor government can choose to leave the task of nominating panel members either to the parliament or the people. In the latter case arbitrators could be elected from a roster by voters. Anyone reaching a minimum of supporting signatures by voters would have to be on this roster. One arbitrator might be chosen by parliament, the other by voters.

The parliament might establish a special committee for this purpose including members of the cabinet, as proposed in a bill drafted on the initiative of Congressman Mario Cafiero by the Argentine opposition party ARI. The bill would establish a Comisión Representativa del Estado Nacional. Consisting of members from both Houses and representatives of the executive power, it would nominate panel members and represent Argentina during the proceedings. In the case of a change of government, which has occurred quite often in indebted countries, a new, incoming government might be prepared to opt for one of these democratic possibilities.

Unsurprisingly, the IMF (2002b, p. 63) tries to find an argument against my ad hoc panels. As claims would have to be verified first 'to be recognized for participation in decision-making . . . the selection of a panel would have to follow, not precede, the verification process. But then who would resolve disputes arising from verification if there was [sic] no panel already in place?'

The answer is simple: all registering creditors nominate their arbitrators who immediately decide on the recognition of claims. Recognized creditors could either confirm their nominees or replace them. The latter could theoretically become necessary if so many claims are excluded that different arbitrators would have been nominated by the remaining creditors, which – though possible – seems unlikely to be the normal case. As creditors are known and organized endorsing or replacing could be done quickly. Creditors whose claims are dismissed are party and should have the same right to nominate arbitrators judging on their case as anyone else. To back up a weak point the IMF adds that creditors might each wish to appoint their own arbitrator, which would make the case unmanageable and 'could distort the balance of power between the debtor- and creditor-selected arbitrators'. This only holds if the nominees are not impartial arbitrators but actually represent and defend the interests of certain groups. In this case, of course, anyone would like to have their own 'defender'. This problem has never occurred in the few cases when private creditors and sovereign debtors agreed on arbitration on debt issues. Compared with the IMF's SDDRF, where creditors have to accept the IMF's choice, my proposal definitely confers more rights on creditors.

Debtor Protection – A Human Right

The idea of internationalizing the basic ideas of US municipal insolvency is to allow the basic function of any insolvency procedure to work in the case of sovereigns. The conflict between legitimate creditor rights and the human right that no one must be forced to fulfil contracts if that causes inhumane distress, endangers one's life or health or violates human dignity must and can be solved in the same way as in all other cases of debt overhang.

What debtor protection means can be illustrated using the example of Malawi. The IMF and the IBRD were accused of having forced Malawi to sell maize from its National Food Reserve to repay debts. The IBRD encouraged the country 'to keep foreign exchange instead of storing grain' (Pettifor, 2002). In a BBC interview Malawi's president said the government 'had been forced [to sell maize] in order to repay commercial loans taken out to buy surplus maize in previous years' (ibid.). The IMF and the IBRD had insisted on it. Malawi sold a substantial amount of maize. After harvest problems in 2002 famine struck, and 7 million of a population of 11 million were severely short of food according to Action Aid. Creditor interest was given priority over survival.

Confronted with it in the House of Commons' Treasury Select Committee (2002, pp. 11–12, see also pp. 18–19) the IMF's Managing Director, Horst Köhler, insisted that this advice had been given by the IBRD and the EU Commission, so 'it is just plain wrong to accuse the Fund that it advised and made even a conditionality out of this'. Köhler suggested that MPs should ask the IBRD and the EU:

> I want to underline: this is an issue in the responsibility of the World Bank and the EU Commission. The IMF was part of this process of giving advice to the Malawi government and the IMF may also not have been attentive enough, but I just tell you that I am not accepting that the IMF is made the culprit for this case . . . I have sent the President of Malawi a letter in which I made clear that he was involved with the World Bank and the EU Commission in this project; that the IMF was part of, say, the kind of international advice and the IMF may, again, not have been attentive enough how they exercised how to run this maize stock, but it was not the responsibility of the Fund to implement the advice. (Treasury Select Committee, 2002, pp. 11ff.)

Obviously, while being 'part of the kind of advice' that resulted in starving people, the IMF did not give this advice at all. In any case, the IMF is innocent. What is important to our argument, though, is that repayment was preferred over the right to live. This precisely would no longer be possible under my model.

Exempting resources necessary to finance minimum standards of basic health services, primary education and so on can only be justified if that money is demonstrably used for its declared purpose. Not without reason creditors as well as NGOs are concerned that this might not always be guaranteed. The solution is quite simple: a transparently managed fund as proposed by Pettifor (2001) financed by the debtor in domestic currency. This would be money that could alternatively be paid to creditors – not phantom debts – but which debtor protection exempts from being seized by creditors. Within my model it would statutorily have to use its resources for anti-poverty measures and financing a fresh start of the debtor economy. Its management could be monitored by an international board or advisory council consisting of members from the debtor country as well as from creditor countries. They could be nominated by NGOs and by governments (including the debtor government). As this fund is a legal entity of its own, checks and discussions of its projects would not concern the government's budget, which is an important part of a country's sovereignty. Aid could also be channelled through the fund, changing the character of money just set apart from the ordinary budget towards a normal fund for the poor.

In analogy to domestic Chapter 9 this fund would finance basic social services essential to the health, safety and welfare of inhabitants. Necessary environmental protection measures could be funded. While this idea had been severely attacked when first presented as part of my sovereign Chapter 9 (Raffer, 1989, p. 59, 1990, pp. 305–306), HIPC II officially incorporates anti-poverty measures. Although actual positive pro-poor effects lag perceptibly behind official declarations, the principle is accepted. Once again, the SDRM rolls this progress back.

Nevertheless, debtor protection is slowly gaining ground. Argentina's President Kirchner quoted the needs of the population as a reason for the debt reduction demanded from creditors. The Caracas Declaration by Ministers of the G24 in February 1998 called for 'domestic social safety-nets as integral elements of stabilization and adjustment programs to protect the most vulnerable elements of the population of crisis affected countries'.

Right To Be Heard

In strict analogy to domestic Chapter 9, the population affected by the solution must have the right to be heard. Taxpayers who have to pick up the bill should indeed have a right to know and to comment on proposed solutions. Both the municipality's employees and so-called 'special tax-payers affected by the plan' may object to the confirmation of the plan. The legal term characterizes a record owner or holder of title to real property against which a special assessment or tax has been levied, whose tax burden the plan proposes to increase. Briefly, taxpayers who have to pick up the bill have the right to know and to comment on proposed solutions. Participation and transparency, other important demands of public creditors vis-à-vis their debtors, are guaranteed within the USA. It should be added that within the USA the court may, but need not, grant the right to be heard to anyone with a direct legal interest in the case, a legal standard that is a far cry indeed from international 'debt management', where neither the affected population nor vulnerable groups have any formal right to voice their views. HIPC II meanwhile recognizes – at least verbally – the participation of affected people and the protection of the poor. The SDRM remained rooted in the ideas of the failed HIPC I and of the 'structural adjustment' models of the 1980s.

Internationally, the right to be heard would have to be exercised by representation. I proposed: '[e]xactly like in Rule 2018, this could be done by trade unions or employees' associations' (Raffer, 1990, p. 305). Furthermore, international organizations, such as the United Nations International Children's Emergency Fund (UNICEF), 'Catholic NGOs, similar organizations of other creeds (especially in countries with non-Christian majorities), NGOs without religious background . . . and – last but by no means least – grass-roots organizations of the poor' would also qualify. Rogoff and Zettelmeyer (2002a, p. 10) seriously misrepresented this proposal: 'trade unions, NGOs or churches could function as arbitrators speaking on behalf of the citizens in the debtor countries'. A right to be heard does not make someone a panel member or a judge in national courts. They corrected this error later (Rogoff and Zettelmeyer, 2002b, pp. 482–3) after I had written to the authors.

Rejected as utopian when first proposed (Raffer, 1989, p. 59), participation officially became part of HIPC II. Civil society is to participate in designing poverty reduction strategies. Obviously, participation is possible after all. Furthermore, one cannot keep people from expressing their views. In Argentina, for instance, civil society 'participated' in the streets by banging pots. Formal representation seems a better way of voicing opinions.

Sovereignty – Governmental Powers

Although the SDRM is designed for sovereigns and sovereignty had been used as an argument against early proposals to emulate Chapter 11, the specific problems of public debtors are not touched upon. Municipal insolvency (Chapter 9) does so.

In her fourth paper Krueger (2002a, pp. 12f.) refers briefly to Chapter 9 as 'In many respects . . . of greater relevance in the sovereign context because it applies to an entity that carries out governmental functions'. She draws attention to differences to the corporate model, suggesting: 'All of these features could be appropriately integrated into a sovereign debt restructuring mechanism' – without providing further details on how to do so. She sees important differences between municipalities and sovereigns that would have implications on the design of the SDRM:

Chapter 9 legislation acknowledges – and does not impair – the power of the state within which the municipality exists to continue to control the exercise of the powers of the municipality, including expenditures. This lack of independence of municipalities is one of the reasons why many countries have not adopted insolvency legislation to address problems of financial distress confronted by local governments.

Her conclusion may be doubted on historical grounds. Virtually all European governments seem to operate on the doubtful premise that public authority cannot go bankrupt, special proceedings would therefore not be necessary. Furthermore, the point that municipalities are subject to constitutional rights of states is presented in a totally misleading way. It seems based on Section 903 'Reservation of State power to control municipalities':

> This chapter does not limit or impair the power of a State to control, by legislation or otherwise, a municipality of or in such State in the exercise of the political or governmental powers of such municipality, including expenditures for such exercise, but –
> (1) a State law prescribing a method of composition of indebtedness of such municipality may not bind any creditor that does not consent to such composition; and
> (2) a judgment entered under such a law may not bind a creditor that does not consent to such composition.

Given the need to reconcile constitutional rights of the federation and states (Kupetz, 1995, pp. 532ff. and 581ff.) Section 903 simply states that insolvency procedures do not invalidate state laws and state rights regarding a 'political subdivision or public agency or instrumentality of a State' (Section 101(34), Title 11 USC) deriving all its rights and powers from the state. Filing for insolvency does not void the constitution, nor the law. Section 903 does not disturb constitutional arrangements (ibid., p. 582). As laws on the subject of bankruptcy are constitutionally reserved to Congress (Article I, Section 10) and states are prohibited to pass laws impairing the obligation of contracts, a state can basically suggest a method of composition. If creditors agree, this might be a useful solution. As the US Constitution is not the constitution of every country it is unlikely that US constitutional concerns are the reason for the lack of municipal insolvency procedures in most other countries. Advised by private Western consultants Hungary adopted an insolvency law for public debtors after the demise of communism.

Krueger's brief objection makes it necessary to point out that corporations are – like municipalities – subject to the law. If justified, her reservation against Chapter 9 would also be valid against Chapter 11. It would not be possible any longer to use domestic legal arrangements as a source of international law. Her rather short passage on Chapter 9, which quotes no legal source and no academic literature on the topic, apparently expresses a certain dislike against Chapter 9, a model which she does not mention again later.

The difference between the two variants is fundamentally important. Chapter 9 is the only procedure protecting governmental powers, and thus applicable to sovereigns. Section 904 titled 'Limitation on Jurisdiction and Powers of Court' states with outmost clarity:

> Notwithstanding any power of the court, unless the debtor consents or the plan so provides, the court may not, by any stay, order, or decree, in the case or otherwise, interfere with –
> (1) any of the political and governmental powers of the debtor;
> (2) any of the property or revenues of the debtor; or
> (3) the debtor's use or enjoyment of any income-producing property.

The concept of sovereignty does not contain anything more than what Section 904 protects. The court's jurisdiction depends on the municipality's volition, beyond which it cannot be extended, similar to the jurisdiction of international arbitrators. Unlike in other bankruptcy procedures liquidation of the debtor or receivership are not possible. No trustee can be appointed (Section 926, avoiding powers, if seen as an exception, is very special and justified). Section 902(5) explicitly confirms: '"trustee", when used in a section that is made applicable in a case under this chapter . . . means debtor'. A US municipality cannot go into receivership and change of 'management' (that is, removing elected officials) by courts or creditors is not possible – nor should this be possible in the case of sovereigns. If any regulatory or electoral approval are necessary under non-bankruptcy law in order to carry out a provision of the plan, Section 943(b)(6) requests that this must be obtained before the court can confirm the plan, a point clearly adaptable to sovereigns. Obviously similar guarantees are absent from Chapter 11.

Public interest in the functioning of the debtor safeguards a minimum of municipal activities. US municipalities are allowed to maintain basic social services essential to the health, safety and welfare of their inhabitants. In the case of railroad reorganization (Subchapter IV, Chapter 11, Title 11 USC) Section 1165 protects public interest 'in addition to the interests of the debtor, creditors, and equity security holders'. Section 1170(a)(2) permits courts to abandon railway lines only if this is 'consistent with the public interest'. There exists a public interest in the preservation of rail transportation that mandates finding a balance between various interests, which economically means that creditors may have to lose more than without such balancing. The plan can only be confirmed (Section 1173(a) (4), Title 11 USC) if consistent with the public interest. No creditor government has shown a similar public interest in avoiding that debt service increases infant mortality within Southern debtor countries.

US Chapter 9 provides viable solutions protecting the governmental sphere of the debtor as well as the best interests of creditors. This is essential as only a totally fair mechanism would be universally accepted, and rightly so. The affected population has a right to be heard. The procedure is as transparent as befits a public entity. Naturally only the basic principles and not all details of domestic Chapter 9 should form the basis of arbitral proceedings. Evidently some important and necessary details of domestic Chapter 9 are unnecessary and inapplicable internationally. Eligibility and authorization to be a Chapter 9 debtor, fundamental and useful as they are within the USA for constitutional reasons, are one example.

Compared with the SDRM the Chapter 9 model has one major drawback – any protection of sovereignty, governmental powers or public interest would limit the IMF's absolute dominance.

Fair and Equal Treatment of All Creditors

Any good and acceptable insolvency procedure has to be absolutely fair to all concerned. This implies that it is in the best interest of creditors and the debtor (which includes debtor protection), but also inter-creditor equity. Present debt management does not live up to this condition. The SDRM is unfair to nearly anyone but the IMF. In contrast, my model contains all these elements of fairness.

Thus I have demanded strictly symmetrical (equal) treatment of all creditors. Generally all creditors of one sovereign debtor – including domestic creditors – should be treated strictly equally. One possible exception may be other heavily indebted SCs. It would not make sense to bankrupt country A by relieving country B. In such cases preferential and differential treatment, strictly according to objective criteria, such as claims affected, the creditor's GDP per head or export income, seems worth considering. Regarding some types of domestic debts, exceptions should be discussed, for example, for pensions funds forced by law to buy government bonds. Securing decent pensions (which does not necessarily mean total exemption) in spite of losses resulting from forced investments could be part of debtor protection. When negotiating the resources for the fund financing the protection of the poor, money could be earmarked for this purpose. Unpaid wages of civil servants should be paid, as meanwhile also suggested by the IMF.

Most, if not all, domestic insolvency laws know different classes of creditors, preferences granted to certain claims (for example, unpaid taxes) or liens on specific assets. My proposal to treat all creditors equally is therefore not technically mandatory. Insolvency models privileging public or multilateral creditors can be as easily designed as mine. My demand for symmetrical treatment is based on economic sense, considerations of equity and the very basics of any legal system, on the necessity to establish the equivalent of national liability and tort laws, on jurisprudence as the *ars boni et aequi* and fairness to other creditors, who like debtors have to pick up part of the bill of IFI failures. As 'Brady' deals showed, even generous reductions by one class of creditors alone are insufficient to regain viability. The losses that private creditors had to accept (occasionally even higher losses than Paris Club members) have not benefitted debtors under the present system of unjustifiable IFI privileges. Including IFIs when it comes to debt reductions for very poor debtors, where their shares are relatively high, was recognized by HIPC. Reductions have remained too small though.

Economic necessity apart, there exists another reason why multilateral creditors must not be treated better. Commercial banks have usually not interfered with their clients' economic policy, nor did bondholders. IFIs have strongly influenced the use of their loans, exerting massive pressure on debtors – to the extent of provoking discussions on whether countries 'owned' what passes as 'their' economic policies. IFIs have routinely taken economic decisions but refused to participate in the risks involved. They insist on full repayment, even if damages negligently caused by their staff occur, which have to be paid by borrowers. A high rate of IFI failures therefore renders adjustment programmes necessary, which are administered by IFIs, just as failed programmes are likely to call for new programmes, as long as unconditional repayment to IFIs is upheld. Economically this is a patently perverted incentive system, logically likely to lead to catastrophes and to hinder quick and proper solutions. Economic efficiency mandates equal treatment of all creditors. There is a need to create a disincentive to misallocation of funds and anti-market behaviour by the international public sector.

Equal treatment would expose them appropriately to the risks involved, rebalancing the economic incentive system, while preference for IFIs would be inequitable and unfair. Even if IFIs only provided consultancy services like other consultants, without dictating or at least co-determining their debtors' policies, there is no reason why liability and financial accountability standards, usual and efficient in the case of normal consultants, should not apply (Raffer, 2005b). IFIs do not deny that they give advice as part and parcel of services paid for by clients. The IBRD even calls itself the knowledge bank.

As mentioned in Chapter 3, IFIs are not preferred creditors, although de facto enjoying privileges. There is no legal need to grant them any preference, quite the contrary, in most cases their own statutes explicitly demand the opposite (see Chapter 13 for details). In sharp contrast to my proposal, one cornerstone of the SDRM is the unconditional exemption of the IMF's own and other multilateral claims. The SDRM would legalize present unjustified practice, surreptitiously changing present legal status and statutes of IFIs in their favour, securing the IMF the coveted legally preferred creditor status it lacks.

For an international Chapter 9 a symmetrical treatment of all creditors follows convincingly, unless subordination of multilateral claims is demanded. Equal treatment is a matter of fairness to debtors as well as to other creditors. Debt reduction must be uniform, the same percentage must be deducted from all debts. Symmetrical treatment or subordination in an insolvency could be the way that the BWIs are held financially accountable. The sad record of violating their own statutes, thus damaging SC members (Raffer, 2008a), has meanwhile made me reconsider my symmetrical treatment demand somewhat. I no longer insist on it, seeing subordination as more indicated and fairer to other creditors, especially the private sector. Compensation for damages done within projects, where determining faults and errors is much easier – which has nothing to do with insolvency, but is an issue in its own right – would reduce the debt burden further (Raffer and Singer, 1996, pp. 206ff., see also Table 6.1).

Sustainability

In a 'Raffer-type procedure' facts and data would be presented by both parties and the representatives of the population in a transparent procedure before the panel, the debtor's capacity to pay and sustainability would emerge fairly reliably from this process. Defending their legitimate self-interests, anyone would present data and facts corroborating their arguments, thus narrowing down the set of feasible options considerably. Decisions – if needed – are unlikely to affect substantial sums of money but rather to solve deadlock situations. For obvious reasons justified opposition by creditors must not be simply overruled. 'Agreements between debtor and creditors would need the confirmation of the arbitrators, in analogy to Section 943' (Raffer, 1990, p. 305; similarly Krueger's, 2002a 'certification'). It would have to take particular care that fairness and a minimum of human dignity of the poor is safeguarded – in analogy to the protection enjoyed by a municipality's inhabitants.

Sustainability would emerge from transparent negotiations. Having all the facts on the table would practically restrict the panel's decisions to break deadlocks affecting minor sums. Unlike sustainability estimates of the IMF in the past (usually based on overoptimistic projections, see Chapter 12), the result – based on all relevant arguments – would be better and more stable.

Speed

Chapter 9-based debt arbitration adapts functioning national and international procedures; it could be implemented immediately if and when important creditors, for example, the G7, agree. Without or against them neither the SDRM nor Chapter 9 could be implemented. No new institution would be created. Panels would dissolve once they had served their purpose. They could be asked to reconvene if disagreements should emerge later on. As insolvency procedures should and hopefully will remain exceptional in the future, a standing institution would soon be severely underemployed.

Stabilizing the Financial Architecture

The mere existence of sovereign insolvency would stabilize financial markets. The wrong assumption that countries cannot become insolvent, on which the lending spree of the 1970s was based, would no longer be possible. But the introduction of an international Chapter 9 should also be used as an opportunity for stabilizing regulatory changes. Regulatory norms unnecessarily harassing creditors (creating so-called legal risk) should be changed. Most important, globalizing the tax deductability of loan loss reserves as presently practised on the West-European continent would be a cheap and efficient built-in stabilizer for the financial architecture. Signalling that lending may be risky and fostering solutions 'in the shadow of the law' as Anne Krueger put it, the Raffer Proposal would provide the right incentives. In addition, the universal introduction of tax deductible loan loss reserves, as practised on the European continent, would allow an economically virtually costless stabilizing feature to function (Raffer, 2005c). The problems that US money centre banks faced in the early 1980s can be easily avoided.

Tax deductible provisions have often been misunderstood as a taxpayers' subsidy. Costs to taxpayers, and hence the benefits to banks, have always been strongly exaggerated. Since 1991 I have repeatedly advocated optional features for eliminating legal risk and stabilizing markets, especially focusing on provisioning (Raffer, 2005c, 2006). Eliminating avoidable problems is advantageous to both creditors and debtors.

Because continental European banks had appropriate loan loss provisions, they were much less affected by the 1982 crisis than US and Japanese banks. Tax deductible loan loss provisioning had encouraged the former to recognize economic reality. Sufficient provisions would have allowed them to realize losses immediately if needed, while US banks had claims vis-à-vis some large countries so high that losses might have wiped out their equity.

Loans still kept at 100 per cent on the books have lower factual or real values once creditworthiness and economic standing of debtors have become doubtful. The existence of secondary markets proves this. From an economic and factual point of view money is actually lost before nominal claims are eventually adjusted downwards in the books. Recognizing diminished values of claims is just another way of stating that the sum of net assets, and thus the tax base, has declined. Reducing claims immediately to secondary market values would make this absolutely clear, but is patently unfeasible. Not least, it would encourage debtors not to honour their obligations in full.

To the extent that provisions reflect actual losses in the values of loans already suffered but not yet booked, they do not economically constitute taxable income. This would be the case if loan loss reserves set aside during one year are equivalent to the change in factual values during that year. Increasing reserves continuously in line with declining factual values would thus not really cost taxpayers a single cent. Should the economic outlook of the debtor improve, these reserves would of course have to be reduced accordingly to keep provisions in line with actual losses. A tax regime without tax deductibility of reserves taxes illusory profits existing only because of tax laws. The Treasury gets an interest-free loan as losses are shifted to the future. An economist can only wonder why banks in jurisdictions restricting or refusing tax deductibility have not protested against paying too much tax.

Because the real world is not an economist's comfortable blackboard, uncertainty will not allow a precise estimate of probabilities (and thus factual values) in practice. One may discuss whether reserves actually match losses already suffered. If reserves are larger, banks get a loan by tax authorities equivalent to this difference between reserves and changes in the values of loans; if reserves are smaller, this difference is taxed as illusory income. The respective amounts are:

$$\$[100(1-p) - \text{reserves}]ti_g \qquad (5.1)$$

where

p	=	repayment probability, hence
$100p$	=	expected value,
t	=	tax rate
i_g	=	interest rate at which the Treasury itself borrows.

The first term in square brackets expresses actual losses. If set aside reserves are smaller than actual losses, the term in square brackets is simply illusory income taxed. If reserves are larger, this would be a temporary loan from the Treasury, which carries no interest in many countries. Such a loan would mean costs to taxpayers that are this difference times ti_g. At $t = 40\%$ and $i_g = 4\%$, a difference of $100 would result in costs of $1.60 per year. In this case delaying crisis resolution over years would increase costs to taxpayers. Assuming that supervisory authorities keep loan loss reserves roughly in line with the decline in value of dubious loans, both costs to taxpayers and taxation of illusory profits will be very low or negligible. A substantial stabilizing effect can be obtained at no or minimal costs to taxpayers.

Economically, provisions have the important function of spreading losses over some years – losses which might otherwise ruin creditors if they had to absorb them in one year. Whether to have tax systems encouraging more prudential provisioning should not be decided without considering the alternatives. Continental Illinois or the case of the Savings & Loan institutions (whose bail-out costs were at least $200 billion dollars) may suffice to show that extremely limited tax deductibility does not necessarily prevent costs to taxpayers. Bail-outs cost money too, on top of the costs of the crises.

The introduction of my international Chapter 9 could be used to change the tax regime regarding provisioning where needed. This would perceptibly de-escalate future debt crises, leaving creditors and debtors more leeway for negotiating their way out of the problem. Economically it would also be fair to creditors.

SIMILARITIES AND DIFFERENCES BETWEEN MY PROPOSAL AND THE SDRM

The following similarities exist (for details and further quotes corroborating the following statements see Raffer, 2005a):

- Recognizing the necessity of sovereign insolvency. Eventually recognizing the need for an orderly framework to determine which part of their debts insolvent debtors can actually pay was quite a break away from the IMF's traditional debt management. So was Krueger's correct statement that this would reduce restructuring costs. There is full agreement as regards this necessity between both alternatives (cf. Raffer, 1989, 1990).
- Verification. After denying the need and even the possibility of

registering and assessing debts in the way usual in any domestic insolvency procedure, the IMF (2002b, p. 68) meanwhile demanded specific checks regarding 'for example, the authority of an official to borrow on behalf of the debtor', echoing what I had demanded in the early 1990s, nearly in my own words.

- Stay-standstill. The idea that the debtor government's demand for an insolvency procedure should automatically preclude further lawsuits and legal enforcement by creditors during insolvency procedures (Raffer, 1990) was taken up by the IMF. Nevertheless, the Fund's position remains unclear. In various documents the IMF has proposed quite different things ranging from an 'implicit support to a temporary standstill' by the IMF or the Fund's endorsing of a stay to variations allowing creditors to vote on it with or without the 'hotchpot' rule. One may, however, say that stays are at least possible in both models – a similarity already including differences. Iraq and Argentina proved, though, how easy immunizing debtors efficiently from lawsuits can be, both de facto and *de jure*.
- (Private) Creditors fully subject to arbitration. Since the 1980s I have always clearly demanded that all creditors should be subject to arbitration. The IMF exempts multilateral institutions from the SDRM, remaining evasive about Paris Club members that are also its main shareholders. Their claims may or may not be covered by the SDRM. All IMF documents, though, are clear that private creditors would be fully subject to arbitration – both a similarity and a difference to my model where private and public (including multilateral) creditors would be treated equally.

However fundamental differences between the two approaches remain (cf. Raffer, 2005a), as shown in Table 5.1.

Table 5.1   Fundamental differences between Raffer and the SDRM

	SDRM	Raffer Proposal
Rule of Law	Not respected	Respected
Problem of sovereignty	Dismissed	Solved
Fairness	Not intended	Part and parcel
Best interest of all creditors	No	Yes
Sustainability	Doubtful	Much improved
Speed	No	Yes
Improving the financial architecture	No concern	One recommended feature

6. Debtor rights and fairness to creditors in Rule of Law-based insolvency systems

According to the Working Group on International Financial Crises (1998, p. 15):

> insolvency laws are designed to balance the rights and interests of various constituencies in apportioning the burdens of insolvency in a manner consistent with a country's policies and goals, including social objectives that may include, for example, the preservation of employment opportunities. While there may be variations in countries' approaches, there are certain key principles and features that could be considered as important to an effective insolvency regime for commercial firms.
>
> A government should consider initiating a temporary suspension of debt payments only when it is clear that, even with appropriately strong policy adjustments, the country will experience a severe fiscal, financial or balance of payments crisis and the government or a substantial portion of the private sector will be unable to meet its contractual obligations in full and on time. In such circumstances, the initiation of an orderly, cooperative and comprehensive workout, while inherently costly, could best serve the collective interest of the debtor, its creditors and the international community.

Such suspension of debt payments is, by the way, a membership right of all IMF members. As repeatedly pointed out above, traditional sovereign debt management differs fundamentally and inexplicably from the mechanisms that became part and parcel of any civilized insolvency procedure. Solutions and techniques tested and developed over centuries before they were finally found optimal are precluded when it comes to SCs. This produces both economic inefficiencies and injustice, as the record of creditor dominated 'solutions' proves.

This chapter discusses the fundamental elements of successful and fair insolvency arrangements in more detail, elaborating further on:

- neutral, fair and disinterested decision making
- debtor protection
- fairness to creditors
- creditor duties and risk.

NEUTRAL AND FAIR DECISIONS

When I presented my proposal at Zagreb University in 1987 my demand for neutral arbitration caused much more surprise and discussion than any other element of my proposal. Arguing that neutral arbitration panels must decide, I used Germany's London Accord 1953 as the illustrating example (Raffer, 1989, p. 60). It stipulated neutral arbitration to settle disagreements between Germany and its creditors. Apparently in former Yugoslavia, a debtor country, the mere thought of what is a matter of course in all other cases was unheard of.

As already explained in Chapter 5, preventing people from being judge in their own cause is the very cornerstone of equity and justice. No legal system worth the name accepts that one party may decide in a lawsuit or any legal procedure where there are conflicting interests. No one would expect debtors entering the courtroom, facing not only judges, who are their creditors, to see that anyone else in the room is also their creditor. This is unthinkable and anyone would see this as a mockery rather than a legal procedure. The right to be judged by personally disinterested persons or entities is firmly entrenched, except when it comes to sovereign Southern debts. Providing an independent judiciary is considered the duty of any civilized government. Present debt management differs fundamentally: creditors are judge, jury, experts and bailiff all in one, sometimes even the debtor's lawyers. Sadly, one cannot contradict critics speaking of an international system of legal apartheid.

Independent decisions are also at the foundation of international law. Both ad hoc arbitration and institutionalized dispute settlement such as the International Court of Justice or the Permanent Court of Arbitration at The Hague (established in 1899 during the first Hague Peace Conference) exist. The United Nations Commission on International Trade Law (UNCITRAL) elaborated rules and norms for arbitration, the UNCITRAL Arbitration Rules adopted in 1976. The General Assembly recommended their use in the settlement of disputes arising in the context of international commercial relations. They are something like a blueprint that may be used either without modification or with modifications that the parties might wish. Arbitration and lawsuits are also part and parcel of international treaties. In fact, arbitration has increasingly become popular to solve international problems. The WTO or the North American Free Trade Agreement (NAFTA) are examples, OECD governments wanted to write it into the Multilateral Agreement on Investment. Only when it comes to Southern debts, arbitration is mostly shunned at present, an intolerable double standard. Loan agreements in the 1930s routinely stipulated it to solve disagreements. Some contracts between countries and private creditors already stipulated arbitration recently, such as in the cases of Nigeria in 1991 and Uruguay in 1990.

In contrast, the members of the Paris Club shun independent decision making and decent legal arrangement. Rocha (1999, pp. 91ff.) reported that Brazil had been legally required not to waive immunities to allow court litigation, but to settle disputes by arbitration. Paris Club members forced Brazil to change this, and to 'exempt specifically . . . Paris Club bilateral restructuring agreements' from arbitration in the early 1990s. A quite disturbing point emerges: laws, even the constitution, do not matter when they are the laws or the constitution of SCs. Nor do the most basic legal principles. An association of creditors, the Paris Club simply dictates debtors the 'solution'. Reportedly they have to leave the room, but are allowed in to hear and accept the decision of their creditors. The efficiency of this practice can be illustrated at Ecuador's example. From July 1983 until September 2000 Ecuador was seven times at the Paris Club, each 29 months on average. On all occasions official creditors could achieve a definite solution to Ecuador's debt problem.

It is impossible to avoid asking why arbitration is good for Germany but bad for a 'developing country', or why official creditors shy away from arbitration even more than the private sector. Logically there is no reason for such legal double standards between North and South, if one believes the Rule of Law should be applied generally. The behaviour of Northern governments and IFIs so far does not suggest that they really believe so.

In spite of the impression created over years, IFIs are by no means legally exempt from this principle of the Rule of Law. At Bretton Woods normal legal redress was seen as a matter of course. Article VII.3 of the IBRD's Articles of Agreement explicitly allows actions against the bank except by members or persons acting for or deriving claims from members. Property and assets are 'immune from all forms of seizure, attachment or execution *before* the delivery of final judgment against the Bank' (emphasis added). Actions may be brought against the Bank in courts of competent jurisdiction in the territories of members in which the Bank has offices, appointed agents for the purpose of accepting service or notice of process, or issued or guaranteed securities. The Bank's founders had no intention to exempt and protect it from legal, and economic consequences of failures. Accountability was not initially meant to be removed. Suing the Bank before national courts was therefore considered normal. Later on MDBs tried to get immunity from lawsuits, as the recent attempt of the IBRD in Bangladesh illustrates. Such attempts go directly against the intentions of the institution's founders. The statutes of IDA, more relevant for the poorest countries, copy the respective IBRD clauses (Article VIII.3).

Members are not allowed to sue the IBRD because they were given another alternative: arbitration. Obviously the reason is the same as in the case of waivers of immunity stipulating courts in OECD jurisdictions for settling disagreements with private creditors: the Bank's founders might well have been concerned that national courts might not be sufficiently neutral. Like the IBRD's former 'General Conditions' (Section 10.04) its present 'General Conditions for Loans' (of 1 July 2005, Section 8.04) stipulate:

> Any controversy between the parties to the Loan Agreement or the parties to the Guarantee Agreement, and any claim by any such party against any other such party arising under the Loan Agreement or the Guarantee Agreement which has not been settled by agreement of the parties shall be submitted to arbitration by an arbitral tribunal as hereinafter provided ('Arbitral Tribunal').

Bank and loan parties appoint one person each. Both sides agree on a third arbitrator. The President of the International Court of Justice or the UN Secretary General appoint this third person if parties fail to agree. Readers might have noted that these Sections describe precisely the same nomination procedure I have proposed for my debt arbitration. IDA's *General Conditions for Credits and Grants* (dated 1 July 2005) repeat the IBRD's nearly literally ('Financing Agreement' instead of 'Loan Agreement' is one difference). Most other IFIs have basically similar statutes. The European Bank for Reconstruction and Development has actually submitted to arbitration.

The IMF differs from all other IFIs. Article IX.3 of its Articles of Agreement grants it total immunity 'except to the extent that it expressly waives its immunity for the purpose of any proceedings or by the terms of any contract'. Obviously, this is explained by the fact that conditionality was not originally foreseen. The Fund was to help member countries to overcome short-term dollar/gold-parity problems by unconditional short-term drawings (= loans). It would be difficult to perceive any need for legal procedures and redress in the case of an emergency helper giving money unconditionally. Nevertheless, its founders did not wish to exclude proper legal dispute settlement totally, but inserted this option. When conditionality became enshrined in the IMF's statutes in 1969, the appropriate change regarding immunity was not made for whichever reason, although its founders would doubtlessly have stipulated the possibility of legal redress as in the case of the IBRD if they had approved conditional drawing. Be that as it may, the IMF may not only submit to arbitration or courts, but contractual clauses stipulating this are expressly allowed. Nothing in its statutes prevents the IMF from applying civilized legal standards. On the contrary, the existence of this waiver may be seen as an encouragement to do so if and when appropriate.

As the long and successful record of national insolvency laws shows, establishing neutral, disinterested entities is not only fair, but also the only economically wise and workable arrangement. Refusing to do so is the main cause of unsuccessful debt management. The powerful position of official and especially multilateral creditors vis-à-vis poor countries, HIPCs in particular, makes an independent entity all the more urgent.

IFIs have not been unbiased when making decisions affecting their own claims as well as those of other creditors. They are party, both creditors in their own right and controlled by majorities of creditor states. Therefore they cannot be arbitrators. Proposing an IMF organ as arbitrator, as the SDRM does, is absurd and unfair to other, particularly private, creditors. The German Commerzbank's publication *Emerging Markets this Week* (26/1999, 15 October) expresses this concern clearly: the BWIs 'will be concerned *with protecting their own balance sheets* rather than with fair "burden sharing"' (emphasis in original). Therefore the 'IMF and World Bank are not suited either as arbitrators or as objective regulators of sovereign insolvency procedures'. Familiar with insolvency as an appropriate means to solve debt problems in other cases, people from the banking community usually see the proposal in a more professional way than official creditors once it becomes clear that this mechanism must be fair to all sides. It would not be generally accepted if it were not. The SDRM proved how justified private sector concerns are.

While very ancient Roman law literally allowed creditors to cut debtors into easily transportable pieces, decent, civilized legal systems have not only opted against physical dismembering, but also for exempting a certain amount of resources to safeguard the human dignity of debtors. However, even in ancient Rome and during the era of debt prisons, only judges, not creditors themselves, had the authority to decide on a debtor's fate. This sets a standard not yet achieved by official SC creditors.

DEBTOR PROTECTION

Although unconditional priority of human life and human dignity is one main principle of all civilized legal systems, debtor protection remained totally absent in international debt management over many years. HIPC II finally introduced this idea, although still in a rudimentary form. Nevertheless its anti-poverty programmes are a move in the right direction and a change from the position held immediately before HIPC II was agreed on. Then it was claimed in discussions on my proposal that debtor protection would be impossible. Sadly the SDRM proposal falls back behind this standard.

Insolvency laws guarantee insolvent debtors a modest, yet humane standard of living, and usually a fresh start by exempting resources that could be seized by bona fide creditors. Interestingly, insolvency laws are not considered uneconomic humanitarianism, but, as US jurisprudence states, a matter of a public as well as a private interest. Insolvency relief is not an act of mercy but a debtor's right, as well as an act of justice and economic reason.

Under domestic Chapter 9 in the USA there is a public interest in the functioning of the debtor, which safeguards a minimum of municipal activities, such as minimum standards of basic health services or primary education. Resources necessary to finance these standards are exempt. In addition, the debtor's population is protected by the right to be heard. Limits to tax increases exist. Tax increases that would depress the standard of living of the municipality's population below the minimum guaranteed to private debtors are clearly illegal.

The protection granted to private insolvent debtors varies from one country to another. Exemptions can sometimes be quite substantial, especially in the USA, a relatively more debtor friendly jurisdiction. For the sake of brevity, examples from the USA will be used to illustrate debtor protection, although similar norms exist in all OECD countries.

Looking at the list of exemptions granted in the USA to individuals and their families we see that Section 522, Title 11 USC allows to exempt 'professionally prescribed health aids for the debtor or a dependent of the debtor', social security and veteran's benefits, unemployment compensation and unemployment benefits, local public assistance benefits, alimony, support, or separate maintenance to the extent reasonably necessary for the support of the debtor or any dependent of the debtor. 'Dependent' includes, by the way, the spouse whether or not actually dependent. Other payments such as pensions enjoy similar preference. Comparing these exemptions with the cuts in public budgets enforced by austerity policies, one notices that social transfers protected for individuals in the North were among the prime targets in the South. As the example of the successful management of Egypt's debt crisis in 1876 (see Chapter 1) proves, one need not destroy existing social safety nets to overcome a debt overhang. The IMF's Managing Director's statement at ECOSOC in 1987 (see Chapter 8) proves that at least the Fund was aware early on of what denying debtor protection meant.

Section 522, however, does not stop here. Household furnishings, household goods, books, pets, tools of trade (such as 26 head of cattle), jewellery, cars and even real property can be exempted up to certain limits. Finally, any property 'not to exceed in value $800 plus up to $7,500 of any unused amount of the exemption provided under paragraph (1) of this subsection' may be exempted pursuant to Subsection (d)(5). In a joint case each debtor can use the full amount of exemptions separately. A waiver of exemptions is unenforceable. The protection of debtors unconditionally overrules the freedom of contracts. Occasionally, surprising exemptions were upheld that may well be seen as unfair to bona fide creditors, such as exempting a mink coat as 'necessary wearing apparel' or diamond rings. Under current law the debtor is permitted to convert non-exempt property into exempt property before filing a bankruptcy petition in order to permit the debtor to make full use of the exemptions to which they are entitled under the law. As shown in Chapter 5, public interest in not abandoning (private) railway lines may also increase creditor losses.

In the case of public debtors, things are of course less clear-cut. Nevertheless, one can say that feasible tax increases are actually much lower than those that would depress the standard of living of the inhabitants below the minimum guaranteed to individuals. Amounts received by creditors have varied substantially, depending on the municipality's financial situation. Insolvency relief produced more or less reductions as under Chapter 11 (corporate insolvency). Naturally, approval of the plan is denied if the municipality has the means to honour all its obligations. In *Fano v Newport Heights Irrigation District* this was done, because the district had assets greatly exceeding its liabilities and there was no sufficient showing of why the district's tax rate should not have been increased sufficiently.

In the 1930s some creditors insisted on financing higher payments by the City of Asbury Park by further tax increases and refused to agree to the plan. The US Supreme Court stated clearly: 'The notion that a city has unlimited taxing power is, of course, an illusion. A city cannot be taken over and operated for the benefit of its creditors, nor can its creditors take over the taxing power.'

To be confirmed the plan presented by a municipality has to be reasonable and also in the best interest of creditors pursuant to Section 943(b)(7), who must be provided with the 'going concern value' of their claims:

> The going concern value contemplates a 'comparison of revenues and expenditures taking into account the taxing power and the extent to which tax increases are both necessary and feasible' . . . and is intended to provide more of a return to creditors than the liquidation value if the city's assets could be liquidated like those of a private corporation.

A court decision further clarified that a plan can only be confirmed if it 'embodies a fair and equitable bargain openly arrived at and devoid of overreaching, however subtle'. This openness and transparency of procedures are of particular interest for sovereign debtors.

Over centuries domestic insolvency norms have established standards of what and how much should be exempt. Although Chapter 9 in the USA has also set appropriate standards for public entities, defining such standards for debtor countries would in all likelihood be a long and troublesome enterprise. International precedents, such as Germany's London Accord, the Indonesian debt reduction after 1968 or Britain's American Loan could provide useful orientation. The IBRD (2000a, p. 25) pointed out that the Paris Club had permitted Indonesia

> under a *bisque clause* arrangement similar to that contained in the Anglo-American Financial Agreement, to defer at its option up to one-half of the principal payments falling due in the early years of the new schedule. These deferred obligations were to be repaid with an interest at 4 percent per annum during the final years of the agreement.

Incidentally, the last years for deferred interest payments included the years 1997 and 1998. One could recall that introducing a Bisque clause into sovereign debt contracts with official creditors would eventually follow the advice of the Pearson Commission, when sovereign debts were practically bilateral debts. However clauses allowing deferral could also be acceptable to private creditors. But deferral would have to be contingent on objective criteria, such as, for instance, the relation between debt service and export revenues, as would be one possibility in the case of insolvency procedures. Oil-indexed payments or payments connected to GDP or terms of trade were stipulated in the past (cf. Rocha, 1999).

The difficulty of determining and agreeing on a standard of what to exempt would be compounded by the fact that these decisions would have to be made while and because concrete cases are pending. As the following chapters elaborate, resources necessary to finance the MDGs can provide a measuring rod and make things much easier, although the MDGs aim – strictly speaking – at less than debtor protection as usual in all other cases. Many people, for instance, would still go hungry. Nevertheless, the MDGs would be a huge improvement. They are globally accepted and UN members (including creditor nations) pledged to spare no effort. Actually improving life substantially within debtor countries, the MDGs could thus play the useful role of avoiding long and difficult negotiations and discussions.

The situation of debt distressed countries shows clearly that resources necessary to finance the MDGs must be freed. Unless one assumes unrealistic ODA increases in the near future, most MDGs cannot be reached without freeing resources presently used for debt service. Money that has to be paid to creditors cannot be used to improve maternal health, to reduce child mortality or the proportion of people without sustainable access to safe drinking water or suffering from hunger. It is not available to finance primary schooling for all boys and girls, nor to finance the elimination of gender disparities in education. One cannot have one's cake and eat it as well. The introduction of user fees and their effects on the poor prove this point clearly and sadly. In analogy to the protection enjoyed by the population of indebted US municipalities, the money to service a country's debts must not be raised by destroying basic social services and the debtor's future. The principle of debtor protection demands exempting resources necessary to finance humane minimum standards for the poor, and a sustainable economic recovery.

As explained in Chapter 5, a transparently managed fund financed by the debtor in domestic currency could provide the money. Naturally financing MDGs would be a prime task of any such fund. This idea was taken up by a bill at Capitol Hill. The Debt Relief and Development in Africa Act (H.R.2232), sponsored by Representative Maxine Waters in 1999, required a Human Development Fund organized in a similar way, fed by money freed by HIPC debt relief. This bill was referred to a subcommittee and did not pass Congress, though.

To put debt obligations and the MDGs in context: the Millennium Campaign (a UN initiative) quotes CAFOD estimates that debt cancellation of $300 billion would be needed by the world's poor. However: 'Debt relief promised by creditors so far: US$ 110bn. Debt cancellation delivered by July 2003: US$ 36bn.' Without a right to insolvency protection, and with promises not to spare efforts unenforceable, resources depend solely on creditor 'generosity', which – in turn – is wholly arbitrary and quite limited.

CREDITOR DUTIES AND LIABILITIES

Like any other market, credit markets depend on functioning economic mechanisms and a framework predefining the rights and duties of market participants. They could not function without these. Within this framework both debtors and creditors have rights and duties and are subject to risk. So far, the focus has been nearly exclusively on debtor duties, virtually disregarding those of lenders, although there is no reason why this one kind of debt should exempt lenders from any responsibility. The anomaly of shifting all responsibilities onto debtors, unique to SC debts, encourages economically and ethically wrong behaviour. It makes focusing on lender responsibilities mandatory. Usually debtors have rights too, unless they are SCs. Even the principle *ex turpi causa non oritur actio* was turned on its head in the case of Southern debts.

Risk and liability are necessary systemic elements of the framework markets need to function (Raffer, 2007). Risk is the hazard of losing money, even without any fault of the lender. It cannot be avoided, neither with sovereigns nor other debtors. Economically risk serves as an incentive carefully to assess debtors' ability to service debts. Errors and negligence in assessment bring about losses. Basic legal principles, such as safeguarding human rights, increase risk by exempting economically recoverable resources. Insolvency laws change the terms of contract, often drastically, also for non-consenting creditors. Insolvent debtors are by definition incapable of honouring all obligations. It is logically and economically impossible to fulfil contracts as stipulated. All civilized legal systems compound this factual creditor risk by granting debtor protection. Laws may terminate, modify or permit a party to terminate or modify contracts, explicitly allowing unilateral changes of contractual rights. Thus, Section 365(a), Title 11 USC empowers the trustee (subject to the court's approval) to 'assume or reject any executory contract or unexpired lease of the debtor'. Pursuant to Section 365(g) this 'constitutes a breach of such contract', a perfectly legalized breach. Injured entities are given a prepetition claim for any resulting damages, and are treated as prepetition creditors with respect to this claim.

Creditors have a duty of care. It is well known, not least from credit relations, that any legal system protects contracts only if both sides have complied with their legal duties. A duty of care is imposed on lenders. They have to observe professional standards, or make checks, such as whether the person signing for a legal entity has the authority to do so. Tortious or illegal behaviour makes creditors liable to compensate damages and may void contracts, unless the victims are SCs.

It must be made clear though: the risk that projects may fail to deliver expected benefits even though professional standards were meticulously observed by creditors remains with the borrower. There are limits to creditor duties. It would be patently unfair to pin all risk on them.

Liability ensures the right of victims to receive compensation contingent upon conditions stipulated in law, such as negligent actions creating unlawful damage. Domestic liability and tort laws serve the purposes of compensating those suffering such damages and of deterring such behaviour.

All legal systems establish duties creditors must comply with in order to enjoy full legal protection of their contractual rights. Not complying with such duties may give rise to damage compensation payments. Establishing and enforcing these principles is the duty of governments, both with regard to domestic and international laws. While the private sector has no further duty but to abide by laws passed by others, governments also have the obligation to preserve the foundation of the Rule of Law, including international law, and to safeguard human rights. Creditor governments have not done so, but have abetted unlawful practices, such as the violation of membership rights of debtor countries by IFIs.

Normally lenders face problems if fully aware that they are financing a debacle or aiding and abetting embezzlement. Regarding SCs this is again different. Official creditors differ from the private sector when it comes to projects that failed to deliver expected benefits. While all creditors are subject to the rule of due diligence, public creditors have virtually always done more than lending by designing and implementing such projects. Public lenders, IFIs in particular, acting in addition to lending as consultants, would be liable to indemnify their clients in case of grave negligence if normal legal principles applied. At present this is turned on its head: IFIs are allowed to profit substantially from their own grave negligence, as analysed in Chapter 13.

In contrast to tort law, insolvency only deals with claims based on solid and proper legal foundations because no insolvency is needed for debts without such proper legal base. So far only Norway has acknowledged creditor co-responsibility. Odious debts, for instance, are null and void. Demands for cancelling apartheid debts were therefore based on the odious debts doctrine. Debts whose existence violates the law, basic legal principles or that are legally null and void are not considered by insolvency procedures but rejected right before relief is even considered. Debts incurred in violation of national laws, of international law, such as in breach of legal obligations or statutes of IFIs, and general universally accepted legal principles, as well as especially debts, whose servicing violates human rights would not have to be serviced in any decent domestic legal system.

No creditor government or IFI has ever defended civilized contract law when many SC governments had been forced to 'assume retroactively' losses of private banks and corporations. One has to emphasize that these were not initially commercial debts voluntarily guaranteed by governments, whose guarantees were eventually triggered, but debts for which there had never been any government guarantee in the first place. It is one of the principles of law that such debts assumed under pressure – obligations not freely entered into – are null and void. If such behaviour by creditors is a criminal act in a creditor country, the criminal code would have to be applied. Creditor governments and IFIs have insisted that these illegal debts be 'honoured', thus supporting and allowing such behaviour. Elected parliamentarians in the USA were more concerned. A bill was introduced by Representatives B.A. Morrsion and S. Levin demanding investigation on the amount of such forced debts and 'the extent to which the assumption of liability for private loans by such countries was a condition imposed by any such banking organization for entering into a rescheduling agreement' (HR 1435, Bill introduced in the House of Representatives, US Congress, 100th Congress, 1st Session, 5 March 1987, Section 4.c.1.B). It did not become law.

What Jeffrey Winters (2004, cf. also Raffer, 2004a, pp. 65f.) called 'criminal debts' would also be illegal. These are debts originating from loans that IFIs disbursed to corrupt governments, such as Suharto's, knowing that large parts of these loans would be embezzled.

Checking whether a person signing on behalf of a legal entity actually has the authority to sign is one obligation of creditors. If the official signing has no authority, the contract does not bind the debtor. Although this is self-evident and such checks are routine for Northern corporate or sovereign debt, this principle has de facto been waived in sovereign lending with Northern government support. There is no valid reason for such discrimination. By basic legal principles substantial parts of sovereign debts are null and void.

Article 75 of the Argentine Constitution, for instance, reserves the authority to incur sovereign debts to Congress. Article 76 prohibits Congress to delegate this prerogative to the administration. Sovereign debts multiplied under the military dictatorship from $7.8 billion in 1975 to $46 billion in 1984 without one single loan raised in the proper, constitutional way. One may argue that the existence of a dictatorship violating human rights obliged creditors in particular to check whether all formal requirements had been obeyed. When a citizen, Alejandro Olmos, started legal proceedings against the government 'and others' the verdict by Criminal Judge Jorge Ballesteros on 14 July 2000 ruled that a large part of Argentine debt resulted from 'measures which were intended to benefit private companies and businesses' (Pettifor et al., 2001, p. 8). This verdict established irregularities in no less than 477 credit operations, as two members of Argentina's Congress, María América González and Mario Cafiero, recalled in a letter (dated 29 July 2004) to the Securities and Exchange Commission, Washington, DC, c/o Mr Russel Clause. No debtor, except developing countries deprived of self-evident rights, would be expected to 'honour' such 'contracts'. Argentina's unilateral debt reduction, though second best from the point of view of economics and the Rule of Law, has meanwhile corrected the debt burden somewhat.

Unfortunately Argentina suffered strongly from these illegal debts. But creditors as a group suffered as well, especially bona fide creditors, because they lost more money eventually than they would have under an early solution and correct application of fundamental legal principles. Ultimately private creditors had to pick up the bill. Protecting claims without proper legal foundations, the public sector is responsible for many of Argentina's troubles and for present creditor losses. While private creditors may have tried to cover up errors, the public sector has allowed and encouraged them to do so, disregarding the very foundations of the Rule of Law.

When I proposed verifying debts as part of my international Chapter 9 approach (Raffer, 1990, p. 309), as is routine in any domestic case, the need and even the possibility of doing so were denied by IFI personnel. Meanwhile the IMF (2002b, p. 68) demands specific checks regarding, 'for example, the authority of an official to borrow on behalf of the debtor', echoing my demand, nearly in my own words (Raffer, 1993, p. 68). Over decades this self-evident obligation was ignored. It still has no practical relevance. Neither the IMF nor any other creditor have encouraged debtors to consider such debts null and void and to act upon that conclusion. It has not even been tried to uphold the basic legal principle that those binding a legal entity must have the authority to do so. The comparatively civilized legal practice of the nineteenth century still remains out of reach.

The IBRD (1988, p. xx) informed early on that 'governments in many of these countries were forced to assume the losses suffered as a result of the external debts of private banks and corporations, which further worsened the burden on the budget'. Chile in the early 1980s is one prominent example of such 'socialized' debts, which had initially been incurred without any government involvement and while the government declared that it would neither intervene in private contracts nor bail out private debts. Banks tried to cover themselves after the crisis broke. Without protection by official creditors, however, this open breach of the law would not have been possible. The BWIs did not even criticize this practice of forcing 'retroactive guarantees' of already defaulted private debt on other, totally different debtors considered less risky because they are denied insolvency protection. Although this *ex post* socialization made debt management more difficult, the BWIs and Northern governments insisted on punctual service of these illegal debts as well, thus anointing them with international 'respectability'. In any case but Southern sovereigns such debts would be legally null and void. The 1997 Asian crisis is another dramatic case of the state bailing out creditors after liberalizing capital flows. Obviously, as a result of the Asian Crisis, the High-level Regional Consultative Meeting on Financing for Development, Asia and Pacific Region (2000, p. 3) called for an international bankruptcy procedure for states. The very next sentence demands that it be 'ensured that private debt does not become government debt'. As long as governments are denied insolvency relief, socializing private losses will remain unduly attractive. As long as official creditors continue to condone and abet the practice of putting pressure on SC governments, forcing them 'to assume' the losses as the IBRD so politely described it, international North-South relations will remain at a standard well below that of ancient Rome.

Banks were accused of helping capital flight, thus rendering the economic situation of their debtors even more untenable. If risk and normal legal responsibility had not been eliminated, banks could not have had an interest in debilitating their debtors in such a way. This problem would not have arisen to the same extent. All legal systems contain norms protecting debtors against either too cavalier attitudes by creditors or against creditors carelessly financing illegal activities, embezzlement or fraud. Such laws may sometimes be quite strict. Unless the debtor is an SC, any creditor suspected of lending with full knowledge that employees (in the case of countries, politicians or functionaries) would redirect these funds into their pockets would face troubles. In the Philippines firms connected to the Marcos clan borrowed government-guaranteed loans to go bankrupt after disbursement, leaving the government to pick up the bill. According to the *New York Times* (30 March, 1986) such loans amounted to $9.59 billion, a very large chunk of the country's total sovereign debt. It is difficult to believe that this practice had gone unnoticed by creditors.

Creditor dominated debt management after the 1970s contrasts vividly with the Rule of Law-based debtor-creditor relations before, as the arbitral award in the Tinoco case in 1922 or the general application of ultra vires proves. Generally domestic laws enforce much higher standards of lender accountability. For example, Lloyd's had to pay damages to a couple its manager had advised and encouraged to borrow to buy, renovate and sell a house at a profit. Because the manager went beyond mere lending by adding advice, the High Court ruled that the manager should have pointed out the risks clearly and should have advised them against the project (*Financial Times*, 5 September 1995). In several countries professional creditors may also be held accountable for damages created by negligently granted credits. In his PhD thesis at the Faculty of Law of the University of Salamanca (finished in 2006), Juan Pablo Bohoslavsky surveyed laws and judicial practice in eight countries with regard to creditor liabilities connected to loose lending in order to extract common principles from national, domestic laws to form the basis for new principles of international law. According to this concept lenders are liable for damages they inflicted on other creditors by their lending with disregard for the most basic principles of risk evaluation, thus postponing the insolvent borrower's crash and thereby increasing other creditors' losses. In particular, French, Belgian and Italian jurisprudence have developed this concept.

FAIRNESS TO CREDITORS

As pointed out above by the example of the USA, domestic insolvency procedures must also protect the best interest of creditors. There is no difference vis-à-vis my proposal. The important point of fairness apart, no biased mechanism would be generally accepted, and rightly so. For a sovereign wishing to have new access to credit markets, the way the debt overhang is dealt with is critical. If creditors feel that they have been treated fairly, they are likely to be as willing to provide new loans for economically promising projects in the future as creditors usually are after corporate insolvency cases.

Unlike present Paris Club practice or under the SDRM my proposal would confer the full rights of a party on all creditors. The Paris Club expects private and non-Paris Club creditors to implement the club's decisions although they had no say and were usually not even heard. This is unjust, and refusals to implement other people's decisions must be understood. Furthermore, the weakest actor, the debtor, is told to gain comparable treatment from other, excluded creditors. Should a recalcitrant creditor take debtors to court in a Paris Club member country, debtors will not be protected by the creditor government but lose the case. Putting an end to such absurdities and injustice is also in the best interest of all bona fide creditors. An international Chapter 9 would do so. It would also prohibit any creditor discrimination in order to finance bail-outs of IFIs, improving recovery rates for the vast majority of creditors.

Introducing universally accepted legal principles would reduce SC debts substantially and improve the functioning of international credit markets. But in addition, differentiating debts and introducing creditor liability is also in the interest of bona fide creditors, who would lose less or nothing if all debtors were equal before the law. If legally unfounded claims were eliminated and damage compensation were paid in those cases where creditors unlawfully caused damages, acting without due diligence, bona fide creditors would recoup larger shares of their claims from insolvent debtors.

Table 6.1 illustrates the effects of undue preference as well as of unfounded claims as presently discussed (classified as odious, illegitimate or in whichever way) if the country is unable to pay. Let us assume that country A has total debts of 100, but is only able to service a debt stock of 50 (50 unpayable), and that A actually gets insolvency protection, no doubt a heroic assumption still when it comes to SCs. To simplify, we only consider a one-off debt stock reduction. If all debts have to be honoured and no creditor is preferred, the haircut would be 50. If 40 were null and void, A would only have a remaining debt stock of 60, of which 10 would still have to go in order to align A's capacity to pay to debt service due. For A this would not really matter: 50 would go one way or another, although based on very different legal titles. For A's creditors, though, the results differ strongly.

In the first case every creditor would receive half their claims. In the latter case those whose claims are voided would receive nothing, while

Table 6.1   Haircuts of bona fide creditors under different assumptions

Differentiation of Creditors	Haircuts of Private Creditors (%)
None	
No preference, all debts fully recognized	50
Claims amounting to 40 null and void	16.67
IFIs exempt	
All other debts fully recognized	83.33
40 null and void, 40 (IFIs) exempt	50
IFIs Treated Lawfully	
40 plus 10 of IFI claims null and void	0
40 plus all IFI claims null and void*	0

Note: * Debtor country still has the money left that would be needed to service a debt stock of 30.

recognized creditors would receive 83.3 per cent of their claims. It is easily seen that bona fide creditors would benefit if some claims were subordinated because of legally improper creditor behaviour. As economic facts eventually assert themselves – what cannot be paid goes unpaid – denying the Rule of Law to debtors has considerable effects on creditors, both bona fide creditors, who are unduly discriminated against, and other, unduly protected creditors, such as IFIs. Public creditors enforcing or supporting the violation of the Rule of Law also trigger substantial negative effects for bona fide creditors. Grave injustice is inflicted if perfectly legal and legitimate debts are treated like debts lacking such solid foundation. Classifying and differentiating debts may thus arguably be seen as more in the interest of bona fide creditors, even though the application of universally recognized legal principles would have avoided substantial damage to debtor countries and their peoples. If clearly illegal debts would no longer unduly harass debtors and the principles of tort law would be applied, reducing multilateral debts in particular, both bona fide creditors and debtors would be perceptibly better off than at present. Identifying such claims and dealing with them properly would make solutions much easier. Abolishing unjustified de facto privileges of those official creditors that substantially contributed to making crises worse would meaningfully contribute to an acceptable and sustainable outcome. Multilateral claims whose very existence violates basic legal principles have to go. After abolishing the undue discrimination of sovereign debtors and bona fide creditors, reinstalled economic mechanisms would again be allowed to play their useful and welcome role.

7. MDGs, debt distress and poverty: theoretical roots of policies protecting the poor in debtor countries

At the UN Millennium Summit in September 2000, 189 countries signed the Millennium Declaration, which set eight goals to be achieved by 2015 that respond to the world's main development challenges. One hundred and forty seven heads of state and governments were present. Meeting these Millennium Development Goals (MDGs) will not eradicate poverty, but if achieved they would improve the living conditions of millions of people, quite often dramatically. The Millennium Declaration promises: 'We will spare no effort to free our fellow men, women and children from the abject and dehumanizing conditions of extreme poverty . . . we are committed to making the right to development a reality for everyone and to freeing the entire human race from want.' Implementing this right requests resources: financing the MDGs conflicts with financing debt service. Achieving the MDGs is directly connected with the idea of debtor protection, thus with a proper and fair solution to the debt problem. Supporting debtor countries in their efforts to achieve the MDGs without creating future debt problems has meanwhile become one of the officially declared aims of debt management.

The eight MDGs drawn from the actions and targets contained in the Millennium Declaration were broken down into 18 quantifiable targets measured by 48 indicators, which will be discussed in the next two chapters. These measuring rods allow the UN, but also the public at large, to monitor whether progress is made towards reaching the MDGs, or not. They automatically produce political pressure. The MDGs are:

- Goal 1: Eradicate extreme poverty and hunger.
- Goal 2: Achieve universal primary education.
- Goal 3: Promote gender equality and empower women.
- Goal 4: Reduce child mortality.
- Goal 5: Improve maternal health.
- Goal 6: Combat HIV/AIDS, malaria and other diseases.

- Goal 7: Ensure environmental sustainability.
- Goal 8: Develop a global partnership for development.

The United Nations Development Programme (UNDP) recalled that the MDGs are not new goals, but 'synthesise, in a single package, many of the most important commitments made separately at the international conferences and summits of the 1990s'. The idea that specific pro-poor policies are necessary can be traced back to Basic Needs, the first approach in development economics that advocated addressing poverty directly, a noticeable break from early orthodoxy. One also notes that achieving the first seven MDGs in heavily indebted countries demands clear decisions between servicing debt and funding these goals. In contrast to the first decades of 'debt management', basic social expenditures must no longer be largely subordinated to payments to creditors if creditor governments want to live up to their commitment. The MDGs are thus a form of debtor protection, officially accepted by all creditor governments. The goal of eradicating extreme poverty sounds like the exemption guaranteeing individual insolvent debtors a minimum standard of living, but not its two targets (halving the proportion of people living on less than one dollar per day and those suffering from hunger). As in the case of municipalities, sovereign insolvency must guarantee the functioning of the public debtor, including a minimum of social expenditures. However, as poverty and underdevelopment in debtor countries existed before the debt crisis, defenders of creditor interests might well argue that an insolvency regime should not and cannot provide the resources needed for overall development. Therefore financing universally accepted goals may solve the thorny problem of determining which level of national welfare should be considered as the minimum to be guaranteed. This is not unlike municipal insolvency, where poor people continue to exist within municipalities while the public debtor stays afloat and minimum social expenditures are exempt.

Critics might argue that quite a few governments have not honoured other commitments, most notably the famous target of ODA of 0.7 per cent of GNP (meanwhile GNI). On the other hand, first signs may inspire hope. Due to NGO pressure, anti-poverty measures were accepted as parts of debt management after the Cologne summit. The Multilateral Debt Reduction Initiative specifically combined debt reduction with the express objective of helping debtor countries to reach the MDGs. Under the heading 'G8 proposals for HIPC debt cancellation' the Final Communiqué of the G8 Finance Ministers in June 2005 explicitly stated that debt relief 'will provide significant support for countries' efforts to reach the goals of the Millennium Declaration (MDGs)'.

Goal 8 does not address social or environmental issues but recalls the

South's demand for reforms of North-South relations within the New International Economic Order (NIEO). Regarding debtor-creditor relations (see Chapter 1) the 'Third World' demanded both debt relief and a new framework to resolve debt issues in the 1970s. So far there is any indication that creditor governments are much more prepared to support achieving MDGs 1–7, the 'social/environmental goals', than to agree to the substantial redesign of present North-South relations that any meaningful move towards a global partnership for development (such as dealing comprehensively with the debt problem) would render necessary.

This chapter traces the roots of these ideas. In the perspective of a brief *dogmengeschichte,* it discusses the Basic Needs approach, the intentional neglect of direct anti-poverty measures during the first decades of 'structural adjustment', and the new anti-poverty focus of the BWIs and other official creditors. It traces the roots of some MDGs to the UNDP's concepts of global public goods (GPGs) and human development. The MDGs themselves are discussed in detail in the following two chapters.

DEVELOPMENT ECONOMICS AS THOUGH PEOPLE MATTERED

In its early period modern development thinking focused on growth, assuming that market forces would eventually spread its benefits to anyone (the following draws on Raffer and Singer, 2001). Direct measures in favour of the poor were considered a diversion of resources from 'investment' to 'consumption', slowing down growth and the trickle down of its benefits to the poor. The ruling trickle down theorem posited benefits would trickle down from the rich to the poor, eventually spreading through the whole economy without government intervention.

During the process of development, income concentration would by necessity become more unequal. As the rate of savings increases with income (the poor have no money to save) and savings equals investments, inequality facilitates investments. After a period of strong growth income distribution would eventually become more equal because rising demand for labour would push up wages, productivity gains would lower prices. This inverted U of inequality was called the Kuznets curve. Absolute poverty for some groups may thus increase. But eventually the turning point is reached. Growing income is then accompanied by greater equality and reduced poverty. Eventually the benefits of development would trickle down. It was thought necessary first to build up capital, infrastructure and productive capacity in a 'backward' economy, which would eventually improve the lot of the poor. For a time – and this could be quite a long period – the poor would have to wait and the rich would receive most of the benefits. If the rewards of the rich were incentives to innovate, to save and to accumulate, this would finally benefit the poor too. Classical, neoclassical and palaeo-Marxist economists all agreed. Caveats on growth were eclipsed by a pervasive emphasis on its techniques. Even the view that the fate of the poor should not be a concern at the early stages of development was fairly common. Inequality became a virtue – presumably not to the displeasure of the rich – and ideas of redistribution or satisfying 'Basic Needs' had to be defended by showing that greater equality did not hinder growth or at least not too much. Quite irritating to many, Ragnar Nurkse and John H. Adler objected convincingly that greater inequality does not automatically engender more investment because the rich might spend their money on luxuries and conspicuous consumption instead.

To avoid an undue caricature it should be mentioned that economic growth was sometimes emphasized as the key to poverty eradication. Even at this early stage, sensible economists and development planners were quite clear that economic growth is not an end in itself, but a performance test of development. 'Arthur Lewis defined the purpose of development as widening our range of choice, exactly as the UNDP's Human Development Reports do today' (Streeten, 1993, p. 16).

Around 1970 doubts began to emerge about the adequacy of accelerating growth as the main thrust of development policy. In 1969 the International Labour Organization's (ILO) World Employment Programme was created to tackle the problem of un(der)employment more directly. For the first time the issue of inequality was officially emphasized. The report of the ILO mission to Kenya was the first international report recognizing the positive side of the informal sector, recommending how its contribution could be made more effective. It was the forerunner of the Basic Needs approach. The mission's head, Sir Hans Singer, sketched the idea that the incomes of the poorest must increase more rapidly than they would by growth and trickle down alone. Redistribution from the increment of growth would mean adding to the incomes and assets of the poor without having to take away from anyone else, an idea that runs counter to the ruling perception of the Kuznets curve. This challenge to achieve greater equality by redistribution *from* growth as formulated in the Kenya Report gave rise to the strategy of 'Redistribution with Growth', based on the joint World Bank/IDS study of the same name, which even spoke of trickle-up effects from greater incomes of the poor. Arguing in favour of investing in the poor became acceptable. The book's title became a widely used catchword at the IBRD. In a way the IBRD present official focus on poverty is a late homecoming – less radical than the 1970s, but arguably better marketed.

Streeten (1993) describes the reorientation from GNP growth via redistribution with growth to Basic Needs. Once it was discovered that the results of redistribution remained modest in practice, at least for low-income countries, basic human needs emerged as the next logical step in development thinking. It had to be argued that better nutrition, health, education and training can be very productive forms of developing human resources, investments in the future, which – with the exception of some forms of education – were considered consumption and therefore neglected.

Basic Needs finally became an accepted approach when the IBRD under McNamara propagated it. Following the Bank many aid administrations adopted poverty orientation. The Basic Needs approach became accepted development policy.

McNamara, the first IBRD president focusing on poverty, forcefully advocated helping the poor. Lending to poor countries, argued McNamara, would not be sufficient. Loans should specifically aim at the poorest within SCs. McNamara had the merit of giving credibility to the idea that helping the poor is not wasting resources but makes economic sense. Quite in line with early US policies, he saw this as a means to fight communism. To do so more efficiently, he increased the volume of IBRD lending considerably, and established country and regional targets that had (and still have) to be met. He established the frequently criticized 'approval culture' of quick disbursing. Due to the IBRD's and IDA's structures the poor were hardly reached, although IBRD money did sometimes trickle a bit further down than before. Even according to its own sources the IBRD did not reach the poorest 20 per cent. Vague terms were used to describe alleged positive effects of projects. Rather than providing verifiable data the IBRD preferred speaking of people 'affected' by its activities or 'benefitting' (or even 'expected to benefit') from them. The exact meaning of benefitting or affecting was nowhere explained, but impressive numbers of people were quoted.

As late as 1982 the conclusions of a working group on poverty calling for measures to alleviate the effects of 'structural adjustment' on the poor were officially approved. But the tide was about to turn. Soon the BWIs insisted that carrying on 'structural adjustment' had positive impacts and was in the very interest of the poor. Special measures to protect them would thus be superfluous if not harmful. Emphasizing human needs might obstruct needed reforms (cf. Raffer, 1994).

'STRUCTURAL ADJUSTMENT' AND POVERTY

This approach of the BWIs can be characterized in a few words:

- Devaluation, which is supposed to reduce imports and increase export revenues. The latter part did not really work, because little or no market shares can be gained if many debtor-exporters devalue at about the same time. This is called the fallacy of composition: strategies that work if one or very few actors pursue them do not work if many actors do so. Increased supply at roughly unchanged demand made export prices collapse. Quite frequently debtors exported more while earning less. Devaluation increased the debt burden in domestic currency. With debts denominated in foreign currency this was a disadvantage to debtor SCs but not to creditors.
- Reducing real wages.
- Cutting subsidies and state expenditures (especially those helping the poor) and increasing regressive indirect taxation in favour of debt service.
- Liberalizing trade and the capital account.

This lemon squeezer approach means that resources are channelled away from the debtor's inhabitants. Less domestic consumption means more resources disposable for debt service. It can be succinctly illustrated. The IBRD (1980, p. 62) described the 'major drawback' of efficient food subsidies as being costly, often using up 'scarce foreign exchange or aid'. In other words, money that could be used to pay creditors was used up to feed the hungry. This was not so much a revisiting of the 1950s, but rather a decision to privilege debt service. In present parlance and plain English: no money to be wasted on MDGs. So-called 'IMF riots' were the result, an expression that does not reveal the important role of the IBRD.

Ernest Stern (1983, p. 91), the IBRD's senior vice president, one of the most influential men in the IBRD and the mastermind behind its programme lending, praised 'structural adjustment' for its 'comprehensiveness', its 'coverage in terms of both macro and sector issues of policy reform; the exclusive focus on policy and institutional reform; and the detailed articulation of the precise modifications in policy necessary to adjust to a changed economic environment'. This form of lending enabled 'the Bank to address basic issues of economic management and of development strategy more directly and urgently', for Stern a 'unique opportunity to achieve a comprehensive and timely approach to policy reform' (ibid., p. 104). For Stern 'structural adjustment' was the response to a 'feasible . . . call for increased sacrifices' (ibid., p. 91) by the population. Of course, Stern explains, there is a need for a 'firm understanding' of monitoring.

The term 'structural adjustment' is used with inverted commas, because the BWIs monopolized it to mean their own specific ideas, or whatever they were doing. While there was evident need for reform, or structural adjustment, in problem debtor countries, this does not mean that the specific set of BWI prescriptions was indicated (Raffer, 1994). Empirical outcome so far rather suggests the opposite. Early attempts to prove success by econometric results were short-lived. Empirical evidence remained, at best, inconclusive. Usually there was no statistically significant difference between 'adjusters' and 'non-adjusters'. Statistical methods, such as country groupings, were repeatedly attacked as purpose serving. One of the extremely few statistically significant results was published by Khan (1990), an IMF econometrician, in the *IMF Staff Papers*: a predicted reduction in growth rates of at least 0.7 per cent of GDP each year that countries had an IMF programme. Others found adverse effects of 'structural adjustment' on growth, particularly in countries with low slippage on conditionality and declining shares of investment in GDP. Eventually the IBRD (1990) itself acknowledged that 'structural adjustment' lending had achieved some success regarding the improvement of the balance of payments (largely due to import compression, critics rightly pointed out) but did not encourage investments nor enable debtors to grow out of debts. The GATT (1986) noted in its *International Trade 1985–86* that 'virtually the entire burden of adjustment' (p. 25) had been put on SCs. 'What is worse, adjustment has involved mostly import contraction rather than export expansion', which threatened to result in a 'vicious circle of reduced imports and reduced export potential'. The GATT's report observed import cuts 'large enough to affect the future productive capacity of these countries' (p. 95). No 'adjusting' debtor recovered sustainably. According to the IMF's *World Economic Outlook* of October 1987 gross capital formation declined by one third between 1979 and 1985. Obviously 'structural adjustment' did impair future production capacity and growth – thus the economic base for financing goals such as the MDGs.

UNCTAD's *Trade and Development Report 2006* (UNCTAD, 2006, p. 47) shows the growth rates of the two regions where 'structural adjustment' was most pronounced. In sub-Saharan Africa (excluding the RSA), where 'adjustment' had started in the mid-1970s, GDP per head decreased by more than 1 per cent per year during 1975–85 and by 1.3 per cent during 1990–95, increasing by 0.2 per cent per annum during 1985–90, a period when Africa suffered a slight decrease. Latin America's GDP per head decreased by 1.6 per cent (1980–85) and 0.2 per cent (1985–90), respectively, during the 'lost decade' of the 1980s. 'Structural adjustment' may not account for the whole negative impact, but it certainly intensified the crisis.

The continuing arguments are nicely summed up by an IMF employee, Wanda Tseng (1984): '"Structural adjustment" costs are unavoidable and lower than the costs of non-adjustment. Efficiency gains will more than make up for "adjustment" costs'. Financial help by the BWIs decreases these costs further. Bringing down inflation is of particular benefit to the poor likely to hold their assets in cash. Successful economic reforms benefit everybody, including the poor. Subsidies have to be abolished, as they are a huge part of public outlays. They discriminate against the rural poor and create incentives for low wages industries, thus leading to rapid urbanization (and slums). To be on the safe side Tseng added that the IMF had no mandate regarding the poor anyway. Considering that the poor are the vast majority in low-income countries, critical minds might ask how proper and successful economic policies disregarding their economic situation could be implemented.

In the September 1986 issue of *Finance & Development* David Beckmann explained the IBRD's policy reversal by changed necessities of SCs: balance of payments equilibria reached by GDP and export growth benefit the rich as well as the poor; relying on market mechanisms does not mean less attention to the poor; planned actions are better than unplanned adjustment; sacrifices are necessary for a better future. The growth crisis made advances in poverty alleviation practically impossible. In line with his employer, the IBRD, he added that many projects benefitted the poor as well, even though the political climate of the 1980s was not conducive to the poor. To prove this he mentions that most IDA and IBRD funds went to poor countries and sectors, whose projects are supposed to benefit particularly the poor – which does not prove any benefit to the poor. However, as the Bank's policy is decided by its members and in consultation with borrowers, the IBRD itself has, the author asserted, limited room for manoeuvring. In plain English: while the Bank helped the poor by not specifically helping them, it was not responsible for what it did as it did not really decide anything.

As 'structural adjustment' was in the very interest of the poor, emphasizing human needs might obstruct needed reforms. This argument, as well as the IBRD's 'major drawback' of efficient food subsidies (using up 'scarce foreign exchange or aid') apply equally when it comes to financing MDGs.

Basically this view was held until UNICEF's *Adjustment with a Human Face* (Cornia et al., 1987) was published, although the BWIs had been confronted with the effects of 'structural adjustment' on the poor as early as 1984 (cf. Raffer, 1994). The proposed changes were initially ridiculed. Pfeffermann's book review of Cornia et al. in *Finance & Development* of December 1988 qualifies the proposed changes of stabilization and 'structural adjustment' policies as a *'cri du cœur'* rather than a serious guideline for economic policy. Seeing the study's merits in raising governments' awareness of poverty, Pfeffermann called for practicable proposals instead of the study's ideas. In spite of his verdict, which was in tune with the general feeling at the BWIs then, Pfeffermann himself had recommended targeting, a method advocated by the UNICEF study, in 1987. Proposals by the UNICEF study, such as targeting, were quickly taken up. The 1988 *World Development Report* wrote about how to target effectively to avoid leakages. Soon special programmes to help those affected by 'structural adjustment' were officially accepted by the BWIs. Suddenly it was argued that special measures in favour of the poor would make 'structural adjustment' more acceptable and thus more efficient – a point steadfastly denied shortly before. Whatever the BWIs did, they always helped the poor – like words always mean what the Red Queen says they do. In practice, though, little was done. While there was a big change in rhetoric, little action followed. Arguments and titles of publications changed, while practice remained essentially unaffected, in spite of severe critique and even though the BWIs could not prove empirically that 'structural adjustment' worked. Quite the contrary, the successful Asian 'tigers' did the opposite of what the representative debtor country was forced to implement. When the 'tigers' decided to follow BWI advice, catastrophe was soon triggered in 1997.

Unlike positive effects, negative effects of 'structural adjustment' and projects on the poor can be proved. Cornia concluded that 'overall, prevailing adjustment programmes tend to increase and aggravate poverty, or in other words, the number of people – and of children – living below the poverty line' (Cornia et al., 1987, p. 66). Although not 'every programme has had an adverse effect on poverty levels . . . on average, this tendency prevails'. Cuts in health expenditures, often part of 'adjustment' led to declines in the health status of the population, reflected, for instance, in increased incidence of infectious diseases and disease-specific mortality. Many illustrative examples can be found. In São Paulo State infant mortality increased sharply in 1984 after a steady decline before. In Mexico average wages in 1992 were half what they had been ten years earlier. Between 1980 and 1992 infant deaths due to malnutrition almost tripled. Faced with reduced real wages and increased school fees, many families withdrew their children from school (Caufield, 1998, p. 153). In 1989 UNICEF estimated 'that at least half a million young children have died in the last twelve months as a result of the slowing down or the reversal of progress in the developing world' (ibid., p. 162). Per capita spending on health in the poorest 37 countries fell by 25 per cent, spending on education halved during the 1980s. Enrolment of children in primary school fell throughout the South, while primary budget surpluses were used to service debts. George (1988, p. 167) showed that 'environmental programmes are among the first to go' when 'the IMF imposes government cuts'.

It must be recalled that the IMF's first 'adjustment measures' were undertaken after 1973. The IBRD claimed the success of 'structural adjustment' in Africa with the famous statement 'Recovery has begun' in 1989 (see Chapter 2). So far no overindebted sub-Saharan country has reached economic sustainability. To economists this should come as no surprise. The IBRD's (1989, p.92) own Operations Evaluation Department (OED) stated: 'conditionalities should take into account the macroeconomic consequences of the policy prescriptions'. It called for an integrated analytical framework to understand better the links between programmes and their expected macroeconomic outcomes: 'Such a framework would also be useful for ex-post evaluations' (ibid., p.6). Briefly, all the neoliberal policies forced upon debtor countries, allegedly to help the poor, had no theoretical basis. Since 'structural adjustment' was jointly controlled by the BWIs one must ask whether the IMF had a theoretical basis and, if so, why and how the Fund kept it secret from the Bank.

In June 1995 a group of NGOs approached the new IBRD president, James Wolfensohn, proposing that the IBRD and civil society jointly assess the impact of 'adjustment' programmes. This led to the Structural Adjustment Participatory Review Initiative (SAPRI), officially launched in July 1997. SAPRI was designed as a tripartite exercise bringing together organizations of civil society, debtor governments and the IBRD in a joint review of 'structural adjustment' programmes (SAPs) and an exploration of new policy options. It legitimized an active role for civil society. In addition to its work with the IBRD and national governments, SAPRIN (the network of participating NGOs) started a parallel initiative known as the Citizens' Assessment of Structural Adjustment (CASA) in countries whose governments decided against participation in SAPRI. This exercise soon produced evidence of devastating consequences of adjustment measures on production, employment and social services in debtor countries. The IBRD's bureaucracy opposed SAPRI. Little of the analysis made its way into country programming. Influences on the Bank's own adjustment assessments and operations remained limited at best. This joint learning exercise eventually ended with two separate final reports, reportedly on the IBRD's request: one produced by the IBRD, the other by NGOs.

The conclusions drawn were highly critical. A 'sharp deterioration in public spending for health care and education, while, in the best of cases, there is inadequate improvement in spending levels' was diagnosed or a deterioration of educational quality due to budget constraints. School fees increased dropout rates in most countries, particularly among girls. The elimination of subsidies for essential goods and services affected the quality of life of the poorest negatively (cf. SAPRIN, 2002).

User fees introduced under BWI pressure reduced access to health services and education for the poor. Social sectors were most severely affected by fiscal discipline to allow higher debt service payments. The BWIs successfully avoided the 'major drawback' of social expenditures the IBRD had identified early on: using up scarce foreign exchange for social policy.

HIPC II: FINALLY ADMITTING THE NEED FOR ANTI-POVERTY MEASURES

While a huge and commendable step towards more efficient debt management, HIPC I did not take the poor specifically into account. The IBRD made a link between the initiative and poverty reduction, but poverty was neither visibly reflected in sustainability indicators, nor in actual creditor decisions. Limiting debt service may be seen as having pro-poor side effects though. It took many years before the Cologne Summit of 1999 officially and explicitly recognized the negative effects of BWI debt management on poverty. Under unprecedented pressure from civil society (the international Jubilee Movement presented over 17 million signatures collected worldwide to the German Chancellor) the G7 admitted that HIPC I had failed and decided to introduce HIPC II. For the first time poverty reduction was incorporated visibly. The Poverty Reduction and Growth Facility (PRGF) proclaims this aim in its name.

Important creditors controlling the BWIs soon accused debtors forced to cut pro-poor public expenditures in favour of higher debt service of neglecting their social sectors. Preparing the Genoa Summit, Italy (Presidenza 2001, p. 19) criticized:

> Health systems should protect people against the financial costs of illness. Yet, many low income countries have in place cost-recovery schemes that imply a regressive burden of user fee payments for health. . . . The empirical evidence in the past decade shows that user fees can discourage in the poorest countries the recourse to formal health services, thereby negatively affecting health performances. Governments need to introduce better incentives, rather than deterrents, to facilitate people's access to health services.

User fees had been forced upon poor countries by the BWIs controlled by the G7, sometimes against debtor resistance, but with the support and applause of G7 countries. The perpetrator turns around to accuse the victim.

The IMF was not designed as a development organization, but to enable (at first practically only industrialized) members of the Bretton Woods system with short-term balance of payments problems to stay within the agreed parity bands. Therefore it refused to take the poor into account. In 1999, however, the IMF (2001) 'embraced a new anti-poverty focus'. The PRGF 'replaced' the Enhanced Structural Adjustment Facility (ESAF), bringing 'with it a number of innovations designed to ensure that lending programs are pro-poor and in line with the country's own strategy for reducing poverty'. This was claimed to be 'more than just a change in name'. When feeling less obliged to document its new poverty culture, the IMF (2003a) finds no difference: 'The Poverty Reduction and Growth Facility (PRGF), formerly known as the Enhanced Structural Adjustment Facility (ESAF) provides loans . . ..'. This contradiction recalls the contradictory statements claiming a pro-poor bias for totally different policies during the 1980s. The IMF (2001) tries to explain contradictions away. The 'PRGF explicitly makes poverty reduction a central goal, whereas under ESAF poverty reduction was an implicit by-product'. This would support the view that – bureaucratic and linguistic niceties apart – the two facilities are identical regarding outcome.

UNCTAD (2002, p. 14) found substantial contradictions between typical Poverty Reduction Strategy Papers (PRSPs) and the 'voices of the poor'. Their demands or the 'aspirations of the poor' result from extensive IBRD field research 'on the perceptions, expectations and experiences of the poor, covering 24 developing countries (including eight in Africa)' (ibid., p. 13). Especially positions on agriculture, labour markets, macro policies, income distribution and the private sector are largely incompatible with PRSPs: 'In these areas, policy preferences of IFIs and/or national governments rather than expectations and aspirations of the poor appear to have prevailed' (ibid., p. 15). While one may logically argue that denying people what they want may ultimately be best for them – many fairy tales illustrate this – such findings do not refute the hypothesis that 'consulting' the poor is but another exercise in lip service.

Once again UNCTAD (2002) identified severe negative impacts on the poor, for instance, via shifts in taxation from corporate, personal income and trade taxes to regressive consumption taxes, falling real incomes of unskilled workers (declines often exceeding 20 per cent), rising input prices for food crops accompanied by declining output and increasing fertilizer prices, the collapse of rural infrastructure such as rural roads, declining levels of rural credits, the transformation of rural property regimes taking away user rights from the poor, user fees in the education and health sectors constituting an important impediment to access for the poor, the 'exorbitant costs of drugs' (ibid., p. 43) or the decline in public service institutions. BWI pressure to liberalize capital accounts have made increased stocks of international reserves necessary, 'one of the widely-used targets of poverty reduction strategies in Africa' (ibid., p. 31), although any IMF member has the right to capital controls pursuant to the IMF's constitution. Only current transactions are to continue if possible. Article XXX(d)(3) includes under current transactions 'payments of *moderate* amount of amortization of loans or for depreciation of direct investments' (emphasis added), Article XXX(d)(4) *'moderate* remittances for family living expenses'. This means that even restrictions on debt service are a membership right. Using these rights, which the BWIs force their clients not to do – the IMF in open breach of its own constitution – would not cost anything, unlike large reserves squirrelling resources away from poverty alleviation, transforming the IBRD's dream of a 'world free of poverty' into a nightmare for the poor. These reserves are money that cannot be used to finance pro-poor policies such as the MDGs.

UNCTAD (2002) repeatedly quotes observations by IBRD sources that BWI reforms have sometimes hurt the poor, even that 'Agricultural market liberalization without the institutional framework . . . could have serious consequences for poor people' (ibid., p. 39–40, quoting the IBRD, 2001, p. 69). But the Bank always comes down on the side of continuing and consolidating reforms rather than in favour of creating the necessary preconditions for reforms to work without hurting the poor. The IBRD (2001, p. 70) officially recognized that the regressive property of VAT hurts the poorest, but did nothing to protect them. Apparently the Bank knows what it is doing and that this diverges considerably from its officially posted goals and dreams.

UNCTAD (2002, p. 21) concluded: 'country PRSPs have so far covered a broad spectrum of macroeconomic policies and structural reforms without assessing their likely impact on poverty', as ministers from HIPCs noted too. UNCTAD (ibid., p. 59) found that 'little attention has so far been given to social impact analysis', echoing other critics and recalling the OED's conclusion about the usefulness of a theoretical framework for 'structural adjustment'. Again poverty is 'fought' without proper analysis but in excellent English and with new acronyms such as PSIA (Poverty and Social Impact Analysis) or an IMF PRSP sourcebook. In 1992 the so-called 'Wapenhans Report' of the IBRD already warned 'the perception that the literary quality of the SAR [Staff Appraisal Report] is in itself a criterion of success' is wrong, that actually accruing returns, not wonderful English, matter and urged 'that point should be driven home'. The BWIs seem to have remained more successful with excellent English than with economic results.

Trying to identify differences between the PRGF and past policies in Africa, UNCTAD (2002, p. 57) concluded that the new poverty focus 'does not replace the development strategies implemented under structural adjustment programmes but complements them'. New conditionalities were added. The effects of largely relying on across-the-board user fees in the areas of education and health (ibid., p. 59) are problematic. In spite of years of HIPC II pro-poor policies are still not properly implemented, although more resources have meanwhile been made available for anti-poverty measures. For the 29 decision point countries UNCTAD's *Trade and Development Report 2006* found a 'rise in poverty reduction expenditures and a fall in debt service, measured as a ratio of government revenue' (p. 94). However this change will not be sufficient to achieve the MDGs. Malawi (see Chapter 5) is a sad recent illustration of what the BWIs' pro-poor focus means in practice.

PRSPs put so much strain on debtor countries' resources and designing them takes so much time that Intermediate PRSPs (I-PRSPs) had to be invented to allow the BWIs to continue disbursements. The 'approval culture' and 'the Bank's pervasive preoccupation with new lending' seem very much alive. HIPC II and the Millennium Declaration, in particular, have refocused attention on policies already proposed or attempted before. Setting specified targets to be reached by a specified year the MDGs provide measurable and internationally agreed targets of anti-poverty policies. Unfortunately present information suggests that they will not be reached globally, although some countries might be able to do so. Undoubtedly, though, the idea of exempting money in order to finance certain basic needs to reach the MDGs is now well established. For the IBRD group it is a homecoming.

HUMAN DEVELOPMENT: GIVING PRIORITY TO HUMAN BEINGS

In 1990 the UNDP produced its first *Human Development Report* (HDR), since then published annually. Introducing the Human Development Index (HDI), a composite indicator covering three dimensions of human welfare (income, education, health), the HDR set a new tone. Going beyond GDP and income it drew attention to a set of social indicators measuring human wellbeing. This helped prepare the ground for the MDGs. The HDR has also published the human poverty index, the gender-related development index and the gender empowerment measure. Regional HDRs have been published, such as the *Arab Human Development Report*, as well as national HDRs. Since 1990 the HDR has continuously published indicators later adopted to measure progress towards the MDGs.

Comparing HDI ranking with ranking by GDP per capita, the UNDP found very interesting differences. Countries with much lower GDP per head might rank close to much richer countries according to the HDI.

Discrepancies vis-à-vis GDP ranking may be even more pronounced with individual indicators. 'The infant mortality rate in the United States compares with that in Malaysia – a country with a quarter the income.' The maternal mortality rate of Kuwait was well below the USA or the UK, both with regard to nationally reported rates and 'adjusted' rates, that is, data based on reviews by UN organizations to account 'for well documented problems of underreporting and misclassifications' (UNDP, 2005, pp. 250ff., p. 58).

As the HDI, like GDP per head, is a national average, the UNDP has always published information on regional, gender, ethnic and social disparities. This might be illustrated with one example: 'Infant death rates are higher for African American children in Washington, DC, than for children in Kerala, India' (ibid., p.59).

To promote improvements in the HDI, the UNDP's *Human Development Report 1994* proposed the 20:20 compact, which was endorsed at the World Social Summit in Copenhagen. The compact's most important targets included universal primary education (for both genders alike), adult illiteracy rates to be halved (the female rate must not be higher than the male one), primary health care for all, elimination of severe malnutrition, family planning services for all willing couples, safe drinking water and sanitation for all and credit for all to ensure self-employment opportunities. This would require SCs to devote at least 20 per cent of their government expenditure to health, education, sanitation, water supplies and other priorities for human development. Donor countries would commit themselves to devoting at least 20 per cent of their aid to these sectors. This list, considered to be the 'very minimum targets' by the UNDP, is immediately recognizable as a forerunner of the MDGs.

While the desirability of human development remains officially unchallenged, the question whether and to what extent aid actually promotes it is strongly debated. The *Human Development Report 1993* presented data showing that – although the range between Denmark's 25 per cent and Germany's 2 per cent was substantial – only 7 per cent of bilateral Development Assistance Committee (DAC) aid went on average to human 'priority areas such as basic education, primary health care, rural water supplies, nutrition programmes and family planning services'. Regarding donor countries the UNDP therefore found 'considerable scope for changing the allocation priorities in their aid budgets in the post-cold war era'. A similar picture emerged for multilateral aid, although multilateral institutions allocated around 16 per cent on average. UNICEF spent 77.8 per cent on human priorities. The African Development Bank was singled out as the multilateral institution devoting the smallest share (4 per cent) to this purpose.

Naturally such figures are not very popular with 'donors', always eager to claim altruistic motives for their actions, as the term 'aid' itself documents. A debate was triggered (Raffer, 1998). The OECD (1994, p. 98) defended its practice against the UNDP, arguing that human priority concerns 'have long been prime areas of interest for the DAC and its Members' and were at the heart of the 1989 DAC's Policy Statement on Development Cooperation in the 1990s.

After confirming its total support for human development, the DAC tackled the problem of aid allocation. It argued that the figure of less than 7 per cent was based on aid loans recorded transaction by transaction in the creditor reporting system administered by the DAC Secretariat. As loans only accounted for 20–25 per cent of bilateral ODA and the 'sectoral allocation' (ibid.) of grants was substantially different, the DAC believed the allowance made by the UNDP for this discrepancy to be inadequate. This belief could never be supported by any data. The OECD referred vaguely to 'other reporting to the DAC (the aggregate reporting system)'. As only donors report to the DAC, this means that donors themselves are not able (or unwilling) to produce more precise data on how much of their aid goes to their prime areas of interest at the heart of their policy concerns.

The OECD asserted that neither the DAC nor its members know how much money benefitted the poor. It went on arguing that aid to the water supply sector was even the subject of a special DAC meeting held in 1994. Its thinking in sectors and the wording 'sectoral allocation' show a further fundamental discrepancy between the DAC and the UNDP with regard to the concept itself. It is the same misperception as between aid to poor countries (which can go to the richest within those countries) and aid to the poor. The UNDP had criticized the wrong weights attached within sectors clearly, although quite briefly. Demanding that ODA allocation be based on levels of poverty, it had explicitly stated that 'ODA should be allocated to people rather than countries.' The *Human Development Report 1993* criticized that higher status projects get preference and that aid does not go to poor people, a criticism repeated more in detail in 1994. The UNDP's focus on need cannot be invalidated by pointing at sectoral figures. Aid to any sector may go to the rich or the poor. Irrigation projects, for example, might be exclusively in the interest of the rich, strengthening their economic position, even enabling them to exploit the poor more thoroughly.

It must not be overlooked that the UNDP demanded 20 per cent for human development priorities, which leaves 80 per cent for financing other activities important for development and debt service. The UNDP did not propose a total redirection to the compact's targets, but a balance between necessary development expenditures and attention to vulnerable groups.

Defending its allocation, the OECD confused the UNDP's developmental concept of high human priority with humanitarian concerns. It is true that aid to refugees and disaster victims is necessary and of high human priority, and it is highly commendable to help in such cases. But this is relief, and by no means what is meant by human priority development. The former helps in emergencies or after disasters, the latter is committed to long-term development, to changing economic and social structures. To illustrate this with the old adage of the fish: relief means giving fish to people, human development means equipping them better to catch their own food. Both activities are necessary, important and laudable, but totally different. They must not be confused.

While part of the confusion could be accidental and arguments might have been phrased differently if things had been clear from the start, one most important and really fundamental divide between DAC donors and the UNDP concept remains. The last counterargument of the OECD brings it to light:

> Even more problematic is the question of how broadly the definition of 'human priority concerns' is drawn and how the various forms of aid interact with human priorities. The UNDP covers only aid going directly to the sectors identified above. But aid which assists general economic development, including aid to support economic stabilization, policy reforms and adjustments to public expenditure priorities, can have a wide impact on the access of poor people to basic education, primary health care and family planning services. (OECD, 1994, p. 98)

This view qualifies everything as human priority concern. In contrast to the UNDP's demand to allocate 20 per cent to human priority concerns, this would mean an actual allocation of 100 per cent. Logically, of course, virtually anything may have positive effects on anything and anyone, including the poor. Logically this means that the OECD considered the very concept of human development, special projects aimed at the poor or other special groups, fatally flawed and logically unnecessary. By this passage the OECD posits that whatever is done by donors is likely to benefit the poor anyway. If this point is accepted there is no need to target any projects specifically on them. It mirrors the BWI view on 'structural adjustment' that whatever is done helps the poor as well as the trickle down approach of the 1950s. Quite conveniently there is no need for detailed statistics on the actual impact of aid, nor for critique either. If accepted this view destroys any logical basis to criticize actual aid policy on the grounds of its (lack of) impact on the poor.

By implying that any ODA and development finance activity benefits the poor, 'aid' is given a philanthropic notion, although it is simply a technical term covering helpful activities as well as greed or – at worst – outright catastrophes creating considerable damage in recipient countries.

GLOBAL PUBLIC GOODS AND MDGS

The idea of global public goods (GPGs) (also called international public goods in the literature) has emerged in the context of increased economic openness and market integration called globalization: public goods initially uniquely discussed at the national level go global. This concept has gained prominence since the UNDP's Office of Development Studies started the research project International Development Cooperation and Global Public Goods in 1998, which produced the first seminal book on GPGs (Kaul et al. eds, 1999). The basic perception is that there exist – similar to national public goods in the textbook sense – non-private goods and services internationally that are able to create global externalities. Thus they cannot be easily provided by the invisible hand. The free-rider problem and prisoner's dilemma situations exist. The familiar problem emerges that market incentives are insufficient to secure provision, exacerbated by the absence of any form of global governance comparable to national governments. Obvious examples for GPGs are the protection of the ozone shield, the prevention of global warming and its effects or the reduction of toxic emissions affecting large parts of the globe. Globalized markets are in need of an equally globalized supply of goods (the term referring also to services, things or conditions) they need but will not produce. Looking at the literature one finds a large range of GPGs, including the preservation of the global environment, cultural heritage, controlling global epidemics, conserving biodiversity, knowledge, peace and security, but also international financial stability or trade agreements that provide the framework of international trade.

Pure GPGs are defined by non-rivalry and non-excludability. This means that the use of such goods by one person does not diminish the use by any other person and that no one can be excluded from it. In a national context streetlights and national defence are usually quoted as examples for public goods. Pure public goods, national or international, are rare. Impure GPGs yield benefits that are partially rival and/or partially non-excludable. Obviously they are more widespread.

The MDGs 3,6,7 and 8 can be traced back to this concept. In the case of the environment (MDG 7) this is obvious, as the discussion on the ozone shield or rain forest, as well as the Kyōto Protocol have clarified. MDG 3 (promote gender equality and empower women) is presented by the UNDP on its home page as 'an intriguing global public good' as 'global norms, including universal human rights, are in effect global public goods par excellence'.

There exists another link between the MDGs and GPGs. People's health, for example, depends on several inputs with a GPG character, such as pharmaceutical R&D, knowledge, the international trade regime (TRIPs in particular) or global disease surveillance. Sometimes, as in the case of HIV/AIDS, the GPG character compounds with other social and economic goals. Helping those suffering from this disease is both humanitarian and may improve economic performance but also fights the 'global bad' of contagious disease.

8. Poverty, debtor protection and the MDGs

The World Commission on the Social Dimension of Globalization (2004) concluded that the eradication of poverty and the attainment of the MDGs should be seen as the first steps towards a socioeconomic 'floor' for the global economy. Without any doubt, debt management must also respect this floor, which means it must not extract resources for debt service that are needed to finance this minimum. In the parlance of insolvency lawyers: the universally accepted idea of resources exempt from seizure by bona fide creditors must finally be applied to the only debtors not benefitting from this protection of human dignity.

The fact that all official creditors have accepted the MDGs and are officially committed to achieve them avoids long discussions on what precisely debtor protection should include. It took national legal systems a very long time to establish what has meanwhile become generally accepted standards in national insolvency cases. Using the MDGs would avoid long discussions on what and how much should be exempt, and it would immediately improve living conditions notably. A difference remains though. While all individual debtors are unconditionally protected from hunger and guaranteed at least a modest minimum of resources, not all people would enjoy this minimum standard after achieving the MDGs. Many people would continue to live on less than one dollar a day or go hungry, as many people did before the debt crisis. This should be of great concern, and development policies must aim at overcoming this inhumane situation. Unfortunately though, this is a long-term enterprise going beyond the MDGs, and beyond debts and debt relief. While sovereign insolvency procedures must mitigate poverty and misery by safeguarding minimum social expenditures, no solution to a debt overhang can simultaneously fulfil all tasks of development policy. Exempting resources needed to finance the MDGs is one advisable and analogous way of implementing debtor protection in a sovereign debt context. Unfortunately this cannot be expected to solve all development problems.

Pettifor and Greenhill (2002, pp. 16–17) connect debt service and financing the MDGs with my debt arbitration proposal:

Debt relief required should be assessed on a case-by-case basis, ideally by an independent arbitration panel with nominees from both debtor and creditor countries. The panel should consider, amongst other factors (for example, the circumstances in which the debt was contracted):

● How much the country will need to spend on a yearly basis to meet the MDGs. Such analysis should ideally be done with the assistance of international organisations such as the United Nations Development Programme (UNDP), UNICEF and the World Health Organization;

● The level of resources available to a country in terms of tax revenues and aid and the other spending requirements faced by the government;

● How much debt cancellation will be required in order to leave the debtor with sufficient resources to meet the MDGs.

Progress towards the MDGs must be seen with the history of earlier 'structural adjustment' policies in mind, as well as the negative effects they had on the poor, on infrastructure, the environment and the economy. There is no doubt that debt management has made reaching the MDGs more difficult. Progress was slowed down or even stopped in some sectors and countries, too often indicators even deteriorated. Pettifor and Greenhill (2002, p. 10) found that progress had been back-rolled in quite a few HIPCs: 'In every area except one (female gross enrolment as a percentage of male enrolment), fewer than half the HIPCs are on track to meet the target by 2015. Many HIPCs are not only off-track but are in fact slipping back from their 1990 levels. For example, at least 7 of the HIPCs are moving away from meeting the target of halving the proportion of people who are under-nourished.' One must, however, not forget that regional or national averages may mask differences from country to country as well as disparities among socioeconomic groups. Even if goals are met nationally, large parts of the population could still be much worse off than the national average. *Time* magazine (12 October 1992), for instance, reported infant mortality in the USA to be 9 per 1000 live births in 1989–90. However, while it was 8.1 for white US-Americans it was 18.6 for black US-Americans – the latter figure comparing unfavourably with Jamaica's national average of 16.

Several estimates of the costs to reach the MDGs have been made. They vary greatly, ranging from an extra $30 billion per year to over $100 (Vandemoortele and Roy, 2005, p. 49). While useful for policy makers, they should all be seen with a grain of salt as the example of education in Uganda (described below) indicates. The UN Millennium Project (2005, p. 250), which also carried out preliminary MDG needs assessments on the country level, projects that 'the cost of meeting the Goals in all countries will amount to $121 billion in 2006 and $189 billion in 2015'. Reaching the MDGs is not equally difficult for all countries. Thus some countries may set higher targets, so-called 'MDG-plus' targets. For countries well in advance of the representative regional or Southern country, this may indeed make a lot of sense. Statistically this would allow other countries to set lower national targets without undermining the achievement of the globally set targets in the aggregate. While arguing for national flexibility, Vandemoortele and Roy (ibid., p. 45) also warn that this statistical property should not be used as an 'escape clause' from the commitment to 'spare no effort' in order to reach the MDGs. Considering the standards set by the MDGs one might well argue that the MDGs as formulated by the UN are the minimum any country should aspire to guarantee to its people. No country should plan at the outset to fall below these levels. Any country must be conscious of the need to check whether the poorest fare perceptibly worse than the average and what can specifically be done to help the poorest.

The US crisis has put both the MDGs and achievements so far at risk. Speculation driving up raw material prices and particularly the increase in food prices have contributed. Quite rightly, the *Global Monitoring Report 2009* (subtitle: *A Development Emergency*) speaks of a 'development emergency that now confronts many poor countries' (IBRD and IMF, 2009, p. 4). The report believes that 'As many as 90 percent of developing countries are assessed to be highly or moderately exposed to the impact of the crisis, as they face slowing growth, high levels of poverty, or both' (ibid., p. 6). Or 'The collapse of world trade and declining net capital flows have led to sharp declines in the availability of foreign exchange resources in emerging and developing countries, causing dismal growth, deteriorating fiscal balances, and sharp declines in private demand.' Resources for the MDGs are less readily available. The source formulates that the prospect of reaching the MDGs by 2015, 'already a cause for serious concern, now looks even more distant'. Up to expectations, the BWIs present their traditional prescriptions: supporting the private sector, maintaining an open trade and finance system, and – last but certainly not least – 'Empowering Multilateral Institutions' (ibid., p. 10).

This chapter discusses the four MDGs with the most pronounced anti-poverty focus. These are:

Goal 1   Eradicate extreme poverty and hunger.
Target 1   Reduce by half the proportion of people living on less than a dollar a day.
Indicators:

1.   Proportion of population below $1 (PPP) per day.
2.   Poverty gap ratio, $1 per day.
3.   Share of poorest quintile in national income or consumption.

Target 2   Reduce by half the proportion of people who suffer from hunger.
Indicators:

4. Prevalence of underweight children under five years of age.
5. Proportion of the population below minimum level of dietary energy consumption.

Goal 2   Achieve universal primary education.
Target 3   Ensure that all boys and girls complete a full course of primary schooling.
Indicators:

6. Net enrolment ratio in primary education.
7. Proportion of pupils starting grade 1 who reach grade 5.
8. Literacy rate of the 15–24 year-old.

Goal 4   Reduce child mortality.
Target 5   Reduce by two thirds the mortality rate among children under five.
Indicators:

13. Under-five mortality rate.
14. Infant mortality rate.
15. Proportion of 1 year-old children immunized against measles.

Goal 5   Improve maternal health.
Target 6   Reduce by three quarters the maternal mortality ratio.
Indicators:

16. Maternal mortality ratio.
17. Proportion of births attended by skilled health personnel.

ERADICATE EXTREME POVERTY AND HUNGER

While the number of people living in absolute poverty worldwide declined significantly from 1237 million in 1990 to 1100 million in 2000, most of this improvement is accounted for by just two very large countries, China and India, where 38 per cent of the world's population live. 'In China alone the number of people living in poverty declined from 361 million to 204 million. Elsewhere, in sub-Saharan Africa, Europe and Central Asia, and

Latin America and the Caribbean, poverty has increased by 82, 14, and 8 million, respectively' (World Commission, 2004, p. 44). Obviously many factors contribute to this result. Debt management, though, has certainly been one key factor in all debt-burdened SCs. Unlike many SCs, both China and India have not undergone years of BWI debt management.

Cornia et al. (1987, p. 27, emphasis in original) pointed out that 'the drop in the *real resources of the poor*' defined as real wages for these poor, was 'greater than the average'. This study also cautioned that 'the relative income distribution' had deteriorated, increasing the number of people below a given poverty line. One has to agree to the IBRD's (2000b, p. 68) conclusions regarding HIPCs: 'Many more infants will die either at birth or before they reach the age of five than in other developing countries, and far fewer will go to school . . . the vast majority of people living in HIPCs have seen no improvement in their lives for more than two decades'. This situation has to be seen in the light of some 20 years of BWI-led debt management. Collapsing real wages meant that the working poor often had to subsist below the poverty line. SAPRIN (2002, p. 86, emphasis in original) concluded '*The **Mexican** minimum wage has lost 69 percent of its purchasing power since the beginning of adjustment in 1982, and the number of people living in extreme poverty (those unable to obtain the basic food basket) rose from 6 million to 30 million between 1994 and 2000.*'

'Many developing countries increased domestic food prices during the period 1980–85 to reduce implicit price subsidies and provide stronger incentives to producers' (Cornia et al. 1987, p. 88). This was quite in line with BWI prescriptions. Although world market prices of some import products such as wheat and rice fell, devaluation automatically drove domestic prices up. This inflationary effect on the income of the poor was frequently compounded by budget cuts. Colombia, for instance, discontinued a food stamp programme in 1982 which had been in effect since 1976 (ibid.)

One may try to defend 'structural adjustment' by arguing that many factors impact on any economy. However IFI staff of the highest level have explicitly and clearly connected 'structural adjustment' with highly negative effects on the poor, recognizing a causal link between the two. As early as 1987 the IMF's Managing Director, Michel Camdessus, admitted at ECOSOC that the poorest 'too often . . . carried the heaviest burden of adjustment' (*IMF Survey*, 29 June 1987, p. 195). Obviously this was not seen as a reason to extend the minimum of debtor protection required by human rights to the South, whose poor have been subject to a treatment that would be impossible in the case of any debtor within any OECD country. Quite the contrary, the IBRD's Senior Vice President, Ernest Stern, praised 'structural adjustment' as the response to a 'feasible . . .

call for increased sacrifices' by the population (see Chapter 7), which the IBRD had to back and ensure by a 'firm understanding' of monitoring.

Sacrifices indeed ensued. In 1989 UNICEF's *State of the World's Children* cited harsh 'adjustment' policies in many SCs as 'a major contributor to the misery of the poor' (quoted from Caufield, 1998, p. 162). Labelling the 1980s as the 'decade of despair', UNICEF estimated 'that at least half a million young children have died in the last twelve months a result of the slowing down or reversal of progress in the developing world' (ibid.).

Cornia et al. (1987, p. 99) found changes in purchasing habits and consumption patterns. Poor households spending 'between 60 and 80 per cent of their incomes on food, are forced, first to increase the proportion of food expenditure in total expenditure; secondly, to concentrate their food expenditure almost exclusively on calories; and thirdly, to substitute cheap for expensive source of calories'. Such substitution, however, cannot be done 'by those already consuming the cheapest nutrients, particularly in insufficient quantities' (ibid., p. 100). The UNICEF study found a 'wealth of evidence' that 'after a long series of adaptations a decline in per capita calorie intake takes place'. At one point belt tightening triggers hunger and, eventually, starvation. The resurgence of diseases leading to death had to be noted (ibid., p. 33).

SAPRIN (2002, p. 16) summarized: 'Overall, however, the greatest emphasis was placed in all the countries on the problems, dislocations and increased poverty and inequities generated by economic adjustment policies through the destruction of domestic productive capacity and through the failure to generate sufficient employment at a living wage.' Or 'as evidenced by the country assessments, the result has been an expansion and deepening of poverty and greater social exclusion' (ibid., p. 169). Arguing that the 'deterioration in health conditions among low-income groups and their inadequate access to quality education translate into an underdeveloped potential and the erosion of the capabilities of individuals and their communities to build sustainable livelihoods' the document concludes: 'These long-term human costs have been the outcome of policies premised on a distorted calculus that considers investments in the social sector as subsidies that can be eliminated, with the assumption that this would lead to greater economic growth' (ibid.). In any case, they made higher debt service payments possible.

'Setbacks on hunger nearly outweigh progress' according to the UN's *Millennium Development Goals Report 2005* – after years of anti-poverty policies implemented by creditors arbitrarily managing the sovereign debt problem as they thought fit. More than 1 billion people still subsist on not more than one dollar per day. The UN's *Millennium Development*

Goals Report 2005 (UN, 2005, p. 6) concluded: 'During the 1990s, extreme poverty dropped in much of Asia, fell slowly in Latin America, changed little in Northern Africa and Western Asia, and rose and then started to decline in the transition economies. But in sub-Saharan Africa, which already had the highest poverty rate in the world, the situation deteriorated further and millions more fell into deep poverty.' For young children, the lack of food can be perilous since it retards their physical and mental development and threatens their very survival.

The report identified progress against hunger, but slow growth of agricultural output and an expanding population, which have led to setbacks in some regions. Since 1990 millions more people are chronically hungry in sub-Saharan Africa and in Southern Asia, where half the children under age five are malnourished. In all SCs 'More than a quarter of children under age 5' are 'malnourished' (ibid., p. 6).

The average daily income of those living on less than $1 a day increased only marginally between 1990 and 2001, from $0.80 to $0.82. Given data problems and error margins one might well wonder whether such small change really signifies an improvement. The poorest of the globe in sub-Saharan Africa saw their average decline from $0.62 to $0.60 during this period. The $1 target is not unproblematic, given climatic, social and economic differences. Nevertheless, it has established itself as an internationally accepted index. It would in any case be difficult to argue that those with less than $1 per day are not extremely poor.

The *Millennium Development Goals Report 2005* (UN, 2005, p. 7) saw chronic hunger (measured in terms of the proportion of people lacking the food needed to meet their daily needs) on the decline. The percentage of people with insufficient food was lower in 2000–02 than in 1990–92 in all regions except Western Asia. However it warned that 'progress has slowed over the past several years, and the number of people going hungry increased between 1997 and 2002'. The *Millennium Development Goals Report 2006* (UN, 2006, p. 5) informed that the worst hit regions showed improvement and rates of hunger declined. However 'progress overall is not fast enough to reduce the number of people going hungry, which increased between 1995–97 and 2001–03. An estimated 82 million people in the developing world were affected by chronic hunger in 2003' (ibid.). In spite of progress made in recent years, 'the number of people going hungry is increasing' in sub-Sahran Africa and Eastern Asia. In the latter region the number of hungry people had declined in the early 1990s but is again on the rise.

Written by the BWIs, the *Global Monitoring Report 2006* (IBRD and IMF, 2006, p. xi) strikes a more positive note: 'Growth continues to be favorable and has helped cut global poverty, in some cases dramatically.'

Nevertheless it admits: 'The bad news is that many countries are off track to meet the human development MDGs.' Impressive gains on a global scale exist. But for 'every success story of rapid growth and job creation in emerging East and South Asian cities, there are disturbing examples of increased poverty in much of Sub-Saharan Africa, and among large groups of people in many other parts of the world. In too many countries, infrastructure is crumbling. Urgently needed investment to modernize water, sanitation, and transportation facilities has proven unavailable.' Apparently infrastructure – rightly called 'a critical element of the invest-ment climate' (ibid., p. xviii) – did not properly survive decades of BWI 'adjustment' and privatization. For both the rural and urban poor in many low-income countries, the gap in access to basic infrastructure is still widening. The US crisis is likely to aggravate this problem.

Infrastructure is not the only example where privatization has worked against those who are not rich. The BWIs were also the engine promot-ing private pension schemes in SCs. In Chile '40 percent of workers in the poorest income decile do not participate in the pension system' (IBRD, 2001, p. 154). But 'Even a well-structured pension system will not initially reach the poor', which is surprising, as Chile had introduced her 'new' system in 1980. The IBRD found that coverage was lowest among the poor. It pointed out that mandatory contributions to public systems might be difficult for them, failing to argue why monthly payments to private institutions should be any easier. The IBRD argued that 'social assist-ance or social pensions should cover the poorest . . . and those without family support'. Apparently the IBRD suggests reintroducing yesteryear's solution, depending on family support in old age. People living on less than the famous daily buck might not be able to pay contributions or to provide much support. Peter Heller, deputy director of the IMF, mean-while admits: 'there is now a consensus that reforms [in Chile] have not only proved costly and inadequate for contributors but have also failed to reduce costs for the government 20 years after their introduction' (*Finance & Development*, June 2006, p. 54). Without reduced costs to the budget, contributors get less. This should be no surprise as administrative costs in SCs are extraordinary, 'a key weakness of the Chilean system' according to Heller. Measured as percentages of contributions administrative charges in Latin America are normally double digit. This reduces yields and ben-efits substantially, and thus the future income of contributors. There are cases where a third of all contributions went to administrators. One may assume further public money needed to fight pension scheme caused old age poverty in the future. Pension reform is quite likely to increase old age poverty, especially in poor countries.

National investment climates rank among the 'six key actions to accelerate progress toward the MDGs' (IBRD and IMF, 2006, p. xvii). The argument that strengthening poverty reduction would require improving investment climates is not wrong. The IBRD's indicators are, however, debatable. The reforms these indicators encourage are more likely to increase than reduce poverty. To give examples: lower minimum wages for first-time employees, no restrictions on night and weekend work, a work week of 50 hours or more, no paid annual vacation or not more than 21 working days per year, quick and easy firing (without undue social frills such as the need to offer retraining options before redundancy termination), no advance notice requirements (called 'firing cost' by the IBRD, although no real costs are caused if notice is given early enough so that workers work fully and normally until leaving), no severance payments, reducing (gross) wages by cutting social security payments (including for retirement fund; sickness, maternity and health insurance; *workplace injury* or family allowance) wrongly and misleadingly called 'nonwage labour costs' (IBRD and IFC, 2006). All this improves the investment climate. Any Manchester capitalist and contemporary of Adam Smith would do very well by these requirements. This methodology induces governments wishing to get good marks from the IBRD to change their laws accordingly.

On 13 October 2006 six US Senators wrote a letter to the IBRD's president, expressing their concern that 'this year's edition appears to discourage countries from upholding established standards of workers' rights as set by the International Labor Organization (ILO)'. Arguing that 'Rewarding lax or non-existent labor standards contradicts ILO policy', the letter recalls that 'the U.S. government also encourages trading partners to abide by these principles', such as minimum wage and working hours laws or freedom of association. The State Department evaluates laws on minimum wages and working hours in preparing its annual report on country human rights practices. Giving concrete examples of violations of the ILO's Fundamental Principles and the reduction or abolition of laws protecting workers, the six Senators conclude: 'The mission of the World Bank is to alleviate poverty. We fail to see how praising countries for failing to guarantee minimum wages and overtime pay lifts people out of poverty. We do not think that discouraging adherence to ILO standards . . . is appropriate or constructive.' One may also wonder whether it works in the purely technocratic sense that lowering prices (= wages) increases demand (= employment). The fallacy of composition that produced disastrous results in the case of commodities might well strike again. If many or all countries lower wage costs, no country gains further competitive advantages, but poverty may increase globally due to lower wages.

In line with the trickle-down theory the BWIs argue: 'More rapid growth is likely to have reduced poverty between 2000 and 2005 significantly – simple projections based on aggregate income growth suggest by as much as 10 percent, or over 100 million people' (IBRD and IMF, 2006, p. 2). Without specifically quoting any, the *Global Monitoring Report 2006* mentions surveys revealing that 'in many countries the poor are more than proportionately sharing in' the progress in human development outcomes (ibid., p. xviii). However whether per capita growth actually reduces poverty remains to be seen. Wisely the report cautions in a footnote: 'These projections come with several caveats. First, they are based on preliminary 2005 estimates of population and national-accounts GDP growth, as well as estimates of income distribution, all of which may be subject to considerable revision' (ibid., p. 43). Also for some 'countries the latest available household data are from 2002'. Considering the 'precision' of BWI estimates of debt sustainability, these estimates of benefits to the poor might just be another example of excessive optimism. Rightly the report's footnote warns: 'All of these caveats mean that the actual poverty estimates for 2005, when they become available, may differ substantially from these projections.'

Caveats notwithstanding, the BWIs think it 'possible to "project" the evolution of poverty through 2005 by combining the most recent household survey data available with data on growth rates of real per capita incomes and assumptions about income distribution. These projections should not be regarded as estimates, but they give some idea of how recent rapid income growth may have translated into lower poverty.' Thus the report mainly argues that growth has picked up, predicting that the 'developing world as a whole' will 'meet the poverty MDG'. It stresses that the 'reduction in the global poverty rate owes the most to impressive advances in China and India' (ibid., p. 21).

Even before the US crisis there was good reason to doubt the optimism of the BWIs. While average incomes in SCs 'have been growing far more strongly since 1990' (UNDP, 2005, p. 18), this growth 'has not put the world on track for the MDGs – most of which will be missed in most countries', because growth was 'unequally distributed between and within countries'. The *Human Development Report 2005* is even more concerned that 'increased wealth is not being converted into human development at the rate required to bring the MDGs within reach'. Human development in some key areas diverges, with inequalities widening. Gaps between rich and poor countries are widening.

The UNDP (2005, p. 68) illustrates the statistically well-known point that high growth rates and increasing inequalities may combine with the example of the UK. In 1998 one out of three children lived below the poverty line, double as many as at the end of the 1970s, one of the highest rates in Europe. The distinctly pro-rich pattern of the 1980s, Thatcherite neoliberalism cutting taxes for higher earners and lowering benefits for the poor, had increased the share of the richest decile from 21 per cent of disposable income to 28 per cent 20 years later – nearly as much as 'the entire bottom half of the population'. Average annual incomes for the richest 20 per cent increased at about ten times the rate for the poorest 20 per cent: the UK's Gini coefficient experienced 'one of the biggest increases in inequality'. There is no reason to assume that growth and immizerization are excluded in debtor countries forced to implement the neoliberal Washington Consensus.

Regarding sub-Saharan Africa the UNDP (2005, p.66) warns of the danger that current growth patterns would leave the poor behind, also by illustrating the importance of income distribution. Tanzania's success in raising overall growth 'has had a negligible impact on poverty rates . . . poverty has been falling far too slowly to achieve the MDGs'. With 1 per cent per capita growth and current distribution patterns, Kenya would not halve poverty until 2030. Redistributing from growth, doubling the share of the poor in future growth, Kenya would halve poverty by 2013 at the same 1 per cent per capita growth rate, meeting the MDG target. With high inequality, much higher growth is needed. The smaller the share of the poor of any increment to income, the less efficient growth is as a mechanism for poverty reduction.

Although relying strongly on average growth rates as the means to justify its optimism, the *Global Monitoring Report 2006* (IBRD and IMF, 2006, p.26) also draws attention to sub-national regions, such as Brazil's northeast or Turkey's Anatolia 'where income and social indicators severely lag national levels', to insufficient growth in Latin America and especially in Africa to make strong inroads into poverty reduction. Only 34 of 143 countries are believed to be on track regarding the proportion of people suffering from hunger, as measured by the percentage of children under five who are underweight (ibid., p.68). In a number of African countries 'nutrition outcomes are worsening, reflecting the nexus between HIV and undernutrition'. Nevertheless, the BWIs also see 'tangible evidence' of 'significant progress' emerging 'in some countries . . . in human development outcomes since the late 1990s' (ibid., p.xviii).

For the the 29 HIPCs that reached the decision point by March 2006 'poverty-reducing expenditures on average have risen from about 6 percent of GDP in 1999 to 9 percent of GDP in 2005, a level more than four times that spent on debt service' (ibid., p.87). One may thus hope that some of the impacts of earlier debt management may be eventually reversed. Undeniably the idea of debtor protection is gaining ground. Unfortunately the 'Impact of Debt Relief after Ten Years of Implementation' on the ground remains less visible than might be wished: 'Although data is limited, debt relief appears to have helped post-completion-point HIPCs advance toward achieving the MDGs. HIPCs have made progress in improving gender equality and reducing child mortality, and have taken some steps in encouraging primary education and ensuring environmental sustainability. However, no measurable changes have been achieved in combating poverty and infectious diseases and in improving maternal health (where data is very limited)' (IDA and IMF, 2006, p. 16).

Pettifor and Greenhill (2002, p. 27, emphasis in original) point out that 'Average life expectancy in Africa has *fallen* since 1980, from 48 to 47 – and in individual countries, the fall is much more extreme.' They mention Zambia, where life expectancy fell from 50 years (1980) to 38 years, or Sierra Leone with a life expectancy of only 37 years. Naturally AIDS currently raging in Africa is one important reason. While AIDS is not necessarily connected to debt pressure, financing measures against AIDS or subsidies for necessary drugs are likely to suffer if there is a debt overhang.

In terms of financing, Goal 1 is the most expensive MDG. Pettifor and Greenhill (2002, p. 22) estimated that the bill for eradicating mass poverty in 39 HIPCs would be approximately $45.7 billion, 27.2 per cent of their combined GDP or 514 per cent of their debt service at that time. All other goals whose costs they could quantify (gender equality and empowering women were, for example, not quantified) were estimated to cost roughly $30.6 billion.

ACHIEVE UNIVERSAL PRIMARY EDUCATION

In 2000 one in three children across the developing world did not complete the five years of basic education which UNICEF believes is the minimum required to achieve basic literacy (ibid., p. 26). This has to be seen with the background of BWI imposed austerity policies in mind.

Caufield (1998, p. 142) found falling school enrolment throughout SCs, a result reflected by many sources. Cornia et al. (1987, pp. 33–4) presented evidence of a decline in literacy and educational attainments. Nigeria's Bendel State might be an extreme illustration, where primary school enrolment fell from 90 per cent to 60 per cent within 18 months. It seems plausible that an increasing number of people having to live on $1 or $2 per day cannot spare money for tuition fees. The dismissal of 7000 teachers in Zaire for budgetary reasons did not promise improvement either. In all countries studied SAPRIN (2002, p. 157) found that the introduction of user fees under cost-recovery and revenue-generation schemes had put serious constraints on access by the poor to education and health care services: 'With children being pulled out of school . . . to help support their families, the primary-school dropout rate had reached 40 percent.' Or 'School dropout rates have risen in most of the countries, particularly among girls, where user fees have been charged' (ibid., p. 184).

The UN (2005, p. 10) reported that 'more than 115 million children of primary school age' were 'out of school . . ... These are mostly children from poor households, whose mothers often have no formal education either.' Between 1990–91 and 2001–02 the net enrollment ratio in primary education increased from 80 to 83. Progress occurred unevenly. Although progress was made in sub-Saharan Africa, this region still has over a third of its children out of school. In five African countries less than half the children of primary school age were enrolled. In Mali, for instance, almost none of the 61 per cent of children out of school have ever attended school consistently.

Enrolment, however, is a necessary but not a sufficient condition for achieving universal primary education. In sub-Saharan Africa just over half the children reach the final grade (UN, 2005, p. 12).

Unsurprisingly and correctly, the UN Millennium Project's list of remedies that could be implemented quickly, dubbed 'Quick Wins', recommends: 'Eliminating school and uniform fees to ensure that all children, especially girls, are not out of school because of their families' poverty. Lost revenues should be replaced with more equitable and efficient sources of finance, including donor assistance.' In plain English this means undoing the 'reforms' debt management had introduced in debt-distressed countries.

Vandemoortele and Roy (2005, p. 49) use this MDG to illustrate the general problem of cost estimates. For Uganda, several cost estimates exist for achieving universal primary education. The authors quote four studies by UNICEF, the UNDP, the IBRD and the UN Millennium Project. Although all studies are based on plausible (but different) assumptions, such as pupil:teacher ratios, the proportion of the budget for teaching materials, or teachers' salaries, 'unit costs for one year of primary education in Uganda' differ by 'a staggering factor of 5:1'. They conclude from this example that caveats about the reliability of estimates are absolutely necessary.

With this caveat in mind, one may well quote one further estimate of the costs of ensuring basic literacy for every child within the HIPC group:

Our calculations showed that the HIPC countries will only need to spend $6.5bn each year in order to ensure that every child gets an education sufficient to ensure basic literacy. While large relative to the incomes of HIPCs, on a global scale this figure is miniscule – representing, for example, less than half of one percent of the projected US defence budget of $1,600bn over the next five years. And only $1.2bn of this is additional to what governments are currently spending. (Pettifor and Greenhill, 2002, p. 26)

REDUCE CHILD MORTALITY AND IMPROVE MATERNAL HEALTH

According to the UN (2005, p. 18) 'every year, almost 11 million children die – that is, 30 000 children a day – before their fifth birthday. Most of these children live in developing countries and die from a disease or a combination of diseases that can be prevented or treated by existing inexpensive means.' The cause may be as simple as no access to antibiotics for treating pneumonia or no oral rehydration salts for diarrhoea. Child mortality is closely linked to poverty and to the quality of health services accessible to the poor, safe water and proper sanitation. Malnutrition contributes to over half these deaths. As the UN's *Millennium Development Goals Report 2005* points out, five diseases (pneumonia, diarrhoea, malaria, measles and AIDS) account for half of all deaths in children under the age of five. Most of these lives could be saved by expanding low-cost prevention and treatment measures. Measles is the leading cause of child deaths. A safe, effective and relatively inexpensive vaccine has been available for over 40 years. Still, measles strikes 30 million children a year, killing 540 000 in 2002 and leaving many others blind or deaf.

Tipping et al. (2005, p. 187) show the connection between rapid urbanization, poverty and child mortality: 'child mortality is higher in cities where the poor have less access to water; a slum penalty'. African cities combine the highest child mortality rates with the lowest levels of access to water.

According to the UN (2005) almost half of all deaths among children under the age of five occur in sub-Saharan Africa, where progress has slowed owing to weak health systems, conflicts and AIDS, and more than one third occur in Southern Asia (Indian sub-continent plus Afghanistan and Iran), despite reduced poverty. Pettifor and Greenhill (2002, p. 10) found six HIPCs to be slipping behind on reducing infant mortality. The UNDP (2005, p. 19) had to conclude 'Progress in reducing child mortality, one of the most basic of human development indicators, is slowing, and the child death gap between rich and poor countries is widening.'

SAPRIN (2002, p. 165, emphasis in orginal) found that '*Drastic government cuts in health-care spending have affected maternal-health services, a factor of pivotal importance for the welfare of children.*' It documented the case of Zimbabwe:

Table 8.1   Infant and child mortality in Zimbabwe (1978–97)

	Infant Mortality Rate			Child Mortality Rate		
	Rural	Urban	Total	Rural	Urban	Total
1978	88	64	83	40	25	57
1981	85	59	79	38	22	34
1984	77	50	69	33	17	28
1986	72	47	64	30	15	25
1988	69	46	61	28	15	23
1990	71	55	66	30	20	26
1997	89	63	80	N/A	N/A	36

Source: SAPRIN (2002).

In 1998, high levels of wasting and stunting in children under five were found, particularly in rural areas, a situation that had worsened since the 1980s. At the same time, infant- and child-mortality rates have been increasing after having shown a steady improvement prior to the implementation of adjustment policies. Several district hospitals and government clinics have been closed since 1995, and there has been a decline in pre-natal services and in immunization coverage. (SAPRIN, 2002, p. 162)

During the period 1978–97 Zimbabwe's infant mortality rate (per 1000 live births) nearly described a perfect U, as Table 8.1 shows (ibid., p. 163). Obviously advances reached before were annihilated by debt management. The child mortality rate increased again as well as an effect of 'structural adjustment' without, however, virtually reaching the value of 1978.

Quoting evidence on the impact of user fees, SAPRIN (2002, p. 158, emphasis in original) illustrated this point with an example: 'With the *establishment of user fees for health care* in **Zimbabwe**, cost increases for patients were dramatic, in some cases exceeding 1,000 percent. This has had a *serious negative impact on the utilization of health-care services* in both rural and urban areas, particularly for the poor.' According to the Zimbabwe study, '. . . immediately after fees were raised in 1991 and again in 1993/94, declines were noted in outpatient and prenatal care sought, prescriptions dispensed, admissions, and X ray, lab and dental services. Most people sought early discharge or absconded to save money.' Such drastic cost increases drive the poor away from health care in general and from services ensuring better health of newborns and their mothers. SAPRIN (2002, p. 162) documented a connection between 'adjustment' and maternal mortality: 'Twice as many women were found to be dying in childbirth in Harare hospitals in 1993 than before 1990.' Understandably the UN Millennium's 'Quick Wins' list requests: 'Eliminating user fees for basic health services in all developing countries, financed by increased domestic and donor resources for health.'

Pettifor and Greenhill (2002, p. 27) warn: 'In Africa, 161 children out of every 1,000 children will die before their fifth birthday; in Niger, this figure is as high as one in four.' Meanwhile Niger joined the Education for All Fast-Track Initiative, achieving impressive improvements (IBRD and IMF, 2006, p. 49). Quite visible financial support from without must be noted: 'Official development assistance (ODA) to Niger has tripled [sic], from about $10 million to $39 million per year' (ibid.) between 2002 and 2005. Pettifor and Greenhill (2002) point out that the Global Commission on Macroeconomics and Health had estimated that each year 8 million lives could be spared if a simple set of health interventions needed to meet the MDGs were put in place. This Commission recommended that, if the MDGs were to be met, the least developed countries will need to spend an average of $41 per capita each year, while other low-income countries would need to spend $37 per capita. The authors compare the $20 billion each year that would have to be spent on health if 39 HIPCs were to meet the MDGs – almost three times their 1999 levels of debt service – with the $17 billion spent each year in Europe and the USA on pet food.

In 2000 the average risk of dying during pregnancy or childbirth in SCs was 450 per 100 000 live births. For more than half a million women each year, pregnancy and childbirth end in death. Twenty times as many women suffer serious injuries or disabilities, which, if untreated, can cause lifelong pain and humiliation (UN, 2005, p. 22). With the lone exception of Afghanistan, very high maternal mortality ratios – defined as more than 550 deaths per 100 000 live births in the year 2000 – were concentrated in sub-Saharan Africa. In countries where women tend to have many children, they face this risk as many times. Avoiding unwanted pregnancies can thus immediately reduce the death toll. The chances of dying during pregnancy or childbirth over a lifetime are as high as 1 in 16 in sub-Saharan Africa, compared with 1 in 3800 in the developed world.

Unfortunately the UN (2005, p. 23) had to report: 'An analysis of the limited data available suggests that significant reductions in the number of deaths have occurred in countries with moderate to low levels of maternal mortality. Evidence of similar progress was not found in countries where pregnancy and childbirth are most risky.' The poorest are once again more afflicted than others. Not only in poor debtor countries, as comparing the infant mortality rate for African-American children in Washington DC with that of Kerala proves.

There were examples as well, where poor countries could improve their rates considerably – the report names Bangladesh and Egypt. Bangladesh was able substantially to reduce maternal mortality by focusing on skilled birth attendants, access to emergency obstetric care and expanded family planning programmes. In Egypt maternal mortality was cut in half in only eight years due to a comprehensive programme to boost the quality of medical care, especially the management of obstetric complications, and to ensure skilled attendants at births. Community support for women during pregnancy and childbirth was mobilized too, and reproductive health needs, including family planning, were addressed (ibid.). Unfortunately information on family planning may be hindered by social or religious opposition, including opposition by donors.

9. Debt distress, global public goods and a global development partnership

This chapter focuses on those MDGs having the character of global public goods (GPGs). Obviously this is a classification that can be discussed because activities such as curing people from malaria can also be seen as anti-poverty measures. Those needing help, especially financial assistance, are usually not the well heeled. One could also argue that alphabetizing the poor, assuring increased access to safe drinking water or improving the lives of slum dwellers may be subsumed under anti-poverty agenda. On the other hand, diseases spread, which means that there can be substantial externalities. Items nowadays understood as GPGs have been financed by ODA over decades (see Chapter 14; Raffer, 1999). Indicator 35 of MDG 8 encourages further increase of these flows.

The Goals discussed in detail in this chapter are 3, 6, 7 and 8:

Goal 3   Promote gender equality and empower women.
Target 4   Eliminate gender disparity in primary and secondary education preferably by 2005, and at all levels by 2015.
Indicators:

9. Ratio of girls to boys in primary, secondary and tertiary education.
10. Ratio of literate women to men 15–24 years old.
11. Share of women in wage employment in the non-agricultural sector.
12. Proportion of seats held by women in national parliaments.

Goal 6   Combat HIV/AIDS, malaria and other diseases.
Target 7   Halt and begin to reverse the spread of HIV/AIDS.
Indicators:

18. HIV prevalence among 15–24 year-old pregnant women.
19. Condom use rate of the contraceptive prevalence rate and population aged 15–24 years with comprehensive correct knowledge of HIV/AIDS.

20. Ratio of school attendance of orphans to school attendance of non-orphans aged 10–14 years.

Target 8   Halt and begin to reverse the incidence of malaria and other major diseases.
Indicators:

21. Prevalence and death rates associated with malaria.
22. Proportion of population in malaria risk areas using effective malaria prevention and treatment measures.
23. Prevalence and death rates associated with tuberculosis.
24. Proportion of tuberculosis cases detected and cured under directly observed treatment short courses.

Goal 7   Ensure environmental sustainability.
Target 9   Integrate the principles of sustainable development into country policies and programmes; reverse loss of environmental resources.
Indicators:

25. Forested land as percentage of land area.
26. Ratio of area protected to maintain biological diversity to surface area.
27. Energy supply (apparent consumption; Kg oil equivalent) per $1000 (PPP) GDP.
28. Carbon dioxide emissions (per capita) and consumption of ozone-depleting CFCs.

Target 10   Reduce by half the proportion of people without sustainable access to safe drinking water.
Indicators:

30. Proportion of the population with sustainable access to and improved water source.
31. Proportion of the population with access to improved sanitation.

Target 11   Achieve significant improvement in lives of at least 100 million slum dwellers, by 2020.
Indicator:

32. Slum population as percentage of urban population (secure tenure index).

Goal 8   Develop a global partnership for development.
Target 12 Develop further an open, rule-based, predictable, non-discriminatory trading and financial system which includes a commitment to good governance, development and poverty reduction – both nationally and internationally.
Target 13   Address the special needs of the least developed countries. Includes: tariff and quota free access for least developed countries' exports; enhanced programme of debt relief for HIPCs and cancellation of official bilateral debt; and more generous ODA for countries committed to poverty reduction.
Target 14   Address the special needs of landlocked countries and small island developing states.
Target 15   Deal comprehensively with the debt problems of developing countries through national and international measures in order to make debt sustainable in the long term.
Target 16   In cooperation with developing countries, develop and implement strategies for decent and productive work for youth.
Target 17   In cooperation with pharmaceutical companies, provide access to affordable essential drugs in developing countries.
Target 18   In cooperation with the private sector, make available the benefits of new technologies, especially information and communications.

Official development assistance

32. Net ODA as percentage of OECD/DAC donors' gross national product (targets of 0.7 per cent in total and 0.15 per cent for least developed countries.
33. Proportion of ODA basic social services (basic education, primary health care, nutrition, safe water and sanitation).
34. Proportion of ODA that is untied.
35. Proportion of ODA for environment in small island developing states.
36. Proportion of ODA for transport sector in landlocked countries.

Market access

37. Proportion of exports (by value and excluding arms) admitted free of duties and quotas.
38. Average tariffs and quotas on agricultural products and textiles and clothing.
39. Domestic and export agricultural subsidies in OECD countries.
40. Proportion of ODA provided to help build trade capacity.

Debt sustainability

41. Proportion of official bilateral HIPC debt cancelled.
42. Total number of countries that have reached their HIPC decision points and number that have reached their completion points (cumulative) (HIPC).
43. Debt Service as a percentage of exports of goods and services.
44. Debt relief committed under HIPC Initiative (HIPC).
45. Unemployment of 15–24 year-olds, each sex and total.
46. Proportion of population with access to affordable, essential drugs on a sustainable basis.
47. Telephone lines and cellular subscribers per 100 population.
48. Personal computers in use and internet users per 100 population.

PROMOTING GENDER EQUALITY AND EMPOWERING WOMEN

As SAPRIN (2002, p. 53, emphasis in original) showed, 'structural adjustment' was not gender blind at all: *'Trade liberalization has also had a gender bias.* The study in *Zimbabwe* found that *women have been the main victims of retrenchments* in the formal sector.' SAPRI's country studies indicated that BWI reforms had substantially different impacts on men and women. Unfortunately gender inequality had already existed before the founding of the BWIs. But the BWIs' policies have deteriorated these inequalities. School fees, for example, increased drop-out rates in general; girls have often been particularly affected. This exacerbated a disturbing gender gap that increases at higher levels of education. To some extent MDG 3 thus only attempts to restore what had been destroyed by 'debt management'.

The UN Millennium Project's 'Quick Wins' advice sheet demands 'Empowering women to play a central role in formulating and monitoring MDG-based poverty reduction strategies and other critical policy reform processes, particularly at the level of local governments.' This would indeed trigger quick and substantial improvements because women can be expected to have a different perspective of how to fight poverty, not least because they are likely to detect gender inequality more readily. This impact would be strengthened by implementing another 'Quick Win', reforming and enforcing legislation guaranteeing women property and inheritance rights.

Donor support for this MDG may not always be forthcoming as readily as official declarations on gender policies. Regarding the education target the UNDP (2005, p. 107) stated: 'Some countries that are farthest off track for the MDG targets of universal completion and gender equity do not receive adequate funds.'

COMBATING HIV/AIDS, MALARIA AND OTHER DISEASES

Speaking of 'The feminization of HIV/AIDS in Sub-Saharan Africa', the UNDP (2006, p. 266) logically connects the two MDGs. SAPRIN (2002, p.163) showed how consultation and admission fees restricted access to hospitals and health care. The document speaks of a 'lack of concern shown by many, including the World Bank, with regard to the spread of the disease [AIDS] in sub-Saharan Africa during the 1980s' (ibid., p. 74).

According to IBRD and IMF (2006, p. 53) 'Both the number of people living with HIV (40.3 million) and deaths from AIDS continued to increase in 2005.' While 'no region has yet achieved a declining rate of new infections, recent data suggest that a few countries have begun to do so', also because of determined government action. The report sees the first signs of decline in HIV/AIDS infection rates emerging in high-prevalence countries such as Haiti and Uganda, as well as Zimbabwe, a country whose situation had been particularly desperate according to SAPRIN. The BWIs were able to report first examples of success. Unfortunately efficient protection techniques, such as high levels of condom use mentioned in the report, frequently meet opposition on traditional or religious grounds, not least in the case of some donors. Disadvantages compound. The *Human Development Report 2006* (p.23) observes 'Inadequate access to water and sanitation restricts opportunities for hygiene and exposes people with HIV/AIDS to increased risks of infection.'

AIDS is not the only killer. Diseases such as malaria, TB, childhood infectious diseases, maternal and prenatal conditions and micronutrient deficiencies abound. Malaria claims some 1.3 million lives a year, 90 per cent of them children under the age of five. Five times as many children die of diarrhoea as of HIV/AIDS according to the *Human Development Report 2006*. Piped water inside houses may lower the incidence of diarrhoea substantially, a reduction of almost 70 per cent is quoted in Ghana. Flush toilets may reduce risk by double-digit percentages. Both piped water and flush toilets are more common in rich than in poor households.

The *Global Monitoring Report* (IBRD and IMF, 2006, p.45) reports: 'Insecticide-treated bed nets (ITNs) are being distributed on a larger scale than ever, and national malaria strategies are getting funding and visibility.' It sees accumulating evidence that ITNs can reduce malaria deaths.

Pettifor and Greenhill (2002, p.27) quoted an estimate by the Global

Commission on Macroeconomics and Health that a simple set of health interventions needed to meet the MDGs could save 8 million lives. Although corruption, mismanagement and a weak public sector are also reasons why these interventions do not reach the poor, the Commission states 'in the vast majority of countries, there is a more basic and remediable problem', namely the fact that the 'poor lack the financial resources to obtain coverage of these essential interventions, as do their governments' (ibid.).

Briefly at least a perceptible part of the problem again boils down to the effects of debt pressure and BWI-enforced reforms that have cut social expenditures and 'slimmed down' governments pursuant to the neoliberal paradigm, thus diminishing their options to intervene. Impoverishment of the poorest caused by BWI policies is another contributing factor. ODA time series would rather not confirm that lack of money really is a remediable problem.

ENSURING ENVIRONMENTAL SUSTAINABILITY

Some aid and part of the money flowing liberally to SCs during the 1970s have financed projects causing ecological catastrophes, such as dams for which huge forest areas were cut down. SC governments, too, have not always acted with environment preservation as their main concern.

The need to repay creditors after 1982 led to considerable ecological damages because of increased exports and severe budget cuts affecting environmental protection. Sometimes it was even argued that SCs should engage in heavily polluting activities because they supposedly enjoy a 'comparative advantage' for polluting industries. Quite famous was a leaked memo by the IBRD's chief economist suggesting that health-impairing pollution should be done in low-wage SCs where compensation for health and lives lost would be cheaper, which was published by *The Economist* (15 February 1992). One may hope that this MDG can bring around fundamental changes of thinking in debtor and creditor countries, as well as within some multilateral organizations.

Interestingly the indicators 30 and 31 (sustainable access to water, access to improved sanitation, respectively) are subsumed under ensuring environmental sustainability in spite of their outstanding importance for disease prevention. Hundreds of millions of urban poor in SCs currently live in unsafe and unhygienic environments, facing multiple threats to their health. However they also pollute the environment. On the other hand, one may interpret this multidimensionality of indicators as a sign of how well and cohesively MDGs were chosen. This sector may serve to illustrate the issues of MDG 7.

The important water and sanitation problem is widely neglected according to the UNDP (2006, p. 62): 'National poverty reduction agendas reflect the pervasive benign neglect of water and sanitation. The sector seldom figures with any prominence in Poverty Reduction Strategy Papers (PRSPs) – the documents that set out national plans and define the terms of cooperation between donors and aid recipients.'

With exceptions obviously confirming the rule (the UNDP singles out Uganda as the case successfully integrating water and sanitation into the PRSP), this sector is normally 'treated dismissively, receiving little more than a few descriptive paragraphs and broad declarations of principle without even a semblance of a strategic reform agenda or financing provisions. The weakness of PRSPs reflect in turn the limited donor interest in water and sanitation.' Budget allocations reinforce this picture, although high social and economic returns from investments in water and sanitation suggest that they ought to be a priority. Improvements in this sector generate wider public goods, such as enhanced gender equity and reduced inequalities in opportunity.

Under the heading 'The poor pay more – and more than they can afford' the UNDP (2006, p. 51) sums up: 'Most are already paying far more than they can afford to pay to meet their basic water needs in water markets that reinforce their poverty.' Water pricing reflects a simple perverse principle: the poorer you are, the more you pay. In Uganda water payments represent as much as 22 per cent of the average income of urban households in the poorest 20 per cent of the income distribution. In Latin America the *Human Development Report 2006* finds that the poorest quintile in several countries spend over 10 per cent of their expenditures on water: 'About half of these households live below the $1 a day threshold for extreme poverty' (ibid.). The UNDP recalls that UK regulatory authorities define any expenditure on water above 3 per cent of total household spending as an indicator of hardship.

The *Human Development Report 2006* sees some encouraging developments in budgets for water and sanitation in recent years, including that spending in 2005–06 was a third higher than in 2002–03. As most of these resources came from national budgets, this evolution does not reflect increased donor interest. State spending is often constrained by large fiscal deficits, also brought about by debt service. Thus the UNDP fears about the sustainability of this trend. The Millennium Campaign, a UN initiative, puts this into perspective: just $5 billion (less than 10 per cent of present ODA, which is itself less than half the promised 0.7 per cent) could 'help give everyone in the world access to safe water and sanitation', while the EU gives $86.8 billion a year to its farmers in subsidies to produce food, including surpluses to be exported at highly subsidized prices. Or the average cow in the EU receives more than $2 per day in subsidies – compared with over 3 billion people in SCs having to survive on less.

Privatization – usually under BWI pressure – was one of the main demands under debt management. A creditor-created rush to sell off public assets made the public interest suffer during and because of privatization. One wonders whether one reason for the neglect of this sector may be the emphasis that official creditors put on privatizing water supply and public utilities in debtor countries.

Privatization often led to reduced access to water, especially for the poor. In Cochabamba (Bolivia) customers not only had to pay more after privatization, but peasants who had previously used free water from public standpipes suddenly had to pay. In any European country using water freely for a sufficiently long period of time would have created a right that could be defended successfully in courts. Obviously in the case of poor peasants in Bolivia that was not an option scrutinized. During the bidding process in Buenos Aires the consortium had indicated the intention to cut tariffs by 29 per cent. In fact, prices were increased six times between 1993 and 2002 after one reduction at first, eventually almost doubling water prices in real terms. The consortium borrowed heavily outside the country, but made no provisions for exchange rate risk, a clear proof of private rationality praised by neoliberals. Such provisions reduce profits available for immediate distribution to shareholders.

Meanwhile political resistance and grave errors by private investors (especially not realizing that borrowing in dollars and cashing fees in pesos might pose those risks textbooks elaborate on) have cooled down investors' appetite. Whether privatization was good business or not depends on the concrete case. For a decade, privatized companies in the UK made profits well in excess of predictions. Dividends were well above average stock market returns. This drained an undervalued asset of scarce capital resources needed for development according to the UNDP (2006, p.92), also pointing out: 'serious problems remain as a result of inadequate investment and high levels of water losses'. The US Environmental Protection Agency estimates that $68 billion will be needed over the next two decades just to restore and maintain existing water utility assets in major US cities.

This might be bad for the country but is definitely good for investors in search of a quick buck (or rather quick quid in Britain), and can be observed in the cases of other privatized activities as well, such as railways or electricity grids. Quite justifiably, private investors want to make money, not to provide water to the thirsty. Business must not be confused with charity. Therefore the will and ability to deliver universal coverage must be doubted, not least in order to be fair to them as well by not demanding what they cannot and need not deliver. The UNDP (2006, p. 93) concludes that if increasing access by the poor had not been 'hugely underestimated . . . public finance and subsidized connections would have figured more prominently'. One may assume public money to be welcome to repair damages done by privatization.

While weaknesses of public providers in many countries are an undeniable fact overly exploited to justify privatization, public success stories have received less publicity. In Brazil, whose water sector is often presented as a model, 25 of 27 state capitals are served by public companies, only two by partially privatized ones. Some public utilities – Porto Alegre in Brazil is an outstanding example – have succeeded in making water affordable and accessible to all. In Porto Alegre utility reform produced gains in efficiency and democratic accountability. Public utilities in Singapore lose less water than private utilities in the UK. Unlike public incompetence, such examples do not support neoliberal and BWI ideology praising privatization.

Fortunately even donor governments have finally opposed conditionality demanding privatization. A report written for Norway's Ministry of Foreign Affairs in preparation for the Oslo Conditionality Conference in 2006 (Bull et al., 2006) sums up the faults of forced privatization. As there have been rarely more than two bidders, public property was usually sold at a discount, and at terms involving major market privileges. The problem of few bidders

> is aggravated by the fact that private firms often have considerably more bargaining power, clout and expertise than their counterparts on the government side. A highly unfortunate situation is found when the World Bank takes an active role on the side of the private firm in such negotiations. Uganda is one country where this seems to have happened, both in the water and in the power sector. This has had nearly disastrous consequences for the power situation in Uganda. (Bull et al., p. 25)

The poor may have to pay higher prices for the same service. As low paying customers they may lose the service. Poorer groups often have to bear a proportionally higher cost of reforms. 'In some cases privatization related conditions appear to have led to rushed privatizations, for governments to get access to aid funds. The time constraints inherent in conditionalities may cut the privatization processes short, for instance by bypassing the establishment of sound regulatory bodies' (ibid., p. 26). Among the infrastructure sectors, the report singled out water supply as the comparatively least successful experiments with private participation. The financial consequences of such failures are to be borne by the poor, not by 'donors'. And they reduce the amount of resources available to debtor governments.

The new Norwegian government firmly opposes undue conditionality regarding privatization, thus economically unfounded links between debt relief and policy actions. In 2006 Britain froze her contribution to protest the conditions the IBRD places on disbursements, but lifted this freeze again in December.

PARTNERS IN DEVELOPMENT?

MDG 8 differs fundamentally from all other Goals. Arguably it is the most important because changes in the global economic framework are necessary to safeguard the financing of MDGs. MDG 8 aims at levelling a playing field too heavily tilted against SCs. Unfortunately the record of North-South relations suggests that this will be most difficult to achieve. The North is much more prepared to 'grant charity' to the 'deserving poor' (while being stern to all those the North considers poor but not deserving) than to accept equal rights and equal treatments of SCs. The record of the never-ending debt crisis proves this clearly.

It has already been pointed out that many demands formulated by SCs as part of the NIEO resurface now in MDG 8. Similarly, addressing the special needs of landlocked and island countries was an important element of the Lomé I Treaty between the EU (then the EEC) and the ACP group of SCs from Africa, the Caribbean and the Pacific. The first target of MDG 8, a rule-based, non-discriminatory trading and financial system, is the very cornerstone of sustainable development efforts. Unfortunately the present system does not satisfy this demand.

The present global economic framework is heavily biased against SCs as the Pearson report already showed (Pearson et al., 1969; see Chapter 1). One has to concur with its finding that structural inequalities and the resource gaps they cause are one important reason for debt crises.

To document these inequalities one may even use OECD sources. Thus the OECD (2000, p. 31) refers to a study according to which 'rich countries' average tariffs on manufactured imports from poor countries are four times higher than those on imports from other developed countries'. Tariff escalation hinders Southern exports: 'OECD tariffs on finished industrial products are about eight times higher than on raw materials . . . . These barriers delay entry into the export-oriented industries, which are most accessible to developing countries – namely commodity processing, light manufactures, and textiles and clothing' (ibid., pp. 31–2). The OECD also mentions the pivotal role of agriculture in development and the damaging effects of Northern agrarian policies that 'impair the role of agriculture as an engine for . . . overall growth'. Non-tariff measures, certain 'behind-the-border' regulations and practices greatly impede trade. The effective US import duty for countries like Viet Nam and Bangladesh is some ten times higher than for most EU countries as the *Human Development Report 2005* (UNDP, 2005, p. 127) points out. In plain English: while creditor countries have demanded full and later on unduly high repayment, these very same creditors have restricted their debtors' earning capacity. While such unfair practices would immediately be stopped within any civilized legal system, this is routine when it comes to SCs.

The debt crisis and the catastrophes caused by 'debt management' – reflected, for instance, by the expression 'lost decade' for the 1980s – have set back development substantially. More important, debtor countries have come under tight control of IFIs and donors that have been able to dictate these countries' policies. The results are anything but encouraging.

It is of course difficult to put a price tag on the disadvantages of SCs under the present framework. Any estimates are liable to be very rough and open to criticism. Thus they have to be taken with a pinch of salt. With this caveat one might quote the *Human Development Report 1992* (UNDP, 1992, p. 67) according to which SCs lost $500 billion in 1990. More recently the Millennium Campaign quotes UN estimates that unfair trade rules deny poor countries $700 billion every year.

Regarding the costs of tied aid, the *Human Development Report 2005* (UNDP, 2005, p. 103) estimated for SCs as a group 'overall current losses at $5–$7 billion – enough to finance universal primary education. Low-income countries as a group lose $2.6–$4.0 billion, Sub-Saharan Africa loses $1.6–$2.3 billion, and the least developed countries lose $1.5–$2.3 billion.' Covering only bilateral aid and excluding technical assistance, the UNDP believes these figures understate real costs by a considerable margin. The *Human Development Report 2005* called the costs of tying, which it believes not to encompass all effects, an 'aid tax'. It concludes: 'Some forms of tied aid fly in the face of a serious commitment to the MDGs.' The UNDP estimated that SC producers of raw sugar alone lost $7 billion a year due to trade barriers.

As debt management receives wide attention throughout this book, and ODA is discussed in detail in Chapter 14, this chapter focuses on trade, the routine violation of membership rights of SCs and the reduction of their policy space.

Violating Membership Rights and Reducing Policy Space of SCs

Arguably the most important reform to reach a global partnership is stopping the violation of membership rights of weaker members in all international bodies. There exists a need to enforce respect of statutory obligations, of bringing the Rule of Law to some international organizations, before any improvements can be envisaged, even if and when major IFI shareholders or WTO players not affected by grave violations of the treaties tacitly agree or even encourage this malpractice.

The problem that contractual rights of SCs are not respected in practice is possibly even more pronounced in the case of the BWIs, most notably the IMF. IFIs have repeatedly created damages to their clients by violating their own constitutions. Introducing the Rule of Law to these institutions is thus a legal, economic and developmental necessity. Without equality and justice no partnership is possible.

Pursuant to its presently valid Articles of Agreement any IMF member has the right to choose policies differing from the usual, fairly uniform IMF prescription. In contrast to conditionality foisted onto members in distress, the IMF's constitution does not only allow capital controls, but even explicitly restricts the use of Fund resources to finance outflows. Article VI(1)(a) even prohibits using the Fund's general resources to meet a large and sustained outflow of capital. Nevertheless, SCs have been forced to liberalize capital accounts, which makes increased stocks of international reserves necessary. Such reserves have meanwhile been anointed one of the widely used targets of poverty reduction strategies in Africa.

The IBRD prefers not to acknowledge open defaults to avoid using reserves to cover such defaults as demanded by its statutes. This does not only mock all acceptable accounting rules, but breaches the Bank's own Articles of Agreement. Statutory mechanisms safeguarding meaningful accountability are suppressed against SC interests (for details see Chapter 13 and Raffer, 2002a).

These violations of membership rights reduce the policy space of SCs on top of international treaties tilting the playing field against development. The *Human Development Report 2005* (UNDP, 2005, p. 126) saw a 'need to revisit agreements and negotiations that limit the policy space available to developing countries, directly threaten human development or skew the benefits of integration towards rich countries'. More radically, Chang (2002, 2005) sees present global arrangements as restricting policy options to the point of 'kicking away the ladder' towards successful development. This in turn restricts the possibilities to overcome debt problems.

The Global Trade Framework

A rule-based system protecting the rights of the weak was one of the main chocolates on the tray to convince smaller and weaker countries to sign the WTO treaties. Installing the one-country-one-vote principle the WTO, like the UN General Assembly, gives SCs representing the majorities of countries and of people also the majority of votes. It was often argued that the WTO's legal framework will put an end to bilateral (and GATT violating) measures such as the US Super 301. Reality differs.

The WTO's Understanding on Rules and Procedures Covering the Settlement of Disputes is very honest, though, expressly stipulating that safeguarding membership rights and enforcing the Rule of Law with impartiality are not the guiding principles of dispute settlement. Its Article 3.7 formulates with utmost clarity: 'Before bringing a case a member shall exercise its judgement as to whether action under these procedures would be fruitful. The aim of the dispute settlement mechanism is to secure a positive solution to the dispute.' The probability of success is explicitly established as the one, only and all important measuring rod. This can be illustrated with the EU's complaint against the US Helms-Burton Act. According to the USA 'the WTO panel process would not lead to a resolution of the dispute, instead it would pose serious risks for the new organization' (WTO, 1996, p. 2). Following US 'advice' to 'explore other avenues' (ibid.) the EC 'requested' the panel to suspend its work. An agreement between the EU and the USA catered to the EU's interests but left other members out in the cold. One may consider the EU's complaint because of its obvious 'unfruitfulness' a breach of its WTO obligations.

The dispute between Canada and Brazil on subsidies to their small aircraft industry is another proof that the WTO does not enforce its own rules against powerful members. Canada, a G7 country, simply refused to provide the information requested by the panel. Declining Brazil's demand to infer that the information withheld was prejudicial to Canada's position, the panel stated that Brazil's evidence was insufficient. The Appellate Body found that Canada had violated its obligation to respond promptly and fully (Article 13.1 of the Understanding), remarking that 'a party's refusal to collaborate has the potential to undermine the functioning of the dispute settlement system' (WTO, 2000, p. 59). The Appellate Body 'might well have concluded that the facts on the record did warrant the inference that the information Canada withheld . . . included information prejudicial to Canada's denial that the EDC had conferred 'benefit' and granted a prohibited export subsidy'. Nevertheless the panel's finding was upheld as it was felt Brazil had not done enough to produce evidence. The Appellate Body did 'not intend to suggest that Brazil was precluded from pursuing another complaint against Canada' (ibid.), without specifying, however, why Canada should then provide prejudicial information it withheld successfully in violation of its obligations before.

Such remarkable 'interpretations' of membership rights and duties are compounded by de facto actions such as the so-called 'Green Room', a mechanism depriving most SC members of their right to proper participation.

The WTO rightly presents itself as a rule-based system – apparently with one rule for the rich and another one for the poor. The present trading and financial system may be predictable, but not non-discriminatory. The WTO (1995, p. 22) itself doubts whether clauses in favour of SCs will be obeyed, warning that agreeing to strengthen multilateral rules and disciplines is not enough: 'A willingness to abide by those rule and disciplines, and to adapt them to changing circumstances is also necessary to a credible system.'

TRIPS – A special concern

Target 17 (affordable essential drugs) seems to result from the WTO regime, highlighting one of its major shortcomings, the unequal treatment of members. Trade-Related Intellectual Property Rights (TRIPS) 'increased the monopoly power of patent holders and limits the ability of generic producers to compete' as Mattoo and Subramanian (2005, p. 20) put it, who argue that the WTO seems to be the 'best vehicle' for advancing Northern corporate interests. It enabled pharmaceutical companies to raise prices far above what many poor people can afford. Its effects should be seen with recent trends of extending patenting in mind. In the USA especially a trend exists to grant patents for simple and obvious ideas, for example, software to order books online by clicking a symbol. Firms already exist that earn money uniquely by registering some dubious patents to harass others 'infringing' on them. If this trend continues and picks up, few things if any might soon be left without 'patents' for which SCs will have to pay. A trend towards monopolization where the interest of powerful industrial countries manifests itself. The effects of TRIPS on human lives have been felt particularly severely in the case of medical drugs. The effects can be clearly illustrated: when Thailand introduced the generic version of fluconazole, a medicine used in the treatment of HIV/ AIDS, prices fell to 3 per cent of the original level. Restricting generica is expensive. The *Human Development Report 2005* quotes estimates by Costa Rica suggesting that her pharmaceutical budget would have to rise fivefold to maintain universal coverage without access to generic drugs.

TRIPS does not protect intellectual property, but specific rights of Northern firms. Local indigenous knowledge remains totally unprotected. The host of tribal knowledge in SCs is put at the North's disposal. Very prominent cases exist of knowledge appropriated under the WTO regime. It would be easy to protect Southern knowledge. One can prove which local procedures or indigenous knowledge exist or not in given regions. Protective mechanisms are easy to design.

TRIPS does exactly the opposite, changing traditional requirements for patenting by dismissing the 'inventive step' (something going beyond mere discovery) as a necessary condition. Article 27 redefines 'inventive step' as 'non-obvious', an important difference. Applying tribal or traditional knowledge obtained in SCs to problems in the North might not involve an inventive step, but may be considered non-obvious. The WTO grants a licence to monopolize certain people's intellectual property. The WTO itself took the acronym of the World Tourism Organization (WTO) although Article 15 of its own TRIPS Agreement explicitly protects combinations of letters (such as WTO).

Shifting the burden of proof in the case of process patents onto defendants, Article 34 compounds the disadvantage of SCs. This inversion of the burden of proof is a highly unusual and dangerous legal practice. Creating nuisance and costs simply by accusing competitors is facilitated. It is easy to see why TRIPS does so.

TRIPS foresees the application of Article XXIII, GATT, which allows for challenging measures in full conformity with the agreement. Such non-violation complaints should have entered into force after five years. But SCs blocked the necessary steps pursuant to Article 64.3. Considering the WTO's record, the opaque formulations of Article 64 (for example, the 'existence of any other situation' impairing benefits) are quite dangerous to SCs. One has to fear that Article XXIII might be used to harass SCs.

TRIPS' basic problem is simple and known. Two legal systems clash. One is used by the more powerful to gain financially instead of trying to reconcile them. Protecting exclusively the North, TRIPS leaves rights recognized by other systems, such as traditional knowledge, unprotected and fair game for Northern interests. Historical parallels are the adoption of Roman law by European nobility to claim peasants' land as their 'property'. Colonialism, when land and property were taken from 'natives' with the 'support' of Northern laws, is another example. The introduction of land registers in SCs was often used to expropriate real owners, who only learned that a register existed at all when they were driven off 'another person's' land.

In April 2001 a group of African countries demanded a special session of the TRIPS Council to discuss the TRIPS Agreement's effects on access to medicines, particularly for treating AIDS. They pointed out that TRIPS had enabled pharmaceutical companies to raise prices far above what a great number of people can afford, claiming the existing model of protecting intellectual property rights to be too heavily tilted in favour of right holders and against public interest. The Republic of South Africa was sued by pharmaceutical companies on the grounds of violating international patent regulations by facilitating access to low-cost medicines. Under strong public pressure the companies ultimately withdrew the lawsuit. Providing the 'cocktail' of needed drugs free of charge Brazil reduced AIDS mortality from 10 592 Brazilians in 1995 to 1700 in 2000. The USA filed a WTO complaint on behalf of its pharmaceutical industry against Brazil, one of the promoters of a declaration on access to low-cost pharmaceuticals to be presented at the WTO. The USA complained against provisions in Brazil's patent law requiring local production of a patented product within three years under threat of compulsory licensing.

On paper the TRIPS Agreement contains a wide range of safeguards to protect public health, including the possibility of overriding patents through compulsory licensing or parallel imports, a flexibility, which, according to the World Health Organization, is not being used. 'Parallel imports' means importing from countries where the product is sold more cheaply without approval of patent owners. Under compulsory licensing governments are authorized to grant the use of patents without the patent holder's consent, especially in cases such as public health emergencies. In many countries AIDS undoubtedly is such an emergency. The *Financial Times* (20 June 2001) explains why safeguards are not used. Over years the USA threatened trade sanctions against countries revising their legislation to incorporate TRIPS safeguards. After AIDS activists dogged Gore's presidential campaign the Clinton administration announced it would no longer oppose *TRIPS-consistent* measures, a policy President Bush pledged to continue. Health groups claim that the USA still exerts pressure on countries to forgo or weaken TRIPS safeguards, for instance, in negotiations on the Free Trade Agreement of the Americas. Over 100 NGOs urged the WTO to adopt a seven-point strategy, including a moratorium on dispute settlement action, an agreement not to put pressure on SCs to forgo TRIPS rights, and an extended TRIPS implementation deadline for the poorest countries.

Not all members face the very same difficulties. Threatening to override Bayer's patent the USA forced Bayer to sell its Cipro tablets at roughly a fifth of its market price. Canada had placed large orders with the local company Apotex for a copy of Cipro before, reopening the debate about patent protection for essential medicines. On the same day (25 October 2001) the *Financial Times* reported both about the US enforced price cut and fierce opposition by a US-led group including Canada against SCs led by Brazil and India, insisting on a declaration by ministers at Doha that 'nothing in the Trips agreement shall prevent governments from taking measures to protect public health'. This is another fine example illustrating the nature of TRIPS and the real value of membership rights under the WTO's rule-based system if members are neither the USA, the EU nor Japan. The WTO has a built-in ratchet effect: its obligations bar SCs from reverting to options of the past, but massive pressure is exerted to prevent them from enjoying 'guaranteed' membership rights. This underlines the need to reform dispute settlement procedures as proposed above to prevent their being used to harass weaker members.

Agriculture: the survival of planned economies at their worst
Not only are members treated differently in breach of treaty, but the WTO treaties themselves were shaped by OECD country interests. Agriculture is the prime example. Describing the Uruguay Round's 'Grand Bargain' as the North's obligation to liberalize agriculture and textiles in exchange for tariff reductions and the acceptance of new rules on investments, intellectual property and services by SCs, Stiglitz (2006) points out that the North did not deliver. He characterizes the WTO treaties as so asymmetric that the poorest countries are worse off than before, quoting annual losses by sub-Saharan Africa of some $1.2 billion.

Subsidized EU sugar exports lower world prices by about one third, while, for instance, Mozambique, a country building a competitive sugar industry employing a large number of agricultural labourers, is kept out of EU markets by an import quota allowing it to supply an amount equivalent to less than four hours' worth of EU consumption. This has to be evaluated considering that Mozambique has also been a 'partner' under the Lomé and Cotonou Treaties over decades and that the EU tots around a programme of free access to the European market, which it calls 'Everything [sic] But Arms'. Although sugar might be anything but arms, when it comes to agriculture there are distinct limits to EU openness.

OECD countries may go on protecting their agriculture. But when countries such as Cambodia and Viet Nam join the WTO, it is a condition of entry to implement deep cuts in tariffs on agriculture and manufacturing. WTO accession is another unique and inequalizing mechanism. Normally countries sign treaties and are then bound by them. In the WTO concessions are extorted from weak would-be entrants. Prior bilateral agreements with all members must be reached, which are used to extract further, individual concessions. Small countries often pressed by 'donors' to join have little choice but to comply, unlike big ones. Deploring high oil prices as depressing its economy, the EU demanded that Russia increase its domestic oil price as a precondition for joining the WTO. Russia declined; it is big enough to do so. Apart from China, few SCs could defend their interests as easily.

The US Department of Agriculture estimates that government payments ($4.7 billion) to 20 000 cotton farmers were higher than US aid to sub-Saharan Africa in 2005. The *Human Development Report 2005* (UNDP, 2005, p.131) rightly observes: 'Subsidies of this order are reminiscent of the state planning systems that characterized the former Soviet Union.' The report points out that these subsidies lower world prices by 9 per cent to 13 per cent and enable US producers to dominate world markets, accounting for about one third of total world exports. The fervently free-market WTO has to turn a blind eye to this because the treaties were formulated to allow such results. Naturally, subsidies increasing while or because world market prices fall create incentives to expand economically unviable production, forcing SCs to bear adjustment costs. In Benin alone the fall in cotton prices in 2001–02 was linked to an increase in poverty from 37 per cent to 59 per cent according to the UNDP. Whole economies are being destabilized by world cotton market distortions, with poor countries bearing the brunt, although cotton exports are of marginal relevance for the USA. Such effects have grave implications for all efforts to achieve the MDGs.

When the Uruguay Round was propagated, some SCs had been given reason to hope for benefits from drastic reductions of Northern agrarian export subsidies destroying their export markets. However the actual outcome remained insufficient to establish a level playing field between SCs and subsidized Northern exports of agrarian surpluses. Expecting higher food prices due to reduced subsidies of agrarian exports Article 16 of the Agreement on Agriculture demands measures in favour of net importing SCs and LLDCs as provided for within the Decision on Measures Concerning the Possible Negative Effects of the Reform Programme on Least-developed and Net Food-importing Developing Countries (NFIDCs). This decision recognizes 'negative effects in terms of the availability of adequate supplies of basic foodstuffs from external sources on reasonable terms and conditions, including short term difficulties in financing normal levels of commercial imports of basic foodstuffs'. Facing increased import bills at a time of scarce convertible currency, these countries were thought to be very adversely affected. Help had to be stipulated before signing the agreement to allay fears of net-importing SCs. The upsurge of agrarian prices starting in the very year the Final Act was signed underlined the need for financial support (Raffer, 1997). New facilities or enhancing existing facilities for SCs experiencing Uruguay Round related difficulties in financing normal levels of commercial imports of basic foodstuffs were considered. Implementing the decision on net importers the WTO approached the BWIs to discuss improved conditions of access to existing facilities, a softening of conditionality, new facilities for net food importers and ways in which it could assist the BWIs to be more forthcoming in these matters. Apparently assistance was not welcome. Although SCs expressed their disappointment regarding the accessibility of existing facilities the BWIs denied the necessity of Uruguay Round related facilities, referring to the range of facilities available. Thus no compensatory mechanism existed that could have cushioned the recent hike in food prices and its effects on the poor, nor is one considered even though it could be easily established and would be necessary to support MDG 1, eradicating extreme poverty and hunger (Raffer, 2008b).

In contrast to the decision's wording, difficulties of most food importers will not be short-term problems, comparable to a phase of illiquidity quickly overcome. *Ceteris paribus*, higher food import prices are likely to create a permanent additional demand for foreign exchange, compounded by impacts of lop-sided liberalization. This non-transitory effect calls for other measures than relatively short-term multilateral loans. Financing consumption by loans is a recipe for disaster in already heavily indebted SCs. Compensatory measures could be financed by donor countries from the large overall gains from trade liberalization and the reduction of expensive agrarian subsidies.

Meanwhile a WTO list of NFIDCs exists. However the Committee on Agriculture underlined that being listed does not confer automatic benefits since donors and international organizations concerned would have a role to play. Unlike negative effects corrective benefits do not result automatically from the treaty. Compensation promised when SC signatures were needed was refused once signatures had been obtained.

In defence of the WTO it has to be said that bilateral treaties or the EU's Cotonou treaty with SCs are usually worse. OECD countries demand 'TRIPS plus' provisions in many regional trade agreements. These provisions explicitly strengthen the protection afforded to pharmaceutical companies beyond WTO provisions and circumscribe the policy space for SC governments.

The Central America Free Trade Agreement grants limited market openings for the six SCs involved. For sugar, a crop in which SCs have a considerable advantage, tariffs will remain at more than 100 per cent and imports will be restricted to a 1.7 per cent market share. Meanwhile the USA has secured extensive market openings for rice, gaining immediate duty-free quotas that rise 5 per cent annually. More than one third of US rice exports will now enter duty free, having previously been subjected to tariffs of 15 per cent to 60 per cent. NAFTA opened the Mexican market without abolishing US agrarian subsidies and import restrictions on agrarian products such as sugar. Mexico is not entitled to defend against subsidized US exports by compensating tariffs, leaving poor Mexican farmers in 'competition' with subsidized US produce (Stiglitz, 2006). On flimsy grounds Mexico was forced to increase the export price of her tomatoes. 'Proofs' of dumping by SCs are so fanciful that Stiglitz concludes that most US firms would commit dumping if the method to determine dumping by SCs were also applied within the USA.

REDUCING SC GOVERNMENT REVENUE

Debt management, new global trade modalities and the long-term decline of ODA shares all leave SCs short of sufficient foreign exchange to finance development, the MDGs or even debt service due. Enforcing the Washington Consensus the BWIs, controlled by the same few countries as the WTO, changed economic and trade policies in SCs fundamentally. 'Structural adjustment' lending forced SCs to open and liberalize their economies – to the extent of making the 'WTO process a "victim" of the success of the World Bank and the IMF' (Mattoo and Subramanian, 2005, p. 20). In plain English: having little to offer when it came to WTO negotiations because of debt management, SCs were once again short-changed.

IFIs compound negative trade effects. When poor rice farmers in Ghana saw their markets squeezed by cheap US imports, the 'IMF has opposed the use of tariffs to restrict these imports on the grounds that there is no evidence of unfair competition. That judgement is hard to square with the fact that US budget payments for rice in 2003 amounted to $1.3 billion, or almost three-quarters of the value of output' (UNDP, 2005, p. 132). In the name of economic efficiency the IBRD pressured Mali to pay local cotton producers this 'world market price' in 2004. The government ultimately refused to bankrupt domestic peasants. Free-tradism boils down to freely subsidized US trade, or export subsidies by OECD countries at large.

After the Asian Crash of 1997 the WTO reported with apparent satisfaction that the process of market opening could be kept on track: most Asian countries had accepted, either unilaterally, as part of IMF-sponsored 'adjustment programmes' or as a result of recent sectoral negotiations in the WTO and in APEC, substantial liberalization and commitments to further liberalization of their trade and investment policies. Not without pride the WTO adds that Indonesia, the country most severely affected by the crisis, liberalized most. With the whole WTO-IMF package implemented as planned, Indonesia was seen as having one of the most liberal trade policy regimes of all SCs. If the WTO is right about the virtual elimination of non-tariff barriers to trade though, Indonesia would also be more liberal than virtually any OECD member. Indonesia could have increased her average applied tariff by 25 per cent without breaching her WTO obligations but – convinced by whatever means – did not do so. Though 'not extensively used' in South East Asia selective tariff increases by some Asian countries remaining within the gap between bound and applied tariffs, thus 'within the flexibility allowed by bindings under the WTO agreements', nevertheless 'give cause for concern to the extent they may distort the pattern of production and trade' (WTO, 1998, p. 28). Using one's contractual rights raises the WTO's concern if done by SCs, in contrast to potential distortions by the Agreement on Textile and Clothing or outright breaches of contract by Northern members, let alone formally legal exercise of contractual rights by these 'more equal' members. Not using their membership rights within the WTO as well as their right to capital controls, Asian countries had to face huge and avoidable financial costs to weather the crisis.

Liberalization has played havoc with government revenues in the poorest countries. Many SC budgets depend heavily on tariff revenues. Especially poorer countries are unable to substitute tariff revenues by relatively complicated income tax or VAT systems. Frequently slashing government employment drastically to produce 'slim' administrations, 'structural adjustment' did not help in implementing the necessary changes. Under pressure in WTO negotiations to slash their budget revenues and by official creditors to honour debt obligations, SCs are driven to desperation exports (by definition exports at unequal exchange conditions; see Raffer, 2005) and lose resources. We witness the spectacle of creditors destroying the revenue base of their debtors while eagerly preaching the necessity of honouring debt commitments.

Tariff income is of limited importance for rich countries' budgets. In sub-Saharan Africa, however, tariffs account for about one third of government revenue, rising to about one half for Lesotho and Uganda according to the UNDP. Theoretically, lower tariffs need not lead to lower revenue if imports react elastically enough. However the potential for a sharp decline in revenue is marked, not least due to creditor enforced austerity measures. In a way this may be a blessing, because steeply increased imports would not contribute to reducing balance of payments deficits. 'One detailed study concludes that three-quarters of the ACP countries could lose 40 per cent or more of tax revenue, with more than one-third of them losing 60 per cent' due to liberalization (UNDP, 2005, p. 138). This means in practice less government income under debt pressure.

An Urgent Need for Reform

As a first step this discriminatory trading system described in detail and repeatedly by the OECD (cf. Raffer and Singer, 2001, pp. 250ff.) must be abolished. Market access must be equal irrespective of whether the exporting country is Northern or Southern. Non-discriminatory barriers, particularly equal tariffs for all goods imported by OECD countries regardless of their origin, is an absolutely minimal demand. It could easily have been negotiated into the relevant WTO agreements, but the North apparently chose not to do so. The economic doctrines which OECD countries use to advocate liberalization are forgotten when it comes to discriminating against Southern suppliers. Abolishing this discrimination is therefore an important demand. The UNDP (2005, pp.147ff.) demands reforms to allow trade to 'deliver for the MDGs', such as compensation for countries losing out. Raffer and Singer (2001) present a list of reforms necessary to rebalance North-South relations and to foster development. Raffer (2002b) proposes specific changes of the WTO framework. Given the present trade framework, these are mandatory. One cannot contradict Pascal Lamy's (2007; emphasis added) expert analysis, which the WTO's director general presented at ECOSOC:

> a number of the current substantive rules of the WTO do perpetuate some bias against developing countries. This is true for example with rules on subsidies in agriculture that allow for trade-distorting subsidies which tends to favour developed countries. This is also true when we look at the high tariffs that many developed counties apply on imports of agricultural and industrial products, in particular from developing countries. *I often say that while the political decolonization took place more than 50 years ago, we have not yet completed economic decolonization.*

10. NGO advocacy for debt reduction cum debtor protection

Reacting to the plight of debtor SCs under 'structural adjustment', NGOs soon took up advocacy in favour of debtors. In the meantime NGO advocacy on debts and other issues such as the WTO has taken off, and their influence on politics has become perceptible. Over years of campaigning for better policies vis-à-vis debtors NGOs have acquired expert knowledge that enabled them to influence policies. They have become accepted players as, for instance, a publication of the IBRD's Operations Evaluation Department (Gautham, 2003, p. 11) shows:

> Many of the ideas inherent in HIPC were proposed by southern states during the New International Economic Order (NIEO) . . . but nothing came of this intense and polarized state-to-state bargaining. One of the striking things about the rise of HIPC is precisely that the debtor states were not a major driving force behind the innovation. Rather, it was made possible by NGOs that shifted the battle from the corridors of power into the domestic political arenas of the Organisation for Economic Co-operation and Development (OECD) industrial democracies. The weak power position of the debtor states and the concomitant strong influence of the NGOs help to explain how the HIPC Initiative eventually became focused almost exclusively on a particular approach to poverty reduction.

This OED publication also speaks of 'the key role played by the international NGO community' (ibid., p. 15) in enhancing the HIPC framework in 1999, and that NGOs' 'suggestions and inputs have helped to formulate new ideas – from process issues, to the introduction of the participatory poverty reduction strategy concept, to technical issues such as retro-fitting the sustainability thresholds'.

The NGO community has both been campaigning at the grassroots level, discussing in international fora and with official creditors, and producing academic papers. Many enjoy consultative status at international organizations, or have continuous contact with governments or IFIs. To give but one illustration, the IMF has regularly published a *Civil Society Newsletter* during the recent past. The UN's *Financing for Development* initiative comprised a Civil Society Forum in order to get input from NGOs (Herman et al. eds, 2001). Both within the UN system and with

IFIs, NGOs have established themselves as visible and important participants in the debate on sovereign debts. The report of the Panel of Eminent Persons on United Nations–Civil Society Relations of June 2004 (UN, 2004, p.26) summarizes succinctly: 'The growing influence of civil society in global policy does not diminish the relevance of intergovernmental processes – it enhances it.' This seems, in particular, true in the case of Southern sovereign debts.

EARLY CAMPAIGNING FOR DEBT REDUCTION

The first campaigns against 'structural adjustment' and demands for debt reductions can be traced back to the early 1980s. The unhealthy link between 'structural adjustment' and debt relief was criticized. Calls for sovereign insolvency were soon taken up by NGOs. The Debt Crisis Network and the World Council of Churches were among the first working on the debt issue. Very often NGOs with a religious base engaged in campaigning. The first big international NGO manifestation against traditional debt management and its effects on people in SCs was organized in parallel with the IMF-IBRD annual meeting in Berlin 1988, as a 'counter-summit'. In the 'largest ever demonstrations against' the BWIs debt cancellation was the 'top demand' (Ambrose, 2005, p. 272). At that time the idea of sovereign insolvency was already spreading after Suratgar's first thrust. It had been propagated by UNCTAD, and several economists, such as myself. In Germany Thomas Kampffmeyer had drawn attention to Germany's forgotten de facto insolvency (London Accord) and Indonesia's debt reduction after 1968, much to the displeasure of the Kohl government that first claimed to have no knowledge of nor documents on this part of Germany's history. A big ecumenical hearing (one would call it a debt tribunal nowadays) was organized by church-based organizations in Berlin to give voice to people from the South suffering under austerity policies enforced by official creditors. They were given the opportunity to testify how 'structural adjustment' affected their own and their neighbours' lives. The BWI representatives presented the usual arguments, such as that 'adjusting' countries had fared better or that debtor governments 'owned' the policies and the IMF was not to blame. The UNICEF study *Adjustment with a Human Face* edited by Cornia, Jolly and Stewart had just been published the year before. As part of this hearing I was invited to present my international Chapter 9 proposal.

In October 1988 the NGO Evangelische Akademikerschaft in Deutschland (Association of Protestant University Graduates in Germany) invited me to their symposion at Bochum to present and discuss my proposal. A resolution was taken, which described my proposal, also drawing attention to the London Accord and the Indonesian solution. A letter was written to the Chancellor, asking him and the government to propagate my proposal. The official answer arrived after quite some time with apologies for the delay caused by the time necessary to study a highly complicated legal matter. It was polite but negative without giving any reason for the refusal to propagate my proposal. Obviously no good point to 'sink' it had been found after intensive searching.

In 1990 the Swiss Working Group Swissaid/Fastenopfer/Brot für alle/ Helvetas/Caritas submitted the idea of an international insolvency to the Swiss *Bundesrat* (government) supported by two papers written by Professor K.W. Meessen (Augsburg/Geneva) and myself. It was taken up and discussed in the Swiss Parliament. Switzerland tried discreetly to advance this proposal internationally, but finally stopped these attempts as no other creditor government signalled any interest. The lack of positive reaction to the Swiss government's initiative around 1990 might at least in part be explained by the official euphoria about new capital flows to Latin America. According to IFIs, but also other international organizations, the debt crisis was over. The 1990s were touted as the years of hope and recovery. Temporarily, discussing mechanisms for debt reduction was eclipsed by unfounded euphoria.

In the year 2000 this proposal was again taken up by the Swiss parliamentarian Christoph Eymann in parliament (the *Nationalrat*). Unlike before, the Swiss government then preferred HIPC to insolvency mechanisms.

In spite of official euphoria of the early 1990s, NGO campaigning did not stop. In June 1992 KAIROS EUROPA, for instance, organized a roundtable on international insolvency with members of the European Parliament in Strasbourg. Formed after the Munich G7 meeting in 1992, the initiative Entwicklung braucht Entschuldung (Development Needs Debt Reduction) actively campaigned for debt reduction, including for the idea of sovereign insolvency.

THE JUBILEE 2000 CAMPAIGN

Jubilee 2000 was without doubt the most influential and prominent NGO advocacy effort to change North-South debtor relations. The first Jubilee 2000 Coalition was founded in Britain by three major Christian aid agencies and by the World Development Movement in 1996. Ann Pettifor, then coordinator of the Debt Crisis Network, was J2K's co-founder, engine and director, both in the case of the British campaign as with Jubilee 2000 International. When the platform for the new Jubilee 2000 UK

(J2K-UK) was formulated by Pettifor and others, the founders invited Peter Mountfield, a Treasury 'mandarin', who had represented his country in the Paris Club over many years, as well as myself to discuss the idea of sovereign insolvency. The organizers wanted to evaluate whether to make it part of their platform and, if so, how. Peter Mountfield had also been the brain behind the Toronto and Trinidad Terms both of course officially proposed by the ministers. As J2K-UK did not exist yet this meeting was held under the auspices of the Debt Crisis Network on the premises of Christian Aid in December 1995.

Some platform members, especially Ann Pettifor, were very much in favour of an independent process modelled after domestic insolvency while taking the specifics of sovereign countries into account. However the idea of an independent process without BWI 'guidance' sounded so radical at that time that quite a few member NGOs had concerns about the realism of depriving the BWIs of their dominating role, going against what all major OECD countries supported. Therefore the compromise found for the platform of J2K-UK described the solution as a 'fair and transparent arbitration process'. This description is both correct and avoids any reference to the BWIs or even to an 'independent' process.

This idea, also dubbed the 'Jubilee Framework', was mocked widely and failed, at first, to win support. However very competent and successful public relations work by J2K-UK finally made debt relief and the injustice of debtor-creditor relations household arguments in Britain. In those days London taxi drivers might start a discussion on SC debts and the sheer injustice of BWI debt management with their clients.

The idea to link the new millennium with the ancient biblical jubilee year originated with Martin Dent, an academic at Keele University in Britain, in 1990 (Pettifor, 2006, p. 299). It recalled the religious notion of the Sabbath year in Christo-Judean cultures, but also very fundamental and universal concepts of justice and fairness common to any culture. Pursuant to the Book of Leviticus, which is part of the Christian Old Testament and the Jewish Torah, social and economic inequalities were to be redressed every 50 years. After seven times seven years the book commands that slaves be freed, debts cancelled and land restored. The year 2000 was declared the year of jubilee, when this redressing of imbalances should be celebrated. As the home page of J2K-UK informs, the All African Council of Churches had called for a Year of Jubilee to cancel Africa's debts in 1990.

Ambrose (2005, p. 273) found it 'a little ironic' that it was difficult to 'ignite' the jubilee message in Muslim countries, since 'injunctions on debt from Qur'an are substantially more direct than those of the bible'. Nevertheless, in Indonesia, the world's biggest Muslim country, the idea of sovereign insolvency was taken up by a big and well-established NGO, the International NGO Forum on Indonesian Development (INFID). Unsurprisingly Indonesia's debt reduction after 1968 was used to prove how easily creditors could solve debt problems.

At first, the idea of Jubilee met scepticism in Britain, being deemed too religious. But, finally, it was adopted. The determination of unpayable debts by a fair and transparent arbitration process in order to cancel them became an essential demand of Jubilee. It turned out to be a powerful request that really influenced North-South relations. Based on the demand of fairness to debtor nations without political or ideological bias and open to anyone subscribing to the platform, the movement eventually comprised an impressively large spectrum of members and supporters. By October 1997 this spectrum's range comprised the British medical profession, the Mothers Union, the Trades Union Congress (TUC), the National Black Alliance, the Muslim Council of Britain, Comic Relief, all major aid agencies except Oxfam and all major faiths (Pettifor, 2006, p. 300).

In February 1996 the Debt Crisis Network invited a group of African leaders to Britain to meet people and decision makers. This tour culminated in an event hosted by Cardinal Hume, who invited another prominent Catholic, Michel Camdessus, then the IMF's Managing Director. Pettifor (2006, p. 299) links this meeting directly to the IMF's 'historically unprecedented step of writing off debts' by participating in the IBRD's HIPC Initiative of 1996.

One early 'offspring' of J2K-UK was the German debt relief movement Erlaßjahr 2000 (internationally spelled *Erlassjahr* to avoid the esszed). In the December of 1996 a meeting was organized at the Catholic Social Academy at Münster by Jürgen Kaiser and others. Ann Pettifor was invited to give her advice based on the experience in Britain. In 1997 Erlaßjahr 2000 was established. Already going further than the British movement Erlaßjahr 2000 was the first expressly to mention my Chapter 9, calling right from the start for the emulation of the basic principles of US municipal insolvency. Latter on, other Jubilee movements followed. In January 1999, when the Latin American and Caribbean Jubilee 2000 Campaign was launched in Tegucigalpa – organizations from 16 countries attended – the Tegucigalpa Declaration explicitly demanded adapting Chapter 9 to sovereigns. The idea of Jubilee spread quickly and developed an incredible impact. After just three years there were Jubilee 2000 coalitions in 69 countries. At the G7 summit in Birmingham in 1998 ten thousands of people demonstrated peacefully for meaningful debt relief, fairness and justice and the cancellation of unpayable debts. According to police estimates, which reputedly are customarily 'cautious' regarding numbers, 70 000 demonstrators formed a 'human chain' in the city to protest against debt management and creditor domination. Meticulous counting by the organizers produced a figure of 100 000 participants. Both figures compare impressively with the 35 000 people demonstrating against the WTO at its famous Seattle meeting.

An anecdote may illustrate the political weight of numbers. J2K-UK had unsuccessfully tried to arrange an appointment with the British Prime Minister, who hosted the G7 meeting, in order to present a long list of signatures in support of debt reduction to him. Even when Muhammad Ali agreed to hand over the list, Downing Street showed no interest. On the day of the human chain, when some 30 000 people had already gathered in the streets before lunchtime (the chain was scheduled for the afternoon), the PM's office called, informing the organizers that the PM would very much like to meet them. Already at a government country house with his guests, the PM had to return to Birmingham for this meeting. Obviously a few ten thousand voters are quite an argument.

In February 1998 the German and UK campaigns marked the 45th anniversary of the London Accord that roughly halved debts. Fake gold bullion were dumped outside Germany's embassy, Christian Aid supporters sent in thousands of postcards. In April 1998 the Jubilee 2000 Afrika Campaign was launched in Accra, Ghana. Delegates from 20 African countries attended.

In November 1998 the Swedish and Italian campaigns organized an international meeting of J2K campaigners in Rome, which was attended by representatives from 58 countries and 12 international organizations (Pettifor, 2006, pp. 302–303). First tensions showed at the discussions in Rome, as representatives from SCs wanted a more radical platform. The final declaration called for the cancellation of unpayable and already also 'odious debts'.

After Birmingham, NGOs started to organize parallel events next to G7 meetings. In 1997 a similar campaign was launched in the USA. In 1999 Cologne was host to the G7 summit and the NGO counter-event. On 18 March 1999 a consultative meeting on SC debts took place in London between the International Jubilee 2000 Campaign, high ranking public servants from all G7 governments except Italy and the BWIs. Cologne was host to the G7 summit and the NGO parallel event. Workshops, demonstrations and discussions were organized by Erlaßjahr 2000. Human chains were coordinated internationally. On 12 June 1999 10 000 people formed a human chain at Edinburgh, one day later 50 000 joined hands around the Thames to call on the PM to 'drop the debt'. Fifty thousand people formed human chains and marched in Cologne and Stuttgart (where Rigoberta Menchú spoke). The organizers of the Cologne NGO meeting met the German Chancellor and presented him with a list of more than 17 million signatures from all over the world backing the Jubilee demand. In 2001 the list finally surpassed 24 million people from 166 countries, who had signed the Jubilee 2000 petition which called for debt cancellation under 'a fair and transparent process'. As expressed by the IBRD publication (Gautham, 2003) quoted above, NGO lobbying was one extremely important factor producing the relative improvements of HIPC II. Most notable, the new PRSPs contained visible trace elements of the idea of debtor protection. Presumably the shifts of HIPC's sunset clause might also not have happened without NGO lobbying.

In Germany lobbying was broad based and highly effective. The two main religions, Catholics and Protestants, supported it. The German Commission Justitia et Pax (an organization of the Catholic Church) published a paper just before and for the Cologne Summit demanding an international Chapter 9. Lobbying opposition parties, the government, commercial banks and the Bundesbank in favour of an international Chapter 9 continued after Cologne. Regarding banks, it was certainly helpful that the CEO of the Deutsche Bank, Alfred Herrhausen, was one of the most vocal advocates of negotiated debt reduction. Visiting their constituencies, MPs were confronted with questions regarding the need for sovereign insolvency mechanisms. In 2000 the Ministry of Development Cooperation (BMZ) felt it had to commission a study on the issue. In spite of NGO demands obviously unaware of Chapter 9, it explored in particular whether the German insolvency proceedings for private individuals and firms could be easily adapted to sovereigns. Analysing a request that had not been made, the study concluded that many hardly surmountable hindrances would make developing HIPC further the better alternative. Surprisingly, the evolutions of HIPC after Cologne were not taken into account. As this study was written before the SDRM, one may well wonder whether the view that adapting private insolvency procedures as such is unrealistic would have been equally held if written after the SDRM was proposed.

One of the patently absurd points of the study was claiming that an 'insolvency agency' comparable to OPEC (a mind-boggling thought devoid of any rational basis) would be necessary because elected politicians cannot be removed from office. Of course such absurdity had never been propagated by any advocate of international insolvency. I myself have repeatedly pointed out that under Chapter 9 courts cannot remove elected politicians from office, which is one good reason why it should be adapted internationally (see Chapter 5). The study itself brought up this unfounded and irrational point in order to 'refute' it 'easily', also oblivious of the fact that Germany had been able to benefit from de facto insolvency relief in 1953 without any OPEC-type institution. This study's problematic views and conclusions were immediately challenged by NGOs and academics. Eventually the BMZ commissioned another study by a professor of law from Berlin, Christoph G. Paulus, which was presented in early 2002. It reached strikingly different conclusions, showing that the US approach to insolvency (where debtors present a plan) made sense for sovereigns and proposing ways of how to implement it.

In April 1999 the Bundestag demanded that the government study the issue of international insolvency. A question (*Kleine Anfrage*) by the CDU/CSU parliamentary fraction in March 2000 requested information about what the federal government had done to fulfil this demand, whether it considered initiating such a mechanism and if so on what basis, and what concrete steps had been taken. The campaign organized a 'Parliamentary Evening' for members of the Finance, Budget and Economic Cooperation committees of the Bundestag on 21 March 2000. Such 'evenings' are a traditional means to discuss issues with MPs outside parliament and in a fairly informal setting. All parliamentary parties were represented and unanimously agreed that a public hearing in parliament should be held. Hearings on this issue by the Bundestag's Finance Committee (*Finanzausschuß*) – also in cooperation with the Committee on Economic Cooperation – took place. In 2002 the second coalition pact of the red-green government led by Chancellor Schröder contained a clause that the federal government would 'vigorously speak out in favour of international insolvency proceedings'. The chapter on the global economy specified that 'the federal government speaks out in favour of fair and transparent proceedings (sovereign insolvency law) including all actors, especially also from the private sector, to reach a solution'. Although actual politics did not visibly reflect this commitment, this was the first time that FTAP appeared in an official document forming the basis of government policies.

The acronym itself resulted from a brainstorming by NGOs forming a working group with the specific aim to promote my proposal. Since the word insolvency has different connotations in various cultures, and Southern NGOs especially did not like this word, another expression avoiding the 'I-word' was sought. After first deliberations at Wuppertal, a meeting in Berlin organized by the German NGO BLUE 21 in 2000 decided to use the description of J2K-UK: Fair Transparent Arbitration Process (FTAP). A FTAP list was created and activities, such as a letter to the G7, followed. NGOs from all inhabited continents took part, Northern Jubilee movements and Jubilee South.

The implementation of the Cologne Initiative, granted under NGO pressure, soon proved disappointing. In 2000 Adrian Lovett of J2K-UK (quoted from Raffer and Singer, 2001, p.190) summed up the harsh verdict of the NGO community: 'The betrayal of Cologne: twelve months of failure.' Comparing promises and results indeed yields a highly negative picture. In September 1999 the Chairman of the International Monetary and Financial Committee, Gordon Brown, predicted that the first country would begin to benefit within weeks. In December 1999 the BWIs still predicted that 24 countries would reach decision point in 2000, a forecast soon corrected to 'up to 20 countries'. When the Okinawa Summit took place in the summer of 2000 only one country, Uganda, had reached completion point, after discussions and delays. However some members of the Paris Club massively arguing for less reduction are reported to have prevailed. NGOs pointed out that Uganda was to receive $15 million less than expected, or 40 per cent of the resources planned for its Poverty Action Fund for 2000 and 2001. The NGO estimate that Cologne would not be fully implemented until at least 2005 was not unsubstantiated. In 2000 Jubilee 2000 expected that no more than $90 billion would ever be cancelled, while $100 billion had been promised at Cologne, as just $15 billion was likely to be cancelled by the end of the year.

Okinawa – 'the climax of our campaigning' according to Pettifor (2006, p. 305) – was accompanied by Jubilee 2000 activities around the world. Meanwhile the G8 tried to find venues as far away from public scrutiny and demonstrations as possible. Okinawa was the most remote Japan could offer, lacking a place amid the wilderness such as Kananaskis. Aided by the Japanese campaign J2K efficiently coordinated by Kitazawa Yōko, the British PM, Tony Blair, and the UK's 'sherpa' were pressured to invite leaders and representatives of the debtor nations 'to their "fireside chat". As a result, a precedent for the G8 was set, and President Obasanjo, accompanied by the presidents of South Africa and Algeria, were invited to meet with President Bill Clinton, Prime Minister Tony Blair, and others in Tokyo' (ibid.). Although these leaders were not invited to the actual 'fireside chat' in Okinawa, but for diplomatic reasons met with the G8 in Tōkyō, Pettifor sees this as another great achievement of the campaign: a broadening of the G8 Summit to include leaders from SCs. The invitation to Southern leaders has been repeated by the G8 every year since then.

In September 2000 the BWI Conference in Prague did not produce a new impetus (cf. Raffer and Singer, 2001). During the concluding press conference with the IMF's Managing Director and the Chairman of the Board of Governors, the IBRD's president answered a question on whether there were moves to simplifying procedures and whether there was progress justifying high expectations for deeper debt relief for the poorest very clearly:

> There were high expectations, indeed, by some, but our expectations were to advance the implementation of the second program of the enhanced HIPC

facilities. There was no indication that I'm aware of, given by Horst [Köhler, the IMF's Managing Director] or myself, that we were going to get deeper or broader. That was certainly something that Jubilee 2000 and many others had been hoping for.

But we have maintained a position that what we want to do between now and the end of the year is to implement, for as many countries as possible, the enhanced HIPC Initiative. We are hopeful that we will reach the target of 20 countries by the end of this year, at which point debt relief can be operative.

Further years of the kind of delay followed, which the IBRD itself had described as so damaging to debtor economies.

An impressive range of well-known people and public figures supported Jubilee 2000, such as Pope John Paul II, Singer Bono of U2 and Bob Geldof. The UN's Secretary General, Kofi Annan (2000, p. 38), put the essence of FTAP wonderfully into a nutshell:

I would go a step further and propose that, in the future, we consider an entirely new approach to handling the debt problem. The main components of such an approach would include . . . establishing a debt arbitration process to balance the interests of creditors and sovereign debtors and introduce greater discipline into their relations.

Allegedly after receiving 'advice', Annan soon withdrew his courageous demand for FTAP, speaking of mediation not arbitration, involving an 'independent' mediator, assisted by the IMF and other experts on a voluntary base. This would not change creditor domination. With the benefit of hindsight one may already recognize one variant of the SDRM. Annan's courageous call for introducing the Rule of Law into international debtor-creditor relations might meet much less resistance nowadays than it did at a time when the IMF still claimed that emulating insolvency for sovereign debtors is impossible, and the very word was taboo.

The host of activities by all Jubilee campaigns and supporting NGOs makes it impossible to go into details. Readers wishing more information are referred to the NGO websites. The illustrative examples of more important events are by no means exhaustive.

In 1998 the Heinrich Böll Foundation and Friends of the Earth organized an Information Conference for Parliamentarians in Washington DC. I presented a paper on 'International Chapter 9 insolvency for countries'. My proposal was incorporated into the 'Global Sustainable Development Resolution' drafted by Congressman Bernie Sanders in 1999, which called for an international insolvency mechanism based on Chapter 9 of US bankruptcy laws, including my arbitration proposal.

In 1999 campaigners in the Philippines formed a human chain around the Asian Development Bank, and the first Foreign Debt Tribunal was organized in Rio de Janeiro. It was not an arbitration panel as demanded by the FTAP model though. In particular, creditors were absent and had had no say in establishing the tribunal. In 2000 Spanish campaigners handed in a petition with a million signatures to parliament, Nigeria added a million signatures to the J2K petition, and the capital Abuja was plastered with 'cancel the debt' signs for Clinton's visit. More than 5 million Brazilians voted against foreign debt payments and a deal with the IMF in an informal referendum.

After the default of Ecuador's Brady-bonds Jubileo 2000 Red Guayaquil was one organizer of a conference on Ecuadorian debts in early December 1999 where my proposal was presented. In a letter to the Paris Club dated 10 September 2000 the Confederación de Nacionalidades Indigenas del Ecuador (CONAIE) – an organization that was also part of the government for a short period of time – demanded debt-to-development swaps of all existing debts, and international arbitration to solve problems of future overindebtedness. Debt service should be replaced by payments into a Fondo Social y Ecológico to finance social, cultural and ecological programmes (including education), essentially the same demand as the counterpart fund proposed by Jubileo 2000 Red Guayaquil in a joint study with the UNDP and UNICEF. Referring specifically to US municipalities CONAIE's demand for arbitration also seconded Jubileo 2000 Red Guayaquil. Quite rightly, CONAIE pointed out that such arbitration procedures result from the very fundamental base of the Rule of Law that no one must be permitted to be judge in their own cause. Stating with clarity that this essential base of the Rule of Law had been violated by creditors being 'judge and party', CONAIE demanded creditor governments to respect the Rule of Law. The document also stated that fundamental human rights had been violated by present debt management denying otherwise customary debtor protection in the case of the poorest. However, as usual in cases of SC debts, neither the Rule of Law nor human rights cut any ice with the Paris Club whose members keenly preach these very principles to their debtors except when it comes to their own claims.

CONAIE blamed the Ecuadorian government with outmost clarity as well, identifying the important role of Ecuador's government and elites in creating the debt overhang. While the country is not simply presented as an innocent victim, the co-responsibility of creditors is properly addressed. The letter referred to Ecuador's successful experience with counterpart funds. Finally it mentioned Germany's London Accord of 1953 offering generous terms to a debtor whose situation was perceptibly better than Ecuador's, the basically similar Indonesian case around 1970, and the more recent cases of Poland and Egypt to show that demands for meaningful debt reduction are technically possible.

Stressing the same concerns as CONAIE, the African Network on Debt and Development (AFRODAD), a platform of African NGOs, has taken up the demand for international arbitration on foreign debt. Speaking of 'institutional imbalances' in a document published in 2000, AFRODAD becomes very explicit, illustrating traditional debt management by paraphrasing a West African adage ('In a Jury of Foxes (the Creditors), the Chickens (the Debtors) are always the guilty'), and attacking the Paris Club as undemocratic and a creditor's cartel acting jointly against one debtor at a time. AFRODAD demanded present practices to be replaced by structures respecting human rights, democracy and the right of the debtor countries and their peoples to be heard. This document goes on, referring to the UN's *Financing for Development* process:

> A proposal for internationalisation of Chapter 9 Insolvency Law of the USA was presented as part of the NGO Hearings to the United Nations in the context of the Financing for Development (FfD) Conference preparations during November 5–9, 2000 in New York by Professor Kunibert Raffer of Austria. Chapter 9 of USA Laws is a procedure for solving the insolvency of a governing body, a Municipality, without violating or undermining its governmental power.

Referring to fears that insolvency procedures might not highlight those unequal power relations at the root of the debt overhang, and that declaring bankruptcy might be seen as suggesting that debtors are solely responsible for the debt crisis, AFRODAD also saw a need for an international arbitration process explicitly addressing the responsibilities of creditor countries and the effects of exogenous factors that might be influenced by creditors, such as denied market access, trade imbalances and declining terms of trade.

Already recognizable in Rome at the end of 1998, a 'schism' of the Jubilee movement occurred. In October 1999 some campaigners from SCs established the Jubilee South coalition. Some Southern campaigns joined. Nevertheless, Jubilee achieved 'an extraordinary north-south alliance' for most of the duration of the campaign, a 'unity, which continued up to 2000' (Pettifor, 2006, p. 313), but according to Pettifor did 'not survive the campaign'. To give an impression of the reach of the Jubilee movement: 'Our Web site in the last years of the campaign was visited by more people than visited those of the IMF and World Bank!' (ibid., p. 302).

Jubilee South distanced itself from the lobbying approach targeting official creditors, calling for immediate, unconditional debt cancellation, even repudiation under the device 'Don't owe, won't pay'. It has focused on the 'recognition of the historical and ecological debts owed by the North to the South for over six hundred years of exploitation, and reparations for those damages and those caused by the perpetuation of the debt crisis' (Ambrose, 2005, p. 276).

CAMPAIGNING AFTER 2000

As the very name indicated, Jubilee 2000 had the goal to achieve debt relief by the turn of the millennium. The campaign had been designed as a 'short-life' organization, one which existed only to achieve the goal of cancellation of 'unpayable debts of the poorest countries. . .by the year 2000' as its global petition stated. Allegedly quite a few people hoped to be able to 'sit it out'. Because of frustration at the failure fully to achieve this goal, many campaigners urged continuation of the campaign. While North-South unity and the coherence of the international Jubilee 2000 Campaign ended in December 2000, campaigning did not stop, although most jubilee members changed their names. J2K-UK was transformed into a research unit, dedicated to monitoring the debt relief promises made by G8 leaders, and holding the BWIs accountable. This work was conducted under the banner first of JubileePlus, and then under the name Jubilee Research, part of the New Economics Foundation. Later still, the Jubilee Debt Campaign, a purely campaigning organization, was established. In 2002, for instance, JubileePlus and the Centre for the Studies of Financial Innovation (CSFI) co-organized a round table on international insolvency in London's Guildhall, which was attended by quite a few people from the banking community. The German campaign just dropped the 2000 from the name. Having no year in it, Jubilee South kept its name, definitely breaking away from the global movement.

One may assume that the IMF's decision to propose the SDRM was also influenced by NGO campaigns for debt reduction and for FTAP. The SDRM was greeted by NGOs as one important step in the right direction, but also met strong criticism from many NGOs because of the strong institutional self-interest behind the SDRM, and the strong increase of the Fund's importance it would have brought about. Concerns were voiced that the SDRM would not change creditor domination but officially install the IMF as the overlord of sovereign debt relief and grant the Fund legal preference as a creditor. Many NGOs therefore countered the SDRM proposal with the Raffer Proposal. In a very open and transparent way, the IMF discussed the SDRM with private creditors and NGOs. NGO representatives were, for instance, invited to an IMF conference on the SDRM in January 2002. Ann Pettifor represented NGO positions as an invited speaker.

The Swiss Federal Ministry of Finance tried to organize a discussion with Anne Krueger on sovereign insolvency. The first event did not take place because Anne Krueger cancelled at extremely short notice. As many NGOs had booked fixed date tickets, this extremely late cancellation caused quite a bit of irritation. Against legal odds – the IMF is immune – some NGOs considered suing the Fund for damages. *Cash*, a Swiss business magazine, pointed out that this had been the second time a discussion between Krueger and myself had been called off, referring to her as 'the quitter'. The Ministry persevered with its efforts, though, and this discussion (with a Swiss banker and myself as discussants) took place in Geneva on 8 August 2002. To the surprise of a Swiss newspaper, the banker and the academic not unjustifiedly seen as the NGOs' nominee, lost no time forming a common front against the SDRM.

In March 2003 the Friedrich Ebert Stiftung Uruguay (FESUR) organized an international seminar on foreign debts under the auspices of the Presidency of the Cámara de Representantes, which took place in Uruguay's parliament in Montevideo. By happenstance, this seminar was held precisely at the time when Uruguay proposed to reschedule. The Friedrich Ebert Stiftung had repeatedly organized events on sovereign debts and my proposal inter alia for politicians and academics in Buenos Aires. Right in the Palacio Legislativo a group of MPs signed the Montevideo Declaration that called for sovereign insolvency. Freddy Ehlers, a Latin American parliamentarian from Ecuador, who had attended the seminar, initiated a decision by the Andean Parliament to promote the discussion of an international arbitration system for sovereign debt. Audits to determine the legitimacy or illegitimacy of external debts were demanded, as well as citizen committees to control and regulate future external debt, and the elimination of preferential treatment of creditors to avoid distortions of international financial markets. Finally the Andean Parliament decided to promote the establishment of a network of representatives of debtor and creditor countries closely cooperating with civil society organizations to encourage the establishment of the international arbitration tribunal of sovereign debt.

Work on sovereign insolvency continued. In 2003 Chr. Paulus proposed a 'model law' formulated by, for instance, UNCITRAL or UNCTAD to be copied by countries in order to avoid different national laws dealing with sovereign insolvency, combined with a neutral entity. The proposal by Acosta and Ugarteche (2003) is probably the most far-reaching: an international arbitration tribunal working on the basis of the Chapter 9 principles I propose plus codifying a legal framework of international financial relations. It was taken up by NGOs, especially in Latin America.

The Jubilee idea is not dead either. Seven years after 2000, Jubilee USA launched the Sabbath Year in January 2007. As the first action, Valentine hearts were addressed to US Treasury Secretary H. Henry Paulson, asking him to 'Have a heart and cancel Liberia's debt!'

During the recent past NGO work also introduced the concept of odious debts into public discussion. Later on NGOs concentrated on the legitimacy of debts. Norwegian NGOs had campaigned especially for cancelling 'dictator debts', claims whose legitimacy are challenged because the money went to undemocratic and often corrupt dictators. The concept of illegitimate debts received a big boost when the new Norwegian government committed itself to supporting international debt arbitration concerning illegitimate debt in 2005, and when Norway declared on 2 October 2006 to cancel parts of the claims deriving from her Ship Export Campaign, which the government classified as a 'development policy failure'. Although the government itself did not use the word 'illegitimate', Norwegian NGOs in particular see this as a result of their lobbying. For the first time a creditor government explicitly recognized part of its claims as improper, and acted upon that conclusion. Although the reason given by Norway's government was creditor co-responsibility for (undiplomatically put) credit pushing, a path-breaking new idea until then shunned by other official creditors, this also boosted the discussion on illegitimate debts. This very laudable attitude is sadly missing with all other official creditors that have steadfastly refused to apply even generally recognized legal standards and principles to SCs so far.

Relations between NGOs, governments and international organizations have usually been quite good, especially during the recent past. Unfortunately rare exceptions exist, as the BWI Annual Meetings in Singapore in September 2006 prove. The BWIs accredited the largest number of NGO representatives ever. There was broad engagement in a process of consultation with Asian NGOs to prepare the civil society forum. 'But, of course, Singapore will be remembered for the controversy surrounding the government's banning of a number of CSOs' legitimately accredited representatives,' as the IMF's *Civil Society Newsletter* of November 2006 informs. This was an open and blatant breach of the agreement with the BWIs that publicly asked the host government to allow all NGO participants to attend the meetings. Both the IMF's Managing Director and the IBRD's President

> urged that all CSOs be allowed to attend because, as they put it, it was critical for the institutions to have the voices of dissent present at the Meetings. The institutions were very disturbed that a number of CSO delegates were detained for questioning upon entering Singapore or, in some cases, deported.

In a letter the Secretary General of the National Confederation of Officers' Associations, India complained to the High Commissioner of

Singapore about the treatment two Indian trade unionists had suffered in Singapore, being treated like common criminals. One delegate

> while in captivity drew inspiration from the fact that in the last century, in South Africa, Mahatma Gandhi was pulled off a train and thrown on to the platform merely because he dared to enter a compartment 'reserved' for whites notwithstanding the fact that he was a legitimate passenger with a valid ticket.

CSO events had to be cancelled because the organizers were not allowed to enter. NGOs called for a boycott. Singapore authorities declared that they had provided ample space for NGO demonstrations and events, according to the police a basement room the 'size of a badminton court'. Due to Singapore's violating their agreement with the BWIs, that room probably did not become too crowded. Allegedly Singapore also tried to hinder civil society to organize their forum at Batam, Indonesia. Upholding democracy and freedom of expression, the Indonesian government decided not to ban this meeting. It went along absolutely peacefully, arguably with more media coverage than it might have enjoyed if everything had gone as smoothly as usual.

CAMPAIGNING FOR TRANSPARENCY

As good campaigning needs information, efforts to increase transparency and to make information customarily withheld more easily available were an important part of NGO work.

To make creditor positions more transparent, EURODAD started to publish its *World Credit Tables* in the mid-1990s, which revealed hitherto confidential information on how much creditor countries were owed by each SC. After the IBRD clamped down on access to confidential centralized creditor information held in its databases, NGO networking still made an 'unofficial' breakdown of creditors' lending possible. Later a follow-up volume called *Taking Stock of Debt* was published, consisting of three parts: EURODAD's latest analysis of the debt issue and HIPC, creditor and debtor profiles.

The increased transparency of the IMF is a result of NGO work. Until the 1990s Article IV reports had never been published. The IMF claimed that it could not publish them since they were documents owned by member countries. After the Swiss Coalition of NGOs lobbied for publication of Switzerland's report, the Swiss government decided to do so in 1994, in line with this country's tradition of high standards of democracy. This unprecedented step provoked harsh criticism by the IMF – suddenly claiming that the document was its property, not the member country's – and other member countries but stimulated new discussions on IMF transparency. Nowadays, these reports can be downloaded, mostly in full, from the IMF's home page.

With the Paris Club, NGO lobbying, strong criticism of its lack of transparency and creditor dominated procedures (see, for instance, Kaiser, 2001) had similar effects. Meanwhile the Paris Club has a home page, an openness unthinkable not that long ago, even though NGOs continue to see this website's information as insufficient. One has to recall that the Paris Club manages public funds – missing information is thus also withheld from the real owners, the peoples of Paris Club member countries.

The role of SAPRIN in making information on the effects of debt management publicly available was already highlighted. Much of what is now freely accessible was secret not that long ago, and would presumably have remained so without NGOs. This in turn would have slowed down progress towards more meaningful debt relief.

11. The concept of sustainability of international financial institutions

The very aim and purpose of any debt reduction – be it arbitrarily granted by some creditors or based on a mechanism respecting the foundations of the Rule of Law – is quite obviously enabling debtors to fulfil their remaining and reduced obligations smoothly and in time. Standing on their own feet, debtors must be able to keep out of debt problems during the foreseeable future. Their debt obligations must remain manageable, or sustainable. Meaningful sustainability estimates are thus the economic base of any economically successful solution. Unfortunately the BWIs have not provided proper sustainability estimates, thus prolonging the debt problem.

Logically the BWIs justified their earliest adjustment programmes as necessary in order to reach sustainability. The IMF approved 88 arrangements between January 1979 and December 1981, all with the officially declared aim to support adjustment policies, particularly measures to reach a sustainable balance of payments position (Crockett, 1982). The 'Baker Plan' wanted to bridge a short period of payment problems to allow SCs to grow into sustainability. Paris Club debt reductions officially purport to want to restore sustainability. The only explanation of the unuseful cut-off point seems to be the idea that debtors are restored to full sustainability after Paris Club treatment, a very unrealistic assumption as the Paris Club's sorry record of debt management proves. Several SCs have visited the Paris Club on what may be called a regular basis to be granted a definite solution of debt problems each time. As mentioned in Chapter 6, Ecuador had to ask the Paris Club for debt relief seven times within less than 20 years. All debt reduction schemes since the late 1980s have had the aim of restoring sustainability, with definitely underwhelming results.

The description of the declared aim of HIPC quoted in Chapter 2 – 'to meet its current and future external debt-service obligations in full without recourse to debt relief, rescheduling of debts, or the accumulation of arrears, and without unduly compromising growth' – perfectly defines sustainability. However, as an OED HIPC review (Gautham, 2003, p. 54) sums up:

It would have been more realistic for the initiative to set the more modest objective of reducing debt to a level that provides countries with a reasonable chance of sustaining their external debts. Even this more modest objective would require full creditor participation to deliver the promised level of relief, and prudent debt management. The initiative assumes that all creditors will participate, but cannot assure this.

The last sentence refers to the fact that creditors, who had no say in determining the outcome, especially the private sector in the case of HIPCs, are not always willing to accept the decisions of official creditors. It is unfair Paris Club practice to make the weakest actor, the debtor, force excluded creditors to comply. If taken to court in a Paris Club country, the debtor is not protected but will lose litigation.

In spite of the problems mentioned above,

The objective related to debt sustainability became more ambitious: from reducing debt as part of a broader strategy to achieve long-run sustainability in 1995; to reducing debt to sustainable levels and thus providing a durable exit strategy from the rescheduling process in the original formulation of the initiative in 1996; to providing a 'robust' exit from debt reschedulings and the achievement of debt sustainability in 1998 . . .; to a 'permanent' exit from the rescheduling process and a 'clear' exit from unsustainable debt in 1999 . . . . The objectives were expanded to specifically target the freed resources to social spending, ostensibly suggesting that debt relief would generate additional resource flows. (Gautham, 2003, p. 11)

One might wonder what the difference between robust, durable, permanent and clear precisely is. This OED document defines 'clear' as removing 'the debt overhang and provide an appropriate cushion against exogenous shocks' (ibid., p. 12), which many people might equally well call a robust, durable or permanent exit. But the meaning of each word is not clear too. The Committee on Development Effectiveness (CODE) 'discussed varying interpretations of what a "permanent exit" from debt rescheduling was intended to mean and suggested caution in automatically linking debt relief to debt sustainability and poverty reduction' (ibid., p. 96). The warning comes as a surprise: logically, achieving sustainability is always linked to debt relief in the case of insolvent debtors.

BWI debt management hardly contributed to providing a robust, clear or permanent exit from debt problems. UNCTAD (2004, p. 5) points out the example of Africa: 'Total external debt then worsened significantly during the period of structural adjustment in the 1980s and early 1990s, reaching a peak of about $340 billion in 1995, the year immediately preceding the launch of the original HIPC.' Over the same period, total debt service paid by the continent increased from about $3.5 billion to a peak of \$26 billion. During the 1980s and 1990s both arrears and multilateral and official debt components of total outstanding debt increased. In 1998 UNCTAD estimated two thirds of the increase in sub-Saharan African debt since 1989 to have been caused by arrears. Such increases and their effects are creditor caused damage.

Among creditor countries, there 'was almost unanimous agreement that expectations about what HIPC can and will achieve are way out of line with what is likely to happen. This poses real dangers for the initiative and for the HIPCs themselves', according to the OED (Gautham, 2003, p. 77). Most creditor countries believed that achieving both debt sustainability at completion point and poverty reduction seemed unlikely: 'Quite generalized agreement existed that HIPC alone would not provide overall debt sustainability for this group of countries as a whole, although it might make some individual countries sustainable, at least for a while.' In other words, creditors declared that the HIPC framework had failed. CODE concluded that 'the HIPC Initiative had objectives that could not be met through design improvements alone' (ibid., p. 96).

In light of these acknowledgements it is all the more remarkable that the BWIs' Debt Sustainability Framework (DSF) redefined sustainability in an alarming way. IMF and IDA (2004, p. 5, emphasis in original) inform:

> *The debt sustainability framework proposed in this paper will have no bearing on the implementation of the HIPC Initiative.* The HIPC Initiative deals with the existing debt overhang in HIPCs and is built upon binding thresholds to achieve debt reduction, which ensures equal treatment of countries under this Initiative. The proposed debt sustainability framework, in contrast, serves the different purpose of informing judgments on appropriate future borrowing policies in low-income countries.

Under their DSF the BWIs should prepare a Debt Sustainability Analysis (DSA) for all IDA-only, PRGF eligible countries every year. 'The objective of the framework is to support low-income countries in their efforts to achieve the Millennium Development Goals (MDGs) without creating future debt problems, and to keep countries that have received debt relief under the HIPC Initiative on a sustainable track' (IBRD, 2006, p. 2). The purpose of the DSA is to assess whether a solvent country's current borrowing strategy may lead to future debt servicing difficulties. Based on this DSA, countries would be classified according to the assessed risk of debt distress. This classification would be used to determine the share of grants and loans in IDA's assistance. This apparently permanent control of debtor SCs as well as the invention of the IMF's Policy Support Instrument (PSI) seem to indicate a clear will of the BWIs to control SCs permanently. In plain English, this means that SCs can virtually never again become fully sovereign countries. This idea is not new. In the mid-1990s the IMF had proposed a permanent ESAF, which it had expected to become operational by 2005.

THE NATURE OF A DEBT OVERHANG

To illustrate the problem of sustainability, it might be useful to return to my concept of phantom debts. Overindebtedness – often called debt over-hang in the literature – describes a situation where parts of the debt stock are unpayable. This can be shown by a simple numerical illustration: 5 per cent interest, no amortization, and $1000 debt stock initially. The example could be complicated, for example, by introducing amortization, variable interest rates or inflation. This would make it less clear, but leave the basic mechanism unchanged. Capitalized arrears increase debt stocks, as anyone familiar with basic mathematics can verify.

During year 1 debts grow by capitalized interest arrears of $25. As the debtor is insolvent not (temporarily) illiquid this problem does not disap-pear. Debts accumulate, amounting to $1279 ($1247 + $32) at the end of year 10 (Table 11.1). The gaps between debt service due and actually paid widen although debt service increases steadily, possibly so because of the lemon squeezer effect of BWI-type 'structural adjustment'. Debts accumulate in the books of creditors with increasing shares of what may be called 'phantom debts'. These exist exclusively on paper, without any economic base whatsoever. They cannot be cashed, they are technically irrecoverable. Creditors record money already lost as though it were still encashable, eagerly calculating and adding interest on this money already lost.

Table 11.1   The evolution of unpayable debts

	Debt Stock	Debt Service Due	Debt Service Paid	New Debt
Year 1	1000	50	25	25
Year 2	1025	51.25	26.25	25
Year 3	1050	52.5	26.5	26
Year 4	1076	53.8	27.8	26
Year 5	1102	55.1	28.1	27
Year 6	1129	56.45	28.45	28
Year 7	1157	57.85	28.85	29
Year 8	1186	59.3	29.3	30
Year 9	1216	60.8	29.8	31
Year 10	1247	62.35	30.35	32

Caused by creditors unwilling to grant needed reduction in time, debts are boosted to ever more unrealistic levels. Debt reduction to sustainable levels appears costlier and costlier on paper. Cancelling $520 after two years would have allowed the debtor to pay as due – if the income level (foreign exchange earnings for sovereigns) assumed for this year can at least be maintained. This is by no means sure if protracted debt service at the cost of necessary replacements had reduced long-run production capacities, as feared by the IBRD or the GATT already in the 1980s. Finally $672 must be cancelled (new stock: $607) to allow honouring all obligations with $30.35. The difference ($152) – pure but not the only phantom debts created by arrears accumulating on top of already unpayable debts – results from creditors' opposition to timely reduction.

From this simple illustration interesting conclusions emerge:

1. Deleting phantom debts simply acknowledges facts. As one cannot lose money one cannot get, this 'reduction' costs creditors not one cent. It is 'generosity for free'. Debtors get no real reduction, although taking away the debt overhang as such is a positive thing. Costs of debt relief are exaggerated by including phantom costs at face value. In talking about debt reduction creditors routinely present costs that sound prohibitively large. Economically, though, these figures are untenable. An example are costs of $34 billion over time – two thirds of HIPC's total costs – estimated officially for 22 Decision Point HIPCs around 2000. The *Washington Post* (16 March 1999) reported that $3 billion of 'forgiven' debt would actually mean a 'maximum budget cost' of $190 million (6.33 per cent of face value), as the rest had been 'essentially written down or written off as incollectible'. A more recent report on HIPC debts informs that the US government – mandated by Congress to estimate the present value of its loan portfolio – applies a 92 per cent discount (UNCTAD, 2004, p. 55). At the Cologne Summit Chancellor Schröder said in an interview that essentially debts were forgiven that could not have been collected anyway – a nice way to define phantom debts.

   More recently non-official estimates by Belgium's Treasury were circulated that put the value of some Belgian claims at 4 per cent of their face value. A Resolution by Belgium's Senate (3-1507/6 of 27 March 2007) demanded that secondary market values of public claims should be published, and cost estimates of relief must no longer be based on nominal claims but that realistic, market values should be used. Proper accounting would of course deflate official 'generosity' perceptibly. It destroys the 'argument' that huge costs prevent further relief down to sustainable levels.

In fact as UNCTAD (2004, pp. 55ff.) shows, HIPC's financial impact on actual total debt service payments was 'quite marginal'. Debt service payments were even higher in 2001 than during the early 1990s, and projected to increase steadily. As countries are not allowed to accrue arrears before reaching decision point, actual debt service was quite frequently higher at that stage than in earlier years. Although countries pay in fact more, deleting phantom claims creates the appearance of generosity. HIPC is characterized by phantom debt reductions creating phantom generosity. In some cases, such as Guinea-Bissau or Tanzania, bilateral creditors provided grants to settle arrears, defending the myth that the country had indeed finally paid.

UNCTAD (2004, p. 55) quotes a paper by Cohen (presented at a joint IMF/IBRD workshop in 2003) suggesting that although the HIPC Initiative had brought the average level of the debt-to-export ratio down from 300 per cent to 150 per cent, this reduction seemed likely just to have eliminated the non-payable portion of debts, or what I call phantom debts.

2. Meaningful reduction must go beyond removing phantom debts. A certain share of remaining claims can be paid if the debtor's future – in US legal parlance: 'fresh start' – is put at risk. In any insolvency case more than $152 would be cancelled to protect debtors and to ensure economic sustainability. Investment needed to ensure viability and 'tools of trade' are exempt. Debtors are also guaranteed a minimum standard of living. Too small reductions – Highly Insufficient Payments Cuts (HIPCs) – expose debtors to relatively small external shocks and are likely to impair their capacity to honour remaining obligations. Rational private investors will be reluctant to invest, fearing the next 'adjustment' programme. Nationals have an incentive to transfer assets out of their country. With phantom costs gone, the situation would still not be sustainable but highly unstable. Of course if and as long as export revenues increase, for example, because of a commodity boom, things will go well.

3. Too small or just sufficient reductions conditioned on additional expenditures by debtors logically produce new crises as lending is needed to finance debt relief. The interest rate of additional borrowing is immaterial. Even 0.5 per cent is unfeasible. If $672 were cancelled but conditional upon the debtor's financing measures (for example, poverty reduction) amounting to $70, the debtor would – *ceteris paribus* – have to finance these programmes by new loans. New arrears would accumulate, even without external shocks and during the grace period. An increase of 35 cents per annum ($70 at 0.5 per cent interest)

is moderate. The arbitrarily assumed swap for poverty reduction of roughly 10 per cent of the reduction is low. But the build-up of arrears starts again, evolving relatively slowly due to the high concessionality of additional borrowing. Demanding softer IDA terms (99 years maturity, 40 years grace) the Zedillo report (Zedillo et al., 2001) was probably aware of this problem.

Poverty reduction and investments necessary for sustainability must be financed from debt reductions beyond $672 – from money creditors could technically collect without debtor protection. Additional financing must obey the restriction

$$\text{Additional Financing} \leq (\text{Total Reduction}) - 672 \qquad (11.1)$$

If equality signs apply debtors remain exposed to minimal shocks and the risk of being unable to maintain perceptibly increased payments ($30.35). Insufficient cancellations create vulnerability. If HIPCs pay more after 'relief' than before other expenditures are crowded out by increased debt service.

4. Delaying relief, creditors have caused damages to debtors, also making things more difficult for themselves. Substantial shares of present debts were caused by creditors delaying necessary reductions over years – as the IBRD's *Global Development Finance* 1997 admitted (see Chapter 2). One cannot but concur with the IBRD's warning in its *World Debt Tables 1992–93* that protracted renegotiations and uncertainty damaged economic activity in debtor countries for several years, and refer to the costs of delaying a solution found by IBRD staff (see Chapter 3).

5. Unlike in the simple example above, the question of whether relief proves sufficient depends in a dynamic economy not only on the haircut creditors take, but also on the future trajectory of the debtor economy. As warned above (point 3), the $672 haircut may only produce a precariously unstable situation, where small changes in variables quite likely to change (such as export prices or interest rates) may again thrust the debtor into insolvency. There are two methods on how to improve the stability of the outcome:

●   Clauses making payments contingent on changes in variables, for example, additional payments to creditors if growth takes off more strongly than expected or a Bisque clause as the Pearson Report had recommended, allowing debtors to pay less if things go worse than assumed. As the IBRD (2000a, p.25, emphasis in original) points out, the Indonesian de facto insolvency after

Sukarno included 'a *bisque clause* arrangement similar to that contained in the Anglo-American Financial Agreement'. Apparently it was less generous, as the Paris Club only permitted Indonesia 'to defer at its option up to one-half of the principal payments falling due in the early years of the new schedule. These deferred obligations were to be repaid with an interest at 4 percent per annum during the final years of the agreement.' Incidentally the last years for deferred interest payments included the years 1997 and 1998. Arguably such a clause might be less attractive to private creditors. But the private sector has occasionally agreed to linking payments to indicators such as growth or the price of crude oil. Well-stipulated contingency clauses can reduce risk and assure a greater fairness to creditors and debtors. It could be one important and helpful feature of international Chapter 9 debt arbitration.

- Forecasting likely changes of important variables, such as export income growth, GDP growth, and calculating how strong external shocks could be absorbed without a new crisis. Assuming real exports earnings of $600 in year 10, which are just sufficient to pay $30.35 to creditors, a fall in export income of 5 per cent in year 11 (or an interest rate increase of five percentage points) would virtually wipe out the capacity to service debts (even without any amortization). Such changes are not unheard of, especially not over a period of several years.

The BWIs have done forecasts and projection. Unfortunately these were routinely (although not always) far too optimistic. Assuming a real growth rate of exports of 9 per cent (not an unrealistic illustration of IFI assumptions for a HIPC) real export receipts are $933.94 after five and $1436.99 after ten years, while a realistic 1 per cent growth rate would have rendered $637.96 and $670.51, respectively. Expressed as percentages of export revenues, strikingly different figures result. Assuming no further interest arrears, and a constant debt stock of $607 (after reduction) the ratio of debts:exports would be either 42.24 per cent or 90.53 per cent of export earnings after ten years. Due to the generosity of the assumed reductions both ratios are officially sustainable (that is, according to the perception of creditors). If debt reduction had been as generous as the so-called '80 per cent Paris Club debt relief', which meant a mere 17 per cent actual reduction (see Chapter 2), the figures would be 73.87 per cent and 158.32 per cent, respectively after ten years, the former clearly sustainable according to HIPC II criteria, the latter not; and both absolutely sustainable under HIPC I. One may complicate the example by introducing temporary arrears that are capitalized but can later be reduced by debt service without problems. In any case, though, overoptimism produces and 'justi-fies' too small debt reductions.

In practice, there is one further complication. Debt stock has tradition-ally been measured in present value terms. Unlike the remaining stock of debts in our very simple example, any discounted value depends crucially on the discount rate. While overoptimism in forecasting growth or export income may 'reduce' debt reduction 'necessary' to reach 'sustainability' – as that obviously has routinely been the case when it comes to SCs – a higher discount rate serves the same purpose. The BWIs, it appears, have combined both ways of reducing 'necessary' debt reductions when calcu-lating debt burdens. UNCTAD (2004, p. 54) pointed out: 'As Uganda's reassessment under the enhanced HIPC Initiative showed, high discount rates combined with overly optimistic export projections can make a country's debt appear sustainable, even though it is not.'

DISCOUNTING WITH COMPLETELY INAPPROPRIATE REFERENCE RATES (CIRRS)

The HIPC Initiative has used six-month averages of the currency specific long-term commercial interest reference rates (CIRRs), which correspond with a maturity of approximately ten years used to calculate present values, or NPVs (net PVs) as the BWIs usually say.

The BWIs see this *'present value of debt*, which – in contrast to its face value – captures the concessionality of outstanding obligations' (IMF and IDA, 2004, p. 14, emphasis in original) as a useful shorthand measure of the future debt service burden inherent in existing debt. 'Reliance on existing NPV-based indicators avoids the need for projections, but is not without problem, as such indicators compare future debt-service obligations with existing repayment capacity without taking account of countries' ability to grow.' According to IMF and IDA (ibid.) 'the appropriate discount rate should ideally capture the long-term return on risk-free assets, suggesting an approach that filters out temporary fluctuations. For this reason, it is proposed that the discount rate for future NPV calculations outside the HIPC Initiative be set initially at 5 percent – the (rounded) current level of the U.S. dollar CIRR' adjusted over time.

If the discount rate actually attempted to be a substitute of projections or to help estimate future sustainability, however, CIRRs are completely inappropriate reference rates. They may measure the difference between what a lender has to pay to raise this amount of money in capital markets and at what conditions it is lent on. They may indeed measure conces-sionality of official lenders, although one may question whether different country specific CIRRs really allow a comparison of official creditors. In the case of export credits a low interest rate simply is a price reduction without which exports could not have been sold.

But sustainability based on such discount rates is meaningless. The NPV concept is used for investment decisions as streams of revenues and outlays can only be compared meaningfully at the same point of time. It makes sense there because $100 today is actually equivalent to $105 in a year's time if one invests this sum at 5 per cent. Discounted values provide useful information for comparing expected streams of payments.

In the case of debts, however, discounting at market interest rates simply states that if the debtor had the NPV today and could invest it at the discount rate(s), all debts would be covered at maturity – logically true but unhelpful. HIPCs qualify as such precisely because they do not have spare money for such investments. Usually they are even unable to honour all financial commitments at concessional terms, which means that these terms are already too tough for them. Using NPVs is like demanding a malnourished, heavily packed person to run 100 metres in 13 seconds, rightly drawing attention to a 30 per cent element of concessionality in comparison with 10 seconds (Raffer, 1998a).

UNCTAD (2004, p. 75) rightly suggests that 'one relatively low level discount rate, such as 3 per cent, could be used for all currencies'. Considering growth rates of some HIPCs in some years, one would have to ask, though, whether 3 per cent might not be too high already.

Discounting future debt service payments with market interest rates reduces debt burdens considerably on paper, just as overoptimistic forecasts reduce the relative burden of future debt payments. Thus the NPV of all HIPC debts was about $190 billion at the end of 1994 according to the IMF, while their nominal debts were $241 billion. At about the same time (in 1995), arrears on principal repayments represented one fifth of the total debt stock of sub-Saharan Africa as UNCTAD (2004, p. 5) points out – a clear sign that debt terms were too onerous.

UNCTAD (2004, p. 54) gives a telling example of the relevance of the chosen rate. In the case of a $10 million loan at 4 per cent, repayable over 40 years (including 10 years grace), a discount rate of 6 per cent produces an NPV of $7.5 million, while 2 per cent results in an NPV of $13.9 million (nearly twice as much). 'In other words, every percentage point difference in the discount rate implies a change in the NPV of about 16 per cent.'

The GAO (2000, pp. 95–6) illustrated differences between discount rates very clearly. A concessional loan having a grant element of 76.5 per cent if the OECD's standard 10 per cent discount rate is applied, shows a grant element of only 51 per cent at a discount rate of 5.25 per cent (July – December 1998 average CIRR, 'the method used by the World Bank and

IMF staffs in analyzing countries' debt profiles under the HIPC Initiative'). Less technically, 'a country may think it has to pay about $19 for debt service when calculated using the DAC but actually has to pay about $40, as calculated under the CIRR method'. Unsurprisingly, UNCTAD (2004, p. 75) explicitly considers the option of discarding the NPV concept, 'as there are some indications that several investors are not as concerned about the NPV of a country's debt as they are about its nominal value'. As investments trigger growth and development it would be wise to take investors' views properly into account, especially so if they are economically sound.

Using PVs allows creditors to shift debt service problems into the future. Warning that 'NPV debt reductions lead to continuously high debt service payments', UNCTAD (2004, p. 58) points out that the 'main problem with such a rescheduling is that it actually increases the total debt service of a country in the long-term'. Putting most debt service payments off to the future provides some relief in the short term, but 'will thus undermine long-term debt sustainability (especially if combined with overly optimistic growth rates, as is the case under the Initiative)'. UNCTAD concludes that debt rescheduling makes the situation worse for HIPCs, as it increases the cumulative amount of debt service payments.

This problem is most clearly demonstrated by long grace periods. This simply means a temporary respite before amortization has to be paid. During these respite periods debt service declines by force of fundamental mathematic rules. Official creditors can provide their NPV debt relief by rescheduling, also for ODA repayments. This politically motivated agreement among Paris Club members may be appropriate for cases of illiquidity but hardly for insolvent debtors, because it simply shifts payments – often also insolvency – into the future.

The economic sense behind a 'solution', such as the debt service option, under which Cologne Terms with 90 per cent NPV reduction on eligible debts are achieved 'through concessional interest rates and a repayment period of 125[!] years, including 65[!] years of grace' (IBRD 2000b, p. 171) remains unclear at best. Similarly, the 'bullet option' with an interest rate of 0.0001 per cent (the IBRD does not dare write over how many years) would be ridiculed in the case of all other debtor-creditor relations. Such debt management does not provide solutions, but affects North-South relations fundamentally. It provides long-term political leverage to the North, allowing creditors to change the policies of debtors.

Discarding the NPV method, using the average interest rate of loans to specific debtor countries or their growth rates as the highest discount rate seems indicated. As actual interest burdens already created problems in the past, one should not imagine any higher discount rate justified. There is concern that discarding the NPV method might be unfair to creditor countries. UNCTAD (2004, p.75) warns that this 'might entail some injustice in the provision of debt relief to countries with sharply diverging maturity structures, as well as some unfairness for creditors providing debt relief on debts with different levels of concessionality'.

It must be noted, though, that *'For private external debt, the NPV is assumed to be identical to the nominal value of debt* (i.e. the nominal interest rate is assumed to be equal to the discount rate)' (IBRD, 2006, p.18, emphasis in original). Thus any haircut agreed on in percentages of NPVs means higher reductions in terms of current dollars by the private sector. Also shifting payments into the future does not reduce NPVs of the private sector – in contrast to public creditors. This does not make it any easier for HIPCs to demand comparable treatment from private sector creditors. Once again the public sector secures itself unfair preferred treatment.

There is no need to go further into distribution and fairness problems of official creditors here, many of whom granted credits in order to foster their own political advantage, thus for very selfish motives. Face values should be used when it comes to debtors. Necessary debt reductions have to be expressed in face values or in PVs that are based on realistic growth rates, or realistic capacities to pay. The distribution of losses among creditors may well be done according to whatever measure creditors prefer. Should a discount rate be wished by official creditors to do so, any value (including zero and infinite) is welcome, as long as it does not reflect on the actual debt relief of debtor countries.

WHICH DEBT LEVEL IS SUSTAINABLE?

In 2003 the IMF's *World Economic Outlook* (2003, p.142) suggested that a 'sustainable public debt level for a typical emerging economy may only be about 25 percent of GDP'. This is much less than the levels of several present problem cases, especially in the case of HIPCs. To compare this view of the IMF with an emerging market and a former model disciple of the Fund, Argentina: when the government announced default, sovereign debts amounted to 53.5 per cent of GDP. After restructuring and repudiation, sovereign debt still recognized in December 2005 amounted to 72 per cent of GDP according to holdout creditors. Logically this means that the haircut was still – by far – not big enough if one accepts the IMF's maximum.

Argentina's case also raises grave doubts about the practical value of sustainability estimates. Well before the September 2001 augmentation, staff estimates had been done on how much debt would have to be cut in order to reach sustainability. As a 'memo to management dated July 26,

2001 noted: "While the results are highly sensitive to the assumptions, the staff estimates that a haircut of between 15 and 40 percent is required, depending on the policy choice" (IMF, IEO 2004, p. 90, fn.95). The IMF nevertheless went on lending, increasing the amount of debt unapayable by its own estimates. Requesting preference over others, this also means that the Fund knowingly increased the haircut private creditors would have to suffer as well as its own income. If the recognition of clear unsustainability just triggers new loans deteriorating catastrophe, one wonders about the usefulness of sustainability estimates.

The IMF (2003b, p. 140) presented research results for the period 1970–2002 that 'suggest that while large debt reductions have often occurred in conjunction with debt defaults there are cases where they have been brought about by a combination of strong economic growth and fiscal consolidation'. Nineteen out of 26 cases 'were associated with a debt default'. Obviously reductions in the past had been insufficient, as the IMF itself acknowledged by proposing its SDRM. This passage also recalls a well-known fact from insolvency procedures: while some debtors believed to be insolvent can overcome their problem, most cannot. It also seems logical to assume that very poor countries, such as HIPCs, cannot manage as high relative debts as emerging markets, that is that 25 per cent of GDP is even less sustainable than in the case of these comparatively richer countries.

This IMF opinion apart, officially established levels of sustainability raise questions. Thus UNCTAD (2004, p. 31) pointed out that two HIPCs (Tanzania and Uganda) had lower debt ratios than some African non-HIPCs (Djibouti, Eritrea, Lesotho, Nigeria, Zimbabwe), based on NPV debt:GNI ratios, and a lower debt burden than Cape Verde, Nigeria and Zimbabwe, using NPV debt:revenue ratios. It is difficult to see an objective, economic base for this phenomenon, especially so as HIPC II assumes one unsustainable debt level for all 'eligible' countries.

One logically possible explanation would be that 'debt thresholds should be established in light of the quality of a country's policies and institutions' (IMF and IDA, 2004, p. 21). In other words, better governed countries using more advanced debt management techniques can cope with a higher debt burden than others. While there is some logic to that, it is the opposite of the one size fits all dividing line of 150 per cent, which – as one must recall – is much higher than the debt burden once considered unsustainable in the case of Germany.

The new, post-HIPC framework officially designed in order to support low-income countries in their efforts to achieve the MDGs without creating future debt problems, and to keep countries that have received HIPC debt relief on a sustainable track, explicitly refers to the 'quality of policies and institutions' as one of the 'pillars' (IMF and IDA, 2005, p. 2). One 'of

Table 11.2   Indicative policy-dependent debt and debt-service thresholds (in %)

	Assessment of Institutional Strength and Quality of Policies		
	Poor	Medium	Strong
NPV of debt-to-GDP	30	45	60
NPV of debt-to-exports	100	200	300
NPV of debt-to-revenue	150	200	250
Debt service-to-exports	15	25	35
Debt service-to-revenue	20	30	40

Source: IMF and IDA (2004, p. 21).

the key elements' of this new framework 'distinct from the HIPC Initiative in important ways' that was 'strongly endorsed by both Boards on the basis of empirical evidence, is that the indicative debt-burden thresholds should depend on the quality of countries' policies and institutions. This feature alone distinguishes the debt sustainability framework from the HIPC approach with its uniform threshold (ibid., p. 11)'. This begs the question why such flexibility was not applied long ago, especially so as HIPC I had already applied some flexibility that was totally lost again by HIPC II.

Based on 'empirical evidence' the BWIs now establish debt thresholds 'in light of the quality of a country's policies and institutions' (IMF and IDA, 2004, p. 21). These are supposed to hold 'Irrespective of what probability of debt distress is considered tolerable'. The document provides an operational matrix translating this notion, 'by defining indicative policy-dependent debt limits, based on the (rounded) results of Bank and Fund staff's empirical analyses' (Table 11.2).

One cannot help noticing that the lowest debt/GDP value is perceptibly higher than what the IMF's *World Economic Outlook* thought sustainable for emerging markets. One might possibly argue that higher average interest rates of emerging markets might account for this difference. Lower interest rates connected with official flows are certainly an argument. On the other hand, the debts of low-income countries have accumulated while the use of funds has been closely, sometimes even intrusively, monitored by official creditors. This raises questions as to the quality of monitoring and finally about the appropriateness of higher thresholds for countries where creditor participation in decision making has co-produced catastrophes. The quality of monitoring may well be seen as a reason not to have higher thresholds.

Except for countries with poor policies and institutions, debt–exports ratios are (far) beyond the values considered unsustainable by both HIPC I and HIPC II. A debtor considered to have strong institutions and good policies would no longer qualify for HIPC I. If the BWIs qualify an SC's policies and institutions as strong/good, this means that less or no debt relief is necessary. In poor countries, where the shares of multilateral claims are relatively high, less debt relief logically means less multilateral relief.

Arguably of more importance is the fact that higher debt levels automatically mean less grants when it comes to financing the MDGs. The BWIs frankly admit this:

> Given the central role of official creditors and donors in providing new development resources to these countries, the framework simultaneously provides guidance for their lending and grant-allocation decisions to ensure that resources to low-income countries are provided on terms that are consistent with their long-term debt sustainability and progress towards achieving the MDGs. (IMF and IDA, 2004, p. 4)

The document also states: 'Given low-income countries' reliance on official flows, debt sustainability depends largely on the willingness of official creditors and donors to provide positive net transfers through new financing' (ibid.). In plain English, a real and definite exit from debt problems is either no longer wanted by official creditors, or was never their real aim.

This conclusion is corroborated by the fact that sustainability is meanwhile differentiated from external viability. The GAO (2000, p. 47) explains: 'According to the IMF, a country is "externally viable" if it is able to pay its external obligations with its own resources (tax revenues, external account surpluses, and nonconcessional borrowing), without recourse to donor assistance.' SCs that cannot achieve external viability are nevertheless pronounced sustainable. One cannot but concur with the GAO that achieving external viability is important because in that case an SC is no longer dependent on concessional financing to meet its debt obligations. This distinction between external viability and sustainability raises questions regarding the real goals of debt management. IMF-style 'sustainability' (with inverted commas) means dependence on official creditors, including multilaterals. Rereading the definition of sustainability presented by the OED's HIPC review at the beginning of this chapter, one notes that such dependence does not contradict this official definition of sustainability. Really overcoming the debt problem is most obviously no longer the aim of debt management, supposing that it ever was. The GAO (2000, p. 47) illustrates the difference between the two terms with absolute clarity: 'Thus, although Tanzania would be considered debt sustainable following HIPC relief, it would not be "externally viable" because it would continue to require some external balance-of-payments assistance to close its financing gap.'

In Uganda's case 'the decision to borrow these resources for poverty reduction results in Uganda never achieving external viability over the projection period' (ibid., p. 48; see also the point about additional financing in the simple numerical example above). If donors were actually prepared to 'spare no effort' in order to reach the MDGs, they would have provided the necessary money as grants.

Some donors, such as Norway, were indeed willing to help ensure durable debt sustainability. Thus they 'have chosen to cancel all their claims, as a supplement to the HIPC Initiative' (Ministry of Foreign Affairs, 2004, p. 31), which required less reduction. The BWIs immediately abused this generosity to bail themselves out:

> In autumn 2001, the World Bank and the IMF began to include this type of extraordinary bilateral debt relief when calculating total debt relief provided under the HIPC Initiative. This means that such unilateral debt relief is computed as part of the coordinated HIPC debt relief, instead of coming in addition to it, and thus does not function as an extra guarantee of debt sustainability. Furthermore, it means that the debt relief provided under the HIPC Initiative itself is less than it otherwise would have been. The creditors that provide 100 per cent debt reduction thereby subsidise those that do not, and the multilateral institutions' proportionate share of total debt relief is reduced. The debtor countries, for their part, are deprived of debt relief that was intended as additional assistance. (Ministry of Foreign Affairs, 2004, p. 31)

If reaching external viability were really the goal, this would not happen. Some years earlier, the GAO points out, IMF staff still saw reaching external viability as the goal of debt management. Obviously this no longer applies. The IMF (2004, p. 52) concluded: 'For low-income countries supported by PRGF resources, as well as the early transition economy programs, the emphasis has been more on structural transformation, poverty reduction, and growth promotion than on external adjustment.' Enforcing one's ideological preferences has been preferred over reaching viability, quite in line with Rodrik's interpretation. If one accepts his view, behaviour such as lending more money to Argentina, while and in spite of already considering debt reductions of 15 to 40 per cent necessary, makes perfect sense as well. Unfortunately the MDGs seem to have become another pretext to justify keeping SCs under creditor control for the foreseeable future. A good idea seems to have been perverted to provide another means of control.

12. Problems of overoptimism and ownership

Sustainability estimates by public creditors discussed in detail below have a rather unique characteristic: they have a sorry record of 'overoptimism'. Unlike estimates in general that are revised once a bias is recognized, BWI forecasts of debtors' export volumes and prices, even of growth in OECD countries, have systematically been biased towards predicting too optimistic trajectories. Published to 'support' the illiquidity theory first, and to 'justify' insufficient debt reductions later on, IFIs have routinely been 'overoptimistic'. Routinely erring in this way leads to higher 'sustainable' debt burdens and thus less debt reduction. In the early 1980s very high growth rates of exports and GDP supported the assertion that countries were only temporarily illiquid, but would soon be able to pay fully, literally 'growing out of debts'. More cautious and more realistic estimates would not have served the purpose of defending the illiquidity theory equally well. Over decades too optimistic forecasts have inflicted damages on debtor countries, rendering strategies based on such forecasts, especially debt reductions, useless. The crisis could not be solved, but has been dragged on. As rightly observed by the IBRD as early as 1992, this has inflicted heavy damage on debtor SCs – creditor caused damage that has especially hurt the poorest.

'OVEROPTIMISM' AT WORK

The point that IFIs have systematically erred on the wrong side is no longer contentious, although examples to the contrary exist. Meanwhile IFIs themselves have repeatedly conceded this fact. IMF and IDA (2004, p. 13) wrote:

> Whether a country – and specifically its government – will be able to service its debt depends on its existing debt burden as well as the prospective path of its deficits, the financing mix between loans and grants, and the evolution of its repayment capacity – namely (the foreign currency value of) GDP, exports, and government revenues. Projections of the debt dynamics provide a link between debt sustainability and macro-economic policies. At the same time, such

projections are only as good as their underlying assumptions . . . The scope for error is large – both on the upside and the downside – with past experience suggesting a systematic tendency toward excessive optimism.[10] Indeed, while the specifics differed across countries, a common theme behind the historical rise in low-income countries' debt ratios was that borrowing decisions were predicated on growth projections that never materialized. This experience points to the need for well-disciplined projections, including by laying bare the assumptions on which they are predicated and by subjecting them to rigorous stress tests that explicitly incorporate the impact of exogenous shocks.

These are very basic requirements of any projection, which IFIs admit not to have observed so far. This passage admits that the BWIs have continuously made overoptimistic forecasts, not well-disciplined projections whose assumptions were not explained and which were not stress tested over decades. In private markets any clients could successfully sue their consultants and get financial compensation. Therefore financial accountability and the principles of tort law need be brought to multilateral institutions as well, as I argue in detail in Chapter 13. Downside errors should not be expected too often, though, as footnote 10 in the text above explains:

An analysis of projections made by Fund staff over the period 1990–2001 suggests a bias toward over-optimism of about 1 percentage point a year in forecasts of low-income country real GDP growth. The bias in projecting GDP growth in U.S. dollar terms, however, was considerably larger, at almost 5 percentage points a year. (IMF and IDA, 2004, p. 13)

Over ten years, and with the period used by IMF and IDA in their illustrative example of a hypothetical low-income country (Country B), 5 per cent annually compounds to 62 per cent off the mark. Or in a simple example where 6 per cent growth is projected but 1 per cent materializes, the debt-GDP indicator at the end of the decade would be around 48.6 per cent instead of 30 per cent, over 20 years approximately 78.8 per cent, or 2.63 times as high.

Interestingly overoptimism continues in this very source, right in the illustrative example of Country B: 'Real GDP growth is projected at around 4½ percent, on average, over 2003–2023; this optimistic forecast contrasts with the recent historical experience (½ percent per annum), but may be plausible under a scenario in which good policies are implemented.' (ibid., p. 71). If wrong and the recent historical rate prevailed, the difference over the period with a real GDP of 100 initially would be 110.5 instead of the anticipated 241.2.

Overoptimism is not restricted to poor countries. In the case of the Commonwealth of Independent States: 'overoptimism by multilaterals contributed to the high debt levels' (Helbling et al., 2004, p. 1). Nevertheless the IMF wants to continue with providing projections under the SDRM. As prolonged crises mean increased income and importance, economists could find economic explanations easily. One does of course hope that these explanations do not apply.

Thus, 'excessive optimism' occurred in Asian crisis countries (IMF, IEO, 2003, pp. 27, 96, 116). According to the IEO, 'Overoptimism appears to be a feature of most large IMF-supported programs' (ibid., p. 30). Regarding Indonesia the Fund had also 'highly optimistic assumptions on growth' to base its programme on (ibid., p. 84, see also p. 30, 77).

An *OED Review of the HIPC Initiative* published by the IBRD's OED (Gautham, 2003) illustrates these errors caused by overoptimism more graphically. This document compares growth assumptions maintained in the Debt Sustainability Analysis (DSA) with historical performance for the 24 countries that reached their decision points by end 2001. It finds: 'The overall simple average of the growth rate assumed in DSAs across all 24 countries is more than twice the historical average for 1990–2000 and almost six times the average for 1980–2000' (ibid., p. 28). One cannot but concur: 'The findings show that there was optimism in the assumptions maintained by the DSAs done at decision point.' Level and terms of new financing assumed by DSAs were also criticized as too optimistic, the document adds. Surprisingly, no appropriate changes were made once the error of being too optimistic had become clear: 'A similar analysis of the assumptions in updated DSAs (for 2003–08) shows that although slightly better, the assumptions continue to be optimistic.'

The OED publication concludes: 'The lack of transparency of the economic models behind these projections and the overoptimistic growth assumptions have made debt sustainability analyses ambiguous, giving rise to the impression that the process is politically manipulable. The threshold levels are also partly a function of the level of resources available to the initiative' (ibid., p. 54). In other words, not the needs of debtors but the generosity of creditors determines debt reduction and thus which debt burden is considered sustainable. Under these circumstances there is little wonder that highly insufficient payments cuts have resulted in the case of HIPCs. This underlines the need to end creditor domination and arbitrariness.

Undue optimism has a long history within the BWIs. It is not necessarily an exclusive characteristic of debt sustainability estimates. In the 1980s, for example, the OED, which had been established because of US insistence, criticized unrealistic scheduling and objectives at appraisal, excessive expectations leading to huge gaps between appraised and re-estimated economic rates of return, enduring errors in implementation rate forecasts of up to 20 percentage points (!) for regional averages (even called 'embarrassing' by the OED).

The entire history of debt management is characterized by too optimistic forecasts and expectations producing too small reductions too late. Assessing HIPC II on congressional request the US General Accounting Office (GAO, 2000) corroborates doubts about the reliability of IFI estimates and thus the professionalism of IFIs. Debt sustainability depended on annual growth rates above 6 per cent in US dollar terms over 20 years – in four cases including Nicaragua and Uganda even above 9.1 per cent. Understandably the GAO doubted whether such rates could actually be maintained for that long, warning also about the volatility of commodity prices – external shocks in technocratic lingo. It pointed out that additional money would be necessary. Like so many creditor initiatives before, HIPC II was apparently again built on fragile, 'optimistic' assumptions and forecasts, whose risks and shortcomings were obvious. Its failure was a logical result, underlining the need for changes in the way sustainability has been calculated. With good reason the Zedillo report stated that HIPC II had 'in most cases' (Zedillo et al., 2001, p. 21) not gone far enough to reach sustainable debt levels, suggesting a 're-enhanced' HIPC III (precisely quoted: HIPC3, ibid., p. 54). More realistic forecasts would no doubt have led to more meaningful reductions.

Four years later, when the GAO (2004, p. 15) assessed HIPC again, it found again that 'projected export growth rates are overly optimistic'. The BWIs had projected that 'all 27 HIPC countries will become debt sustainable by 2020 if their exports grow at an average of 7.7 percent each year, they receive debt relief under the HIPC Initiative, and donors provide their expected assistance'. The GAO thought growth rates at the historical annual average of 3.1 per cent more likely, less than half the rate the BWIs projected. The GAO thus estimated 'the total amount of the potential export earnings shortfall over the 2003 to 2020 projection period to be $215 billion'. It also provides an estimate that 'every percentage-point increase (decrease) in export growth rates from the historical average, the export earnings shortfall would decrease (increase) by about $35 billion' (ibid.). The GAO assumes high export growth rates unlikely because of these countries' heavy reliance on primary commodities. While one cannot prove before 2020 who will definitely have been right, historical records and its arguments suggest the GAO's assumption of a substantial shortfall to be much more likely.

Unfortunately the clear perception of past errors due to overoptimism does not seem to trigger an appropriate learning effect. According to its self-description, the reliability of its sustainability estimates touches on the IMF's very reason to exist. One should therefore expect this problem to be tackled. This seems not the case. The external evaluation panel of the IEO (Lissakers et al., 2006, p. 19) noted that they were 'struck by the IEO's focus on process rather than on the substantive issues underlying the process'. They wondered why the most important question 'why the Fund's policy advice had failed to restore the country's external viability', already raised by another report some years before, was not answered. It must be emphasized that the IEO is by far the most critical unit of the IMF, having the merit of exposing grave shortcomings of IMF activities. The IMF, however, has not followed up such findings appropriately so far. The panel concluded

> IEO evaluations to date are generally considered of high quality, but several criticisms were repeatedly made to the panel: they do not isolate and analyze in depth the most important questions such as *why the IMF misdiagnoses exchange rate trajectories and over-estimates growth*, nor do they tackle strategic institutional questions such as the IMF's role in low income countries . . . . The analyses instead focus heavily on IMF processes and procedures. (Lissakers et al., 2006, p. 5, emphasis added)

The panel wondered about the lack of will to learn from the past, mentioning a side remark in the report *IMF and Recent Capital Account Crises* that the IBRD had a far more accurate estimate than the Fund of the depreciation of Brazil's real if the currency were allowed to float:

> Since exchange rates are the IMF's bread and butter and this question was central to the design of the Brazil stabilization package one would expect the IEO to explore why the World Bank got it right and the Fund missed the mark. It does not. As Peter Montiel [commenting on IEO activities in 2003] points out, evaluation teams neither try to explain how the Fund went wrong on its exchange rate analysis nor analyze why the staff's growth projections were 'wildly off the mark'. . . . The chronological narrative approach used for the country case studies does not lend itself to stepping back and honing in one or two central questions. (Lissakers et al., 2006, p. 19)

In spite of past record, thorough analysis in order to improve results does not seem to be seen as important. This can be explained by the fact that IFI clients have to pay for their consultants' negligence, which increases unpayable debts. They have to carry the costs of decades of negligent debt management, of continuously 'overoptimistic' forecasts and estimates which 'proved' initially that no debt overhang existed and served later as the justification for insufficient debt reductions prolonging catastrophe, inflicting easily avoidable damage on the poor.

ERRORS ON THE PESSIMIST SIDE: RAISING EMBARRASSING QUESTIONS

As already mentioned in passing above, the IMF has erred on the low side as well in the past, though obviously not at all as frequently as on the optimist side. Unfortunately, rather than balancing its customary overoptimism, these errors also raise embarrassing questions.

As Rosnick and Weisbrot (2007) show, the IMF's projections for GDP growth in Argentina since 1999, and in Venezuela since 2003, raise serious questions about the objectivity of these estimates. Closely analysing IMF publications the authors find an extremely disturbing error pattern. Their Table 1 (Table 12.1) visualizes the problem clearly.

A clear dividing line emerges. Before the default of 2001– when Argentina served as the model the IMF used to justify its policies – the Fund had always erred in its customary way. However, once Argentina had defaulted, the Fund immediately started to err in the other direction. While optimism before the default was helpful in 'proving' how well one of the model pupils of the IMF did – thanks to IMF advice, of course – forecasts after that event were once again helpfully playing down the effects of default. It might have been a huge success in practice as regards restarting growth, but not according to the forecasts (possibly wishes?) of the Fund. Rosnick and Weisbrot (ibid.) point out: 'These repeated under-estimates of Argentina's growth, as well as the ones for Venezuela (below), depart from the historical bias of IMF growth projections, which have tended toward overestimation.'

The authors then document in detail that the IMF had a very different attitude toward the government of Argentina and her economic policies

Table 12.1   IMF projected GDP growth for Argentina vs actual growth

Fall WEO	Projected Growth (following year)	Actual Growth (following year)	Error in Forecast (percentage points)
1999	1.5	−0.8	+2.3
2000	3.7	−4.4	+8.1
2001	2.6	−10.9	+13.5
	Default and Devaluation (end of 2001)		
2002	1.0	8.8	−7.8
2003	4.0	9.0	−5.0
2004	4.0	9.2	−5.2
2005	4.2	8.5	−4.3

Source: Reproduced from Rosnick and Weisbrot (2007, p. 4, Table 1).

before the default as compared with the period after it. Not everyone shared the IMF's optimistic view. Moody's Investment Service downgraded Argentina's bond rating in 1998. The Fund's Managing Director, Michel Camdessus, expressed his certainty that Moody's would soon see the error of its ways and embrace the IMF's optimistic views (cf. ibid., p. 5).

These optimistic projections for economic growth 'proved' IMF advice right – a 'success' the IMF busily waived around. One notes that Argentina's GDP had dropped by 15.5 per cent, from 100 to 84.5, during these three years, instead of the projected value of 108. On the basis of this projected 'success' the Fund pushed for deeper reforms including more fiscal tightening, privatization and deregulation aimed at restoring market confidence. The optimistic 2.6 per cent growth was forecast as late as October 2001.

IMF optimism must have had effects on the private sector. Its optimist declarations and forecast painted an unrealistically bright economic future. Obviously private lenders took this into account when deciding to buy Argentine bonds. IMF lending to Argentina before default further corroborated that impression. Thus the IMF is responsible for some of the problems of private creditors and Argentina. Granting drawings – even when fully knowing that this would deteriorate the situation – the IMF granted 'abusive credit'. This is a concept in particular familiar to French, Belgian and Italian jurisprudence. Juan Pablo Bohoslavsky (2006) surveyed laws and judicial practice in eight countries establishing creditor liabilities for loose lending in order to extract common principles from national, domestic laws to transform the theory of the responsibility for abusive granting of credit into a general principle of international law. He argues that such 'abusive credits' should also have consequences in international law, and thus be made applicable to cases of sovereign insolvency. This concept holds lenders liable for damages inflicted on other creditors by lending with disregard for the most basic principles of risk evaluation, thus hiding the debtor's real situation and postponing the insolvent borrower's crash, and thereby increasing other creditors' losses. In private business such behaviour triggers an obligation to compensate damages. In contrast, the IMF thrives on crises that are deeper than they would have been without its involvement.

Bohoslavsky (2006) argues that loans granted without following the most elementary prudential guidelines in the analysis of credit risk, attempting by such means to obtain an unfair advantage over previously existing creditors, should be subordinated to those not classified as abusive. Subsequent creditors, in particular those harmed by having been induced to make loans because of abusive lending to a party that could not or would not repay them, could file claims against the abusive grantors generating such false appearance. However this concept is in a very early stage at present. It still needs be made applicable to cases of sovereign insolvency. It should be noted though that the IMF could be taken to court because of such abusive conduct (see Chapter 13). Rosnick and Weisbrot (2007) prove by citations that IMF officials were aware by 1998 that the convertibility system (including the peso's one-to-one peg to the US dollar) was unsustainable. Yet the Fund continued to act as if this were not true. This further corroborates the case against the IMF.

After default had been announced the IMF fell out with Argentina. The government's point that this was the only path left to restore fiscal solvency and revive economic growth cut as little ice with the IMF as did actual growth after 2001. Immediately the bias in forecasting turned around by 180 degrees. Incidentally these wrong forecasts made believe that Argentina had been wrong not to obey the IMF. Statements on Argentina suddenly differed fundamentally from those before default, usually shifting blame – such as for the 1:1 peg – on the country as though the IMF were wholly innocent and had never advocated and proposed currency boards to SCs.

Although less clear-cut than Argentina, the authors show that the 'IMF has continued to lowball Venezuela's economic growth ever since 2003' (ibid., p. 11). Or Chávez's presidency seems to have made the IMF lose its customary overoptimism. Rosnick and Weisbrot support the view that politics influence decisions by pointing out that two days after the IMF was concerned about the Rule of Law in Argentina it offered the military, who ousted the democratically elected President Hugo Chávez in a coup, to 'stand ready to assist the new administration in whatever manner they find suitable' (quoted from ibid., p. 8). This is no newly found love for military putschists. Argentina's fascist military junta was as eagerly and quickly embraced by the IMF as Chile's. In Chile's case the question of accuracy of statistics used to support praise for the dictatorship's policies looks very similar to the pattern discernable with IMF forecasts (see Annex on Data).

'OWNERSHIP'

The issue of 'ownership' is another peculiar feature of BWI interventions. Depending on occasions and audiences, they either claim to be only supporting a country's own programme or to make a country adopt 'sensible' policies – one but not the only clear logical inconsistency. The claim of country 'ownership' is heard more often recently than in the past, when more pride was expressed on how tightly SCs were controlled. Both official sources and publications by leading BWI staff show that countries do not 'own' programmes.

Discussing 'ownership' directly leads to discussing conditionality, 'ownership's' exact opposite. It raises the question of why conditionality should be imposed. If countries genuinely considered the conditions as in their own best interests, there would be no need to impose these conditions in the first place. A simple declaration of intent would be sufficient. The very existence of conditionality proves that something is forced down a struggling client's throat.

Interestingly conditionality did not exist originally in the IMF's Articles of Agreement. Keynes opposed it (cf. Raffer and Singer, 2001, p. 3). Quite logically there could be no ownership debate before conditionality crept in. The Fund started applying it since 1952 as a matter of a board policy decision, but without any basis in the Articles of Agreement, thus technically breaking its constitution. As late as 1969, conditionality became explicitly enshrined in the Articles of Agreement. It has been strengthened over time.

The IBRD has never made unconditional loans, even when financing concrete projects some conditions required policy changes (cf. Mosley et al., 1991, p. 27). When starting programme lending, conditionality was increased. '[T]he Bank felt that it needed a place at the top policy-making table' (ibid., p. 34) beyond what it could expect from mere project monitoring.

Even official IBRD publications confess quite frankly that the IBRD imposes economic decisions on borrowers. The Bank has frequently complained about lack of 'ownership', or lack of client interest in 'IBRD-supported' operations. The Wapenhans report (IBRD, 1992b) identified insufficient 'ownership' as one major and frequent problem in need of redress. This would be impossible if projects and programmes were indeed the client's own, and the IBRD's role were restricted to financial support and expert opinion where and as demanded.

The IBRD's OED (1989, p. 26) concluded: 'Finally, borrower preferences are not always seen as important in supervision management, although the outcome often has a critical impact on the borrower.' Or to quote one of the Bank's executive directors: 'The challenge for the Bank is to change the ways it interacts with borrowers, from *a pattern dominated by prescription, imposition, condition-setting, and decision making* to one characterized by explanation, demonstration, facilitation, and advice' (IBRD, 1993, p. 12, emphasis added).

The impression gained from reading official IBRD documents is corroborated by quoting Ernest Stern's description of structural adjustment lending (SAL) published in 1983 (quoted in detail in Chapter 7). This IBRD top executive was appointed Vice President in 1978, Senior Vice President in 1980 and even served briefly as Acting President. He praised both the 'comprehensiveness' and the possibilities to intervene in detail. With the availability of funds entirely dependent on progress in implementing policy reform SAL enables 'the Bank to address basic issues of economic management and of development strategy more directly and urgently'. Explaining the need for 'firm' monitoring, Stern explicitly mentions a Letter of Development Policies referred to in the loan agreement and tranching of disbursements, allowing preconditions for the release of the next tranche. Stern concluded: 'While this procedure may be called 'conditionality', it is in principle no different from the relationship involved in Bank sector or project lending'.

Quite naturally the Structural Adjustment Facility (SAF) introduced in 1986 for poor countries shows a similarly stern understanding of conditionality. Finally the Enhanced SAF (ESAF) introduced soon after SAF is subject to even stricter conditionality (Polak, 1991, p. 7).

Jacques J. Polak was no less outspoken. He was Director of Research, subsequently a member of the IMF Executive Board. More important, he is the 'chief architect' of the IMF's monetary model according to *Finance & Development* of December 1997, a model that had been adapted to changing circumstances since its inception (in the 1950s) but 'still remains useful'. In other words, he was the father of the IMF's approach to balance of payments problems. Polak (1991, p. 12) wrote: 'The purpose of the Fund's conditionality is to make as sure as possible that a country drawing on the Fund's resources pursues a set of policies that are, in the Fund's view, appropriate to its economic situation in general and its payments situation in particular.'

This could still be wrongly interpreted in the sense that the IMF – like a stern Victorian governess – chastises debtor countries for their own good, forcing them to do what is objectively best for them. Speaking about the Compensatory Financing Facility Polak obliges by destroying such erroneous assumptions. This facility is the best illustration of how conditionality crept in and was strengthened. Initially introduced to compensate shortfalls in export earnings beyond the control of SCs, it was de facto unconditional. Technically, its

> conditionality was limited to an obligatory statement by the member to 'cooperate with the Fund . . . to find, *where required*, appropriate solutions for its balance of payments difficulties.' . . . Over the years, however, the Fund has increasingly come to the realization that *even though a country's export shortfall was both 'temporary' and largely beyond its control the country might still have balance-of-payments difficulties attributable to inappropriate policies and that*

large amounts of unconditional credit might cause the country to delay adopting needed policy adjustments. (Polak, 1991, p.9, emphasis added)

There is no way to express with greater clarity that conditionality is not necessarily linked to remedying a crisis. Even if the country's economic policy is not at all the reason for the temporary problem, the country still has to change it if the Fund wishes so. The IMF may use conditionality to force its ideological predilections of the day (usually of a neoliberal kind) on debtors in distress. The IMF has routinely done so. From a logical point of view this is quite strange unless the real reason is increased leverage rather than the elimination of economic inefficiencies. To be able really to evaluate IFI interventions one must recall that the IBRD stated after the Asian crash that Mexico had fulfilled most of the consensus conditions, but East Asia had not. The IBRD (1999, p.2) reached the 'conclusion: Washington consensus policies were neither the cause of high growth, nor the cause of the crisis.' This begs the question: why implement them if the country's recovery were the issue?

To assess the influence of the Fund appropriately, prior actions, which means changing policies in accordance with the Fund's views before receiving money, must not be forgotten. Reliance on prior actions had become popular when Polak (1991, p.13, emphasis added) suggested that these can be used to the country's advantage 'to minimize the policy commitments it must make in its letter of intent and thus to *present itself as opting for adjustment on its own rather than under pressure from the Fund'.*

In plain English: a distressed country may choose whether to accept the IMF's conditions openly or by 'cleverly' disguising them as its own 'free' choice. One wonders how often the IMF applied Polak's advice. Not surprisingly IFIs have repeatedly complained about insufficient borrower commitment or have stressed the need that programmes should be clearly 'owned' by affected governments. Such phrases are absolutely inexplicable if IFIs had simply supported the affected governments' own proposals.

Naturally an IMF programme or IFI lending may also be used by one faction of the government against another or as a means to implement policies disliked by the population by claiming that one was forced by IFIs. For Indonesia, for example, internal documents show that both IMF staff and management perceived the crisis as an opportunity to assist the reformist economic team in carrying out financial sector reform and deregulation, both areas that were earlier emphasized in IMF surveillance. The IMF assisted one faction. Or Korea used IMF interventions to serve the agenda of domestic interest groups by changes in labour regulations regarding redundancies to make firing easier. Such coincidence of interest has no doubt existed occasionally. Conditionality enforcing privatization might be especially appealing to some people in SCs, hoping to get a slice of the cake on the cheap. In Europe anecdotes abound about political friends having struck a good deal when European governments started their neoliberal privatization spree. Similar political connections could well play a role outside Europe too. Bull et al., (2006, p. 25) found that there were rarely more than two bidders in auctions for major concession contracts in SCs, that many public enterprises were 'thus sold at a discount and to terms that involve major market privileges'. The situation was found to be particularly bad in Africa, as well as 'highly unfortunate . . . when the World Bank takes an active role on the side of the private firm in such negotiations'.

But more often IFIs have overruled the 'client' –for example, in the case of privatizations by siding with a foreign bidder – as the very discussion on ownership proves. Obviously countries are not necessarily keen on projects or programmes, rightly so if one considers the lack of success of debt management over decades. If IFIs had a record of not forcing their policies on their debtors under duress, the claim that debtors only act under pressure would not be credible.

The Group of 24 criticized the increasing restrictiveness of Fund lending and the proliferation of performance criteria in number and scope 'under one pretext or another' (*IMF Survey*, Supplement, 19 August 1987). During 1983–85 nearly 80 per cent of the arrangements contained, on average, more than eight performance criteria, sometimes as many as 14, a number dwarfed by the over 100 conditions of the IBRD's second SAL to Thailand. Quite often they extended to microeconomic variables such as prices of specific products or services. Reviews became standard for all except SAF programmes to fill in performance criteria that could not be specified at the outset and to reset targets. Performance criteria were specified quarterly and semi-annually. While a host of conditions will make a programme unimplementable, there is one advantage to it. The IMF or the IBRD may or may not pardon non-compliance by granting a waiver.

This has not changed fundamentally. EURODAD (2006, p. 3) summarized:

> On average poor countries face as many as 67 conditions per World Bank loan. However, some of the countries faced a far higher number of conditions. Uganda, for example, where 23 per cent of all children under 5 are malnourished, faced a staggering 197 conditions attached to its World Bank development finance grant in 2005.

This astonishing number dwarfs Nicaragua's 107 conditions (First Poverty Reduction Support Credit, 2003) and Rwanda's 103 conditions (Second Poverty Reduction Support Grant, 2005). It refers to Uganda's Fifth

Poverty Reduction Support Credit of 2005. EURODAD (2006, p. 8) explains in a footnote:

> The WB justifies the number of conditions for Uganda on the fact that the whole PRSP monitoring matrix was attached to the loan document and say [sic] that the Bank will not be monitoring all benchmarks. This in fact results in less transparency as the Bank has not clarified which benchmarks it will be monitoring and which ones it will not.

Such openly admitted arbitrariness reinforces the point that countries do not own 'their' programmes. In practice, all these many conditions simply cannot be fulfilled. But seen from the angle of increasing leverage a vast amount of conditions that cannot be fulfilled does in fact make sense. On top of financial impunity for their own torts, too many conditions allow IFIs unrestrained arbitrariness in deciding whom to call to account for non-compliance. This situation is certainly not in line with the objectivity criteria for decision making processes espoused by the ideas of good governance or the Rule of Law. Such arbitrariness in monitoring increases IFI leverage. That many conditions would definitely not be necessary if IFIs simply financed programmes urgently wanted by SCs anyway.

A tendency to shift 'ownership' of the project or programme in the sense of accountability for it – on paper – exclusively on to the borrower is discernible. The BWIs have increasingly adopted formulations such as IBRD (or IMF)-supported programmes to indicate that one talks, in fact, about a client's programme, for which the SC, not the BWI, is financially accountable.

IFIs sometimes try to use HIPC II in order to shift the blame for failures on to SCs under their thumb: 'PRSPs [Poverty Reduction Strategy Papers] have been produced by the country authorities, and not by Bank and Fund staff' (IMF, 2000). Logically the country is to blame for the action it 'owns', even though: 'Greater ownership is the single most often cited, but also the least tangible, change in moving to PRGF-supported programs. There is no single element of program design or documentation that will signal this change' (ibid.).

When presenting HIPC II, IFIs have remained somewhat contradictory on ownership. The IMF, for example, informed that the PRGF 'replaced' the Enhanced Structural Adjustment Facility, bringing 'with it a number of innovations designed to ensure that lending programs are pro-poor and in line with the country's own strategy for reducing poverty'. In 2001 this was presented as 'More than just a change in name' by the IMF's home page under the heading 'IMF Lending to Poor Countries – How does the PRGF differ from the ESAF?' Such formulations seem to suggest an increased involvement of debtors. When feeling less obliged to document change, the IMF finds no difference. The *IMF Financial Activities – Update August 15, 2003* informed: 'The Poverty Reduction and Growth Facility (PRGF), formerly known as the Enhanced Structural Adjustment Facility (ESAF) provides loans . . .'.

The OED report by Gautham (2003, p. 43) describes the link between HIPC II and 'ownership' quite clearly: the 'original design was essentially developed by the staffs of the World Bank and the IMF', the international NGO community has played a 'key role' after 1999. However,

> The debtors had no explicit role in the O-HIPC design, and limited influence on the E-HIPC. This is noteworthy, since the HIPC process envisages the debtor government and the civil society in poor countries firmly taking the driver's seat and owning the process. Their limited input into the design of the process may affect the initiative's outcomes.

Regarding emerging markets and middle-income countries, 'ownership' is not envisaged by the IMF. Putting the IMF's role in a nutshell, Krueger summed up the SDRM proposal in a clear way: 'The Fund would only influence the process as it does now, through its normal lending decisions.' This and the IMF's idea of enabling its board to determine sanctions against an indebted member country (see Chapter 3) indicate to what extent 'ownership' by debtors is really desired. In contrast, analysing the 'ownership' issue strongly supports Rodrik's interpretation that the debt crisis was used as an opportunity to force the Washington Consensus on debtor countries in distress (see Chapter 2).

The report on conditionality prepared for the Norwegian Ministry of Foreign Affairs by Bull et al. (2006, p. vii) concluded from case studies

> that there is a stronger sense of national ownership of the programs today than before the guidelines on conditionality were reviewed. All the programs studied are based on government plans. However, this sense of ownership is weakened by three factors. First, the quality of the participatory processes varies significantly across the countries. Second, policies have been elaborated with significant input from the IFIs and foreign consultants, and there has been a lack of local input. Third, there is a perceived lack of 'policy space' stemming in part from lack of analysis of policy alternatives. A fourth factor that has been brought up in the case studies is that when government institutions have had differing views (as is often the case), IFI representatives have used these differences strategically to promote their own view.

In such cases IFIs might at least claim partial ownership by the debtor country's authorities.

The question of ownership and transparency affects the relationship between SC governments and the BWIs. If the programme fails or is abandoned, the government might blame them and say that the conditions were wrong or unfulfillable and unrealistic. They might also then claim that they never really wanted the programme to which the conditions were attached and that it was forced upon them by the BWIs. Bank and Fund on their part might say that the failure or abandonment of the programme was due to a lack of political will or competence on the part of the government or the result of political manoeuvring and instability in the recipient country. In this way governments may use the BWIs as scapegoats, pinning the blame for failure on them; whereas the BWIs will use the governments as scapegoats, blaming them for failure rather than the programmes and conditions. This is clearly an unhealthy situation, even though crushing BWI domination is the rule.

EASY REMEDIES

Both problems could be remedied very easily. Regarding sustainability, the debtor's capacity to pay and sustainability would emerge fairly reliably from my form of debt arbitration presented in detail in Chapter 5. Uncertainty would of course always remain. But it could be further reduced by clauses connecting additional payments to creditors to the economic performance of debtors after debt reductions restore economic health. This is as fair as it is useful. It encourages creditors to agree to larger cuts than they might otherwise be willing to, which increases the debtor's chances of full and sustainable recovery. Sharing the economic fruits of this success, which might not have happened if reductions had been smaller, is but fair. Creditors would receive what they can rightly expect under the circumstances. If the debtor economy does not experience visible growth, the reduction was obviously not too large. Creditors could not reasonably have expected more money anyway. If the economy takes off successfully after my arbitration process – as Germany did after the generous reduction of 1953 (where creditors did not share in success) – creditors, without whose cooperation this boom could not have happened, would also get what is rightly theirs, a share in the growth they contributed to. Clauses linking payments to GDP growth or export performance already exist. There is no reason why they should not be used more widely in order to solve the problem of determining payment capacity and to safeguard creditor rights.

The ownership issue could be remedied in two ways, namely by:

1. Copying the success of the Marshall Plan: regional cooperation and self-monitoring. European recipients of Marshall Plan aid were

encouraged by the USA to monitor one another's performance. This is something unthinkable so far in the North-South context, in spite of the undeniable success of the Marshall Plan and its procedures. Each Western European government submitted a plan which was inspected, vetted and monitored by other European recipient governments in the Organisation for European Economic Co-operation (OEEC). Streeten (1994, p. 126), who proposed emulating this in development cooperation, specifically mentioned that 'the heavy hand of the US government [the only donor] was kept out of it'. Streeten does not fail to point out that 'Control by peers rather than superior supervisors is also a principle advocated in business management.' SCs could copy this successful feature to produce plans on how to adapt their economic structures. They could form groups according to geographical or, if this should be more advisable, also according to other, economic criteria. Self-monitoring groups, for instance, in sub-Saharan Africa, could focus on the specific needs and problems of their regions, which will often diverge from those of other regional groupings (cf. Raffer and Singer, 1996, pp. 197ff.). Regarding economic success, beating the historic record of the BWIs should not be difficult.

2. Independent dispute settlement. Although IFIs and SCs are technically both parties to a contract, one party alone has usurped the power to decide and to deny the other side any legal relief or protection. This could easily be amended by making IFIs financially and economically accountable, as initially foreseen for virtually all of them by their founders. This issue is treated in greater detail in Chapter 13. The important point, though, is that disputes between the parties would be settled by an independent entity. Or the Rule of Law, so fervently preached by public creditors would be brought to bear even when it came to protecting SCs and the poor of the globe against infringement by these fervent preachers of the Rule of Law.

One could draw a parallel between ways in which structural changes have been tackled, depending on who was the 'adjuster'. The terms 'adjustment' or 'structural adjustment' were initially used to describe adjustment of a totally different type: industrial countries adjusting their economic structures to increasing imports from Southern exporters, especially in the textiles and apparel sector. The fact apart that adjustment has taken decades and this sector could not yet be fully liberalized by the North, disputes between 'adjusting' industrial importers and exporting SCs have never been solved by exporters deciding what should be done. At present, dispute resolution exists under the WTO umbrella. SCs, poorer and by definition economically less advanced, are expected to restructure their whole economies quickly, and liberalize more rapidly and fully than the North have done for one sector that is a small part of their industrialized economies. Also, in practice there exists no procedure to settle disputes regarding IFI programmes between SCs and IFIs at all. One might wonder which logical reason for this difference exists. One might also wonder whether a fair balance between IFIs and SCs could not increase 'ownership' substantially.

13.   MDGs and preferred creditor status

Since the very start of debt management by the BWIs they have asserted that they were preferred creditors and could therefore not be expected to 'forgive' any debt. Once debt reduction had become unavoidable, IFIs claimed that others would have to grant them. Over the years, this claim, strongly supported by the Paris Club, gained more and more credibility. For SCs with large shares of multilateral debts this meant an important, additional difficulty. Even after James Wolfensohn had broken the taboo by pushing for the introduction of HIPC, IFIs have remained privileged. Under HIPC all other creditors are supposed to take haircuts first. Only if this would still be considered insufficient by the BWIs, their own claims can be touched. If so, as much as possible has been shifted on to other creditors via the HIPC Trust Fund, which refunds debt relief provided by IFIs under HIPC. Although it has always been financed in part by the IBRD – Wolfensohn immediately proposed the windfall surplus in 1995 as one source of money – this fund largely shifts the financial burden. Nordic countries especially, such as Norway, have picked up the bill. In 1988, on the initiative of the Nordic countries, a debt relief mechanism called the Fifth Dimension was established to provide relief for newly turned IDA countries still having to service old loans on market-based IBRD conditions.

Unsurprisingly under the MDRI, the BWIs were again able to shift the financial burden on to others. To avoid misunderstanding: the initiative by Nordic countries to help the poorest SC debtors via the Fifth and Sixth Dimensions or the HIPC Trust Fund is laudable. It has contributed perceptibly to reducing misery in these countries, and it may be the optimal strategy under present political circumstances – a humane realpolitik, so to say. On the other hand, it shows how cleverly IFIs have been able to organize their bail-out based on the argument that they are preferred creditors and must be shielded from the consequences of their own lending.

Showing that IFIs are not preferred creditors and that they know it, this chapter discusses the problem of an economically perverted incentive system allowing IFIs to profit from their (grave) negligence or even from wilfully inflicting damage. If this could be stopped, and the Rule of Law as well as economic sense could finally be brought to bear in the case of IFIs, the burden of debt would be substantially reduced. This in turn would perceptibly facilitate both financing the MDGs and in the longer run successful development at large.

PREFERRED OR NOT PREFERRED – A QUESTION EASY TO ANSWER

Although the status of preferred creditor is alien to the statutes of IFIs, the impression has quite successfully been created over decades that multilateral claims are entitled to preferential treatment. This perception is completely unfounded and at odds with the truth. In fact, IFIs have undone their founders' intention, reversing it into its opposite. Granting bilateral reductions, the Paris Club has demanded comparable losses from the private sector, but not from multilaterals. However such decisions by some creditors to extend preferential status de facto to IFIs differ fundamentally from a legal right of being exempt, even though the private sector has usually acquiesced. There exists no legal obligation to grant such treatment.

Checks of the IBRD inter alia by Canada's auditor-general, concluded that it had no preferred status. Under pressure from private business the IBRD even waived the negative pledge clause in its loans in 1993 (Caufield, 1998, p. 323). If it had been *de jure* preferred there would have been neither need nor scope for such clause, nor for pressure to waive it, as legal norms always prevail. It is one rare occasion where private creditors asserted their rights vis-à-vis IFIs. By waiving this right, the IBRD acknowledged that its claims should not be treated in the same way as private claims, but should be subordinated to them.

As a rule, Multilateral Development Banks (MDBs) have a statutory obligation to grant relief. Rather than stipulating any preference the IBRD's Articles of Agreement contain the legal obligation to grant debt relief if and when needed. Article V.3 of IDA's statutes is similar. Article IV, Section 6 obliges the IBRD to provide a special reserve providing for what Article IV, Section 7 ('Methods of Meeting Liabilities of the Bank in Case of Defaults') requests. Detailed rules on how to proceed follow. As the IBRD is only allowed to lend to members or with repayment fully guaranteed by member states (Article III.4), the logical conclusion is that default of member states was definitely considered a possible, and maybe even an occasionally necessary, solution. The IBRD's founders understandably wanted lending to be subject to some market discipline, and designed mechanisms that would allow the Bank to shoulder its fair share of the risks involved. In contrast, other creditors, especially the private sector, have no similar obligation. As sovereign insolvency procedures do not exist, this is a clear indication that its founders wanted to subordinate the IBRD's claims.

But the IBRD's statutes go even further. Article IV.4.c confers a right onto members suffering 'from an acute exchange stringency' (viz. threatening default) to ask for relief. It stipulates:

> If a member suffers from an acute exchange stringency, so that the service of any loan contracted by that member or guaranteed by it or by one of its agencies cannot be provided in the stipulated manner, the member concerned may apply to the Bank for a relaxation of the conditions of payment. . . . (ii): The Bank may modify the terms of amortization or extend the life of the loan, or both.

Article IV.4.c specifically demands taking both the Bank's and such member's interests into account. One notices that no conditions are stipulated for such relief, except the member's urgent need for help. Similarly IDA's Article V.3 demands to take decisions on relief 'in the light of all relevant circumstances, including the financial and economic situation and prospects of the member concerned'.

The country has the right to ask for relief. The IBRD may – but need not – grant it. While this does not mean that the Bank has to grant relief whenever asked, it certainly constitutes a general obligation to grant relief when and where appropriate, an obligation hardly reconcilable with the purported preferred creditor status and the Bank's behaviour in the past. Other creditors, most clearly the private sector, have no such obligation. The often heard 'argument' that relief for multilateral debts cannot be granted or would make development finance inoperable was not shared by the IBRD's and IDA's founders formulating their respective Articles of Agreement. Steadfastly denying debt relief and claiming to be a preferred creditor the IBRD is definitely at severe odds with its statutory duties and the truth. Acting in this way, the Bank and IDA have inflicted gravest damage on members under duress, SCs forced to turn to them for help because of acute foreign exchange stringency. Using the possibilities allowed, even suggested by their statutes – thus obviously intended by their founders – would no doubt have defused quite a few crises.

The Agreement Establishing the Inter-American Development Bank provides for 'Methods of Meeting Liabilities of the Bank in Case of Defaults' (Article VII, Section 3). Charges should first be made 'against the special reserve provided for in Article III, Section 13', which is to meet the Inter-American Development Bank's liabilities in the case of debtor default. The Agreement Establishing the Asian Development Bank similarly demands a special reserve to meet liabilities in the case of default (Article 17). Article 18 gives the detailed description of how to proceed (Raffer, 2004a, p. 69).

The case of the African Development Bank (AfDB) is slightly different. The first version of the agreement establishing the AfDB, dated 4 August 1963, contained the arrangements known from other MDBs. Article 22 even foresaw reserves to cover special funds. The agreement's present version (after the last revision of July 2002) eventually became available after some years on the AfDB's home page. Article 22 still refers to 'any reserve established for this purpose' (that is, meeting liabilities). The text of Article 20 (Special Reserve) was completely deleted (its heading remained), possibly in reaction to the AfDB's downgrading from triple-A by Standard & Poor's in the 1990s, and its reform. At that time African members were certainly not in a position to oppose Northern requests. Article 21 still stipulates what should be done in the case of default by borrowers. But referring to calling capital early on rather than to using reserves first could be intended as a disciplining measure on borrowing members. Article 21 and the history of the statutes do not support the argument that unconditional full repayment is intended.

The European Bank for Reconstruction and Development writes off losses and submits to arbitration (also foreseen for the IBRD) – which proves that MDBs, if properly managed, can survive financial account-ability and market risk. It has no clients from the South though.

The IDA's Articles of Agreement are somewhat vague. Pursuant to Article V.3, titled 'Modifications of Terms of Financing', IDA may 'agree to a relaxation or other modification of the terms on which any of its financing shall have been provided'. In the case of maturities of 35, 40, or even 20 years with ten-year grace periods and 'no interest charge' (IDA prefers to call its 0.75 per cent interest rate a service charge, apparently in line with Islamic banking principles) this leaves little realistic alternatives but outright reductions. IDA is a fund fed by periodic replenishments and reflows. Reducing reflows is immediately possible without endangering the fund. The argument that amortization is needed to refill IDA, which would preclude debt relief, is definitely no longer valid since IDA started to distribute grants. Like cancelled IDA debts, grants do not create reflows. If grant financing does not endanger the functioning of IDA, debt relief cannot do so either. The common problem of debt relief persists of course. Unless reductions are financed additionally, loanable funds decrease. Real lending capacity has to be assessed on a 'net base' though. Programme credits just granted to allow reflows 'on time' must not be counted. Merely substituting (over)due credits by new ones, they do not constitute new resources. In quite a few cases IDA debt reductions would in all likelihood not mean reduced net flows to a country. It remains to be seen how big the net effect would be for all IDA countries. The additionality problem also exists with official development assistance (ODA). If debt reductions are covered by ODA budgets without making additional resources available, net ODA decreases. The G8 decision at Gleneagles to cancel the debts of some countries vis-à-vis IDA and the African Development Fund (but not vis-à-vis their Inter-American equivalent) proves that debt reduction is possible in the case of such funds. The choice of countries and institutions once again highlights creditor arbitrariness.

The original statutes of all MDBs clearly subordinated multilateral claims. Their founders obviously meant MDBs to grant relief well before others. Their task of fostering development would explain this decision of their founders. Over the years MDBs have reversed this decision in violation of their own statutes. Unlike private creditors they all are statutorily obliged to reduce debts in case of default, but prefer breaching their statutes by not granting debt relief. This is done both to the detriment of debtor member states and of other creditors, who have to accept much larger haircuts than legally necessary.

The IMF knows that it enjoys no legal or contractual preferred creditor status, as can be read on its very own home page (Boughton, 2001, p. 820). When problems with SCs unable to service their debts to the IMF in time could no longer be ignored around 1988, preferring the IMF was discussed. It was attempted to find arguments in favour of preference. But the fact that the IMF had no legal or contractual status as a preferred creditor could not be denied. Supporting their institution's drive for undue preference, its 'Executive Directors stressed the . . . need . . . in practice . . . to treat the Fund as a preferred creditor.' In September 1988 the Interim Committee endorsed this position and 'urged all members, *within the limits of their laws*, to treat the Fund as a preferred creditor' (ibid., p. 821, emphasis added). The qualification 'within the limits of their laws' shows that even this IMF organ could not bring itself to demand unconditional preferred creditor status for the Fund from its members. The committee accepted that national laws may forbid any such treatment. In contrast to the impression IFIs (and especially the IMF) try to create, there is no legal hindrance to equal treatment. Therefore the IMF's SDRM proposal attempted to obtain *de jure* preferred status for IFIs in an extremely self-serving way.

Some clarifying facts must be mentioned in the case of the IMF. When it was established, conditionality did not exist. Loan loss provisions were considered unnecessary. Acting as an emergency source of finance providing short-term liquidity on a comparatively small scale without any strings attached justified unconditional repayment. Nevertheless, no preferred creditor status was enshrined in its statutes but the possibility to waive its immunity. This is all the more interesting as it is difficult to think of reasons for lawsuits under these circumstances of unconditional emergency lending. Payments such as 'criminal debts', or drawings not disbursed to help a member in balance of payments difficulties but helping dictators to embezzle funds might be one logically possible case.

Before the Second Amendment, the IMF's Articles of Agreement 'contained a provision suggesting that others would have preference on the Fund' (Martha, 1990, p. 825). The author refers to Schedule B, paragraph 3 on the calculation of monetary reserves on which repurchase obligations were based. It seems logical that the exclusion of holdings 'transferred or set aside for repayments of loans during the subsequent year' was done 'to give preference in repayment to lenders other than the Fund'. He argues that the intention of deleting this calculation and with it Schedule B, paragraph 3 from the statutes by the Second Amendment 'was not to repudiate the underlying thought that it was beneficial to encourage bank lending by giving banks and others a preference in repayment' (ibid., p. 814). Unfortunately the initial intent was blurred when conditionality was introduced, rather than making the IMF financially accountable as indicated by economic reason, and legally and ethically proper.

One has to concur with Martha (1990, p. 814) that the IMF's statute contains 'a presumption against a preferred creditor status', and that 'general international law contains no compulsory standard of conduct requiring the preferential treatment of any external creditor, including the Fund' (ibid., p. 825). However the IMF has no explicit statutory obligation to grant debt relief, which can again be explained by its initial role as a helper without conditionality. Important multilateral development banks violate their own constitutions by not giving members in default relief as stipulated. The IBRD simply refuses to acknowledge default, even if countries have not paid anything for six or seven years (Caufield, 1998, p. 319). Claiming no default as long as such countries stay 'in mutual respectful contact' (ibid.) with the Bank, the IBRD mocks all acceptable accounting rules.

This open breach of their statutes makes meaningful and sustainable solutions of overindebtedness more difficult, inflicting damages on borrowing members. The fact that members' statutory rights have repeatedly been infringed is a big problem unless one accepts a global system of legal double standards.

CHARGING WITHOUT DELIVERING – PAYING FOR WHAT ONE DOES NOT GET

There is one argument valid for all IFIs including the IMF though. All MDBs have built up loan loss provisions as demanded by their statutes, but refuse to use them as intended and when needed in spite of statutory obligations. Forced by external auditors, the IMF started to provide for non-payment by building up loan loss provisions. The 1986 audit raised the possibility that the next one might have to be qualified (meaning that the audit would have to warn about the real value of some debts still booked at face value, with negative effects on the IMF's standing as a creditor because it had failed to provide against losses) if the Fund did not take clear steps to recognize the poor quality of some assets and claims (Boughton, 2001, p. 814). These reserves are not called loan loss provisions, presumably because that might lead people to conclude that the IMF thinks that losses are unavoidable. Rather, they are called 'precautionary reserves'. As, for instance, the IMF's Public Information Notice 03/64 (22 May 2003) expresses it quite ornately, the IMF's margin includes a surcharge to 'generate resources for a SCA-1, established specifically to protect the IMF against the risk of loss of principal resulting from arrears'. What all this complicated wording means is rather simple: the IMF has already charged clients the costs for providing against loan losses. This surcharge was, for instance, 0.1 per cent on average in fiscal year 2003. While charging members the costs of defaults, the IMF refuses to use this money when members become incapable of paying.

All IFIs have charged their clients for the event of default, but also claim they cannot use these reserves for the very purpose for which they were established. As IFIs have charged such margins and built up reserves, but have refused to use them for their intended purpose, their clients have been made to pay insurance premia without getting benefits once damage has occurred. This is like an insurance company charging necessary fees but refusing to cover damages once they occur. Unlike IFIs, no insurance company could get away with such behaviour, in spite of the example of debt management, not even if the clients were SC governments.

One must not criticize IFIs for providing against loan losses. On the contrary, provisioning is a normal, economically sound and commendable business practice among lenders. Lenders routinely face a certain amount of losses – just as grocers must cope with the fact that some apples rot before they can be sold. Prices or fees charged to clients must include margins to cover such losses, since they are part and parcel of doing business. Although the IMF's Articles of Agreement do not demand it – it is not prohibited, in contrast to making capital account liberalization a loan condition – this is economically sound. As of the end of October 2003 the IMF's 'precautionary balances' were about SDR 6 billion, or 8.5 per cent of credit outstanding. The Fund had decided to bring them up to SDR 10 billion. In April 2005 the IMF had 13.9 per cent of outstanding claims covered by loan loss reserves. After the wave of repayments by big clients these 'precautionary balances' meanwhile cover a much larger share of claims outstanding in 2007, enabling the IMF to take much larger hair-cuts. After the imploding of its lending volume, the Fund's precautionary balances cover more or less its total exposure. Under HIPC II the IMF has already, though reluctantly, agreed to reduce its claims via grants. All other IFIs have much higher 'precautionary balances'. As of the end of October 2003 they ranged from slightly more than 20 per cent (IBRD) to over 30 per cent (Asian Development Bank) of credit outstanding.

THE TOTAL LACK OF LIABILITY, TORT AND FINANCIAL ACCOUNTABILITY

One further, and very powerful, argument for not treating IFIs better than other creditors is their substantial involvement in debtors' economic decisions. So far they can do so without shouldering appropriate risks and liabilities. IFIs have largely abolished the risk of losing money by making other creditors lose more. The argument that IFIs charge interest below the debtor's market rate is generally (but not always) true, but economically flawed and legally irrelevant.

In a market economy anyone must face the economic consequences of their actions and decisions. If consultants give advice negligently or without obeying minimal professional standards, they can be sued and have to pay compensation for the damage they have caused. National liability and tort laws serve the purpose of compensating those suffering unlawful damages, such as those resulting from negligent or unduly risky conduct or from providing dangerous products. But they also deter such behaviour. Knowing that one must pay for the damage done by sloppy work or wrong advice that could be avoided if professional standards were obeyed thus serves as a strong incentive to improve the quality of products and services. The success of market economies is based on linking deci-sions and risks. The systemic point is not that people receive indemnities – which is necessary and good – but that liability and tort laws make pro-viders of goods and services work more carefully. As a result, only a small fraction of all market transactions gives rise to lawsuits. Central planners in former communist countries, in contrast, knew that their institution would never be held financially accountable. The designers of the system, who claimed that these central planners would work in the best interest of the party and thus the people, thought this perfectly correct. This seems a striking parallel to IFIs claiming that they only work in the best interest of development and thus of the poor. As could be expected, the lack of financial accountability produced extremely bad results in both cases.

Two types of financial accountability can be distinguished: external accountability of corporations to their customers, or state agencies to people; and internal, between firms or legal entities and their own staff. Employees may under certain conditions be liable to refund to their employers damages that they have caused and that their employers had to pay for, but this is an internal matter not of interest here. The focus is on external accountability, the possibility of suing IFIs, not their employees, or on the relation between IFIs and their clients as well as people who suffered damages because of unlawful IFI behaviour. External accountability can and usually will strongly support conscientious staff opposing negligent or otherwise improper lending. Being able to point out financial consequences to the IFI will in all likelihood be a good argument against such lending.

Given the importance of these principles, it seems reasonable to demand that efficient management also be required from bilateral aid and multilateral development cooperation institutions. To remain consistent with their commitments, one would expect donor countries to have introduced appropriate management and accountability standards at their own national agencies and at all IFIs they control by voting majorities. This, however, has not occurred. Indeed, since the demise of communist economies, IFIs and aid donors are alone in escaping financial accountability. Consequently SCs and the poor remain totally unprotected against negligently or even willingly inflicted damage. Even worse, errors and negligently done damage may increase the importance of IFIs, since damages caused by one project or adjustment programme call for a new loan to repair them, thus increasing IFI income: in other words, an incentive structure exists that might cynically be described as 'IFI-flops securing IFI-jobs' (Raffer, 1993a, p. 158).

Such perverse outcomes are economically unjustifiable. Several telling examples demonstrate the difference in legal standards applied to normal market actors and IFIs. In 2003 a German court at Münster ordered a bank to compensate a client whom it had advised to buy Argentine bonds as high yielding yet safe investments. The court followed the plaintiff's argument that the bank did not explain Argentina's well-known difficulties adequately. It ordered the bank to indemnify fully its client because of the advice it had given. Similarly Italian banks were ordered by courts to indemnify small investors they had advised to invest in Argentine bonds because these banks did not provide advice with due diligence.

In another case a British couple that borrowed money from Lloyds sued the bank successfully because its manager had advised and encouraged them to renovate and sell a house at a profit. The High Court ruled that the manager should have pointed out the risks clearly and should have advised them against the project. Because the bank had gone beyond mere lending by giving advice, Lloyds had to pay damages when prices in the property market fell and the couple suffered a loss.

In contrast, the IMF may advise (or force, as sceptics may formulate) SCs to implement programmes that it had 'known to be counterproductive . . . or that had proved to be "ineffective and unsustainable everywhere they had been tried"' (IMF, 2004, p.91). This does not result in damage compensation but in increased earnings and more control over the client.

Brazil's Polonoroeste illustrates the glaring difference perfectly. *Time* magazine (12 December 1988) reported that a loan of $240 million granted, despite warnings from the IBRD's own experts (see also Rich, 1994, pp.141ff.), had caused considerable environmental damage. Bank officials admitted that they had erred and lent another $200 million to repair the damage done by the first loan. Brazil's debts increased by $440 million, the IBRD increased its income stream.

The Bank claimed that Brazil had failed to comply with conditions of the loan agreement, while NGOs and Brazil pointed at failures by the Bank. But this is immaterial to the argument. Brazil suffered financial consequences while the Bank gained financially. Delinking decisions and risk triggers economically inefficient practices by destroying the normal system of economic incentives. (Co)determining its clients' policies and decisions, the IBRD refuses to share risks appropriately, insisting on full repayment, even if and when damages are caused by grave negligence of its staff.

The only exception of the generally accepted principle that someone inflicting damage unlawfully must compensate their victims is unfortunately development cooperation, the last sphere where damage can still be inflicted with impunity and even financial gain. If normal accountability standards applied to Southern debtors there would in all likelihood be no multilateral debt problem. The difference may be illustrated with the famous story told by Stiglitz (2000a) 'of one unfortunate incident when team members copied large parts of the text for one country's report and transferred them wholesale to another', leaving the initial name in some places. Any private consultant would be liable to pay damage compensation. In most countries penal consequences would not be wholly unlikely.

As described in Chapter 2, the Asian crisis was allowed to develop although at least the IBRD had known 'the relevant institutional lessons' for years. One of the engines of Chile's crash in the 1980s, the IMF knew or should have known them as well. Nevertheless, the BWIs encouraged Asian countries to liberalize as they had encouraged Chile's military junta around 1980.

Examples of doubtful behaviour abound. May some very few further illustrations suffice:

- Blumenthal report: in 1982 the German expert Erwin Blumenthal, seconded by the BWIs to Zaire's central bank, warned most outspokenly and in writing that Zaire should not get any further money due to widespread corruption. In 1983 the IMF allowed Zaire the largest drawing ever by an African government. Predictably the money disappeared. Until 1989 the IMF trebled the volume of Zaire's drawings. Zairians had to pick up the bill.
- Haiti: According to *Time* magazine (2 July 1984) $20 million disbursed to alleviate balance of payments problems vanished without a trace, although the movement of a similar amount into the Duvaliers's palace account could be noticed. *Time* also reported the IMF's reaction: it '*threatened to halt aid* to the country *until Haiti made sure more money would not disappear the same way*' (emphasis added). Searching for this money and ensuring its repayment was apparently not mentioned. Bruce Rich pointed out that Haiti received the largest number of IMF standby agreements over the past half century: 22 IMF loans, of which 20 went to the regimes of Papa and Baby Doc.
- Nicaragua: the IMF disbursed money to Somoza just before the Sandinista victory, when the dictator was about to flee; just in time to take this money with him. Nevertheless, the IMF expected the country to 'honour' these debts.
- Trinidad and Tobago: in 1989 the country documented grave irregularities and deficiencies in the IMF's assessment of its economy, which created the impression of economic mismanagement and led to a 'structural adjustment' programme. After the IMF became aware of these substantial errors no correction was published in spite of the importance to the country. Because of the government's need for the IMF's 'seal of approval' Trinidad's own expert advised them not to pick a fight with the IMF.
- Somalia: Jamal (1992, p. 149) presents the example of Somalia in the 1980s where absolutely inappropriate policies were prescribed by the IMF, apparently because of insufficient assessment of the country's economy. After detailed criticism the author sums up: 'All in all, the

spectacle is one of the IMF trying to impose the trappings of a free market economy on Somalia whereas one already exists in all but name.'

The establishment of the IMF's internal evaluation office and its frank reports are a huge and commendable step forward. Evaluating the Fund's role in Argentina, it found many cases of grave negligence at the least, if not worse (IMF, 2004). It found that a 'program was also based on policies that were either known to be counterproductive . . . or that had proved to be "ineffective and unsustainable everywhere they had been tried"[41] . . . Nor did the program address the now clear overvaluation of the exchange rate.' Footnote 41 further clarifies that the IMF was fully aware of proven ineffectiveness and unsustainability: 'As expressed by FAD [the IMF's Fiscal Affairs Department] at the time' (ibid., p. 55). Another 'critical error' (ibid., p. 46) which occurred in 2001 was that there was no sufficiently clear understanding of what to do should the approach fail. The board supported 'a program that Directors viewed as deeply flawed' (ibid., p. 50). The 'September 2001 augmentation suffered from a number of weaknesses in program design, which were evident at the time. If the debt were indeed unsustainable, as by then well recognized by IMF staff, the program offered no solution to that problem' (ibid., pp. 54ff.). In a footnote the IEO corroborates this last point by quoting a 'memorandum to management dated July 26, 2001', stating that IMF 'staff estimates that a haircut of between 15 and 40 percent is required'. The IMF not only 'failed to use the best analytical tools' (ibid., p. 66), but '[a]vailable analytical tools were not used to explore potential vulnerabilities in sufficient depth' (ibid., p. 67). It goes without saying that the IMF was again unduly 'optimistic' in its forecasts, as the report documents. This is just a small selection from a limited part of the period evaluated. It should be sufficient to show that – if the IMF were a consultancy firm and Argentina its client – the plaintiff's lawyers would have a feast. But the IMF is not a consultant and Argentina has to pay for programmes that – as the IMF must have known, judging from its own evaluation report – contributed to her ruin. The IMF gets more interest income from Argentina than it would have got if it had refrained from such strategies. One cannot but concur with the statement of the Argentine Governor: 'Recognising errors is, however, just the first step in a healthy self-criticism exercise. The second step is bearing responsibility for failures, namely sharing the burden of redressing their consequences' (ibid., Annex). Equal treatment of all creditors would be a first, yet important step (for further corrective measures, see Raffer, 2004a) to provide incentives for good institutional governance and for applying due care.

Arguably the so-called Wapenhans report (IBRD, 1992b) is the internal critique of IBRD lending that drew most publicity. The report's disturbing result – which can be corroborated by other sources including the Bank's own – is that available knowledge and evidence have simply not been used to avoid financial consequences disastrous to borrowers. The points raised were not new. The Bank's OED, answering directly to the president, established because of US insistence and frequently quoted by the report, had published the same criticisms for quite some time. Quite often, as the OED itself states, without any result on the actual implementation of projects, although only about half the projects could be judged likely to sustain their benefits. The sector water supply and waste disposal, for instance, did not heed the OED's critique since the earliest appraisal in 1970 – a sobering result, the OED remarked correctly.

Similarly the Report of the External Evaluation of the Independent Evaluation Office by Lissakers et al. (2006, p.4) 'found little evidence that findings and recommendations of specific IEO reports are being systematically taken up and followed up by senior management and the Board'. No corporation subject to market discipline would behave like this. Under normal liability rules there would be a vivid interest in finding and correcting errors. In contrast, the panel even had to warn that 'the IEO must be assured full access to records and information within the IMF. Management has taken certain steps to limit access and the panel believes these constraints may impede the IEO's ability to do its work' (ibid., p.3).

The Wapenhans report (IBRD, 1992b) repeated the OED's criticisms, frequently even in the same wording. Unsurprisingly water supply and sanitation was once again identified as particularly problematic (ibid., p.ii), and remained so. Raffer (1995) discusses the Wapenhans report in detail. Suffice it here to recall its most appalling criticism. It was thought necessary to emphasize expressly: 'the perception that the literary quality of the SAR [Staff Appraisal Report] is in itself a criterion of success' is wrong. Actually accruing returns matter, not wonderful English. Apparently thinking this novel, unheard of idea that economic returns, not the language of reports matter in banking might not be immediately acceptable to IBRD personnel, the report added 'that point should be driven home' (IBRD, 1992b, Annex A, p.8). It follows logically from this passage that costs could be avoided if the Bank used remedies more appropriately and acted with greater care.

The Wapenhans report stated clearly that the IBRD's limited use of remedies is sending the wrong signals to both borrowers and staff. Employees are subject to a pressure to lend (also called 'approval culture' by the Wapenhans report). This was also the case with regional MDBs.

If economic incentives are overridden, other criteria (even the beauty of language) become fundamentally important. It is difficult to imagine how any management could become more attentive to the economic effects of its decisions under such circumstances. Unless decisions are linked with financial accountability, in other words, unless the most basic mechanism of a market-friendly economy is introduced, one cannot expect a real and fundamental change of the IFIs' business culture. As already mentioned, financial accountability would also support staff that try to change this business culture.

The IBRD's reaction deserves mentioning: the Bank changed its method of evaluation once again in 1997. Soft criteria became more important, such as more emphasis on social impact, with-without project comparisons, qualitative observations and judgements on institutional development. In spite of claims to the contrary, no stringent rules for judgement can be found, even in material sent on request by the OED. Particularly after the Wapenhans report the IBRD reinforced its strategy of immunization against accountability and blame, shifting towards financing projects without clear economic returns, even activities practically escaping economic scrutiny. In contrast to the first reform of the mid-1980s, this new method increased the share of satisfactory projects sustainably, a remarkable improvement according to the IBRD (cf. Raffer, 2005d).

As early as 1985–86 the IBRD had introduced a new methodology, less mechanical and characterized by subjectivity of assessments, which increased the weight given to evaluators' perceptions, some of which were difficult to explain fully, as the OED itself formulated. This somewhat subjective method reduced the share of unsatisfactory projects from 28 per cent according to the old method to 12 per cent with unsatisfactory or uncertain performance in 1987. 'Uncertain' was a euphemism, defined as 'Project achieves few objectives, if any, and has no foreseeable worthwhile results.' In spite of this innovative change the share of satisfactory operations went on declining perceptibly. Hence the necessity to change methodology once again. Apparently this is much easier than changing the implementation of projects and programmes. As the IBRD is virtually totally delinked from success or failure of its projects and programmes this is possible – unlike in the case of actors subject to market discipline.

Unsurprisingly rules and norms proudly presented in Washington do not seem to trickle down to those actually working in the field. The cases studied by Bull et al. (2006, p. vii) 'show that the new Good Practice Principles (GPP) and the World Bank's Conditionality Review [which to a great extent overlap with the IMF 2002 Guidelines] are not well known among the local IFI representatives'. Or 'A recent World Bank review recognizes that the World Bank work on trade has been based on weak analyses of poverty and distributional incomes, and weak analyses of the impact of external shocks' (ibid., p.33). As success diminishes earnings while flops increase it, microeconomic analysis suggests this to be the better strategy.

Particularly the IBRD has been keen on stressing that it has learned for some time. It was recently joined by the IMF. But one has to ask: at whose cost? Why must the poorest pay their tuition fees?

The statutes of most IFIs foresee legal liabilities comparable to private consultants, which are indeed a necessary part of any civilized legal system: whoever causes damages by negligent or tortious action must provide financial redress. Commercial banks have usually not interfered with their clients' economic policy. Bondholders even less so. In contrast, IFIs have strongly influenced the use of loans, exerting massive pressure on debtors, to the extent of provoking questions over whether countries actually 'own' these economic policies. IFIs have routinely taken economic decisions but refused to participate in the risks involved. They insist on full repayment by clients, even if damages negligently caused by their staff have occurred. A high rate of IFI failures therefore renders adjustment programmes necessary, which are administered by IFIs, just as failed programmes are likely to result in new programmes, as long as unconditional repayment to IFIs is upheld. No protection granted by contract or tort law to anybody else applies to the poorest of the world. Even wilfully and unlawfully inflicted damage does not presently confer any right to compensation. In spite of official declarations on human rights and equality of human beings, there exists one law for the rich in OECD countries and another law for the poor in the South. Minds more critical than mine might be tempted to speak of juridical apartheid. This perverted incentive system is also a severe market imperfection, totally at odds with any market economy – with unsurprising results.

Like any other creditor, IFIs must carry the risk of losses. Like consultants, they must be financially responsible for their decisions, connecting these to the risks involved, as well as for observing minimum professional standards. The most basic condition for the functioning of the market mechanism demands it. If this link is severed, market efficiency is severely disturbed, as former communist economies clearly prove. Economic efficiency but also fairness to the debtor and to other creditors demands that IFIs, at least co-responsible for the mess, should no longer be treated with preference.

As the example of the European Bank for Reconstruction and Development shows, writing off losses and submitting to arbitration, as well as obeying one's statutes do not necessarily ruin an MDB. The IMF's economic interest in legalizing the present unlawful discrimination of other creditors is immediately clear and reflected in the SDRM proposal.

IMPLEMENTING FINANCIAL ACCOUNTABILITY

When introducing financial accountability it is advisable to differentiate between programmes and projects. As it is practically impossible to determine an IFI's fair share in programmes that went wrong – clear cases such as some of those cited above notwithstanding – identifying tortious behaviour is easier in the case of projects. Naturally, legal redress mechanisms already discussed and statutorily foreseen can be immediately used. Thus arbitration pursuant to the statutes of MDBs (see Chapter 6) could be implemented at once.

Programmes

Regarding programmes, there is an easy way of holding IFIs financially accountable. Instead of attempting to determine precise shares in failed programmes all IFIs should lose the same percentage of claims as other creditors once a country becomes unable to repay fully. Instead of wrongly claimed 'preferred creditor' status, IFIs must be treated symmetrically as the Raffer Proposal requests. In SCs with high IFI involvement, which have been forced to orient their policies according to IFI 'advice' for some time, this solution is particularly justified. As the shares of multilateral debts are relatively higher in the poorest countries, protecting IFIs from losses is done at the expense of particularly poor clients, whose scarcity of experts has often made them extremely dependent on solutions elaborated by IFI staff. As shown above, there is even a clear case for going beyond Raffer's initial proposal of equal treatment by subordinating IFI claims by subordinating them.

Projects

Economically viable projects, which means projects that earn their amortization and interest payments, pose no problem. But if a project goes wrong, the need would arise to determine financial consequences. In the simplest case borrower and lender(s) agree on a fair sharing of costs. If they do not, the solution used between business partners, transnational firms and countries, or within NAFTA and the WTO in cases of disagreement could be applied: arbitration. This concept is well introduced in the field of international investments. If disagreements between transnational firms and host countries can be solved that way, there is no reason why disputes between IFIs and borrowing countries could not be solved by this mechanism as well. Present attempts to use the IBRD group's arbitration mechanism the International Centre for Settlement of Investment Disputes (ICSID) for conflicts on debts – which have not been understood as investments so far – such as by Italian bondholders of Argentine debts, show how unjustified resistance to arbitration is. The Rule of law does, however, mandate that such arbitration mechanism be not itself part of a creditor group.

A permanent international court of arbitration – different from temporary insolvency arbitration under FTAP, although it could be composed in the same way – would be one good idea. SCs and IFIs could be permitted to nominate the same number of members. These members would then elect one further member to reach an uneven number to assure majorities in order to avoid deadlocks. If necessary, this court might consist of more than one panel. Arbitration on projects could of course also be a panel ('chamber' in the terminology of Article 26) of the International Court of Justice or part of another, appropriate international entity.

Arbitrators would decide on the percentages of loans to be waived to cover damages for which IFIs are found responsible. The right to file complaints should be conferred on individuals, NGOs, governments and international organizations. As NGOs are under less pressure from IFIs or member governments their right to represent affected people is particularly important. Giving non-official entities the right to start cases is not new. The IBRD's Inspection Panel and the IDB's investigation mechanism were specifically established to allow NGOs to file formal complaints. IFIs just stopped short of real redress. Official recognition that one was wronged alone does not cover damages. The court of arbitrators would of course have the right and the duty to refuse to hear poorly prepared or obviously ill-founded cases. The need to prepare a case meticulously would deter abuse. The possibility of being held financially accountable would act as an incentive for donors and IFIs to perform better and protect the poor from damages done by ill-conceived projects. Last but not least, enabling victims of aid projects to receive damage compensation would force donors and IFIs to respect human rights and fundamental legal norms when financing projects.

The close scrutiny of how loans are used, which would result from implementing the proposals made above, does not mean the end of concessional lending. Projects and programmes actually financed under these conditions of accountability would have a much better rate of success and much more positive impacts on development. Totally lacking any form of financial accountability, IFIs and sometimes donors have neglected appropriate care, a textbook-type moral hazard problem that must not be allowed to continue.

Financial accountability would also be highly beneficial to IFIs themselves. It would give their staff a good argument against pouring money into regions just because of lending targets as well as against political interference by important shareholders, including demands to bail out other creditors.

14. Lending or granting: ODA and the MDGs

The need of additional ODA in order to enable poor countries to reach the MDGs has always been obvious. In the Summit Documents of Gleneagles the G8 promised to double aid to Africa by 2010. Somewhat less clearly, they formulated with regard to other SCs: 'Aid for all developing countries will increase, according to the OECD, by around $50bn per year by 2010, of which at least $25bn extra per year for Africa.' This is neither an agreement nor a commitment by the G8. However, they announced that a 'group of G8 and other countries will also take forward innovative financing mechanisms including the IFF for immunization, an air-ticket solidarity levy and the IFF to deliver and bring forward the financing, and a working group will consider the implementation of these mechanisms.' Finally they 'agreed' on a leading role of the IBRD 'helping to ensure that additional assistance is effectively co-ordinated'. As the 'G8 has also agreed' on MDRI debt relief, aid increases are logically additional.

While further multilateral debt relief has occurred, though slowly, arbitrarily, and in a way that is definitely not beyond criticism, the G8 have clearly failed to live up to their pledge of additional aid. In May 2007 the Executive Coordinator of the Millennium Campaign, Evelyn Herfkens, answered the question very clearly on what people working on the implementation of the MDGs could expect from the Heiligendamm G8 meeting: 'Not much.' In this interview granted to a German NGO, she recalled that ODA had not increased substantially, but was rather about to fall again, and that a 'massive share' of ODA had been debt reduction counted as aid. Without counting debt cancellations, aid to Africa would be stagnant. Herfkens called the check of the Gleneagles promises 'quite devastating'. Singling out the unwillingness of the G8 to check progress, she pointed out that Heiligendamm would have been an ideal opportunity to monitor progress and implementation of the Gleneagles announcements. Herfkens thought that such unwillingness might be explained by the knowledge that no results could be presented.

One of the big problems of ODA is that present practice encourages dubious recording. Increases in ODA do not mean that more money to finance the MDGs is necessarily available. ODA figures produced by each

Debt management for development

member state itself are reviewed by other DAC members. Participation by recipients or independent experts has never been deemed necessary. DAC donors have exercised the privilege of self-control, called 'peer review' in their publications. This double monopoly on data production and performance evaluation explains why aid cannot be expected to live up to expectations. 'Donors' have often included items that are clearly not ODA by their own definition, they have 'broadened' – an expression coined by the DAC – ODA by incorrectly recording flows.

Debt relief was clearly and repeatedly classified as not meeting the DAC's ODA criteria by the OECD DAC itself as long as it was only done by communist countries. With communism history and the impossibility of full repayment obvious, DAC members now have included debt relief at face values in order to boost figures. Arguably worse still, projects destroying the environment and chasing people away from their land, 'food aid' of vermin ridden maize or thousands of rolls of toilet paper brought to Africa for a US-AID employee first and then back to his US home after his assignment were labelled aid by official 'donors' (cf. Raffer and Singer, 1996). The way aid figures are produced is already the first important cause of criticism, disillusion and caution.

Clarifying what can be expected from ODA, this chapter describes the evolution of payments labelled ODA by the DAC. Analysing what the figures regularly published by the DAC actually mean, it draws attention to perceptible shifts in ODA towards financing remedies against global issues that respect no borders. These new tasks are less or not developmental in the strict and traditional sense, but rather tasks of common global interest, remedial action against international externalities. Some of the global public goods (GPGs) financed are also MDGs. Financing MDGs and 'ODA' as defined by the DAC may differ substantially.

THE EVOLUTION OF ODA

In April 2007 an official OECD document by its OECD Secretary-General and the Chairman of the DAC (Gurría and Manning, 2007, p. 3) called the performance against ODA targets 'a matter of some concern in the light of the 2005 G-8 and Millennium+5 Summit commitments, recently reconfirmed by G-8 development ministers, to increase aid by $50 billion in real terms between 2004 and 2010, and to double aid to Africa over the same period'. The document notes that '[M]ost of the recent increase in aid is due to debt relief', with some increase also in humanitarian aid after the Indian Ocean tsunami of 2004, which is not expected to continue at 'the exceptional levels of 2005–2006'. The present rate of increase of 'core development aid' will have to 'triple over the next four years' to fulfil 'donor' pledges in 2010: 'other forms of aid will now have to increase very substantially in 2007 and 2008 if there is to be a realistic prospect of meeting the 2010 targets through planned and manageable increases'. Annual real growth required over this period is 12 per cent (ibid., p. 4). Excluding debt relief and humanitarian aid, aid to Africa 'has barely increased since 2004'. Quite rightly, both authors see a need for donors to speed up disbursement in order to preserve the 'credibility of their promises to double aid to the continent' by 2010. It should be recalled that this document 'compares aid in 2002, the year donors committed to substantial aid increases at the Monterrey International Conference on Financing for Development, with the 2006 outturn and the level required in 2010 if donors are to meet their current aid pledges'. The G8 are not alone in failing to fulfil their pledges.

In 2006 net ODA from DAC members fell by 5.1 per cent in real terms to $103.9 billion (ibid., p. 2). The document explains (emphasis in original): 'This overall figure, however, exaggerates the fall, since exceptional debt relief to Iraq and Nigeria, while still substantial, was less than in 2005. *Excluding debt relief, ODA fell 1.8% in real terms.*' Even with doubtful recording, aid disbursements move in the wrong direction.

The distinction made by two OECD representatives of the highest rank between core aid and debt relief and humanitarian assistance deserves comment. It recognizes that not everything the OECD records as ODA is proper aid and of the same quality. It also reflects a necessary, more detailed distinction between flows officially recorded as ODA and ODA pursuant to the OECD's own definition, to which Raffer (1998b) first drew attention. He already singled out debt relief and humanitarian assistance as not properly qualifying as ODA. This distinction was severely attacked by the OECD in the past. Now it adopted this view itself.

The important point for our purposes is that there is a necessary distinction between what the OECD calls 'aid' (or ODA) and aid in the sense of help. Unfortunately ODA may be 'all aid short of real help' (Raffer and Singer, 1996, p. 3). Increases in ODA are therefore not a sufficient condition at all for reaching the MDGs. They might just be 'well-managed' data. Resources actually financing MDGs must be increased. Real help not OECD-type aid is needed.

The OECD (2007, p. 1) proudly announced that ODA 'from DAC members rose by 32% in 2005 . . . a record high', while 'Core development programmes rose by 8.6% between 2004 and 2005, but most of this increase was accounted for by only two countries, Afghanistan and Iraq.' Both countries are known to be of specific interest to the West, especially the G1. One may well doubt whether this aid 'is administered with the promotion of the economic development and welfare of developing countries as its main objective', as demanded by the DAC as its own condition for qualifying as ODA. In plain English, this can only be understood in the way that core ODA remained nearly constant. The OECD speaks of an increase of 2.9 per cent if these two countries are excluded, quite different from the 32 per cent trumpeted out as a record high.

The *Global Monitoring Report* 2006 (IBRD and IMF, 2006, p. 7) sees a 'need to shift' aid allocation 'if support for the MDGs is to be the objective'. Aid

> is often not channeled to where the impact on the MDGs is likely to be greatest . . . . For example, over 60 percent of the increase in ODA between 2001 and 2004 was directed to three countries – Afghanistan, the Democratic Republic of the Congo, and Iraq, although these three countries collectively account for less than 3 percent of the poor people in developing countries.

In addition, 21.26 per cent of ODA in 2005 was debt relief. This exceptional debt relief 'pushed the *bilateral share* of DAC members' ODA to 76.9%, the highest level since 1973' (OECD, 2007, p. 2, emphasis in original). Clearly this is unsustainable, because debt once cancelled cannot be cancelled again (although one should not short-change the OECD's 'innovative' capacity when it comes to ODA statistics). On the other hand, for the 'third successive year, net ODA loans were negative (repayments of principal exceeded new disbursements by USD 1 billion)' in 2005. If we subtract debt relief (on whose quality as ODA even the OECD has repeatedly expressed concern) from total ODA, we receive 0.26 per cent of GNI. This subtraction still does not correct for politically motivated flows, nor in the case of Iraq, for the 'substantial waste, fraud, and abuse' an official document of the US House of Representatives (see Chapter 3) found in the case of billions of dollars withdrawn in cash from the Federal Reserve and shipped to Iraq. One wonders how much of that has ended up as US ODA to Iraq.

The OECD's (2007, p. 1) assertion that ODA amounting to 0.33 per cent of its members' combined GNI in 2005, up from 0.26 per cent in 2004, represented 'the highest ratio since 1992' needs comment. In 1992 0.33 per cent was indeed recorded as well. But compared with GNP percentages of the 1950s and 1960s – above 0.5 per cent in several years (peaking at 0.54 per cent of GNP in 1961) – this ratio is quite small. Including claims already lost as though they were still worth their face values as debt relief, and after declarations to spare no effort to reach the MDGs and to increase aid substantially, total ODA in 2005 was still less than half the famous 0.7 per cent target accepted and pledged early on by most but implemented by few DAC donors. This target compares quite modestly with the amounts the USA had channelled to Europe for several years under the Marshall Plan: between 2 and 3 per cent. The 'highest level ever' of ODA in 2008 ($119.76

billion), which the OECD proudly announced to the press on 30 March 2009, was 0.30 per cent of GNI, less than in 2006 and 2005. Optimistically the OECD reported that 'with some further effort, most donors are within reach of their 2010 targets', a DAC average of 0.39 per cent according to the OECD. However, only one paragraph later, realism returns: 'Only a special crisis-related effort can ensure that the 2010 targets for aid are met, which is even more important now that the economic crisis is reducing developing countries' growth prospects and their ability to make progress towards the Millennium Development Goals.'

If the famous 0.7 per cent target had been reached, the OECD would have provided $226.5 billion (calculated from OECD, 2007, p. 9) in 2005 instead of slightly less than $106.8 billion, or $119.72 billion more in just this one year. Recalling that estimated costs of implementing the MDGs vary greatly, ranging from an extra $30 billion per year to over $100 billion, just living up to one's pledge might have solved the problem. In this case, there might have been no need for spectacular summit announcements such as doubling aid to Africa. This difference in 2005 is approximately the size of the estimate by the UN Millennium Project that meeting the Goals in all countries would cost $121 billion in 2006. As some money is already used for the MDGs, this difference should be more than sufficient to cover all the costs of the project's estimate.

In spite of all tricks 'increasing' ODA (discussed in detail below), a need for more financing is obvious. Once again, Britain took the lead in proposing change. In 2003 the Chancellor of the Exchequer, Gordon Brown, proposed an International Finance Facility (IFF). The IFF's problem is that it was designed to frontload aid to help meet the MDGs. The question of what might happen after 2015 is eschewed. According to HM Treasury the IFF is to 'provide up to an additional $50 billion a year in development assistance between now and 2015'. Arguing that 'traditional increases in donor aid budgets will not be enough to provide these additional resources and meet the aid targets that have been set', the Treasury (undated) argued that frontloading would be a solution. However, since the IFF 'would leverage in additional money from the international capital markets by issuing bonds, based on legally-binding long-term donor commitments' (ibid.), the question remains how repayment after 2015 would be financed. According to this proposal, 'donors' would borrow to increase ODA flows. So far, so good. But would interest payments before amortization be counted as ODA? What would happen once repayments have to be made? In all likelihood this would reduce proper aid, and the just achieved MDGs (if actually achieved by the IFF) would immediately be undone by lack of financing, once and if (as extremely likely) ODA budgets would have to start repaying IFF loans. The IFF proposal refers to the fact that donor countries pledged to increase their aid budgets as a reason to expect ODA flows to continue to rise after 2015, during the IFF's repayment-only phase. Considering several past official pledges of aid targets this is courageous. Increases of aid effectiveness brought about by the IFF are mentioned as another reason. Interestingly the 'emergence of major donors, such as China, after 2015' is specifically used as another reason why aid need or might not fall drastically during the repayment phase in the proposal once available at the Treasury's home page – quite a different view from present 'rogue aid' perceptions. Meanwhile this document has disappeared from the Treasury's home page, which hardly suggests continued strong support by HM Treasury for its own brainchild.

Trying to increase ODA, the IFF initiative acknowledges the insufficiency of present ODA or aid. Problems of what passes as ODA compound the quantitative aspect. If one looked the OECD's gift horse in the mouth this should not be a surprise.

LOOKING A GIFT HORSE IN THE MOUTH

Honouring the old English saying that all's grist that comes to the mill, 'donors' have always included an array of activities as ODA, such as rewarding voting behaviour in international organizations, supporting military allies or simply promoting exports by lowering prices. The IBRD (1990a, pp. 127ff.) concluded: 'Many "aid" programs in donor countries cover an assortment of activities (including commercial and strategic initiatives) which often have, at best, a tenuous connection with development.' It even saw the borderline between military and development aid 'sometimes blurred; the definition of the country of origin usually prevails' (ibid., p. 253). Donors made special efforts to assist friendly countries during 1990–92 because of the Gulf War, in some countries even explicitly called 'Gulf aid'. A 'Gulf War peak' is clearly visible, which critical minds might call paramilitary expenditures, whose main objective is definitely not the promotion of development or the welfare of SCs, as required for ODA by the DAC itself. In particular, this peak is very similar to the relative concentration on Afghanistan and Iraq more recently.

Gunnar Myrdal criticized the OECD's recording in the 1960s, pointing at the malpractice of regularly and systematically blurred distinctions between ODA and 'flows' in official DAC statistics. He criticized that Portugal, one of the poorest European countries and itself an 'aid' receiver at that time, had the place of honour in DAC statistics. It fought a protracted and costly colonial war in Africa, recording substantial flows of resources to Angola and Mozambique. Myrdal's critique contributed greatly to a change of perception and to a comparatively clearer definition of ODA, formulated in 1969, which is still *de jure* valid, but was eroded considerably in the 1990s. Furthermore, the DAC has never totally dropped the notion that flows across the North-South divide must always be conducive to development (that they are always aid rather than business) which was somewhat down-tuned after Myrdal's critique. It is reviving this perception forcefully at present.

The DAC's present ODA definition demands the promotion of the economic development and welfare of SCs to be the main objective and a minimum grant element of 25 per cent. The definition is so vague that critical minds might call it well chosen. The first criterion allows practically anything to pass. People do disagree on what 'welfare' or 'economic development' means. There is even more disagreement on what measures promote them. Actual increases in welfare or an actual promotion of development are not necessary. The intention suffices. There is no logical reason not to include military activities if soldiers shoot or kill mainly to promote welfare and economic development. Possibly as a result of Myrdal's remark on Portugal any kind of military assistance is now excluded officially according to the DAC. This is not quite true, as Raffer and Singer (2001, pp. 91–92) showed. Unless the donor's main intention to the contrary (such as doing harm, having another main objective) can be conclusively proved, which is next to impossible, this criterion applies automatically, even if substantial damage is inflicted upon recipient countries and the people affected by a project. At present no mechanism of assuring damage compensation exists. If one looks at the standards considered normal and demanded by the Rule of Law within any OECD country, such a mechanism should be introduced.

Obviously the donor club is not very keen on enforcing its own rules strictly, allowing cosmetic tinkering with aid statistics to make them look better. Some members have continuously reported export credits as ODA, a practice routinely condoned by the DAC. Austria is probably the best example to illustrate this point. Although by no means the only DAC member using aid to promote exports, the share of export credits in total ODA was traditionally perceptibly above other DAC members. This fact has been criticized by researchers, NGOs, the Austrian aid administration itself and the OECD DAC for quite some time, but to no avail. In 1983 even the official report on ODA published by the Austrian Federal Chancellery stated that the OECD found fault with export credits 'evading primarily development oriented planning, structuring (intention), assessment as well as international ODA-comparison and used with an orientation towards competitiveness' of exports (for quotes see Raffer and Singer, 2001, pp. 73ff.). A few lines further down the Chancellery stated that 'the benefit of the developing country [is] a secondary effect after all'. A few pages above it declared: 'Presently no application of developmental criteria. Review urgently needed.'

In its peer review of 1996 the OECD calculated that a 'stricter interpretation' of ODA would have reduced Austrian aid by 0.06 GNP percentages in 1993 and by 0.11 in 1994, or by two fifths and one third, respectively. In 1994 Austria's Federal Chancellery stated in its main official publication on ODA that if reporting 'according to the reporting practices applied by the majority of DAC-members the volume would be about 0.25% of GNP' in 1992. Officially it was 0.30 per cent. The following table contains a row specifying the ODA subtotal considered 'in accordance with DAC [criteria]' ('davon "DAC-gemäß"'). Both the competent Austrian authority and the DAC declared publicly, officially and repeatedly that these flows were not ODA because they violated the first DAC-criterion of being 'administered with the promotion of the economic development and welfare of developing countries as its main objective'. Nevertheless, with extremely few exceptions these credits have been recorded as ODA by the DAC – a fact that bodes ill for connecting higher, officially recorded ODA flows with more resources available to finance the MDGs.

The history of ODA recording is, in fact, a history of tinkering and cooking data. Particularly after 1989, the end of the Cold War, 'donors' busily undermined checks of what passes as ODA, moving downwards to pre-Myrdalian recording practices.

Claiming that the definition of ODA had not changed, the OECD conceded in the 1990s that changes in interpretation have tended to 'broaden the scope' of the concept. What this means is quite simple: while a certain amount of flows that did not satisfy the OECD's definition of ODA had always been tolerated as 'aid', this incorrect share started to increase steeply. The DAC's performance would have been noticeably worse without this broadening. There are two types of broadening:

1. Suddenly including flows not included before, although they might be defended as ODA; examples are administrative costs (ODA since 1970), or inclusion of official contributions to private voluntary agencies. This practice creates statistical breaks, in the OECD's words a 'major break' in continuity. The graph of ODA over time is changed by pushing up ODA from one year to the next by such inclusions. Appropriate corrections have not been made. The OECD (1985, p. 173) called revising historical records for 'substantial' changes as 'not always feasible'. From a purely statistical point of view consistent time series cannot be considered unfeasible. The OECD's time series

on ODA are thus flawed. The falling trend must be more pronounced if data had been corrected properly.

2. Perceptibly increasing the share of outlays that are not ODA pursuant to official statements by the DAC itself, but which routinely have been included anyway.

In the jubilee edition of the OECD's annual report on aid, the so-called Chairman's Report (women have never been allowed to chair so far, although the word chairman was removed some years ago), the OECD (1985, p. 173) defines 'in particular export credits extended by an official sector trade promotion body . . ., debt relief funded by the National Treasury or other government departments' as Other Official Flows (OOF), explicitly denying them qualification as ODA. Practice was softer on DAC members than official statements. In the case of communist donors the OECD (1985, p. 118) stated consistently that debt cancellations and debt reschedulings softening outstanding loans to more concessional terms were 'not taken into account'. A few years later the situation had changed. With the Cold War and its exigencies matters of the past, and DAC members forced to write off their claims, debt 'forgiveness' including non-ODA export credits was readily recorded, increasing total ODA, without any change in definition, as the OECD has insisted.

In its 1994 report on ODA published in 1995, the OECD even called aid to refugees and disaster relief 'extreme examples of the way circumstances can thwart intentions'. It explained: 'The definition of ODA requires that, to be eligible for inclusion, resources should be "for the economic development and welfare of developing countries".' Such payments are laudable and necessary expenditures helping to alleviate human suffering, thus real help. But these flows do, strictly speaking, not contribute to development and are – as the OECD rightly observed – not really development aid. Thus the two main outlays causing the recent increase in aid, debt relief and humanitarian aid are not ODA according to official OECD statements. Belatedly but still the expression 'core aid' acknowledges that statistics have not been handled correctly.

As many critics have pointed out, double counting occurs in the case of debt cancellations. If debt cancellations are automatically and wrongly counted as ODA, any debt cancellation automatically 'increases' aid. There is no additionality at all. It should go without saying that debt relief is counted at face values as though debts could be recovered without problems. Recalling the economic values estimated for outstanding official debts – 8, 6.33 or 4 per cent of face value – further incorrectness is added to double counting. As in the case of 'broadening' ODA, as the OECD elegantly describes data cooking, 'donors' appear more generous than

Table 14.1   ODA by DAC members; broadened and deflated totals

	(Percentage of GSP)					
	1989	1990	1991	1992	1993	1994
Official DAC value	0.32	0.33	0.33	0.33	0.31	0.30
Deflated ODA	0.260	0.245	0.239	0.235	0.221	0.211
ODA inflator	*1.231*	*1.347*	*1.381*	*1.404*	*1.403*	*1.424*

they actually are. In the case of an economic value of, say, 4 per cent of the nominal, 'forgiving' the 'whole' claim means logically a grant of 4 per cent to the HIPC (or other debtor country), combined with a bail-out financed by the 'donor' for itself of 96 per cent. Doubtlessly, one may call this aid, not in the sense of development aid, but in the sense of donors helping themselves.

It should be clear that recording as such is not of too great importance. If enough money were provided to finance reaching the MDGs, it would matter little whether, in addition, flows that do not qualify are also counted. This would exaggerate aid but not detract from real help. The problem is that such non-ODA flows are used as substitutes for proper aid to boost figures. Proper aid is thus much smaller than official, untrue figures, as even the OECD has eventually come around to admit.

Encouraged by official OECD statements on 'broadening', Raffer (1998b) tried to estimate this 'broadening' effect. Referring readers wishing for a detailed account and description to my paper (initially presented at the Annual Conference of the Development Studies Association at Reading, UK, in 1996), one may sum up its results (cf. Raffer and Singer, 2001, pp. 83ff.). I called the relation between official (broadened) figures and deflated ('unbroadened') ODA, ODA inflator. This 'ODA inflator' (official ODA figures divided by ODA figures corrected for broadening) was 1.23 in 1989. It increased to 1.42 in 1994 (Table 14.1).

According to Table 14.1 officially recorded ODA was 42 per cent higher in 1994 than justified by the OECD's own definition or what it would be if the original concept would still have been applied without what the OECD called 'major breaks in the continuity of the long-term series' and without including non-ODA in violation of one's own definition.

Furthermore, broadening almost doubled over the six years shown. In other words, what the OECD itself initially considered and still considers proper development aid decreased quite visibly, particularly so if one assumes that sums that could not be included because of lacking information, such as debt determined 'aid' bailing out other creditors, were likely to have been substantial. Most of the figures necessary for the calculation of Table 14.1 were readily accessible, particularly so in the reports of the early 1990s, itemizing ODA disbursements in detail. Although admitting that the amounts involved can be 'substantial', the OECD refused to provide estimates of the quantitative impact of broadening. Logically two possibilities exist. Either no corrections could be made to produce consistent time series, because the DAC could not quantify these factors – which would be surprising, considering that it had been able to do so on several occasions – or it is unwilling to disclose these sums because they are too 'substantial'. In both cases ODA time series are flawed.

The OECD's statement that quantifying broadening would be impossible is plainly wrong. Its assertion that no statistical evidence existed to support my conclusions is absurd, unless the OECD does not consider its own data as statistics (for quotes and details see Raffer and Singer, 2001, p. 88; the OECD quoted my unpublished conference paper, not Raffer, 1998b, which is readily available for the public to check). This statistical growth of volume due to boosting factors reveals a disturbing trend.

A clear political effect is recognizable though. 'Broadening' kept ODA 'constant' during a period when SCs expressed justified fears that aid would shift eastwards, when it was discussed whether post-communist economies should simply be added to the list of recipients, and when what the DAC, later labelled Official Aid (to the East), took off remarkably.

After Gleneagles a new age of broadening started. Once again, debt relief and humanitarian assistance are important broadening items, pushing up ODA data. Calculating only the 'broadening' effects of humanitarian aid and debt relief from OECD (2007) renders nearly the same ODA inflator as for 1994 in Table 14.1 (1.417). However my calculation in the 1990s included nine factors, not two, even though these two factors above were certainly of high quantitative importance in 2005. Taking account of 'core development programmes' to Iraq and Afghanistan, which the OECD (2007) specifically singled out, would render an ODA inflator of over 1.5, which means quite a few items singled out by Raffer (1998b) are still not netted out. Briefly 2005 seems to have been the all time high of ODA figure cooking.

One should note that recording resources financing GPGs as ODA has also been done in violation of the OECD's own ODA definition because in such cases the promotion of the economic development and welfare of SCs is definitely not the main objective, as demanded by the DAC definition. In recent years substantial shares of what was presented as ODA financed GPGs, thus fighting global problems under the cloak of ODA (for estimates of the shares of GPGs in ODA, see Raffer, 1999, 2009).

Tendencies of shifting ODA even more towards donor interest are all too perceptible. Shifting away from the 'main objective' of fostering development has become more pronounced after 9/11. In 2003 the DAC introduced the new focus 'prevention of terrorism' as 'a relevant development objective'. Quite a few donors have already placed counterterrorism in their new aid priorities. It seems doubtful whether all money spent for that purpose can help reach the MDGs.

LOANS OR GRANTS

About a decade ago, Raffer and Singer (1996, pp. 209–210) proposed financing institutional reforms and a social agenda exclusively by grants. Institution building, a social agenda and projects for the poorest must be financed by grants unless a recipient is sufficiently liquid, which is however extremely unlikely in the case of most poor SCs.

This would not mean the end of concessional lending. Loans at concessional interest rates allow their debt service to be covered with relatively lower income streams. In countries where debt service already puts heavy strains on the government or money is scarce for other reasons, (new) loans that do not earn their own amortization and interest service are bound to worsen the country's debt situation further or to lead to the next debt crisis if granted on a larger scale. The highly negative economic consequences of such lending are apparent. The 'near-market' interest rates of the IBRD or regional development banks will often be too high in many countries if loans are not self-liquidating, as lending for pro-poor activities usually is. Therefore urgently needed anti-poverty projects must be financed by other means, preferably by grants, often even in relatively richer SCs. If the evolution of democratic institutions or human development is really as important to donors as their rhetoric claims, they should be prepared to finance these commendable activities. As economic theory holds that the willingness to pay reveals an actor's true preferences (called 'revealed preference' by microeconomics textbooks), this would also be an opportunity for donors to prove the honesty of their concern for the poor or values such as democracy or the Rule of Law.

RELIABILITY OF INFLOWS AND PERMISSION TO USE THEM

While increases in ODA, be they real or due to imaginative recording, are loudly heralded to the public, implementation creates its own problems. As *The Economist* (7 April, 2007 p. 55) pointed out 'The OECD reckons that, between them, 31 poor-country governments received 10,837 donor "missions" in 2005, almost one a day. Even those that explicitly asked for "quiet periods" to get on with their real work were not spared.'

In spite of so many checks, reliability is not the main characteristic of ODA: 'Only about 65% of aid actually arrives on schedule, according to the OECD. Finance Ministers must cope with shortfalls and windfalls. Zambia was due to receive $930m in 2005, but ended up with just $696m. Vietnam which was expecting about $400m, got roughly $2 billion.' This might well be a reason why SC governments do not dare make full use of aid, and why, for instance, Ghana collected $1.2 billion of an extra $1.3 billion 'in the vaults of its central bank' (*The Economist* 7 April 2007, pp. 55–56).

Aid backlogs might be quite substantial, as the EU's example illustrates. By the end of 1999 the backlog of outstanding commitments had reached over 20 billion euros. During the last five years the average delay in disbursement of committed funds had increased from 3 to 4.5 years. For some programmes the backlog was equivalent to 8.5 years of 'payments' (IDC, 2000, p. xvi). Disbursements for the much less bureaucratic treaty Lomé I (signed in 1975) were not completed until 1990, when the highly bureaucratized Lomé IV was signed (Greenidge, 1999, p. 111). According to Commissioner Nielson, ACP countries fared better than the Mediterranean programme regarding the general overall time lag (IDC, 2000, p. 37) even though some states have practically collapsed in Africa. Lomé's partnership concept was efficient in comparison with other EU actions 'unhampered' by such partnership.

Reliability of commitments was so bad that one committee member suggested 'some form of compensation' for consultants and NGOs if something goes wrong through no fault of theirs. A lot of organizations ceased to apply for EU funds, he stated, because they could not afford the administrative risk involved regarding payments arriving in time. Commissioner Nielson called the case of 'the fabulously well organized and successful agricultural research network' CGIAR 'very embarrassing'. The Commission was 'unable to pay because the dossier was moved from one Directorate-General to another and the patient did not survive that transfer' (ibid., p. 41). In plain English: the delicate task of transporting a document within reasonable time from one Directorate-General to the other proved too much for the EU. Arguably so, because the Commission was too heavily engaged in preaching the importance of good governance or high standards of public sector management to ACP countries.

Lack of reliability is one reason why aid cannot be put to best use. It is nonsense to hire and fire teachers as money arrives or does not, or starting and stopping anti-AIDS programmes dependent on whether promised money continues to arrive. Increases in ODA lose much of their impact under such volatility. Unable to plan properly, one cannot put inflows to good use. But this is not the only problem regarding increased ODA inflows. The country may receive ODA, but may not be allowed to use these resources, a very clear indication of what 'ownership' really means.

The IMF has made many countries use ODA inflows to build up reserves. BWI pressure to liberalize capital accounts have made increased stocks of international reserves necessary. They are meanwhile one of the widely used targets of poverty reduction strategies in Africa, although any IMF member has the right to capital controls pursuant to the IMF's Articles of Agreement. Only current transactions are to continue. Using these rights, which the BWIs force their clients not to do – the IMF in open breach of its own constitution – would not cost anything, unlike large reserves squirrelling resources away from poverty alleviation and from financing MDGs.

Evaluating the IMF and aid to Africa, the IMF's (IMF, IEO, 2007, pp. viii, 40) own IEO found: 'PRGF-supported macroeconomic policies have generally accommodated the use of incremental aid in countries whose recent policies have led to high stocks of reserves and low inflation; in other countries additional aid was programmed to be saved to increase reserves or to retire domestic debt.' Increased disbursements are literally sterilized, while many poor countries fell behind schedule to meet the MDGs. The IEO found this practice so common that 'outside observers perceive the Fund as "blocking" the use of aid' (ibid.). Countries with reserve levels below 2.5 months of imports were programmed to use almost all of the anticipated aid increases (95 per cent on average) to raise reserve levels. But the amount of reserves is not the only indicator, inflation plays an important role too: 'The estimated inflation threshold for determining whether the country got to spend or save additional aid lies within the 5–7 percent range' (ibid.). Economists call this a trade off. Fighting inflation is privileged: tough luck for underweight children under five years of age or infants dying if the country's inflation is above this critical range, maybe only by fractions of a percentage point. Even though the money is there, it must not be used to help them.

One cannot but understand the shock suffered by the General Director of Médecins Sans Frontières in Belgium, G. Ooms, when reading this IEO Report:

> It really was an eye-opener. It reveals, almost casually, that the IMF did not block the reception of additional aid at all; it simply blocked the use of additional aid. . . . On the one hand you have hundreds if not thousands of organizations and individuals pleading their government to provide more aid to provide better health care or education, to realize the MDGs, to keep children from starving and to keep people with AIDS from dying perfectly avoidable deaths; and on the other hand you have the IMF making sure that 80% of all that aid is not being used. This picture is too grotesque for my imagination, and yet it

is what has happened since 1999, and as far as I know it simply continues to happen. (Rowden and Thapliyal, 2007, pp. 1–2)

Some SCs have at least a fair chance to be allowed to use these reserves to iron out aid volatility, which means going on financing their fight against poverty and infectious diseases: 'Countries with very high initial levels of reserves are, on average, allowed to finance the aid reductions to avoid fiscal adjustments, mainly through the depletion of reserves' (IMF, 2007, p. 56). This is, however, asymmetrical: countries 'with very low initial levels of reserves, by contrast, have to fully bear anticipated reductions in aid, in the form of full fiscal and current account adjustments. The programmed fiscal response to aid reductions does not depend on inflation levels.' Who could any longer doubt official IFI claims that countries actually 'own' their programmes?

This IEO evaluation documents one further interesting point: 'Case study analysis indicates that debt sustainability concerns may be an additional factor reducing the programmed level of absorption – and increasing the programmed build up of reserves – in response to an increase in aid' (ibid., p. 6). Thus at least the IMF assumes that debt relief has not been sufficient in quite a few cases and that reserves therefore also have to serve as a cushion. Similar to the case of outright debt cancellation such funds are in a way double-counted: 'aid' technically substitutes proper reductions.

Seen with this IMF strategy in mind, the attacks on new creditors and donors, culminating in the hypocritical phrase 'rogue aid' gain a wholly new perspective. These flows do not only increase poor countries' policy space, but they may also allow continuous financing of the MDGs not guaranteed by 'old' donors.

NEW IDEAS FOR DEVELOPMENT COOPERATION

To assure that increases in ODA are actually help, not just ODA but not help, changes in present practices are necessary. Raffer and Singer (1996, 2001) presented several suggestions of how this could be achieved.

One important proposal, first made by Paul P. Streeten in the early 1990s, is copying one extremely successful feature of the Marshall Plan: self-monitoring of recipients. Unfortunately this characteristic and successful feature, which could have easily been copied, was never considered by Northern donors vis-à-vis the South, not even within the relatively progressive framework of Lomé I. The Marshall Plan had the clear intention of promoting regional cooperation among recipients by joint assessments of needs and joint requests, and the principle of self-monitoring by recipients.

In 1948 the recipients of Marshall Plan aid signed the convention establishing the Organisation for European Economic Co-operation (OEEC), which was reconstituted as the OECD at the beginning of the 1960s. The OEEC served as a monitoring agency for Marshall aid recipients. Europeans were encouraged by the USA to monitor one another's performance, and – as Streeten put it – 'the heavy hand of the US government was kept out of it'. Each Western European government submitted a plan which was inspected, vetted and monitored by other European recipient governments in the OEEC. Streeten did not fail to point out that 'Control by peers rather than superior supervisors is also a principle advocated in business management.'-

Since other features of Marshall aid were emulated by development aid, this difference is difficult to explain unless one accepts the view that the relatively democratic and open structures the USA encouraged in Western Europe are at odds with Northern governments' intentions to use development aid to their own narrow political and economic advantage. Here the Marshall Plan has still something to teach.

Additional aid pledged to allow reaching the MDGs, in fact technically all ODA, could be put into regional funds or funds organized according to other criteria, such as income per head. Within these groups SCs would act as the Europeans once did. This process of self-monitoring and joint requests to the donor community should and could be further enhanced by integrating NGOs into the process. Present institutional contacts between official donors and NGOs could serve as a starting point. Public discussions including affected people, open information policies and thus strong transparency should be encouraged.

This structure would change North-South relations radically, quite in line with official declarations of donors always speaking of ownership, partnership and cooperation. As the generosity of the USA is very unlikely ever to be matched (2–3 per cent of GDP over years), one could at least implement the other successful US innovation, self-monitoring. The present situation of largely unhampered donor power would give way to a much more open, transparent and democratic structure of development cooperation, which would go beyond the concept of partnership within the first Lomé Treaty, before the backswing towards 'normal' donor-recipient relationships between the EU and the ACP countries occurred. This would not mean the end of any donor influence, but this influence would be counterbalanced. Naturally new donors would be welcome to participate, which should immediately annihilate present concerns of donors and IFIs.

FINANCIAL ACCOUNTABILITY OF DONORS

One main shortcoming of present development cooperation is that aid recipients are denied any form of protection usual in all other cases. Thus damage done by grave negligence has to be compensated in all cases unless this is done in the context of development cooperation. Donors must be held financially accountable for grave negligence like anyone else. In essence, this means simply making the public sector with regard to development cooperation accountable in the same way that anyone else already is, eventually bringing the most essential principles of law to development cooperation. The right of victims to make donors accountable for what they facilitate is needed to improve the lot of the poor, whose human rights and sometimes whose lives are too often considered not important enough to be properly taken into account. There is still a long way to go before the victims of development finance will be treated in an equally decent way in which transnational firms or individuals within OECD countries are treated as a matter of course. The mechanisms needed are easy to introduce and have already been described in Chapter 13 for IFIs. Arbitration could as easily be used to hold donors accountable for tort. This proposal can be summed up: fair treatment for SCs and the globe's poorest instead of treating them as fair game. The principles of tort law must finally be introduced to 'development cooperation'.

INDEPENDENT REVIEWS OF ODA

ODA statistics produced by the DAC suffer from inconsistencies, and too often activities are recorded as ODA that do not even satisfy the DAC's own criteria for inclusion. As Raffer (1998b) showed the DAC has always been prepared to allow doctoring of aid statistics within limits, presumably as long as this remained within proportions considered acceptable by the donor community.

To improve aid statistics, their consistency and comparability some form of independent auditing would have to replace present peer reviews. Ideally this should be done by a group of independent experts from both donor and recipient countries. This new form of reviewing would not mean large additional costs since it would replace present peer reviews. These also cost money that could be used to cover the expenses of independent auditing instead. Independent auditing would secure a minimum of statistical correctness. Although it cannot be expected to correct all the numerous problems of present ODA it would be an important improvement. It would constitute a barrier against reporting and recording flows that are not ODA by the DAC's own definition. The quality of aid and aid statistics would substantially improve. It could be reported which part of ODA goes into financing the MDGs, and checked in a preliminary way whether this aid is likely to contribute effectively towards reaching them.

Annex on data: Caveats on debt statistics and indicators

When discussing debt issues, one should always keep in mind that published data and widely used indicators may be misleading, simply wrong or unreliable, wrongly interpreted, or – if worst comes to worst – be abused to back untenable arguments. Before interpreting data or drawing practical (political) conclusions one should therefore examine debt statistics critically to see what precisely can be deduced from them, what they tell us and whether they are fully reliable. One should always heed the IBRD's warning, expressed, for instance, in its *World Debt Tables 1992–93* (vol. 2, p. v) that conclusions drawn from debt indicators will not be valid unless accompanied by careful economic evaluation.

Various data problems, such as the use of specific discount rates, their use when it comes to determining sustainability, differences between secondary market prices (economic values) and face values of loans, differences between cost estimates for the MDGs or data reliability have cropped up earlier. The official euphoria of the 1990s about Latin America having put the debt crisis behind was backed by pointing out that conventional debt indicators, such as the debt service ratio (DSR), had returned to pre-1982 levels. The IBRD's *World Debt Tables 1992–93* (vol. 1, p. 59) declared, under the subheading 'Beyond the crisis': 'Although several middle-income countries are still heavily indebted, the debt crisis affecting middle-income countries worldwide is past. While the legacy of the crisis will cast a shadow on their prospects, their debt-to-export ratios, which have declined substantially since 1986, are now below 1981 levels.'

Naturally the next sentence restricts this good news to 'Those countries pursuing sound policies of economic reform', meaning countries obediently following BWI advice.

Widely used debt indicators, such as the DSR or the interest service ratio (ISR), are important, often serving as the basis on which decisions such as debt reductions are taken. Unfortunately looking only at them may often hide the real debt problem in a misleading way. This Annex will therefore discuss data problems. Due to their importance within HIPC or for the general assessment of debtor economies, the focus must by necessity be specifically on the DSR. The most prominent case of wrong conclusions,

Latin America in the early 1990s, is presented in some detail because of its didactic merits. Analysing this particular case produces useful information for debt overhang situations in general. It will be contrasted with sub-Saharan Africa. In addition problems of other debt data are discussed briefly, such as data on Chile's capital flight and capital repatriation.

DSR-BASED EUPHORIA: THE EXAMPLE OF PRE-TEQUILA CRISIS AMERICA

Suffice it to quote the IBRD's *World Debt Tables 1992–93* (p. 3), where the Bank concluded with regard to 'a number of' Latin American countries: 'With debt indicators now back to pre-1982 levels, most of these countries are emerging from the debt crisis, helped in some cases by the catalytic effects of reductions in their commercial bank debt' (for other statements by the IBRD and other official creditors, cf. Raffer, 1996).

The IBRD's claim that debt indicators were back to pre-1982 levels should have been evaluated with the IBRD's warning on data in the very same publication in mind. As Table A.1 shows, traditional debt indicators had actually declined. However, as the IBRD measures payments on a cash basis (payments made), not on the basis of payments due, low ratios of debt service or interest payments to exports or GNP can result from two diametrically different cases. A country without any debts logically has ratios of zero. But so would a country with huge debts that is not paying a single penny. If used to describe a country's indebtedness, both DSR and ISR can be highly misleading. Dividing actual payments (cash base) by export earnings, both ratios are equally low for debt free countries and heavily indebted countries unable or unwilling to pay. The less debtors pay – the more accumulating arrears boost the debt overhang – the lower these indicators are. Using payments contractually due, calculated by adding arrears to actual payments, rather than the IBRD's traditional indicators is thus more meaningful. It would have shown the real and substantially different picture of pre-Tequila Crisis Latin America. Calling debt service obligations 'the real measure of debt burden' the IBRD (1989, p. 21) had recognized this fact just before euphoria started, although for sub-Saharan Africa. Nevertheless, the IBRD was soon afterwards misled by its own indicators for Latin America.

While manifestly wrong, any corroboration that the debt crisis was over was perfectly in line with the IBRD's euphoria of the early 1990s. With few exceptions, Latin America's low debt indicators simply mirrored huge arrears. Interestingly sub-Saharan Africa's indicators were dramatically lower than Latin America's during those years, but were not interpreted with similar optimism. Regarding Africa, the IBRD heeded its own warning. This raises questions as to why IFIs interpret the same indicators that differently.

The IBRD's debt ratios (DSR and ISR) convey the useful information which share of export earnings is used for debt service. But they must not be used to measure debt pressure in the situation of a debt overhang. To measure this in a meaningful way, one has to follow the IBRD's caveat and look beyond its traditional debt indicators, as the IBRD itself apparently did in sub-Saharan Africa. It is possible to reflect a debt overhang relatively well by one single indicator. To solve the problem of a hidden debt overhang I proposed a new indicator in 1994 (Raffer, 1996). As nonpayment and arrears are both reason and clearest sign of a debt overhang, relating actual payments to all payments contractually due provides a simple, useful index:

$$0 \le DSR/DSR_d^* \le 1 \qquad (A.1)$$

DSR is the IBRD's cash-base ratio. The denominator, DSR_d^* is debt service paid plus payments due but not effected. My index – which for the sake of brevity and want of any better name might be called Raffer index – is 1 if all payments are made on time, zero if nothing is paid. Multiplied by 100 it shows actual payments as percentages of debt service due. It does not suffer from the ambiguity of conventional indicators. A similar indicator for interest payments (ISR/ISR_d^*) can be calculated, but it is of less interest. As the IBRD had started to publish data on arrears some years before I proposed my debt indicator, this correction – which I had already suggested in the German language *Zeitschrift für Lateinamerika, Wien* in 1993 – can be done easily.

Theoretically DSR_d^*, which may be called the real debt service ratio, should include all payments due but not effected: all arrears (including of short-term debts), capitalized interest, rescheduled arrears for every year, and new loans only obtained to pay (over)due debt service. Unfortunately such detailed data are not easily available. For this practical reason I had to restrict DSR_d^* to data published by the *World Debt Tables* (now *Global Development Finance*), basically DSR plus interest capitalized, reschedulings of amounts due or in arrears, and arrears on long-term debts. While an improvement over traditional debt indicators, this may still understate the debt burden.

Assuming exports earnings of $600 in the simple numerical example of phantom debts in Chapter 11, conventional debt indicators based on actual payments are 5.06 per cent in year 10 (DSRs are identical to ISRs in this example). They hide accumulating arrears. The less the country pays – the higher a debt overhang grows – the lower DSRs become. If debt service actually due were divided by export revenues (DSR$_d$*) 10.4 per cent would result, more than double the conventional ratio of 5.06. In our illustrative example the unambiguous Raffer index, obviously useful to assess the capacity to pay, is 0.487. Less than half of debt service due is actually paid. Compared with actual figures this is not unduly low. Calculating DSR$_d$* with readily available IBRD data for sub-Saharan Africa and low-income countries during the 1990s produces values around 0.2 and 0.4, respectively. In 1992 sub-Saharan Africa's Raffer index was 0.126 (Raffer, 2001a): the region paid roughly one eighth of its contractual obligations. The situation improved after 1992, reflecting that even insufficient debt relief is better than none.

Based on IBRD data the Raffer index warned in the summer of 1994 that the perceived end of the debt crisis in Latin America during the early 1990s was basically due to the toleration of extremely large non-payments, or breaches of contract. If creditors had accepted much lower, let alone similar arrears in 1982, there would have been no debt crisis. The debt overhang had not gone before 1994–95, but had perceptibly grown since the 1980s.

Although it is neither possible nor intended to analyse Mexico's special case here in depth, some remarks seem advised. The country benefitted from a unique, special relation to the USA. Already under Baker the USA abandoned insistence on full repayment in the case of its Southern neighbour. The Brady Plan was executed first and generously there, expectations of NAFTA and higher oil prices during the first Gulf War benefitted Mexico. In 1982 huge reschedulings took place. As early as 1985 Mexico could reschedule a debt stock equivalent to 54.3 per cent of her long-term debt. Between 1985 and 1992 Mexico was allowed to reschedule every year. The cumulative amount of these reschedulings is $136.4 billion or 120.3 per cent of her total debt stock in 1992. Mexico rescheduled soon after the beginning of the debt crisis, a fact recognized by *World Debt Tables 1992–93* (p. 47) in a graph. Thus Mexico paid more or less punctually. Her Raffer index was nearly 1 in the years before the Tequila Crisis.

But her current account deficit more than trebled during 1990–92 (179 per cent per annum), hardly a sustainable growth trajectory. Presented at the Development Studies Association Conference, Lancaster, on 7–9 September 1994, Raffer (1996) warned before the Tequila Crisis against the general euphoria mainly fuelled by low debt indicators. The data on which my calculations were based continue to be published in *Global Development Finance*, as this IBRD publication has been called over the more recent past. Reflecting the real debt burden, my index would be equally useful to assess other, future cases properly.

To illustrate the dimension of the problem and the information produced by the Raffer index, Table A.1 shows the differences in debt indicators resulting from the two approaches. As the figures differ between *World Debt Tables* issues, it should be added that latest available data were used at that time (in 1994).

Interest and principal arrears were only available on long-term debt. Actual arrears would be higher unless short-term debts – which were around 18.5 per cent during 1989–91, or around $67 billion in 1990 and 1991 – were always serviced fully on time. This might not be as assured as with regard to the other component of total debts, IMF drawings, which exploded between 1980 and 1991 from slightly less than 0.6 per cent of total debts to nearly 4 per cnet, or multiplied (in current dollars) by 12.3. Furthermore, total debt service does not include principal repayments of short-term debt.

For 1992 only estimates of interest arrears were available in the *World Debt Tables 1992–93*. The $21 625 million interest and $25 484 million principal arrears of *World Debt Tables 1993–94* would mean a slight increase of arrears to $47 109 million. Adding these (26.0 per cent of export earnings) to the 29.8 per cent debt service ratio of the *World Debt Tables 1992–93* the real ratio in 1992 would have been 55.8 per cent, well above the ratio of 1980. The contractual interest service ratio would have been 24.4 per cent, nearly double the 12.6 per cent or 12.1 per cent of the *World Debt Tables 1993–94* and *1992–93*, respectively. The estimates for 1992 published in *World Debt Tables 1992-93* produce a contractual interest service ratio of 24.6, also well above the value of 1980. The IBRD's opinion on lower debt indicators quoted above thus only held for the region if one disregarded arrears.

According to the last issue of the *World Debt Tables 1993–94* available when I wrote this paper, the projected 1993 figures for interest payments showed a contractual interest service ratio which was actually equivalent to 1980 (as no arrears were published for 1981 in the issues used, this is the only pre-debt crisis year that can be referred to). The contractual debt service ratio, however, the more important indicator for foreign exchange needs, was still well above 50 per cent and the level of 1980.

It is of particular importance to note that arrears of interests were perceptibly higher than actual interest payments in 1990 (113.6 per cent) for the first time, in 1991 (115.4 per cent), and nearly as big in 1992 (94.3 per cent). Principal arrears were higher than repayments in 1990 (111.5 per cent), 1991 (121.7 per cent) and 82 per cent in 1992 (*World Debt Tables 1993–94*). Not surprisingly – considering the unduly privileged position of some official lenders – private creditors accounted for most of these arrears, between 83 per cent and 87.8 per cent in the case of interest, and

Table A.1 Latin America's arrears and debt service 1980–93 (million US$/%)

	1980	1982	1983	1984	1985	1986	1987	1988	1989	1990	1991	1992	1993ᵖ
Arrears of													
Interest	66	332	1198	3286	2873	3711	8554	9014	17077	26019	27782	21625	14995
Principal	623	n.a.	n.a.	n.a.	6969	9563	12394	15073	18495	25933	26460	25484	23694
Sum	689	n.a.	n.a.	n.a.	9842	13274	20948	24087	35572	51952	54242	47109	38689
Actual Payments													
INT⁺	24580	37572	34760	35254	34750	30371	28850	33834	26313	22830	24082	22931	23946
TDS⁺⁺	46265	59045	50237	51627	47691	48373	47019	55464	51307	46094	45816	54284	57342
Payments due (Arrears + Actual Payments)													
INT_d	24646	37904	35968	38540	37623	34082	37404	42848	43390	48849	51864	44556	38941
TDS_d⁺	46954	n.a.	n.a.	n.a.	57533	61647	67967	79551	86879	98046	100058	101393	96031
DSR and ISR (Cash Base)*													
ISR	19.7	30.3	29.8	27.2	27.9	27.4	23.4	24.3	16.9	13.3	13.6	12.6	12.3
DSR	37.1	47.6	43.0	39.9	38.2	43.7	38.1	39.8	32.9	26.9	25.9	29.8	29.5
Contractual DSR and ISR**													
ISR_d	19.8	30.6	30.8	29.7	30.2	30.8	30.3	30.8	27.8	28.5	29.3	24.4	20.0
DSR_d	37.7	n.a.	n.a.	n.a.	46.1	55.7	55.1	57.1	55.7	57.1	56.6	55.6	50.4

Notes:
⁺ interest; ⁺⁺ total debt service = interest payments plus principal repayments (cash base: actual payments irrespective of contractual oligations);
* DSR = debt service ratio: (actual) total debt service/exports of goods and services; ISR = interest service ratio: (actual) interest payments/exports of goods and services; ** _d indicates that payments contractually due (not actually made) are used in the numerator; ᵖ projected.

Source: Raffer (1996); calculations based on the IBRD's *World Debt Tables* (various issues).

from 69.7 per cent to 73 per cent in the case of principal. This is a patently unfair discrimination of the private sector.

Until 1991 Latin America's contractual debt service ratio was markedly worse than sub-Saharan Africa's (*World Debt Tables 1993–94*). As no arrears are shown for the big debtor Mexico (nor for Chile and Uruguay) the situation for Latin America excluding Mexico (LA-Mexico in Table A.2) is even more drastic. Its contractual interest service ratio was 27.2 in 1992, its contractual debt service ratio 59.5.

Actually 'interest capitalized' increased dramatically in the region during the last years: it more than doubled from $606 million in 1989 to $1.312 billion in 1990, grew to $2.857 billion in 1991 and $9.278 billion in 1992. For 1993 $8.6 billion are projected in the IBRD's explanation of debt stock changes (debt stock-flow reconciliation), which easily accommodates the fall in arrears of $6.629 billion. In 1992 most of the reduction resulted from the clearance of arrears, especially by Brazil. However her $9 billion settlement was immediately followed by new arrears of $2.7 billion in the same year (*World Debt Tables 1993–94*, p. 32). According to the *World Debt Tables*, the 'clearance of arrears' in Latin America was not due to an economic improvement, but simply to rescheduling and capitalization of unpaid interest.

The perceived and officially heralded end of the debt crisis in Latin America was basically due to the toleration of extremely large non-payments, or breaches of contract. Mostly private creditors have to carry the burden. Rather than a recovery, these figures recall Maddison's (1985, p. 28) description of Latin America in the 1930s when 'debt default eased payments constraints', and creditors acquiesced to the situation.

Naturally the global decline in interest rates since their apex in the 1980s had had beneficial effects, lowering interest service ratios perceptibly. The importance of interest rates is immediately clarified by pointing out that average rates of new commitments were 11.6 per cent in 1980 and 7.2 per cent in 1992. With 53 per cent of long-term debts at variable rates in 1992, an increase to the level of 1980 would have meant about $9 billion more to pay. Eventually this shift would also be reflected in higher interest rates of non-variable rate loans. Each percentage point increase of the average interest rate was equivalent to roughly $5 billion. Contractual debt service ratios, however, which are most important from the point of view of foreign exchange needs, have remained nearly constant during 1986–92, above 55 per cent. Even with the IBRD's optimistic projection of interest arrears for 1993 available in early 1994, every other Latin dollar would have had to go to creditors if contractual obligations were honoured.

The evolution of Latin America's debt overhang measured by the Raffer index is depicted in Table A.2. For 1980 no data on capitalized interests

Table A.2   Evolution of the debt overhang (DSR/DSR$_d^*$)

	1980[a]	1988	1989	1990	1991	1992	1993[p]
Latin America	0.9853	0.6918	0.5865	0.4639	0.4452	0.4905	0.5480
LA-Mexico	0.9809	0.6181	0.4979	0.3950	0.3606	0.3736	n.a.
Argentina	1	0.5493	0.3501	0.3328	0.2860	0.2606	n.a.
Costa Rica	0.9944	0.2829	0.2044	0.5536	0.5854	0.8097	n.a.
Mexico	1	0.9999	0.9917	0.9825	0.9885	0.9963	n.a.
Philippines	1	0.8876	0.9068	0.8957	0.8705	0.8979	n.a.
Venezuela	0.9915	0.9946	0.9871	1	1	0.8422	n.a.
Brazil	0.9691	0.9023	0.7337	0.3800	0.3321	0.3449	n.a.

Note: [a] capitalized interest not available; [p] projected.

Source: Raffer (1996), data from *World Debt Tables* 1993–94.

were available when Raffer's (1996) paper was finalized in the summer of 1994. We shall return to this particular year and its data below. Uruguay is not shown among the 'Brady countries' because, like Chile, she always produced an index of 1 according to BWI data.

Some interesting facts emerge from presenting the IBRD's own data if used to produce the Raffer index. First, one needed not be a 'good child' to be eligible for so-called Brady-type relief, as Argentina, Costa Rica and Brazil prove. Second, except in the case of Costa Rica, these time series do not reflect positive impacts by Brady-type reductions on debt servicing in the early 'Brady countries', not even in the Philippines that had a second helping. Costa Rica and the Philippines still could not service their debts correctly.

Third, if a region honours only about half its contractual obligations (34.97 per cent if one deducts Mexico, Chile and Uruguay), one can hardly call the debt crisis over or the debt overhang overcome. The IBRD's statement 'Latin America has benefited from strong inflows of foreign direct investment and portfolio investment thanks to reforms and dealing with its debt overhang' (*World Debt Tables 1993–94*, p. 5) is definitely contradicted by its own figures.

Finally, Argentina, Brazil, Mexico and Venezuela were the main countries in the region able to place bonds (*World Debt Tables 1993–94*). Honouring only one fourth of her contractual obligations, Brazil obtained large reschedulings in 1992 and was second in attracting new bonds, right after Mexico and before Argentina in 1992 and 1993. Apparently new bonds worth billions of dollars can be placed by debtors with huge arrears.

Recalling that a new wave of creditors was encouraged to enter the market in the form of a Ponzi scheme, this should be less surprising.

SUB-SAHARAN AFRICA AND LATIN AMERICA IN THE EARLY 1990S: AN INTERESTING COMPARISON

Although sub-Saharan Africa's (SSA) conventional debt indicators were dramatically lower than Latin America's at the beginning of the 1990s, IFIs did not interpret them as optimistically as in the case of Latin America. This a very interesting fact to be taken into account when evaluating their optimism on Latin America's recovery. If 'better' traditional indicators are a reason for euphoria in one region, why not in the other? Or if one has to interpret them cautiously in SSA, why not apply the same caution in the Western Hemisphere? These are questions difficult to answer, supposing (as we all do) that no deliberately different interpretation and use of the same indicators was intended. The fact remains, though, that if the standard of caution applied in SSA would have been used in Latin America too, this would not have triggered such massive inflows from a wholly new group of creditors.

Table A.3 illustrates the dubious character of official data on debts, particularly on SSA. It compares debt indicators for the same years taken from two consecutive years of the IBRD's *World Debt Tables*.

From one year to the next debt indicators and data for SSA 'improved' dramatically, but without any explanation. After 1988 the first effects of the Toronto Terms could offer an explanation but that would have to be checked. In any case, one wonders why a publication by creditors did not most clearly draw attention to that explanation, if it applied. The country grouping of SSA had not been altered. DSR_d differs from DSR_d^* used in Latin America. It is lower, because it does not include interest capitalized and reschedulings. DSR_d for 1993 was finally 77.6, definitely higher than the optimistic estimate. After two decades of IMF adjustment, SSA's arrears were nearly five times the amount of debt service actually paid in 1995 and 1996 according to *Global Development Finance* (1998).

Debt reductions in the recent past improved the picture of course. Nevertheless UNCTAD (2004, p. 5) had to point out that principal arrears represented one fifth of SSA's total debt stock in 1995. For the period 2000–02, principal arrears alone were on average double the amount of debt service paid (ibid., p. 6). Although an improvement over 1997–98, no doubt due to various debt reduction schemes, this is still not a sustainable situation.

Evaluating HIPC, the Zedillo report (Zedillo et al., 2001, p. 51) pointed

Table A.3   Sub-Saharan Africa's arrears and debt service 1980–93 (%)

	1980	1986	1987	1988	1989	1990	1991	1992	1993ᵖ
DSR and ISR on Cash Base*									
WDT 1993–94									
ISR	6.2	11.4	9.4	10.3	9.7	9.0	9.2	8.6	7.3
DSR	9.7	24.9	19.6	21.0	18.0	18.0	17.1	16.9	13.5
WDT 1992–93**									
ISR	5.7	11.6	9.2	11.5	10.2	8.9	10.0	8.8	–
DSR	10.9	28.2	22.1	24.7	21.8	20.0	19.8	18.5	–
Contractual DSR and ISR***									
WDT 1993–94									
ISR_d	6.4	15.8	16.3	19.7	20.5	20.9	23.4	25.7	26.8
DSR_d	11.2	39.4	39.1	50.5	48.0	50.2	56.7	64.9	68.0
WDT 1992–93**									
ISR_d	6.1	18.7	20.3	26.9	27.7	27.2	32.6	34.5	–
DSR_d	11.2	49.4	49.4	67.9	64.6	64.0	76.6	–	–

Notes: * DSR = debt service ratio: (actual) total debt service/exports of goods and services (TDS/XGS); ISR = interest service ratio: (actual) interest payments (INT/XGS);
** Data for 1992 provisional estimates;
*** $_d$ indicates that actual payments plus arrears are used in the numerator;
ᵖ projected.

Source: World Debt Tables 1992–93, 1993–94.

out succinctly: 'The official estimate is that debt service will decline by $1.1 billion a year from what would otherwise have been paid, and by $2.4 billion a year from what would have been due.' Careful reporting draws attention to such differences. Apparently looking beyond traditional indicators, the report already wondered whether debt relief had been pushed far enough, pointing out that 'at best, debt relief will offset only a small part of the estimated shortfall in ODA'.

Although statistics provided by the BWIs are used by practically everyone working on debts and the BWIs have used them to support their own conclusions, these data have not received the scrutiny they deserve. Doing so both questions the reliability of statistics and casts doubt on whether they are produced with due care. As shown for Latin America as well, unexplained changes occur. The ratio total debts/GDP published in various *World Debt Tables* display great and unexplained differences of up to 10.1 percentage points for the same year in the case of years long before the issue was published. Both size and time elapsed do not prima facie suggest that this is likely to result from the usual correction of very recent data that understandably undergo some changes between the first published values (usually still estimates) and more exact data presented quite some time later, when further checks could have been made.

THE YEAR 1980: A VERY INTERESTING CASE

This year is one example posing interesting questions. First, *World Debt Tables* only provided data on interest arrears. *World Debt Tables 1989–90* published interest arrears on long-term debt outstanding and disbursed (LDOD) for all SCs and SSA of $791 million and $188 million, respectively.

It seems understandable that debt statistics had not been as well developed before 1982 as they became after the debt crisis officially started. One also understands that computing the relevant data took some time, especially so as the BWIs took some time before they realized that there actually was a crisis. By any account or source, arrears were not as widespread as they would become later. So they were not the main statistical concern after August 1982. The whole system of debt statistics was revamped and improved during the 1980s. Thus one should not criticize the fact that producing data on the arrears in the year 1980, which did not play a major role in the debt issue, were not immediately available. Eventually they were.

It took somewhat longer until arrears in amortization were published. *World Debt Tables 1992–93* produced the first data of principal arrears for the year 1980. All SCs and SSA both had none. This issue (p. v) informed that 'principal in arrears on long-term debt outstanding is identified and shown as a memorandum item in section 1 . . . beginning with 1985'. However there is a zero for 1980 in the tables, which according to BWI custom means zero, not dots indicating 'not available'. In *World Debt Tables 1993–94* principal arrears in the year 1980 were $1922 million and $1121 million for all SCs and SSA, respectively, a visible change from zero. To recall, we are speaking here of a year (1980) that was at that time already history for well over a decade.

To cut a long story short: over the years (more precisely over the different issues of the *World Debt Tables* and later of *Global Development Finance*) arrears kept growing steadily though not always very steeply. The arrears shown for 1980 in, for instance, 2000 were much higher, $2507 million and $1726 million (principal), and $2475 million and $1710 million (interest) for all SCs and SSA, respectively. They stayed rather stable, increasing by some few millions. Eventually *Global Development Finance* dropped the year 1980 from its summary tables.

Disregarding the values of zero published 12 years later as printing errors (although there is no information justifying this assumption), principal arrears officially existing in the year 1980 grew from $1922 million to $2548 million (*Global Development Finance* 2003) for all SCs, and from $1121 million to $1730 million for SSA, by 32.57 per cent and 54.33 per cent, respectively over one decade.

Comparing interest arrears from the first publication mentioned above to *Global Development Finance 2003* shows even larger differences. For all SCs interest arrears multiplied 3.13 times, for SSA 9.11 times – they nearly increased tenfold. If the region itself had grown as fast as SSA's arrears in 1980 did over ten years, SSA's debt problems would be perceptibly smaller if not gone.

This protracted and substantial increase of data for 1980, starting nine (interest) and 12 years (principal) after 1980 poses questions regarding their reliability. This evolution definitely goes beyond usual and necessary statistical corrections of first and preliminary data, especially so as it occurred over quite a few years, starting several years after the year on which data are reported. In the case of all SCs, named differently in various issues, one could argue that new countries joined. However communist governments (North Korea being the exception confirming the rule) were widely known as punctual and reliable payers. Including former communist countries or new countries coming into existence after the demise of communism can thus hardly account for such change, especially so in and after the late 1990s.

Regarding SSA one might point out that the Republic of South Africa (RSA) and Namibia joined the group after apartheid had been overcome. In fact, both countries appear on the list of debtor countries after its demise. However all issues until *Global Development Finance 2003* show two dots (= data not available) for RSA. Namibia is not included in the country tables, no data are published for her. Apparently SSA totals do not include these two countries. The statistical region must have remained unchanged as far as countries producing the total for 1980 are concerned. In parenthesis it may be said that if any amounts for these two countries had actually been included in the totals (for which there is absolutely no indication) that would raise even more problematic questions.

Could it be that it took creditors a couple of years before they realized that they had in fact not been paid fully on time – or at all – and that their debtors had thus been in arrears over years without their realizing this? While Rip van Winkle slept away 20 years in Irving's tale, and we cannot exclude that the one odd out creditor might be blessed with the same capacity to relax, it appears difficult to believe that a substantial percentage of creditors woke up, say, in the year 2000, suddenly realizing that there had been arrears to them in 1980, then duly reporting this fact.

Regarding the experience of the year 1980, where more and more arrears accrued the further away in the past this specific year was, gives us hope that future verification of end of 2004 data determining whether countries not yet eligible for debt relief under HIPC by meeting the income and indebtedness criteria may join the group of eligible SCs, will produce equally growing numbers of eligible SCs.

A FURTHER CAVEAT ON DATA

The problem of the reliability of data also emerges if one simply compares time series of different issues of annual statistics. A comparison of time series published in various *World Debt Tables* issues shows the following values for the ratio total debts/GSP for Latin America (Table A.4):

World Debt Tables 1993–94 displays a more pronounced improvement, which can be interpreted as more successful 'adjustment' policies. Comparison with other *World Debt Tables* suggests that the *World Debt Tables 1993–94* figure for 1988 results from an error regarding GSP. Nevertheless, differences of four to five percentage points – considering that we speak of percentages of the gross social product of Latin America, which is anything but a negligible difference – should raise questions.

More interesting even are the slightly different time series in the IMF's *World Economic Outlook (WEO)* on ratios of external debt (total debt without liabilities to the IMF) to GDP (Table A.5).

Table A.4   Ratios of total debts/GDP for Latin America

	1986	1987	1988	1989	1990	1991	1992
World Debt Tables 1990	62.0	64.2	53.6	46.7	47.9ᵖ	–	–
World Debt Tables 1992	63.2	64.9	55.6	47.8	42.6	41.4	37.6ᵖ
World Debt Tables 1993	66.7	68.8	43.5	51.0	46.7	45.0	41.7

Note: ᵖ projected.

Table A.5   Ratios of external debt and GDP

	1984	1985	1986	1987	1988	1989	1990	1991	1992	1993
WEO 1989	46.3	45.4	44.1	43.8	38.8	37.0	35.8	–	–	–
WEO 1993	53.0ª	53.6	51.6	57.3	50.6	43.9	41.1	43.6	37.3	36.5

Note: ª from IMF, *World Economic Outlook 1992*.

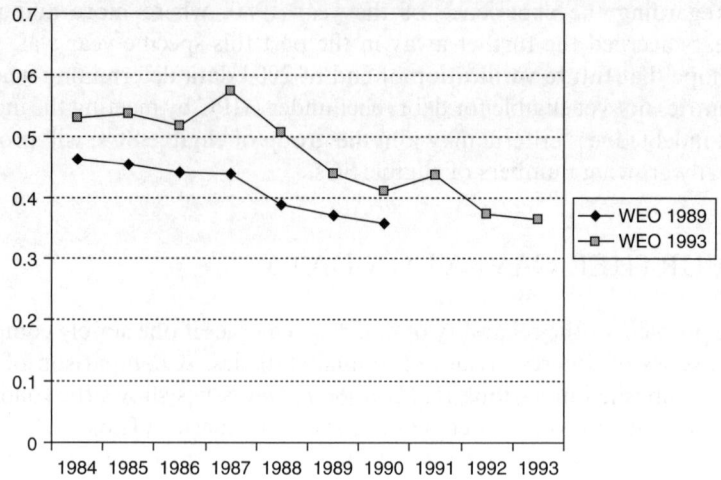

Figure A.1   Ratios debt/GDP according to World Economic Outlook (WEO)

Values for 1989 and 1990 in the *World Economic Outlook 1989* as well as the figure of 1993 are estimates or projections, naturally subject to estimation errors, and in need of checks and corrections. The substantial difference for years long gone by such as 1985 or 1986, though, and the very different picture drawn by the two time series (see Figure A.1), do justify questions. The first line displays a constant (and monotonously falling) reduction of the debt burden, while the second peaks in 1987, falling afterwards. The value of 1989 displayed by the *World Economic Outlook 1989* is again approximately reached in 1992 according to the *World Economic Outlook 1993*. If one assumes a necessary time lag until 'adjustment' policies can show effects, the series of *World Economic Outlook 1989* would by coincidence more readily support claims of successful 'adjustment' policies before Brady. Slowly but persistently, things are getting better in this series, due to BWI advice, one may well assume.

In contrast, the line from *World Economic Outlook 1993* shows a relatively steep increase to the peak in 1987 that makes the need for Brady relief very plausible, although the quick fall in 1988 could not yet be explained by Brady schemes. In any case, even the shapes of the two time series differ considerably, as shown graphically in Figure A.1. Obviously, depending on which figures are correct, wholly different conclusions and policies are justified.

THE PUZZLE OF CHILE'S CAPITAL FLOWS

Suffice one more illustration for the problem of data. The Chilean situation improved drastically between the *World Debt Tables 1992–93* and the *World Debt Tables 1993–94*. While the former publishes a debt service ratio of 33.9 for 1991, the latter shows 23.1 for the same year. The interest service ratio nearly halved from 24.3 to 13.3 for 1991. These differences are not easily explicable by usual adjustments of recent data, particularly so as Chile never had any arrears.

Regarding repatriated flight capital, Chile is a good example too. During the 1980s when capital flight was – quite correctly – seen as a sign of wrong economic policies, statistics on Chile showed no capital flight, even a slight inflow into the country. This was repeatedly quoted as a proof of the military junta's sound economic policy based on IFI advice. All estimates of this 'atypical' Latin American country, for example, Pastor (1990) using IMF and IBRD data or Duwendag (1986), rendered essentially the same result. Estimating capital flight for 25 big sovereign debtors, Duwendag found an unexplained inflow of capital of $2.4 billion for the period 1970–83, or 19 per cent of all net credits borrowed during this period. He pointed out that existing data showed the opposite of capital flight for Chile, arguing that one could therefore not classify Latin America sweepingly as a capital flight region. A detailed case study on Chile by Arellano and Ramos (1987), estimating capital flight in several ways, finds relatively clear outflows for a very limited period (1982 and partly in 1983). But the sum amounting 'in all likelihood to no more than $1 billion (or 5 percent of foreign debt)' (ibid., p.153) is more than compensated by inflows in either 1985 alone or during 1979–80. The authors expressly regretted that Chile would not be able to benefit from repatriated capital: 'Unfortunately the modest size of capital flight means that its repatriation – even if it all returned – could reduce Chile's debt no more than 5 percent' (ibid.).

But the tide turned eventually. Repatriation of flight capital became the touchstone of good economic policies. Fortunately and against mere logic, Chile was able to benefit massively from repatriation too, once this had become the characteristic of sound economic policies. The IBRD's *World Debt Tables 1993–94* (p. 4) particularly stressed the importance of repatriation as contributing to the recovery in Latin America. Capital was now flowing back because of sound economic policies (ibid., p. 11). Naturally statistics on capital flight in particular cannot be very precise, and there is certainly reason to believe that repatriation does occur once an economy improves. Chile, though, had her cake and ate it: after serving as a model of how to avoid capital flight, it could also serve as a model of repatriating flight capital. A logical explanation of how money that had never left could return is still needed.

As these examples show, a great deal of caution regarding the data base on which conclusions regarding debt policies rest is indicated. Also such examples do justify more research on the reliability of official data, and some caution when using them.

Glossary

amicus curiae: (Latin, literally: 'friend of the court') someone not a party to the case but believing that the court's decision may affect their interests. They may file a written statement (brief) if all parties consent or the court gives leave to do so. The US government does not need consent or leave.

Article IV report: produced by the IMF on the base of regular visits (usually each year) to member economies. After discussion in the IMF's Executive Board it is transmitted to the member and normally available (in full or at least as a so-called short Public Information Notice (PIN)) at the IMF's home page nowadays. The name derives from its legal base, Article IV, IMF statutes.

avoiding powers: right to demand the return of payments made shortly before the petition to the detriment of other creditors. As elected officials usually continue in their capacities, they would have to do so (which might also be awkward for them). Therefore Section 926 enables creditors to request the court to appoint a trustee to pursue avoiding powers if the municipality refuses to exercise them.

Basel I: In 1988 the Basel Committee on Banking Supervision (established by the central bank governors of the Group of Ten countries in 1974 (home page http://www.bis.org/bcbs/index.htm)), decided to introduce a capital measurement system commonly referred to as the Basel Capital Accord or Basel I. Depending on perceived risk, loans were assigned specific weights reducing or increasing the costs of lending in a way strongly encouraging short-term flows to Asia.

basis point: 1/100 per cent (0.01%).

child mortality rate: probability of death between a child's first and fifth birthdays, expressed per 1000 live births.

Commercial Interest Reference Rate (CIRR): currency specific reference rate used by the OECD for officially supported export credits of OECD countries and by IFIs to calculate present values of debt stocks of HIPCs and other SCs. See also http://www.oecd.org/LongAbstract/0,25 46,en_2825_495663_2428234_1_1_1_1,00.html.

Committee on Development Effectiveness (CODE): one of the committees on which executive directors of the IBRD serve; helps the board discharge its oversight responsibilities.

Cotonou Treaty: signed between the EU and SCs from Africa, the Caribbean and the Pacific (ACP group), successor of the 'Lomé Treaties', undoing ACP rights achieved under Lomé, making the EU-ACP relationship 'WTO compatible' (cf. Raffer and Singer, 2001).

Country Policy and Institutional Assessment (CPIA): this index is a summary measure of a country's policy and institutional performance, as assessed by the IBRD, covering 'a broad range of areas, including macroeconomic and structural policies, public sector management and service delivery, and policies for equity and social inclusion. The CPIA ratings are used, among other things, to allocate IDA resources' (Gautham, 2003, p. 102).

cross acceleration clause: stipulates that delays in meeting payment obligations of one bond issue immediately trigger the obligation to reimburse the principal of this and all other bond issues.

debt service ratio (DSR): total debt service (interest and amortization) actually paid divided by export revenues of goods and services (in official statistics, especially the IBRD's, usually abbreviated as TDS/XGS); traditional indicator of the debt burden.

Debt Sustainability Analysis (DSA): assesses how a country's current debts and prospective new borrowing affect its ability to service debts in the future (see IBRD, 2006, p. 3). According to the IBRD it is the general expectation that one DSA will be prepared annually for each country.

Enhanced Structural Adjustment Facility (ESAF) established in 1987 to provide concessional IMF lending to poor countries; superseded the Structural Adjustment Facility (SAF, established 1986).

executory contract: contract which has yet to be carried out.

ex turpi causa non oritur actio: principle that courts may refuse to enforce a claim based on the claimant's own illegal or immoral conduct or transactions. The Latin sentence says that no action is possible on the basis of disreputable causes.

Fifth Dimension: mechanism using new IDA credits to meet interest due on earlier market-related IBRD loans.

global public good (GPG): public goods are defined by the properties of non-rivalry (consumption by one person does not diminish or detract the consumption possibilities of others) and non-excludability (benefits/effects are available to all once the good is provided). Kaul et al. (1999, pp. 509–510) define GPGs as public goods 'with benefits that are strongly universal in terms of countries (covering more than one group of countries), people (accruing to several, preferably all, population groups), and generations (extending to both current and future generations, or at least meeting the needs of current generations without foreclosing development options for future generations)'.

Human Development Index (HDI): measures a country's average achievements in three basic dimensions of human development. The performance in each dimension is expressed as a value between 0 and 1. The dimensions combined to produce the HDI are life expectancy at birth, education (adult literacy rate weighted with 2/3, combined gross enrolment ratio weighted with 1/3) and GDP per head (PPP US$).

IDA-only countries: IBRD members exclusively financed by credits from IDA, the IBRD's concessional arm for low-income countries.

indebtedness criterion (under HIPC): a country meets the indebtedness criterion if its debt ratios are above the relevant HIPC thresholds after the notional application of traditional debt relief mechanisms.

infant mortality rate: probability of dying before an infant's first birthday, usually expressed per 1000 live births.

Institute of International Finance, Inc. (IIF): global association of financial institutions created in 1983 in response to the international debt crisis, see http://www.iif.com/about/index.quagga.

interest service ratio (ISR): (actual) interest payments dived by XGS (INT/XGS).

Jubilee (Year): religious demand in the Bible/Torah to rebalance economic and social relations every 50 years, which includes debt cancellation and redistribution of land. Used by NGOs (including non-religious ones) as the title of their debt reduction campaign.

LIBOR: London Inter-Bank Offer Rate, rate at which the most influential banks offer each other credits.

majority voting clause: permits majorities to vote on proposals to alter the terms of debt contracts.

Meltzer Commission: International Financial Institution Advisory Commission established by Congress (1998), named after its chair, Allan H. Meltzer, a conservative economist who had advocated abolishing the IMF; published its report in March 2000, in which the majority recommended a dramatic scaling back of the IMF's activities. See http://www.house.gov/jec/imf/meltzer.htm.

municipality: defined by Section 101(40) US Code as a 'political subdivision or public agency or instrumentality of a State'. In practice, cities, irrigation districts, sewer operators, counties, even a hospital subject to control by public authority. Due to constitutional specificities within the USA (Union–State) state law may prohibit a municipality from proceeding under Chapter 9.

negative pledge clause: guarantees that no creditor's claims in the future will have preference over present debt.

OED: IBRD's Operations Evaluation Department, established on 1 July 1973 after US Congress and the GAO had started to press for evaluations from the IBRD, also considering the alternative of evaluating on their own (prior activities by McNamara). Now renamed Independent Evaluation Group (IEG), in spite of this name an internal IBRD unit.

Organisation for European Economic Co-operation (OEEC): formal organization of Marshall Plan recipients established after World War II. In 1961 the OEEC became the OECD.

Paris Club: informal cartel of bilateral creditors founded in 1956 when Argentina needed debt relief. It has neither legal basis nor status, but meanwhile a home page describing it as a 'non-institution'. See http://www.clubdeparis.org/en/presentation/presentation.php?BATCH =B01WP01.

phantom debts: nominal debts accumulated in creditors' books that cannot be repaid or cashed because they are technically irrecoverable (thus economically non-existent, money already lost), but still treated as though perfectly sound. Raffer coined this expression in 1998 to highlight exaggerated and make-believe costs of debt reduction.

poverty gap ratio: mean distance separating the population from the poverty line (with the non-poor being given a distance of zero), expressed as a percentage of the poverty line.

present value: sum of all future payments or income streams discounted at an appropriate rate of interest. Shows how much future payments are worth at present given a certain rate of interest.

prior actions: measures that must be implemented upfront, prior to IMF Board approval of a programme; the IMF also interprets them as a way of testing programme ownership.

proportion of births attended by skilled health personnel (doctors, nurses or midwives) expressed as a percentage of live births: The UN's MDG Indicator website clarifies that traditional birth attendants, even if they receive a short training course, are not included.

quintile: one fifth of a distribution (for example, richest 20% of a country's income distribution).

real interest rate: nominal interest rate deflated by the rate of inflation or, for example, raw material export prices.

SAF: see Enhanced Structural Adjustment Facility.

Sixth Dimension (aka IDA Debt Reduction Facility): facility established by the IBRD to help poor SCs, and funded by the Bank and bilateral donors. It finances buybacks of commercial debt at reduced prices in the secondary market.

spread: surcharge upon LIBOR, which anyone else but those determining LIBOR must pay.

target(ing): aiming social expenditures at vulnerable groups who need them (most) instead of subsidizing across the board; reduces costs and increases efficiency. Schemes may be targeted by income (for example, food stamps provided to people below a certain income), needs (for example, food for underweight children), commodity (subsidizing basic food items unpopular with richer people), age or region. These elements can be combined (for example, food to children in low-income households in a certain region).

tort: breach of duty leading to liability for damages (other than breach of contract). Tort law typically includes negligence.

trustee (in debt instruments): person acting on behalf of bondholders, thus representing them vis-à-vis the debtor, embodying the collective interests of creditors, who can no longer act individually.

trustee (in insolvency cases): person appointed to manage the property of the debtor (estate) during bankruptcy proceedings, in particular 'for the purpose of general administration of such property for the benefit of the debtor's creditors' (Section 101.11.c US Code).

under five mortality rate: probability of death before a child's fifth birthday.

Bibliography

Acosta, A. (2001), 'La increíble y triste historia de América Latina y su perversa deuda externa', in C. Jochnick and P.P. Freire (eds), *Otras caras de la deuda, Propuestas para la acción*, Quito and Caracas: CDES and Nueva Sociedad, pp. 17ff.

Acosta, A. and O. Ugarteche (2003), 'A favor de un tribunal internacional de arbitraje de deuda soberana', available at http://www.globalizacion. org/docdiscusion/DocDisc1TiadsUgartecheAcostaC.pdf (accessed on 9 August 2009).

Adams, P. (1991), *Odious Debts: Loose Lending, Corruption, and the Third World's Environmental Legacy*, London: Earthscan.

Adams, P. (2002), 'The doctrine of odious debts: using the law to cancel illegitimate debts', available at http://www.odiousdebts.org/odiousdebts/ index.cfm?DSP=content&ContentID=4909 (accessed on 9 August 2009).

AfDB (African Development Bank Group) (2006), 'Brief on the multilateral debt relief initiative: ADF implementation modalities', Commonwealth Secretariat (CHMF(06)3).

Ambrose, S. (2005), 'Social movements and the policies of debt cancellation', *Chicago Journal of International Law*, **6**(1), 267ff.

Annan, K. (2000), 'Freedom from want', in *We, the Peoples, the Role of the United Nations in the 21st Century*, Millennium Report by the Secretary General, available at http://www.un.org/millennium/sg/report/full.htm (accessed 10 August 2009).

Arellano, J.P. and J. Ramos (1987), 'Chile', in D.R. Lessard and J. Williamson (eds), *Capital Flight and Third World Debt*, Washington, DC: IIF, pp. 153ff.

Barry, C. and M. Peterson (2009), 'The G-20's global hit-and-run', *Policy Innovations* (Carnegie Council), 24 April, available at http://www. policyinnovations.org/ideas/commentary/data/000123 (accessed on 10 August 2009).

Bohoslavsky, J.P. (2006), 'Consecuencias jurídicas y económicas del crédito abusivo (Especial referencia al endeudamiento soberano)', PhD thesis (Doctorado Europeo), Facultad de Derecho, Universidad de Salamanca.

Boote, A.R. and K. Thugge (1997), *Debt Relief for Low-income Countries, The HIPC Initiative*, IMF Pamphlet Series No. 51.

Boughton, J.M. (2001), *Silent Revolution: The International Monetary Fund 1979–1989*, Washington, DC: IMF; Chapter 16 also available at http://www.imf.org/external/pubs/ft/history/2001/ch16.pdf (accessed on 12 August 2009).

Bucheit, L.C. and G.M. Gulati (2000), 'Exit consents in sovereign bond exchanges', *UCLA Law Review*, **48**(1), 59ff.

Bull, B., A.M. Jerve, E. Sigvaldsen, with inputs from H. Gulli, K.A.S. Murshid, P. Rebelo and O. Saasa (2006), 'The World Bank's and the IMF's use of conditionality to encourage privatization and liberalization: current issues and practices', Prepared for the Norwegian Ministry of Foreign Affairs as background for the Oslo Conditionality Conference, Centre for Development and the Environment, Oslo University (SUM Report No. 13).

Caufield, C. (1998), *Masters of Illusion, The World Bank and the Poverty of Nations*, London: Pan.

Chang, Ha-Joon (2002), *Kicking Away the Ladder, Development Strategy in Historical Perspective*, London: Anthem.

Chang, Ha-Joon (2005), 'Policy space in historical perspective – with special reference to trade and industrial policies', available at http://www.networkideas.org/themes/industry/sep2005/in05_Policy_Space.htm (accessed on 24 March 2009).

Cheru, F. and C. Bradford (eds) (2005), *The Millennium Development Goals, Raising the Resources to Tackle World Poverty*, London, New York and Helsinki: Zed in association with the Helsinki Process on Globalisation and Democracy.

Cline, W.R. (1985), 'International debt: from crisis to recovery?' *American Economic Review*, **75**(2), 185ff.

Committee on Foreign Relations (of the US Senate) (1977), Bretton Woods Agreements Amendments Act of 1977, US Senate, 95th Congress, 1st Session, Report No. 95-603, Washington, DC: Government Printing Office.

Cornia, G.A., R. Jolly and F. Stewart (eds) (1987), *Adjustment with a Human Face*, 2 vols, Oxford: Oxford University Press.

Crockett, A. (1982), 'Issues in the use of Fund resources', *Finance & Development*, **19**(2), 10ff.

Diaz-Alejandro, C. (1985), 'Good-bye financial repression, hello financial crash', *Journal of Development Economics*, **19**(1–2), 1ff.

Dobbs, Michael and Paul Blustein (1999), 'Lost illusions about Russia', available at http://search.washingtonpost.com/wp-srv/wplate/1999-09/121861-091299-idx.html (accessed on 14 September 1999).

Duwendag, D. (1986), 'Kapitalflucht aus Entwicklungsländern: Schätzprobleme und Bestimmungsfaktoren', in A. Gutowski (ed.), *Die internationale Schuldenkrise; Ursachen – Konsequenzen – Historische Erfahrungen*, Berlin: Duncker & Humblot, pp. 115ff.

Eichengreen, B. (1999), *Toward a New International Financial Architecture: A Practical Post-Asia Agenda*, Washington, DC: IIF.

Eichengreen, B. and A. Mody (1998), 'Interest rates in the North and capital flows to the South: is there a missing link?', *International Finance*, **1**(1), 35ff., also available at http://www.blackwell-synergy.com/doi/pdf/10.1111/1468-2362.00003 (accessed on 4 August 2009).

Eichengreen, B. and A. Mody (2000), 'Would collective action clauses raise borrowing costs?', NBER Working Paper no 7458, available at http://www.nber.org/papers/W7458.pdf (accessed on 5 August 2009).

EURODAD (1995), *World Credit Tables 1994–95, Creditor–Debtor Relations from Another Perspective,* Brussels: EURODAD.

EURODAD (2006), 'World Bank and IMF conditionality: a development injustice', available at http://www.eurodad.org/uploadedFiles/Whats_New/Reports/Eurodad_World_Bank_and_IMF_Conditionality_Report.pdf (accessed on 10 August 2009).

Fischer, S. (1997), 'Capital account liberalization and the role of the IMF', IMF Seminar, Asia and the IMF, Hong Kong, 19 September, available at http://www.imf.org/external/np/apd/asia/FISCHER.HTM (accessed on 10 August 2009).

Galbraith, J.K. (2003), 'The Brazilian swindle and the larger international monetary problem', available at http://www.jubileeresearch.org/analysis/articles/brazil240103.htm (accessed on 10 August 2009).

GAO (US General Accounting Office) (2000), 'Developing countries: debt relief initiative for poor countries faces challenges' (Chapter Report, 29 June 2000, GAO/NSIAD-00-161), available at http://www.gao.gov/archive/2000/ns00161.pdf (accessed on 10 August 2009).

GAO (2004), 'Achieving poor countries' economic growth and debt relief targets faces significant financing challenges – report to congressional requesters' (GAO-04-405), available at http://www.gao.gov/new.items/d04405.pdf (accessed on 10 August 2009).

GAO (2005), 'Rebuilding Iraq, status of funding and reconstruction efforts', Report to congressional committees (GAO-05-876), available at http://www.gao.gov/new.items/d05876.pdf (accessed on 10 August 2009).

GATT (1980), *International Trade 1979/80*, Geneva: GATT.

GATT (1986), *International Trade 1985–86*, Geneva: GATT.

Gautham, M. (2003), 'Debt relief for the poorest, an OED review of the HIPC Initiative', OED, IBRD, available at http://lnweb18.worldbank.org/oed/oeddoclib.nsf/b57456d58aba40e585256ad400736404/86dd1e3dca61e0b985256cd700665b1c/$FILE/HIPC_OED_review.pdf (accessed on 10 August 2009).

Gelpern, A. (2005), 'What Iraq and Argentina might learn from each other', *Chicago Journal of International Law*, **6**(1), 391ff.

George, S. (1988), *A Fate Worse than Debt*, London: Penguin.

Greenidge, C.B. (1999), 'Return to colonialism? The new orientation of European development assistance', in M. Lister (ed.), *New Perspectives on European Union Development Cooperation*, Boulder, CO, and Oxford: Westview, pp. 103ff.

Gurría, A. and R. Manning (2007), 'Statement', 15 April, available at http://www.oecd.org/dataoecd/29/3/38435815.pdf (accessed on 10 August 2009).

Helbling, T., A. Mody and R. Sahay (2004), 'Debt accumulation in the CIS-7 countries: bad luck, bad policies, or bad advice?', IMF Working Paper no. WP/04/93, available at http://papers.ssrn.com/sol3/papers. cfm?abstract_id=878916#PaperDownload (accessed on 12 August 2009).

Helleiner, E. (2005), 'The strange story of Bush and the Argentine debt crisis', *Third World Quaterly*, **26** (6), 951ff, available at http://www. socioeco.org/forums/d_read/intreg/LR_951-969.pdf (accessed on 10 August 2009).

Herman, B., F. Pietracci and K. Sharma (eds) (2001), *Financing for Development, Proposals from Business and Civil Society*, Tokyo, New York and Paris: UN University Press.

High-level Regional Consultative Meeting on Financing for Development, Asia and Pacific Region (2000), 'Session 1: Issues in domestic resources mobilization in the Asia-Pacific context', Jakarta, 2–5 August, available at http://www.unescap.org/drpad/projects/fin_dev/reportses1.htm (accessed on 10 August 2009).

Hurley, G. (2007), 'Multilateral debt: one step forward, how many back? EURODAD report on the G8 debt deal 2 years-on', available at http:// www.eurodad.org/uploadedFiles/Whats_New/Reports/Microsoft_ Word__Eurodad_MDRI_Update_April07_FINAL.pdf (accessed on 10 August 2009).

IBRD (1980), *World Development Report 1980*, Washington, DC: IBRD.

IBRD (1988), *World Debt Tables 1988–89*, vol.1, Washington, DC: IBRD.

IBRD (1989), *Sub-Saharan Africa – From Crisis to Sustainable Growth*, Washington, DC: IBRD.

IBRD (1990a), *World Development Report 1990*, Oxford: Oxford University Press.

IBRD (1990b), *Adjustment Lending: Ten Years of Experience*, Washington, DC: IBRD.

IBRD (1992a), *World Debt Tables 1992–93*, vol.1, Washington, DC: IBRD.

IBRD (1992b), *Effective Implementation: Key to Development Impact, Report of the World Bank's Portfolio Management Task Force*, Washington, DC: IBRD.

IBRD (1993), *Getting Results, The World Bank's Agenda for Improving Development Effectiveness*, Washington, DC: IBRD.

IBRD (1996), *World Debt Tables 1996–97*, vol.1, Washington, DC: IBRD.

IBRD (1997), *Global Development Finance 1997*, Washington, DC: IBRD.

IBRD (2000a), *Indonesia, Managing Government Debt and its Risks*, Washington, DC and Jakarta: IBRD.

IBRD (2000b), *Global Development Finance 2000*, Vol.1, Washington, DC: IBRD.

IBRD (2001), *World Development Report 2000/2001*, Washington, DC: IBRD.

IBRD (2006), 'How to do a debt sustainability analysis for low-income countries', available at http://siteresources.worldbank.org/INTDEBTDEPT/Resources/DSAGUIDE_EXT200610.pdf (accessed on 10 August 2009).

IBRD (2007), 'HIPC at-a-glance guide, spring 07', available at http://site resources.worldbank.org / INTDEBTDEPT / Resources / Debt_Pocket Broch_Spring07.pdf?resourceurlname = Debt_PocketBroch_Spring07.pdf (accessed on 10 August 2009).

IBRD (various years), *World Debt Tables*, Washington, DC: IBRD.

IBRD, OED (1989), *Project Performance Results for 1987*, Washington, DC: IBRD.

IBRD, OED (1999), *1998 Annual Review of Development Effectiveness* (Task Manager: Robert Buckley) available at http://lnweb18.worldbank.org/oed/oeddoclib.nsf/11d38e62c269811285256808006a0022/56f245888 62d25d8852567f200568e93/$FILE/arde98.pdf (accessed on 10 August 2009).

IBRD and IFC (2006), 'Employing workers', available at http://www.doingbusiness.org/ExploreTopics/EmployingWorkers (accessed on 31 October 2006).

IBRD and IMF (2006), 'Global Monitoring Report 2006, Millennium Development Goals: strengthening mutual accountability, aid, trade, and governance', available at http://www.imf.org/external/pubs/ft/gmr/2006/eng/gmr.pdf#search = %22World%20Bank%20MDG%20%22 Global%20Monitoring%20Report%202006%22%22 (accessed on 12 August 2009).

IBRD and IMF (2009), Global Monitoring Report 2009: a development emergency, available at http://web.worldbank.org/WBSITE/

EXTERNAL/EXTDEC/EXTGLOBALMONITOR/EXTGLOMON REP2009/0,,contentMDK:22141578~menuPK:5924426~pagePK:6416 8445~piPK:64168309~theSitePK:5924405,00.html (accessed on 10 August 2009).

IBRD and UNDP (1989), *Africa's Adjustment with Growth in the 1980s*, Washington, DC: IBRD.

IDA (2005), 'The Multilateral Debt Relief Initiative: implementation modalities for IDA', 18 November, available at http://siteresources. worldbank.org/IDA/Resources/MDRI.pdf (accessed on 10 August 2009).

IDA (2006a), 'Additions to IDA resources: financing the Multilateral Debt Relief Initiative' (35768 vol. 2 rev., Attachment I), available at http:// siteresources.worldbank.org/INTDEBTDEPT/Resources/35768_2.pdf (accessed on 10 August 2009).

IDA (2006b), 'IDA countries and non-concessional debt: dealing with the "Free Rider" problem in IDA14 grant-recipient and post-MDRI countries', 19 June, available at http://siteresources.worldbank.org/IDA/ Resources/Seminar%20PDFs/73449-1155322341160/Freeriderboard paper.pdf (accessed on 12 August 2009).

IDA and IMF (2006), 'Heavily Indebted Poor Countries (HIPC) Initiative and Multilateral Debt Relief Initiative (MDRI) – status of implementation', 21 August), available at http://www.imf.org/external/np/pp/ eng/2006/082106.pdf (accessed on 10 August 2009).

IDC (International Development Committee, House of Commons) (2000), *The Effectiveness of EC Development Assistance*, Session 1999–2000, Ninth Report, London: Stationery Office; also available at http:// www.publications.parliament.uk/pa/cm199900/cmselect/cmintdev/669/ 66902.htm#evidence (accessed on 10 August 2009).

IMF (2000), 'Key features of IMF Poverty Reduction and Growth Facility (PRGF) Supported Programs', available at http://www.imf.org/ external/np/prgf/2000/eng/key.htm#P31_2132 (accessed on 10 August 2009).

IMF (2001), 'IMF lending to poor countries – how does the PRGF differ from the ESAF?', available at http://www.imf.org/external/np/ exr/ib/2001/043001.htm (accessed on 10 August 2009).

IMF (2002a), 'Sovereign debt restructuring mechanism – further considerations', 14 August, available at http://www.imf.org/external/np/pdr/ sdrm/2002/081402.pdf (accessed on 10 August 2009).

IMF (2002b), 'The design of the sovereign debt restructuring mechanism – further considerations', 27 November, available at www.imf.org/external/np/pdr/sdrm/2002/112702.pdf (accessed on 10 August 2009).

IMF (2003a), 'IMF financial activities - update August 15, 2003', available at http://www.imf.org/external/np/tre/activity/2003/081503. htm (accessed on 27 September 2006).

IMF (2003b), *World Economic Outlook (September)*, Washington, DC: IMF.

IMF (2004), 'Fund-supported programs – objectives and outcomes', 24 November, available at https://www.imf.org/external/np/pdr/2004/eng/ object.pdf (accessed on 10 August 2009).

IMF (2005), *World Economic Outlook (September)*, Washington, DC: IMF

IMF (2006), *Factsheet – April 2006,* available at http://www.imf.org/external/np/exr/facts/mdg.htm (accessed on 12 May 2006).

IMF, IEO (2003), 'Evaluation report, the IMF and recent capital account crises: Indonesia, Korea, Brazil', available at http://www.imf.org/external/np/ieo/2003/cac/index.htm (accessed on 10 August 2009).

IMF, IEO (2004), 'Report on the evaluation of the role of the IMF in Argentina, 1991–2001', available at http://www.imf.org/external/np/ ieo/2004/arg/eng/pdf/report.pdf (accessed on 10 August 2009).

IMF, IEO (2007), 'An evaluation of the IMF and aid to sub-Saharan Africa', 12 March, available at http://www.imf.org/external/np/ieo/2007/ ssa/eng/index.htm (accessed on 10 August 2009).

IMF and IBRD (2006), 'Review of low-income country debt sustainability framework and implications of the MDRI', 24 March, available at http://www.imf.org/external/np/pp/eng/2006/032406.pdf (accessed on 10 August 2009).

IMF and IDA (2004), 'Debt sustainability in low-income countries – proposal for an operational framework and policy implications', 3 February, available at http://www.imf.org/external/np/pdr/ sustain/2004/020304.pdf (accessed on 12 August 2009).

IMF and IDA (2005), 'Operational framework for debt sustainability assessments in low-income countries – further considerations', 28 March, available at http://www.imf.org/External/np/pp/eng/2005/032805.pdf (accessed on 10 August 2009).

IMF and IDA (2006a), 'Heavily Indebted Poor Countries (HIPC) Initiative – issues related to the sunset clause', 16 August, available at http://www. imf.org/external/np/pp/eng/2006/081606.pdf (accessed on 10 August 2009).

IMF and IDA (2006b), 'Heavily Indebted Poor Countries (HIPC) Initiative – list of ring-fenced countries that meet the income and indebtedness criteria at end-2004', 11 April, available at http://www.imf.org/external/ np/pp/eng/2006/041106.pdf (accessed on 10 August 2009).

Inter-American Development Bank (1992), *Economic and Social Progress in Latin America, 1992 Report*, Washington, DC: IDB, p. 1.

Jamal, V. (1992), 'Somalia: the Gulf link and adjustment', in K. Raffer and M.A. Mohamed Salih (eds), *The Least Developed and the Oil-rich Arab Countries – Dependence, Interdependence or Patronage?*, Basingstoke and New York: Macmillan and St. Martin's Press, pp.128ff.

Jochnick, C. and F.A. Preston (eds) (2006), *Sovereign Debt at the Crossroads, Challenges and Proposals for Resolving the Third World Debt Crisis*, Oxford: Oxford University Press.

Kaiser, J. (2001), 'Debt management à la Louis XVI – a short promenade through the programme and practice of the Paris Club', available at http://www.jubileeresearch.org/analysis/articles/J_Kaiser_Paris%20 Club.htm (accessed on 10 August 2009).

Kaiser, J. (2003), 'Debts are not destiny, on the 50th anniversary of the London Debt Agreement, 1953–2003', mimeo.

Kampffmeyer, T. (1987), *Towards a Solution to the Debt Crisis: Applying the Concept of Corporate Composition with Creditors*, Berlin: German Development Institute (DIE).

Kaul, I., I. Grunberg and M. Stern (eds) (1999), *Global Public Goods: International Cooperation in the 21st Century*, New York: Oxford University Press.

Kersley, H., A. Pettifor and J. Bush (2005), 'What does the Paris Club deal mean for Nigeria?', Advocacy International, mimeo.

Khan, M. S. (1990), 'The macroeconomic effects of fund-supported adjustment programs', *IMF Staff Papers*, **37** (2), 195ff.

Khor, M. (2002), 'The WTO, the Post-Doha agenda and the future of the trade system: a development perspective', available at http://www.networkideas.org/featart/may2002/fa28_Post_Doha_Agenda.htm (accessed on 10 August 2009).

Krueger, A. (2001a), 'International financial architecture for 2002: a new approach to sovereign debt restructuring', 26 November, available at http://www.imf.org/external/np/speeches/2001/112601.htm (accessed on 10 August 2009).

Krueger, A. (2001b), 'A new approach to sovereign debt restructuring', 20 December, available at http://www.imf.org/external/np/speeches/2001/122001.htm (accessed on 10 August 2009).

Krueger, A. O. (2002a), 'A new approach to sovereign debt restructuring', available at http://www.imf.org/external/pubs/ft/exrp/sdrm/eng/index.htm (accessed on 10 August 2009).

Krueger, A. (2002b), 'Sovereign debt restructuring and dispute resolution', 6 June, available at http://www.imf.org/external/np/speeches/2002/060602.htm (accessed on 10 August 2009).

Kupetz, D.S. (1995), 'Municipal debt adjustment under the bankruptcy code,' *The Urban Lawyer*, **27**(3), 531ff.

Lamy, P. (2007), 'The Doha Round at a crossroad [sic]', WTO News: Speeches – DG Pascal Lamy, available at http://www.wto.org/english/news_e/sppl_e/sppl64_e.htm (accessed on 12 January 2009).

Lissakers, K., I. Husain and N. Woods (2006), 'Report of the external evaluation of the Independent Evaluation Office', 29 March, available at http://www.imf.org/External/NP/pp/eng/2006/032906.pdf (accessed on 10 August 2009).

List, F. ([1841] 1920), *Das nationale System der politischen Ökonomie*, Jena: Fischer.

Maddison, A. (1985), *Two Crises: Latin America and Asia in 1929–38 and 1973–83*, Paris: OECD.

Martha, R.S.J. (1990), 'Preferred creditor status under international law: the case of the International Monetary Fund', *International and Comparative Law Quarterly*, **39**(4), 801ff.

Mattoo, A. and A. Subramanian (2005), 'Why prospects for trade talks are not bright', *Finance & Development*, **42**(1), 19ff.

Meltzer Allen H. et al. (2000), *Report of the Meltzer Commission*, available at http://www.house.gov/jec/imf/meltzer.htm (accessed on 10 August 2009).

Millennium Campaign (undated), 'About the Goals; Goal 8 develop a global partnership for development', available at http://www.millenni-umcampaign.org/site/pp.asp?c=grKVL2NLE&b=186389 (accessed on 7 October 2006).

Ministry of Foreign Affairs (of Norway) (2004), 'Debt Relief for Development, A Plan of Action', available at http://www.regjeringen.no/upload/kilde/ud/rap/2004/0225/ddd/pdfv/217380-debtplan.pdf (accessed on 12 August 2009).

Mosley, P., J. Harrigan and J. Toye (1991), *Aid and Power, The World Bank and Policy Based Lending*, vol. I, London and New York: Routledge.

Murshed, S.M. and K. Raffer (eds) (1993), *Trade, Transfers, and Development, Problems and Prospects for the Twenty First Century*, Aldershot, UK and Brookfield, VT, USA: Edward Elgar Publishing.

Norwegian Government (2005), *The Soria Moria Declaration on International Policy* (English version), available at http://www.sv.no/partiet/regjering/regjeringsplattform/kapzengelsk (accessed on 6 November 2007).

OECD (1970), *Development Cooperation, Efforts and Policies of the Members of the Development Assistance Committee, Review 1970*, Paris: OECD.

OECD (1972), *Development Cooperation, Efforts and Policies of the Members of the Development Assistance Committee, Review 1972*, Paris: OECD.

OECD (1983), *Development Co-operation, Efforts and Policies of the Members of the Development Assistance Committee, 1983 Review*, Paris: OECD.

OECD (1985), *Twenty-five Years of Development Cooperation – A Review, Efforts and Policies of the Members of the Development Assistance Committee, 1985 Report*, Paris: OECD.

OECD (1994), *Development Cooperation, Efforts and Policies of the Members of the Development Assistance Committee, 1993 Report*, Paris: OECD.

OECD (1996), *Development Cooperation, Efforts and Policies of the Members of the Development Assistance Committee, 1995 Report*, Paris: OECD.

OECD (2000), *Development Cooperation, Efforts and Policies of the Members of the Development Assistance Committee, 1999 Report*, Paris: OECD.

OECD (2007), 'Final ODA data for 2005', available at http://www.oecd.org/dataoecd/52/18/37790990.pdf (accessed 10 August 2009).

Ortiz Martinez, G. (1998), 'What lessons does the Mexican crisis hold for recovery in Asia?', *Finance & Development*, **35**(2), 6ff.

Oxfam (2007), 'The world is still waiting, broken G8 promises are costing millions of lives', Oxfam Briefing Paper no.103, available at http://www.oxfam.org.uk / resources / policy / debt _ aid / downloads / bp103 _ g8.pdf (accessed on 10 August 2009).

Pastor, M. Jr. (1990), 'Capital flight from Latin America', *World Development*, **18**(1), 1ff.

Pearson, L.B. *et al.* (1969), *Partners in Development: Report of the Commission on International Development*, New York: Praeger.

Pettifor, A. (2001), 'Concordats for debt cancellation: making debt relief work twice – first, as money to the poor; second, for empowering the poor', New Economics Foundation, Jubilee Research, mimeo.

Pettifor, A. (2002), *Debt is still the lynchpin: the case of Malawi*, mimeo, version 2003 available at http://www.politicsofhealth.org/main/debt_is_still_the_lynchpin (accessed on 12 August 2009).

Pettifor, A. (2006), 'The Jubilee 2000 Campaign: a brief overview', in C. Jochnick and F.A. Preston (eds), *Sovereign Debt at the Crossroads, Challenges and Proposals for Resolving the Third World Debt Crisis*, Oxford: Oxford University Press, 297ff.

Pettifor, A. and R. Greenhill (2002), 'Debt relief and the Millennium Development Goals', Background paper for HDR 2003, Human Development Office, UNDP, available at http://hdr.undp.org/docs/publications/background_papers/2003/HDR2003_Pettifor_Greenhill.pdf#search = %22greenhill%20Pettifor%20%22Debt%20Relief%20and

%20the%20Millennium%20Development%20Goals%22%22 (accessed on 12 August 2009).

Pettifor, A., L. Cisneros and A. Olmos Gaona (2001), *It Takes Two to Tango: Creditor Co-responsibility for Argentina's Crisis – and the Need for Independent Resolution*, Jubilee Plus, NEF: London, available at http://www.jubileeresearch.org/analysis/reports/tango_exec.htm (accessed on 10 August 2009).

Polak, J. J. (1991), *The Changing Nature of Conditionality,* Essays in International Finance no. 184, Princeton, NJ: Princeton University Press.

Presidenza (del Consiglio dei Ministri, Ministero del Tesoro, del Bilancio e della Programmazione Economica) (2001), 'Beyond debt relief', mimeo.

Raffer, K. (1987), 'Tendencies towards a "Neo Listian" world economy', *Journal für Entwicklungspolitik*, **3**(3), 45ff.

Raffer, K. (1989), 'International debts: a crisis for whom?', in H.W. Singer and S. Sharma (eds), *Economic Development and World Debt*, Basingstoke and New York: Macmillan and St Martin's, pp. 51ff (Papers of a conference held at Zagreb University in 1987).

Raffer, K. (1990), 'Applying Chapter 9 insolvency to international debts: an economically efficient solution with a human face', *World Development*, **18**(2), 301ff.

Raffer, K. (1993a), 'International financial institutions and accountability: the need for drastic change', in S.M. Murshed and K. Raffer (eds), *Trade, Transfers, and Development, Problems and Prospects for the Twenty First Century*, Aldershot, UK and Brookfield, VT, USA: Edward Elgar Publishing, pp.151ff; also available at http://homepage. univie.ac.at/Kunibert.Raffer/net (accessed on 8 August 2009).

Raffer, K. (1993b), 'What's good for the United States must be good for the world: advocating an international Chapter 9 insolvency', in Bruno Kreisky Forum for International Dialogue (ed.), *From Cancún to Vienna, International Development in a New World*, Vienna: Kreisky Forum; also available at http://homepage.univie.ac.at/Kunibert.Raffer/ net (accessed on 8 August 2009).

Raffer, K. (1994), '"Structural Adjustment", liberalisation, and poverty', *Journal für Entwicklungspolitik*, **10**(4), 431ff.

Raffer, K. (1995), 'Good governance, accountability, and official development co-operation: analyzing OECD-demands at the example of the IBRD', in K. Ginther, E. Denters and P.J.I.M. de Waart (eds), *Sustainable Development and Good Governance*, Dordrecht: Nijhoff, Kluwer, pp. 343ff.

Raffer, K. (1996), 'Is the debt crisis largely over? – a critical look at the data of international financial institutions', in R. Auty and J. Toye (eds), *Challenging the Orthodoxies*, Basingstoke: Macmillan, pp. 23ff (Paper presented at the Development Studies Association Conference, Lancaster, 7–9 September 1994).

Raffer, K. (1997), 'Helping Southern net food importers after the Uruguay Round: a proposal', *World Development*, **25**(11), 1901ff.

Raffer, K. (1998a), 'The necessity of international Chapter 9 insolvency procedures', in: EURODAD (ed.), *Taking Stock of Debt, Creditor Policy in the Face of Debtor Poverty*, Brussels: EURODAD, pp. 25ff.

Raffer, K. (1998b), 'Looking a gift horse in the mouth: analysing donors' aid statistics', *Zagreb International Review of Economics & Business*, **1** (2), 1ff, also available at http://homepage.univie.ac.at/kunibert.raffer/ZAGREBP.pdf (accessed on 8 August 2009).

Raffer, K. (1998c), 'Hunger, poverty, and human development: analysing the debate between the UNDP and the OECD', in H. O'Neill and J. Toye (eds), *A World Without Famine? New Approaches to Aid and Development,* Basingstoke: Macmillan, pp. 335ff.

Raffer, K. (1999), 'ODA and global public goods: a trend analysis of past and present spending patterns', ODS Background Paper, Bureau for Development Policy, Office of Development Studies, UNDP.

Raffer, K. (2000), 'New forms of dependence in the world system', in A. Müller, A. Tausch and P.M. Zulehner (eds), *Global Capitalism, Liberation Theology and the Social Sciences*, Huntington, NY: Nova Science, pp. 169ff.

Raffer, K. (2001a), 'Debt relief for low income countries: arbitration as the alternative to present unsuccessful debt strategies', Paper presented at the WIDER Conference on Debt Relief, 17–18 August 2001, Helsinki.

Raffer, K. (2001b), 'Solving sovereign debt overhang by internationalising Chapter 9 procedures', Arbeitspapier no. 35, Oesterreichisches Institut fuer Internationale Politik (OeIIP) and Austrian Institute for International Affairs, Vienna, updated version available at http://homepage.univie.ac.at/Kunibert.Raffer/net.html (accessed on 8 August 2009).

Raffer, K. (2002a), 'Reforming the Bretton Woods Institutions', *Zagreb International Review of Economics and Business*, December, 97ff.

Raffer, K. (2002b), 'Ways and suggestions of reform of the multilateral trade negotiations', in Arab Thought Forum and Bruno Kreisky Forum (eds), *WTO Trading System – Review and Reform*, Amman: Arab Thought Forum and Bruno Kreisky Forum, pp. 122ff.

Raffer, K. (2002c), 'The final demise of unfair debtor discrimination? – comments on Ms Krueger's speeches', Paper prepared for the G24 Liaison Office to be distributed to the IMF's Executive Directors representing Developing Countries, available at http://homepage.univie. ac.at/Kunibert.Raffer/net.html (versión española también en ese lugar; version française aussi en ce lieu; accessed on 8 August 2009).

Raffer, K. (2002d), 'Schemes for resolving the sovereign external debt problem', in OPEC Fund for International Development (ed.), *Financing for Development, Proceedings of a Workshop of the G24 held at Nigeria House, New York, September 6–7, 2001*, Pamphlet series no. 33, pp. 141ff.

Raffer, K. (2003), 'The present state of the discussion on restructuring sovereign debts: which specific sovereign insolvency procedure?', Paper presented at the 4th Inter-regional Debt Management Conference, DMFAS, UNCTAD, Geneva 11–14 November, available at http://r0.unctad.org/dmfas/pdfs/raffer.pdf (accessed on 8 August 2009).

Raffer, K. (2004a), 'International financial institutions and financial accountability', *Ethics & International Affairs*, **18**(2), 61ff; also available at http://www.cceia.org/resources/journal/18_2/articles/5019.html (accessed on 8 August 2009).

Raffer, K. (2004b), 'Measuring the real debt burden: proposing a new debt indicator', *DMFAS Newsletter*, The Newsletter of the Debt Management DMFAS Programme, UNCTAD, no.16, 1st Semester 2004, p. 9 (version française dans *Infosygade* – Bulletin du programme de gestion de la dette – SYGADE, p. 9; version española en *Infosygade* – Boletín del programa de gestión de la deuda – SYGADE, p. 9); all three versions available at http://homepage.univie.ac.at/kunibert.raffer/net. html (accessed on 8 August 2009).

Raffer, K. (2005a), 'The present state of the discussion on restructuring sovereign debts: which specific sovereign insolvency procedure?', in UNCTAD(ed.), *Proceedings of the Fourth Inter-regional Debt Management Conference and WADMO Conference 10–12 November 2003*, Geneva and New York: UN, UN Sales no. E.05.II.D.11, pp. 69ff; also available at http://r0.unctad.org/dmfas/pdfs/raffer.pdf (accessed on 8 August 2009).

Raffer, K. (2005b), 'Considerations for designing sovereign insolvency procedures', *Law, Social Justice & Global Development Journal*, **1**, available at http://www.go.warwick.ac.uk/elj/lgd/2005_1/raffer (accessed on 8 August 2009).

Raffer, K. (2005c), 'Internationalizing US municipal insolvency: a fair, equitable, and efficient way to overcome a debt overhang', *Chicago Journal of International Law*, **6**(1), 361ff.

Raffer, K. (2005d), 'Multilateral debt management and the poor', in John-ren Chen and D. Sapsford (eds), *Global Development Policy and Poverty*

Reduction, The Challenges for International Institutions, Cheltenham, UK and Northampton, MA, USA: Edward Elgar Publishing, pp. 179ff.

Raffer, K. (2005e), 'Reinforcing divergence between North and South: unequal exchange and the WTO framework', *Journal für Entwicklungspolitik*, **21**(4), pp. 6ff.

Raffer, K. (2006), 'The IMF's SDRM – Simply disastrous rescheduling management?', in C. Jochnick and F.A. Preston (eds), *Sovereign Debt at the Crossroads, Challenges and Proposals for Resolving the Third World Debt Crisis*, Oxford: Oxford University Press, pp. 246ff.

Raffer, K. (2007), 'Risks of lending and liability of lenders', *Ethics & International Affairs*, **21**(1), 85ff; reprinted in C. Barry, B. Herman and L. Tomitova (eds) (2007), *Dealing Fairly with Developing Country Debt*, Malden, MA and Oxford: Blackwell, pp. 127ff.

Raffer, K. (2008a), 'Bretton Woods Institutions and the Rule of Law', *Economic & Political Weekly*, **XLIII** (38), 49ff 20–26 September, also available at http://homepage.univie.ac.at/kunibert.raffer/KR-acc.pdf (accessed on 8 August 2009).

Raffer, K. (2008b), 'A food import compensation mechanism: a modest proposal to reduce food price effects on poor countries', G24 Paper, available at http://www.g24.org/raff0908.pdf (accessed on 8 August 2009).

Raffer, K. (2009), 'Global public goods', in P.A. O'Hara (ed.), *International Encyclopedia of Public Policy, Vol. 1, Global Governance and Development* (associate editors K. Raffer and G. Segell), Perth: GPERU, pp. 219ff.; also available at http://pohara.homestead.com/Encyclopedia/Volume-1.pdf (accessed on 8 August 2009).

Raffer, K. and H.W. Singer (1996), *The Foreign Aid Business: Economic Assistance and Development Co-operation*, Cheltenham, UK and Brookfield, VT, USA: Edward Elgar Publishing (paperback: 1997).

Raffer, K. and H.W. Singer (2001), *The Economic North-South Divide: Six Decades of Unequal Development*, Cheltenham, UK and Northampton, MA, USA: Edward Elgar Publishing (paperback 2002, 2004).

Rich, B. (1994), *Mortgaging the Earth, The World Bank, Environmental Impoverishment and the Crisis of Development,* London and Boston, MA: Earthscan and Beacon.

Rocha, B.M. (1999), *Development Financing and Changes in Circumstances, The Case for Adaptation Clauses*, London and New York: Kegan.

Rodrik, D. (1996), 'Understanding policy reform', *Journal of Economic Literature,* **24**(1), 9ff.

Rogoff, K. and J. Zettelmeyer (2002a), Early ideas on sovereign bankruptcy reorganization: a survey, IMF Working Paper WP/02/57, also available at https://www.imf.org/external/pubs/ft/wp/2002/wp0257.

pdf#search = %22IMF%20WP%2F02%2F57%20%22Early%20Ideas%20on%20Sovereign%20Bankruptcy%20Reorganization%3A%20A%20Survey%22%22 (accessed on 8 August 2009).

Rogoff, K. and J. Zettelmeyer (2002b), 'Bankruptcy procedures for sovereigns: a history of ideas, 1976–2001', *IMF Staff Papers*, **49**(3), 470ff; also available at http://www.imf.org/External/Pubs/FT/staffp/2002/03/pdf/rogoff.pdf (accessed on 8 August 2009).

Rosnick, D. and M. Weisbrot (2007), 'Political forecasting? The IMF's flawed growth projections for Argentina and Venezuela', Center for Economic and Policy Research, Washington, DC, available at http://www.cepr.net/documents/publications/imf_forecasting_2007_04.pdf (accessed on 12 August 2009).

Rowden, R. and N. Thapliyal (2007), 'IMF still blocking progress on HIV/AIDS, health, and education: new report outrages aid advocates', *Policies and Priorities*, **2**(1), Actionaid, available at http://www.action aidusa.org / pdf / PoliciesandPriorities-IFIs-Spring2007issue-1008.pdf (accessed on 26 April 2007).

Sack, A.N. (1927), *Les effets des transformations des Etats sur leurs dettes publiques et autres obligations financières,* Paris: Sirey; also available at http://www.odiousdebts.org/odiousdebts/publications/dettes_publiques.html (accessed on 12 August 2009).

SAPRIN (2002), 'The policy roots of economic crisis and poverty: a multi-country participatory assessment of structural adjustment' (published in 2004 by Zed under the title *Structural Adjustment: The SAPRI Report*), available at http://www.saprin.org/SAPRI_Findings.pdf (accessed on 12 August 2009).

Steneri, C. (2003), 'Voluntary debt reprofiling: the case of Uruguay', Paper presented at the 4th Inter-regional Debt Management Conference, DMFAS, UNCTAD, Geneva, 11-14 November, available at http://r0.unctad.org/dmfas/pdfs/steneri.pdf (accessed on 12 August 2009).

Stern, E. (1983), 'World Bank financing and structural adjustment', in J. Williamson (ed.), *IMF Conditionality*, Washington, DC: IIF and MIT, pp. 87ff.

Stiglitz, J. (2000a), 'What I learned at the world economic crisis: the insider', *New Republic*, 17 April, 56ff; also available at http://www.mindfully.org/WTO/Joseph-Stiglitz-IMF17apr00.htm (accessed on 12 August 2009).

Stiglitz, J. (2000b), 'Democratic development as the fruits of labor', Keynote Address, Industrial Relations Research Association, Boston, January, available at http://www.lera.uiuc.edu/meetings/Annual/2000/StiglitzSpeech.PDF (accessed on 12 August 2009).

Stiglitz, J. (2006), *Making Globalization Work*, New York: Norton.

Streeten, P. (1993), 'From growth via basic needs, to human development: the individual in the process of development', in S.M. Murshed and K. Raffer (eds), *Trade, Transfers and Development, Problems and Prospects for the Twenty First Century*, Aldershot, UK and Brookfield, VT, USA: Edward Elgar Publishing, pp. 16ff.

Streeten, P. (1994), 'A new framework for development cooperation', in *Benessere, equilibrio e sviluppo, Studi in onore di Siro Lombardini*, a cura di T. Cozzi, P.C. Nicola, L. Pasinetti, A. Quadrio Curzio, con la collaborazione di G. Marseguerra, vol. I, Milano: Vita e Pensiero, pp. 111ff.

Tan, C. (2006), 'Who's "Free Riding"? A critique of the World Bank's approach to nonconcessional borrowing in low income countries', CSGR Working Paper no. 209/06, available at http://www2.warwick.ac.uk/fac/soc/csgr/research/workingpapers/2006/wp20906.pdf (accessed on 12 August 2009).

Taylor, J.B. (2002), 'Sovereign debt restructuring: a US perspective', 2 April, available at http://www.iie.com/publications/papers/print.cfm?doc=pub&ResearchID=455 (accessed on 12 August 2009).

Tipping, D.C., D. Adom and A.K. Tibaijuka (2005), 'Achieving healthy urban futures in the twenty-first century: new approaches to water and basic sanitation', in F. Cheru and C. Bradford (eds), *The Millennium Development Goals, Raising the Resources to Tackle World Poverty*, London, New York and Helsinki: Zed in association with the Helsinki Process on Globalisation and Democracy, pp. 181ff.

Torres, H.R. (2007), 'Reforming the International Monetary Fund – why its legitimacy is at stake', *Journal of International Economic Law*, **10** (3), 1ff; also available at http://www.networkideas.org/featart/aug2007/fa10_Hector_Torres.htm (accessed on 12 August 2009).

Treasury (HM) (undated), 'International Finance Facility', downloaded from http://www.hm-treasury.gov.uk./documents/international_issues/international_development/development_iff.cfm, 24 June 2007.

Treasury Select Committee, House of Commons (2002), 'Treasury – uncorrected evidence', Thursday, 4 July, available at http://www.publications.parliament.uk/cmselect/cmtreasy/uc868-iii/uc86801.htm (accessed on 5 May 2008).

Tseng, W. (1984), 'The effects of adjustment', *Finance & Development* **21**(4), December, 2ff.

UN (2004), *We the Peoples: Civil Society, the United Nations and Global Governance, Report of the Panel of Eminent Persons on United Nations – Civil Society Relations*, UN document A/58/817

UN (2005), *Millennium Development Goals Report 2005*, available at http://unstats.un.org/unsd/mi/pdf/MDG%20Book.pdf (accessed on 12 August 2009).

UN (2006), *The Millennium Development Goals Report 2006*, New York: UN.

UN Millennium Project (2005), *Investing in Development: A Practical Plan to Achieve the Millennium Development Goals*, London: Earthscan.

UN Millennium Project (no year), 'Quick wins', available at http://www.unmillenniumproject.org/press/press3.htm (downloaded 7 September 2006).

UNCTAD (1986), *Trade and Development Report 1986*, Geneva: UN.

UNCTAD (2002), *Economic Development in Africa: From Adjustment to Poverty Reduction: What is New?*, Geneva: UN.

UNCTAD (2004), *Economic Development in Africa. Debt Sustainability: Oasis or Mirage?*, Geneva: UN.

UNCTAD (2006), *Trade and Development Report 2006*, Geneva: UNCTAD.

UNDP (1992), *Human Development Report 1992*, New York, Oxford: Oxford University Press.

UNDP (2005), *Human Development Report 2005*, New York: Oxford University Press.

UNDP (2006), *Human Development Report 2006*, New York: Oxford University Press.

US House of Representatives (2005), Committee on Government Reform, Minority Staff Special Investigations Division, 'Rebuilding Iraq, U.S. mismanagement of Iraqi Funds', Prepared for Henry A. Waxman, available at http://www.democrats.reform.house.gov/Documents/20050621114229-22109.pdf (accessed on 12 August 2009).

Vandemoortele, J. and R. Roy (2005), 'Making sense of MDG costing', in F. Cheru and C. Bradford (eds), *The Millennium Development Goals, Raising the Resources to Tackle World Poverty*, London, New York and Helsinki: Zed in association with the Helsinki Process on Globalisation and Democracy, pp. 44ff.

Weiss, M.A. (2005), 'Iraq: Paris Club debt relief', CRS Report for Congress, Congressional Research Service, 19 January, available at http://fpc.state.gov/documents/organization/44019.pdf (accessed on 12 August 2009).

Winters, J. (2004), 'Criminal debt', written statement for Combating Corruption in the Multilateral Development Banks, Hearing before the Committee on Foreign Relations, US Senate, 108th Congress, 2nd session, 13 May, available at http://foreign.senate.gov/testimony/2004/WintersTestimony040513.pdf (accessed 12 August 2009).

Working Group on International Financial Crises (1998), 'Report', October, available at http://www.bis.org/publ/othp01d.pdf (accessed on 12 August 2009).

World Commission (on the Social Dimension of Globalization) (2004), 'A fair globalization: creating opportunities for all', available at http://www.ilo.org/public/english/fairglobalization/index.htm (accessed on 12 August 2009).

WTO (1995), *International Trade 1995 – Trends and Statistics*, Geneva: WTO.

WTO (1996), *WTO Focus*, no.14, December.

WTO (1998), *Annual Report 1998*, vol.1, Geneva: WTO.

WTO (2000), *Annual Report 2000*, vol.1, Geneva: WTO.

Zedillo, E. *et al.* (2001), 'Recommendations of the high-level panel on Financing for Development', UN, General Assembly, 26 June (A/55/1000), available at http://www.un.org/esa/ffd/a55-1000.pdf (accessed on 12 August 2009).

Bibliography

Index